Gender, Sexuality and Feminism in Pakistani Urdu Writing

Gender, Sexuality and Feminism in Pakistani Urdu Writing

Amina Yaqin

ANTHEM PRESS

Anthem Press
An imprint of Wimbledon Publishing Company
www.anthempress.com

This edition first published in UK and USA 2026
by ANTHEM PRESS
75–76 Blackfriars Road, London SE1 8HA, UK
or PO Box 9779, London SW19 7ZG, UK
and
244 Madison Ave #116, New York, NY 10016, USA

First published in the UK and USA by Anthem Press in 2022

Copyright © Amina Yaqin 2026

The author asserts the moral right to be identified as the author of this work.

All rights reserved. Without limiting the rights under copyright reserved above, no part of this publication may be reproduced, stored or introduced into a retrieval system, or transmitted, in any form or by any means (electronic, mechanical, photocopying, recording or otherwise),
without the prior written permission of both the copyright
owner and the above publisher of this book.

British Library Cataloguing-in-Publication Data
A catalogue record for this book is available from the British Library.

Library of Congress Control Number: 2025947399

ISBN-13: 978-1-83999-802-7 (Pbk)
ISBN-10: 1-83999-802-4 (Pbk)

Cover Image: Naiza Khan ©'Henna Hands' 2006

This title is also available as an eBook.

To my father and grandmothers

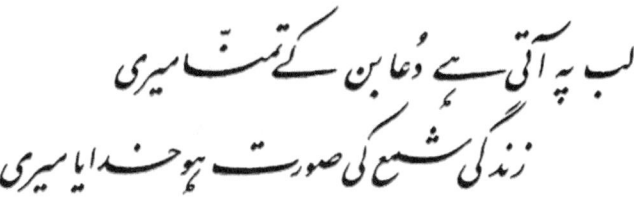

Lab pe ati hai dua ban ke tamanna meri
Zindagi shama ki surat ho khudaya meri

My ambition comes to my lips in the form of a prayer
Dear God, I wish my life is like an incandescent flame
Muhammad Iqbal, 'Bache ki dua'
(A Child's Prayer) 1902.

CONTENTS

Foreword	ix
Acknowledgements	xi
A Note on Transliteration	xv
1. Introduction: Poetry, Politics, Women	1
2. Form, Education and Women: Rekhti, Reform and the Zenana	39
3. Progressive Aspirations: Sexual Politics and Women's Writing	67
4. Fahmida Riaz: A Woman Impure	119
5. Kishwar Naheed: Dreamer, Storyteller, Changemaker	179
Conclusion	253
Bibliography	259
Index	275

FOREWORD

I must begin by congratulating our talented and industrious author, Amina Yaqin, for this incredible labour of love. It is an important pioneering work that was badly needed.

I felt touched and honoured to learn from Amina that her book is inspired by a collection of Urdu feminist poetry in translation that I put together many years ago, entitled *We Sinful Women*, a tribute to Kishwar Naheed's wonderful poem of that name. The title was apt, catchy and above all it seemed marketable to the Women's Press team responsible for guiding it into the world. The book received plenty of attention from academics, but it also built up a cult following among younger women in the diaspora. Fahmida Riaz and Kishwar Naheed, whose work formed the core of my book of translations, are the subjects of the last two chapters of Amina's book. She takes us into the inner worlds of the poets, and her sensitive close readings of some of their iconic poems give us a deeper insight into the intertextualities of feminism in Urdu writing.

Reading this book took me back to my own research into the women's movement in Pakistan in the 1980s and my search for related poems. It took me two or three years to assemble the material I needed, but it was an immensely gratifying task. As far as activism was concerned, the Women's Action Forum in Lahore and Tehrik-e-Niswan in Karachi and Sindh were both doing impressive work in consciousness raising and also dealing with women's issues head-on, defying General Zia-ul Haq's brutal martial law with the promulgation of Hudood Ordinances in 1989. These laws spelt an ideological implementation of Sharia law authenticating Pakistan's identity as an Islamic state. They dealt with theft, drunkenness, *qazf* (bearing false witness) and *zina* (unlawful or 'immoral' sexual intercourse, including rape). When I wrote the introduction to the poems to flesh out the socio-political context and set the scene for that battle, I could not have dreamt that some 30 years later a book would emerge that would offer a credible literary history to the Women's Movement that stirred Pakistani women writers in the 1980s.

What Amina begins in this new work is an exploration of the historical roots of secular modernity that flowered in the work of Pakistani feminists since the late twentieth century, despite the watchful constraints of the reactionary society in which they have operated. Constructing a literary history of gender in Urdu literature, she takes into consideration the popular form of the *ghazal*, the performative mushaira and the nurturing of a new feminine voice. Significant female figures such as Habba Khatun and Lalla Ded are situated within the Sufi tradition; experiments in form that mark a shift in taste from fantasy to realism are eruditely analysed.

Reform paves the way for a new modernity with the formation of the anti-colonial resistance movement heralded by the work of the Progressive Writers Association in the 1930s. In this context, Amina charts the progress of gendered representations in the twentieth century through the torch bearers of a new feminist aesthetic: Rashid Jahan and Ismat Chughtai. For me, the evolution of progressive ideas into the finest examples of feminist writing is best seen in the works of the two major poets, Riaz and Naheed, who will, I hope, fascinate you as much as they fascinated me. This is a book that grounds you in its stories and the twists and turns of Urdu in post-Partition Pakistan; its conclusion offers a much-needed glimpse into the future direction of emergent, grittier modes of writing from the margins.

In so doing, it promises to break the shackles of a highly patriarchal, state-orchestrated patriotism based on nostalgic nationalism, charting a path for new feminist futures in the twenty-first century.

Rukhsana Ahmad

ACKNOWLEDGEMENTS

When I started exploring feminism and its relationship to Urdu I never imagined how long the journey would be and how many relatable moments there would be in the process of being a woman in the academy. The work wouldn't have been possible without the generosity of academics, friends, writers, mentors and family, who have been a constant source of support and inspiration. Two individuals who nurtured a love of Urdu despite my convent education are my grandmother and father: the former used to recite Iqbal's poetry verbatim when we were growing up and my father always had a *sher* or a couplet to emphasize a life lesson from a variety of sources ranging from his multilingual knowledge bank of Persian, Siraiki, Punjabi and Urdu. He insisted on Urdu *sabaq* in sweltering Lahore afternoons to fill the gaps of an English education. I will always be grateful to Maulana Haroon Rashid, who insisted on t*arbiat* alongside *talim*. In the learning of Urdu there has been no discrimination of sect, gender or political grouping and I have learnt from a variety of teachers including Zaidi sahib, whose passion brought the *marsiya* to life. So for Abbu a very special thanks for your unconditional love and commitment to literature and for going out and finding books for me when I needed them. My Kashmiri maternal grandmother Ismat Qayum's early morning recitations of Iqbal instilled a familiarity with her verse from an early age and I am told that my grandfather was the last GP to treat Iqbal as his life ebbed away. This brought the poet close to home and writing this book has reminded me of how much I learnt from her. It has also made me curious about my paternal grandmothers, Bashirunnisa and Sahibzadi Begum, who lived in Sirsa pre-Partition India and who I never met. They were not formally educated and it is hard to find an archive of their lives beyond oral stories.

The women scholars who brought this project back to life and to whom I owe a huge debt of gratitude are Professor Donna Landry and Professor Geeta Patel. They have been incredibly generous with their time and patiently listened to the book in its various stages helping me to flesh out my argument over sumptuous cakes and coffee. Geeta Patel has also kindly sourced documentaries I requested from Delhi. I will remain indebted to Professor Kumkum Sangari for conversations about the book on one of her many visits to SOAS. Aamer Hussein has been a good friend and listened to the book outline many times. He has always been behind this project and his writings and our conversations have been a source of motivation and learning. Iftikhar Arif has been very kind and generous over the years, helping me out with sourcing material in the early years of the project. I am grateful to Dr Ayesha Siddiqa for her valuable insights and for making her mother's book available to me. Kishwar Naheed, the late Fahmida Riaz and Zehra Nigah have always been accessible for interviews and conversations; their input has been invaluable. The late Asif Furrukhi invited me to translate some of Kishwar Naheed's work and was always helpful whenever I reached out to him. Thanks are also due to Fatema Hasan for sharing her knowledge of Ze Khe Shin and for off-the-record conversations about the poets. I'd also like to acknowledge the support I was given by the late Ranjana Ash and how thrilled she was to learn about this project. Rukhsana Ahmad has been incredibly generous with her support and it was her translations of Urdu feminist poetry that reinvigorated my interest in Urdu poetry as a postgraduate student. I owe thanks to the late Mahmood Jamal and Farida Jamal who kindly shared information about their aunt Sughra. I am thankful to colleagues at the Oriental Department, University of Punjab and the English Department for their conversations and time. Thanks are due to the late Ahmad Nadeem Qasimi, Dr Mashkur Husain Yad, Intizar Husain, Ashfaque Ahmad, Bano Qudsia, Dr Waheed Qureshi, Dr Jamil Jalibi, Ahmad Faraz, all of whom patiently listened to the project and shared their views on the Progressives and women's writing. Muhammad Umar Memon gave valuable feedback on my translations. Thanks also to Pragya Dhital, Mehr Afshan Farooqi, Ayesha Khan for sharing publications. My dear friends, Kulsoom Hussein Saiyid and her daughter Amena Hussein Saiyid have kindly shared valuable family insights on Nazir Ahmad and his great granddaughter's diary as well as giving me access to the diary in its pre-publication stages.

Dr Qamar Khan and his family in Karachi helped me navigate the city and provided sustenance, facilitating my conversations with Fahmida Riaz, Dr Jamil Jalibi, Dr Sahar Ansari and others. I am grateful to driver Muhammad Taj for transporting me to many parts of Lahore for the project. My khalas, Muneera Javed and the late Farida Bashir and their families in Islamabad have all been very kind to the project and to me. A special thanks to my mamoo Farooq Malik and to his family for helping out when needed. I am also very grateful to my aunt, the late Qamar Bashir who shared overviews of Urdu poets and poetry who she hosted at her house as friends of her husband, Mir Bashir.

ACKNOWLEDGEMENTS

At SOAS I am grateful to friends and visiting speakers for their generosity in helping me to refine my ideas over the years. SOAS library is of course a treasure house, as is the British Library, and I am thankful to all the South Asia subject librarians especially Farzana Whitfield. I'd also like to acknowledge my students at SOAS who have been a continuous source of inspiration.

Heartfelt thanks are due to Neelam Hussein and Zareena Saeed for their mentoring, company and friendship in Lahore. Muneeza Shamsie has been a constant source of knowledge and inspiration. I'd like to thank Yasmeen Hamid for lending her ear to the book and for sharing her knowledge of the field as a poet and a critic. My school and college friends Beena Kamran, Amena Hussein Saiyid, Gul Bukhari, Saadia Toor, Shefali Chandra, Arpita Das, Cheryl Wadasinghe, Sadia Tariq, Nadine Zubair have sustained me over the years despite long distances. Jugnoo Rahi has always been available for advice and support. I'm also grateful to friends and interlocutors who have lent their ear to the project in its different stages: Alex Tickell, Anshuman Mondal, Munizha Ahmad-Cooke, Kai Easton, Rehana Ahmed, Claire Chambers, Stephen Morton, Reina Lewis, Kath Weston, Jeevan Deol, Ed Simpson, Nadje Al-Ali, Kelly Pemberton. To get to this stage wouldn't have been possible without amazing friends and babysitters for Maleeha and Laila, so thank you, Nuzhat, Amber, Alaya. A special thanks goes out to my mother, my sister Faiza and my brothers Moin and Amin and their families who have put up with my writing habits and been a constant source of support with babysitting as has the extended family.

I would like to thank the commissioning editor Professor Ranjan Ghosh for his enthusiastic reception to the book proposal. I am deeply grateful to Megan Greiving, the Acquisitions Editor at Anthem, and the production team especially Jayashree Prabhu and Ashwathy Chandrasekar for overseeing the book through all its necessary stages. A massive thanks to Rachel Goodyear for her tireless and meticulous copyediting. I am indebted to Bilal Zahoor and Folio Books for taking on this book for publication in Pakistan. And my grateful thanks to Bilal and Irfan Ahmed who kindly organised last minute Urdu scans of poems.

The chapters are based on conference presentations and have benefitted from the generosity of many who have engaged with the work and made suggestions for improvement. I am particularly grateful to Ameena Saiyid and Asif Furrukhi for the honour of interviewing Kishwar Naheed at the Karachi Literature Festival. I would also like to thank Fiona Tolan and Rachel Carroll, the organizers of the Beyond Western Eyes: South Asian women's writing symposium held at Liverpool John Moores University in 2019, for inviting my keynote on feminism and the secular sacred divide that came at just the right moment in the book's last stages. The translations of poems from Kishwar Naheed, Zehra Nigah and Fahmida Riaz have appeared as part of journal articles and independent translations in the following publications and I am grateful to be able to reproduce them in this book. Selected translations of Kishwar Naheed's poetry in *Salt in Wounds: Poems of Kishwar Naheed*, edited by Ali Kamran (Lahore: Sang-e meel, 2020); *Selected Poetry of Kishwar Naheed*, selected by Baidar Bakht (Lahore: Sang-e meel, 2018); 'Breaking the Mirror of Urdu Verse: Speech and Silence in the Poetry of Kishwar Naheed', *Moving Worlds: A Journal of Transcultural Writings* 4 (2004): 34–46, ISBN: 978-0-9553060-3-7. Zehra Nigah's poetry in *Critical Muslim* 4 (2012); 'Fahmida Riaz: Translated Poems', *Annual of Urdu Studies* 19 (2004); 'Kishwar Naheed: Translated Poems', in *The Distance of a Shout* (Oxford: Oxford University Press, 2002); 'Issues of Translation: Three Contemporary Urdu Poems', *SOAS Literary Review*, 1 November 1999, http://www.soas.ac.uk/soaslit/home.html.

Some of the content in Chapter 2 is based on 'Truth, Fiction and Autobiography in the Modern Urdu Narrative Tradition', in 'Novelization in the Islamic World', special issue, *Comparative Critical Studies* 4, no. 3 (2007): 379–402, ISSN 1744-1854; selective reflections on autobiography in Chapter 5 are in conversation with my article on 'Autobiography and Muslim Women's Lives', *Journal of Women's History* 25, no. 2 (2013): 171–84, ISSN: 1042-7961. Part of the discussion in Chapters 2, 4 and 5 is derived from my journal article '"*Badan darida*" (The Body Torn): Gender and Sexuality in Pakistani Women's Poetry', *Pakistan Journal of Women's Studies (Alam-e Niswan)* 13, no. 1 (2006): 45–66, ISSN: 1024-1256.

Where possible, we have sought permission from publishers to include source Urdu text. I am deeply grateful to Naiza Khan for allowing me to use her exquisite 'Henna Hands' artwork for the book's cover image. It has been an absolute pleasure to connect with her over mutual and shared interests relating to feminism, women's writing and activism.

Lastly, Peter, Maleeha and Laila's love, support and patience with the never-ending deadlines for this project have sustained me. Peter has read and heard many drafts over the years and been a critical friend to the project, helping me to improve the clarity of my argument at all stages. The criticism has been mixed with much-needed shared chocolate, coffee breaks and care.

A NOTE ON TRANSLITERATION

The transliteration of Urdu in this book is based on commonly standardized forms of Romanized Urdu available in textbooks and digital platforms. I have devised my own system based on established systems in the *Annual of Urdu Studies*. My method is simple and consistent to maximize access and readability. In the pandemic I have had limited technology access; therefore I have not used diacritics. I have provided original poems in Urdu from Kishwar Naheed, Fahmida Riaz, Zehra Nigah and Parvin Shakir where I engage with them in depth and where possible. Translations from Urdu to English are my own unless indicated otherwise. Words of English origin in Urdu are reproduced in standard English. Arabic and Persian origin words are transliterated as pronounced in Urdu.

Chapter 1

INTRODUCTION: POETRY, POLITICS, WOMEN

In India and Pakistan, Urdu poetry connects a multiplicity of voices in the public domain, appealing to an elite class, and extends beyond that 'ashrafization' in its formulation as an everyday lived experience offering different trajectories across a variety of spaces.[1] It is a signifier of national, local and gendered cultures, forming a cross-cultural mosaic across multiple identities and identification. You will find examples of phrases and poems cited and quoted in a variety of places: television channels will devote hours of primetime viewing to cultural discussion programmes and performances of poetry and song; politicians will quote well-known poems in the certainty that their significance will be broadly understood; and even the drivers of rickshaws and trucks will have adapted poetic phrases painted on their vehicles. Other cultural forms, including devotional music such as the *qawwali*, folk art and street theatre, engage a cross-section of society, offering a cultural aesthetic that draws from everyday life. Poetry thus advances an activist medium of self-expression in which authority and ownership of symbols, metaphors and personifications can be overturned and class politics questioned. In this landscape, it is necessary to think about the place of women and their intersectional relations to class, nation and culture.[2] Nosheen Ali has written about the plural diversities of poetic knowledges in South Asia and a decolonized approach to poetry through a region-led cross-cultural knowledge of poetic traditions in order to understand the culture of emotions and affect that are part of everyday life.[3] Poetry as both an oral and a written medium in the subcontinent was utilized by reformists, anticolonialists, progressives and nationalists. How do we make sense of the different types of narrative that are embedded in this politics of conformity and resistance? In her book *Self and Sovereignty* Ayesha Jalal has emphasized the role of poetry in the 'construction of narratives of identity' in late nineteenth-century India and its notable presence in the vernacular press of the period.[4] The spirit of Urdu poetry was inflected with influences from *bhakti* and Sufi traditions underlining Indic and Islamicate aesthetic qualities.[5] Jalal uses the political poetry of protest to illustrate the politics of changing

Muslim subjectivities. Her reference to the poetry of protest indicates how language was becoming a place for ethnic identification and contributing to a modern political identity formation.

In this book, I wish to consider how poetry, politics and activism are intertwined in women's writing in the twentieth century.[6] I investigate the story of Progressive women poets in Pakistan, a story that has not been recounted in detail, in order to interrogate the narratives that were unfolding around these women: of nation, community and gender. The account of literary women in the postcolonial nation taking up the mantle of public poets reflects Urdu's engagements with political and philosophic ideas of the secular and sacred through histories of reform, anticolonial resistance and the longer trajectory of Islamic and Indic aesthetic influences. I examine how the state and patriotic national affiliations have influenced and profoundly affected narratives of and about gender, transforming the representation of sexualities in Urdu poetry to a heteronormative narrative of family. I suggest that women writers have negotiated liberal and Islamist ideologies, articulating a self-positioning that is neither secular nor religious. As performative subjects, they engage with an ethical, moral and political landscape, moulding it to a terrain of dialogic encounter that is inclusive of gender difference. My methodological approach is interdisciplinary, engaging with women's subjectivities across class, nation, religion and gender from a variety of sources ranging from postcolonial studies, gender studies, politics and history that helps me to illustrate the dynamics of power negotiated by women both on the frontlines and via the backdoors of political agency. As part of my critical overview, I foreground Urdu's linguistic hybridities, the legacy of nineteenth-century reform and canonical texts written by men to educate women at the turn of the century in colonial India. This contextual scrutiny reveals how gendered identities were shaped in the lead-up to Partition. With the rise of anticolonial nationalism, the Indian women's movement gathered force and the bodies that had been spoken for previously as representatives of the private sphere took to the public realm as active speaking subjects, participating in activism and in the writing and production of local as well as English literatures. Their cosmopolitan and local synergies articulated new modernities that were in conversation with the secular and sacred across different Indian literatures. The presence of women's voices from the *zenana* was evident in Urdu literature with the publication of late nineteenth-century modest writings by Zahida Khatun Sherwania and Haya Lakhnavi, as the rules of seclusion were gradually relaxed. Their quiet verse compositions contrasted with the revolutionary and activist prose writings of Rashid Jahan and Ismat Chughtai in the first half of the twentieth century. They were at the vanguard of the radical Progressive Writers' movement, energized by anticolonial resistance, influenced by Communist ideology and part of a global response to fascism. Urdu literature was at the heart of this political and literary protest movement, speaking out against social hierarchies while advocating a new kind of writing that emphasized secular modern storytelling.

I suggest that the legacy of Progressivism can be found in the voices of women poets from Ada Jafri in the 1940s onwards to Zehra Nigah, Fahmida Riaz, Kishwar Naheed, Sara Shagufta and is present in the work of regional writers such as the Punjabi poet Nasreen Anjum Bhatti and the Sindhi poet Amar Sindhu.[7] These poets express transnational and global feminist aspirations with a view to transforming local narratives of women's subservience extending beyond the national project to participatory politics and a rights-based discourse.[8] Their work can help us to engage meaningfully with the activism and aesthetics of the women's movement in Pakistan.[9] There are many poets who are part of this journey and I have selected the works of those Urdu poets who I think are representative more broadly and with whom I have had a chance to connect and interview in depth over the years.

Elite, Folk and Sufi Developments

In order to understand the spirit of *taraqqi pasand adab* (Progressive) writing and how it influenced women writers in particular, it is necessary to look at a longer history of women's relationship to the colonial state in nineteenth-century India. Historically, the first woman poet with a recognized publication to her name was a *tawaif* (courtesan) from the southern Indian Deccan region by the name of Mah Laqa Bai Chanda (1768–1824),[10] Chanda being her *takhallus* (pen name).[11] Scott Kugle argues that the main audience for Mah Laqa Bai Chanda's poetry was men and intimacy with powerful men of the court such as Aristu Jah (the prime minister) and Nizam Ali Khan gave her recognition and status.[12] Mah Laqa was, as biographers have shown, a powerful woman and held in high regard by figureheads of the Asaf Jahi dynasty (Nizams of Hyderabad). She was also a woman of property and considerable means.[13] Courtesans at the turn of the nineteenth century embodied a premodern Indic mood of *sringara rasa*, celebrating erotic love unencumbered by the later reform-led strictures of moral censure that would regulate sexual conduct in accordance with the demands of colonial society.[14]

Prior to the eighteenth-century poetry of Mah Laqa was the elite and aristocratic Mughal voice of the seventeenth-century Zebunnisa Begum, the daughter of the Mughal emperor Aurangzeb. Their prominent presence has been acknowledged in *tazkiras* (historical biographies) but the moral dynamics of the colonial and postcolonial period asked for a new kind of modernity from women that was subservient to the colonial state. Beyond the courtesan and the princess, South Asian women's cultural representations have taken different forms from folk heroines to powerful queens, ranging from Sita to Draupadi, Hir to Sohini, Mira Bai, Razia Sultana to Chand Bibi, reiterating the presence and resilience of women in fact and fiction. The sixteenth-century Punjabi folktale of Hir and Ranjha illustrates the plight and centrality of women to tales of romance and retribution.[15] *Hir Ranjha* provides a classic local example of how love is forsaken for social gain and honour, and orthodoxies maintained over heterodox positions through the bodies of women.[16]

Thus folktales combined with poetic secular and devotional Sufi representations have been a noteworthy influence on Urdu writers.[17] The Islamic Studies scholar Anemarie Schimmel reminds us of the feminine voice in Sufi poetry and how the *nafs* (soul) is connected to feminine traits, although it can also allude to vice and temptation. But she also points out that the occurrence of unfixed sexualities in Sufi poetry complicates its relationship to gender. Referring to a longer history that includes Rabia al-Adawiya, an eighth-century female Sufi poet, Schimmel makes the observation that when a woman walks in the path of God she transgresses her gender and becomes an ideal human: 'The noun "man" can be used to designate any individual who earnestly strives toward God, without making direct reference to the biological gender of the individual in question'.[18] Schimmel's philosophic analysis transforms perceptions that consider Adawiya to be a symbolic man. In South Asia the presence of women as protagonists extends to the legend of the sixteenth-century female Sufi poet from Kashmir, Habba Khatun. Habba Khatun (Loved Woman) was a peasant girl from the village of Tsandahar, who married King Sultan Yusuf Shah in Kashmir and became queen. Known for her beauty, she was tutored in Persian by a Sufi mystic and learnt to compose her own songs in Koshur. In the words of the critic Tariq Ali, she 'gave the Kashmiri language a literary form and encouraged a synthesis of Persian and Indian musical styles'.[19] Ali is of the opinion that what made her unique was the syncretism of her identity, which brought together Sufi mysticism and pre-Islamic practices. He argues that the orthodox clerics saw in her connection to music and bodily tattooing an aberration of Islam and a symptom of Sufi blasphemy. This division between the clergy and the love-crazed Sufi poet is a long-standing tradition in Islamic poetry. A woman before Khatun who also left her mark on Kashmiri Sufi poetry was the famous poet and saint Lalla Ded (1320–1392). These connections across Indian women Sufi poets are part of an Indic context that shows how Sufi and Hindu devotionalism connect 'between extreme forms of hierarchy and separation in gender roles, and moments when these boundaries were blurred and transgressed'.[20] According to Rosalind O'Hanlon, an example of this blurring can be found in representations of the self, the *nafs*: '[It] becomes the equivalent of the Hindu *virahini*, the loving spouse parted from her Lord, just as Vaishnava devotees expressed their passionate love in the feminine imagery of Radha and the *gopi* playmates of Lord Krishna.'[21] The aesthetic attachment to the Sufi feminine is illustrated in a translation from one of Habba Khatun's short lyrics:[22]

> I left my home for play
> Nor yet again
> Returned, although the day
> Sank in the West.
> The name I made is hailed
> On lips of men,
> Habba Khatun! Though veiled,
> I found no rest.[23]

Thus, Habba Khatun, Hir and Mah Laqa offer divergent historical and legendary connections for this book because their voices echo a combined Islamicate Sufi aesthetic and an Indic erotic love.[24] Habba Khatun's removal from the court evidences how power hierarchies were symbolically played out through gender and class. In essence, this trio of women allow me to emphasize the interplay between elite and non-elite culture that resonates in the language of Urdu poetry, women's identities and narratives of power as they evolve in the twentieth century. Coupled with the folk legends of Hir Ranjha, Sohini Mahiwal and Noori, they show the resilience, power and devotion of women despite social and/or class restrictions.[25]

Reform, Women's Rights and Education

In colonial India, the shift from a plural notion of communities to communalized religious nationalisms begins to materialize after the 1857 Rebellion against the British East India Company. After this historic moment of resistance, British rule was formalized and Indians became official colonial subjects of the British Crown. Nineteenth-century Muslim reformists targeted women as metonymic signifiers of the 'plight of their community' and the courtesan became a symbol of the regressive past.[26] The reformists situated themselves in a pro-Western modernist discourse and their strategy for women was not markedly different from that which was prevalent in Victorian England, prescribing 'sexual restraint and moral uprightness'.[27]

Urdu literature was deployed as a vehicle for utilitarian models of moral and social improvement by Muslim reformers with encouragement from colonial administrators and the formidable Muslim women rulers of Bhopal. As Indians responded to the modernizing and civilizing mission of the colonial state, the zenana and women were particularly targeted for reform through educating the family. This 'oriental' zenana was read by the colonizers as a product of a backward religio-moral culture in need of reform, and indeed Victorian feminists and Western women saw it as a space that highlighted civilizational differences confirming the necessity of the imperial mission. Another reason the zenana came under scrutiny was because it was seen as a place of protest and revolutionary activity that threatened the colonial state.[28]

A particularity of gender takes shape in nineteenth-century colonial India as 'modernizing' notions of masculinity and femininity, upholding middle-class family values, influenced a new moral code that reinforced heteronormative notions of sexuality.[29] The gender politics of this 'enlightened modernity' can be traced in reformist negotiations with the colonial state. For instance, the postcolonial critic Gayatri Chakravorty Spivak has analysed the legislation around the practice of *sati* (widow immolation), highlighting the double policy adopted by the colonial state to appear both benevolent and progressive. The colonial state appeased religious conservatism by negotiating an agreement that permitted voluntary sati but not forced sati, with the aim of saving 'brown women from brown men' but without losing agency or power with local communities.[30] Partha Chatterjee has argued that nineteenth-century reformers sought to resolve the 'women's question', including issues such as sati, in tandem with their 'preferred goals' of nationalism. These goals included an aspiration for the material progress of Western civilization alongside the retention of an 'authentic' spiritual culture of the East.[31] For Indian nationalists, the struggle for the preservation of cultural authenticity became a matter of uncompromising national pride in the face of colonial oppression and they chose to identify Western morality as the 'other', representing the 'other' women as out of control and beyond respectability. Thus, while the reformists in their public life participated in the civil service, their wives, sisters and mothers at home began to symbolize an 'inner' spiritual identity.[32] Their spiritual inner world, a protected sanctuary, was underpinned by the moral rectitude of their women. Chatterjee's conclusions suit the material/spiritual dyad underlying the educated Indian Muslim male elite's drive for modernity, and their key to 'resolving the ticklish problems posed by issues of social reform' was to nominate women as keepers of a true religious and spiritual identity. Meanwhile the political background to twentieth-century creative writing shows how a universalizing sisterhood engendered by Indian women's activist groups blossomed quickly, although there were inevitably differences of caste and religion.

The turning point for women's rights came in the 1920s when they gained the support of provincial legislatures. Political mobilization was nurtured through organizations such as the Women's India Association (WIA) and some of the prominent delegates agitating for equal rights from the Raj included writers and intellectuals such as Sarojini Naidu, Annie Besant and Begum Hasrat Mohani.[33] Naidu's political activism drew from the suffragette campaign in England and she went on to become the president of the Indian National Congress in 1925 and later the governor of Uttar Pradesh.[34] Appropriating the 'mask' of English writing alongside her political career, she published three collections of poetry, gaining accolades for her writing in English and recognition as the 'Nightingale of India'.[35] Naidu's journey as a poet was marked by multilingual influences including Urdu, and her political life was touched by her attachment to Gandhi.[36] Her writing emphasizes romanticism with its 'shifting moods of *vipravalamba* (love in separation), a sub-category of *sringara rasa* (the mood of love or eroticism)', a quality that appealed to Western publishers.[37] But at the same time she reinvigorated some of the traditional Indic representations of Sita and sati in the spirit of the devotional bhakti poetry of Mira Bai for contemporary purposes. In doing so, she accentuated the self-belief and activism amongst cosmopolitan Indian women who saw themselves as role models and protagonists in India's fight for independence.[38]

Naidu's progressive modernity and the unknowability of the zenana contributed to some tensions between women's activism and the civilizing mission of the colonial state. The Parsi Christian writer Cornelia Sorabji, in her speech to the Royal Empire Society in 1932, stated: 'The great struggle of the future will be between the modern and the old fashioned woman'.[39] Sorabji, as someone who was not an anticolonialist, helped to create an archive of zenana life for the colonial state. Burton notes that Sorabji did not hold the feminist movement in high regard and was, in her private letters, critical of Sarojini Naidu and her peers for being anti-British. Sorabji remained a loyal colonial subject, and her professional engagement with the zenana as an authentic Indian space accentuated her need to be recognized as a modern, secular subject.[40] These differences emphasize why we need to look at the individual stories of women within the broader movement to see how they negotiated the mantle of authenticity as colonial subjects and as activists.

The multiple narratives of women activists from Naidu to Sorabji writing in English are tinged with split perceptions, and their creative writing indicates some of the challenges they encountered as native informants to the West and as role models for indigenous communities caught between religious and secular transformations. In contrast to the cosmopolitan Anglicized public lives of the Hindu Naidu and the Parsi Christian Sorabji and belying the assumptions of an unknowable zenana are examples of women who were *purdah nashin* (secluded), writing in Urdu from the interiority of the zenana. The Muslim Urdu poet Zahida Khatun Sherwania of Aligarh (pen name Ze Khe Shin; 1894–1922) could not access public life, although she thought about politics as keenly as her male counterparts. She was not allowed to step outside the boundaries of the zenana because of family restrictions.[41] Ze Khe Shin published her verse by masquerading as a male poet, keeping her female identity a secret in order to respect her family's need for privacy thus protecting them from social ostracism. Her concern for women's education was no less than her male contemporaries and she wrote at length about it in her 60-stanza-long *Musaddas Aina-e Haram* (The Mirror of Sanctum). In this long poem she speaks as an advocate for Muslim women's education, arguing for their emancipation from the oppression of men. She writes:

Un ko reh reh ke satata hai ye be-asl khayal
Ghar men parh likh ke khawatin ka rukna hai mahaal
Kahin uthay na musawaat ka gham khez sawwal
Kahin ho jai na mardon ki hakumat ka zawaal

Hai in khud gharzon ko nahin itni bhi khabar
Zoja-e jahila hai afat jan shohar

Aiyye jahila ka ap ko dikhlaon ghar

[They are again and again disturbed by this unnatural thought
Educating women and keeping them at home is hard
It might raise the beleaguered question of equal rights
What if it brings an end to the rule of men

Oh my, these arrogant people are deeply misinformed
They don't see that an uneducated wife is disaster for her husband

Come let me show you the house of one such uncouth woman][42]

The poem gently chides Indian Muslim men, reminding them of their greater moral duty to Islam: 'Barq girti hai to bechare musalmanon per' (When lightning strikes, it falls on poor Muslims). Ze Khe Shin is deeply committed to reform through women's education and she echoes the dilemma of the period where emancipation for women in the public sphere was advocated by a particular elite rooted in community affiliations, seeking to be modern while retaining authenticity through their women.[43] A critique of this modernity came from the scepticism of Muslim traditionalists, the most vocal of whom was the poet Akbar Allahabadi (1846–1921). His satirical verse in the form of a *qita* (fragment) adopted a moral tone that was critical of the benefits of Western education for Muslim women:

> Be parda nazar aaiin jo kal chand bibian
> Akbar zamin men ghairat-e qaumi se garh gaya
>
> Puchha jo main ne ke ap ka parda vo kya hua
> Kehne lagin ke aql pe mardon ki par gaya
>
> [Yesterday when he saw some ladies without the veil,
> Akbar was thunderstruck for the modesty of the nation!
>
> When [he] asked them 'What has happened to that veil of yours?'
> They began to reply that, 'It has fallen upon the wits of [our] menfolk!'][44]

In another untitled poem, Allahabadi foretells the perils of Westernization and modernization that come with women's education:

> Ilm-e maghrib parh ke hon gi aisi khudsar bibian
> Bibian shohar banen gi aur shohar bibian
>
> Kya bataon kya karen gi ilm parh kar bibian
> Hon gi sab dipti se lekar ta governor bibian
>
> Admi kya chiz hai hewan sar charh jaen gi
> Jab pari ban jaen gi saya pehn kar bibian
>
> In ke dam-makr se abhi bachna dushvar hai
> Aur afat dhaen gi science parh kar bibian
>
> Han magar talim se ye faida hoga zarur
> Hon gi essai mission men ja ke nokar bibian
>
> Jin ke pale panch guz malmal ki qimat bhi nahin
> dal den gi un ke sar saya ka langar bibian
>
> Han magar talim un ko chahiye itni zarur
> Mard ki gham khwar hon, bachon ki rahbar bibian.

[[From] studying the knowledge of the West, [our] ladies will
  become so wilful
[That] the wives will become husbands, and the husbands will
  become wives!

What should [I] say: what will [these] ladies do after acquiring
  knowledge?
The ladies will become [everything] from deputies to governor!

What to say of men – [The ladies] will tyrannise over animals too,
When [these] ladies will put on skirts [and] become fairies!

Even now it is hard to escape from their snares and deceits;
The ladies will create even more calamities after studying science!

Yes, but there will certainly be this benefit from [their] education:
The ladies will go [and] become servants in the Christian missions.

Who does not have even the price of five yards of muslin in their pockets,
[Their] wives [too] will burden them with the cost of skirts!

Yes, but they certainly do need this much education:
[That they] should be the consolers of [their] husbands, the guides
  of [their] children!][45]

Allahabadi exaggerates the effect of Western education on women's identity, in particular, the danger of women forgetting their traditional roles. Predicting the inevitable sequence of future events, he foresees a change in women's dress, the locus of traditional identity, beginning with the loss of the 'veil' – the most prized possession in a *sharif* Muslim woman's wardrobe – symbolic of the loss of innocence. And if this is not enough Allahabadi embellishes further, predicting a women-only workforce of deputies, governors and even scientists. He caricatures Eastern masculinity whose strongest asset, it seems, are its women who, pushed outside their 'natural' environment, will encounter the unnatural Western world and succumb to it. Female vulnerability will be replaced by male vulnerability and the world will be turned upside down. The skirt-wearing fairies turning into agents of tyranny, the women scientists stirring cauldrons of witchery, others forsaking their religion for the mission, all symbolize the anxieties of a colonized masculinity. His satirical verses indirectly comment on the patriarchal manifestation of the British Raj, which succeeded in establishing a male gendered hierarchy over their dominion, leading to a feminization of the colonized male identity.[46]

Speaking out for Muslim women was the Bengali Muslim feminist activist, educationist and writer Rokeya Sakhawat Hossain. Using the form of the short story, she wrote 'Sultana's Dream', a tale that subverted the conservatism of Allahabadi with a utopian emancipatory insight from a futuristic place called 'Ladyland', inhabited by women while men are relegated to the '*mardana*'. 'Sultana's Dream', a satire in English, was published in the *Indian Ladies Magazine* in 1905. 'Ladyland' reversed women's experience of purdah and patronage to one in which they were in charge of political affairs, gaining ascendancy through scientific knowledge. The story bears testimony to her prowess in the English language as a tool of influence and progress as well as a medium in which she could mock the customs of seclusion, an exercise that she also undertook in her essay-writing in the vernacular.[47] This feminist fantasy inevitably led to doubts over Hossain's authenticity as a Muslim woman.[48]

In contrast, Altaf Husain Hali, Akbar Allahabadi and later male prose writers' varying responses to the women question underline two extreme positions on women, speaking of them and for them, but never allowing them to inhabit a space of their own. In her study of Muslim reformist writings, Gail Minault has showcased both the representation of women by men and writings by women in the nineteenth century that illustrate them to be 'symbolic of the plight of their community: its backwardness, its ignorance of the faith, its perilous cultural and historical viability, particularly when faced with the loss of political power'.[49] Minault argues that a sharif class of North Indian Muslims, 'the former Mughal service gentry', were actively involved in the production of these writings.[50] The 'sharif urban literati of Upper India' collectively savoured the dream of reforming the Indian Muslim elite which had been in decline since the time of the last Mughal emperor, Bahadur Shah Zafar.[51]

Therefore the speaking out of Ze Khe Shin from within the zenana is even more noteworthy. Her main difference as an Urdu writer in contrast to English authors is her complete absence from the public sphere. Another prominent veiled elite woman who wrote poetry was Fatima Sughra Haya of Lucknow's Firangi Mahal, but, unlike Ze Khe Shin, her poetry was published for public consumption in the 1930s. This led to objections from the family and thereafter she wrote as Haya.[52] Some of Haya's poetry is introspective, focusing on family and devotion to the Prophet, while other poems reflect her views on contemporary themes. It has been noted that she was unable to reach a wider community initially due to familial constraints and latterly because of her deteriorating mental health.[53]

The concerns of public and private, purdah and polygamy are detailed in the English writings of Iqbalunnisa Hussain, which argue for Muslim women's education and express reservations about religious practices that confined women to the domestic sphere. In her essays, she speaks more generally of the condition of Muslim women advocating modern education and worldliness:

> The purdah system in uncivilized circles is taken as a mark of social distinction as it necessarily makes a woman virtuous. But the purdah system observed in our country is an artificial one. It is just an external force which compels an individual to live a secluded life. […] the purdah system observed by uncivilised women has not made them at all virtuous. This artificial purdah is neither possible nor supported by modern girls. Modern education aims at the real purdah, the development of character, personality, and the discipline of one's emotions and instincts. One can imagine the sad plight of modern girls in the family that observes artificial purdah strictly and indiscriminately, to the ruination of their health, education, and personality.[54]

Hussain writes polemically and also experientially to challenge the discourse of purdah as a signifier of a traditional society. She expresses some of the frustrations that were felt by intellectual women in purdah who lived in 'civilized circles', such as Haya and Ze Khe Shin, and like them her emphasis is on the lack of education/civilization amongst the lower classes.[55] Thus we see how the challenges of public performativity affected ashraf women Urdu poets alongside their English counterparts. While they aspired to a Western-style education, the West's identification of Muslim women as a community in need of saving from the zenana led to clashing views. The poet of the East, Muhammad Iqbal, warned against Western feminism in his magnum opus *Javidnama* (The Book of Eternity), setting up Western women as constructs of secular liberalism who advised against maternity and advocated for abortion in contrast to the pious and obedient daughter of the Islamic world Sharaf Al-Nisa, a devotee of God and the Qur'an.[56] This rejection of secular liberalism was translated through the literal separation of the public and the private in some spheres echoing a reformist mistrust of modernity. Muslim women representatives such as Begum Jahan Ara Shahnawaz, the daughter of Mian Mohammad Shah Nawaz, was encouraged by her husband to give up 'purdah'.[57] Kumkum Sangari and Sudesh Vaid have highlighted the importance of understanding the shifting meaning of public and private across social classes and how they affected women differently. In their analysis, the common denominator setting the agenda in both cases was the middle-class family. They suggest that 'modernizing movements' including social reform and nationalism offered a much more 'liberal space' for middle-class women in colonial India while 'democratizing movements' worked toward altering the 'social structures of patriarchal formations'.[58]

By the 1930s, the Indian women's movement had lost its political momentum as an Indian collective, and solidarity gave way to separatist communal associations.[59] Nationalism imposed its own demands and women's roles became redefined in the process of resistance, representing ideals of honour and shame, protecting the family according to ethnicity. In the meantime, an avant-garde literary movement instigated by the Progressive Writers' Association (PWA) and the modernist group Halqa-e arbab-e zauq (The circle of aesthetics) brought a new consciousness to textual representations of gender and sexuality which forever changed the stereotyped ideal of the honourable and chaste woman. Literary groups such as these marked a radical transformation in the literary depictions of gender roles in the first half of the twentieth century, while the presence of women themselves as active participants in the vanguard of the Progressive Writers' movement transformed the older conception of women's writing as a hobby inhabited by the aristocracy or a by-product of male writing. Progressive liberalism advocated a change in the articulation of women who carried the burden of honour and shame in a traditional society and had previously been confined to the zenana. The discursive role of the Progressive Writers' movement instigated a delineation of class and gender boundaries and facilitated the emergence of women poets in a public arena that had traditionally belonged to men. For these poets, the sexual freedom advocated by the Progressives meant that they were no longer inhibited by the spectre of being caricatured as courtesans. Thus the advent of modernity and the formation of a new urban middle class led to a visible change in the perception of women as inhabitants of a secluded sphere. Their visibility increased and the anonymity of print media allowed them a textual space on a par with their male contemporaries. The Progressives, a hybrid group of writers and intellectuals, were committed to a shared future for India, envisioning a nation that was inclusive across caste, class and religion. With the onset of Partition the ethos of Progressive writers was split across two nations and the writers were left with a nostalgic vision of a borderless world.

Feminist Voices and the Legacy of Progressive Writing

In her book *The State of Islam: Culture and Cold War Politics in Pakistan* Saadia Toor unpicks the divide between liberal patriotic writers, who she argues subscribed to the 'key values of "progressivism"' and became part of an anti-Communist intellectual agenda, and those with a socialist vision who were picked off by the state, for instance the international award-winning Urdu poet Faiz Ahmed Faiz.[60] Habib Jalib, who took over the mantle of revolutionary poetry while Faiz was incarcerated, used poetry as a platform to comment critically on Ayub's sponsorship scheme for 'establishment' writers. Jalib became known as the 'people's poet' and was a strong presence in the women's marches of the 1980s protesting against Sharia laws.[61] Jalib's spirit of irreverence is regenerated in the work of two prominent twentieth-century poets, Fahmida Riaz and Kishwar Naheed, but with the key difference that their kind of writing could not garner a listening public in the same way because it broached taboo topics. To understand Jalib's story fully, we need to include the counternarratives of women Urdu poets who were marching alongside men and shifting the landscape of Pakistani culture, together with human rights and women activists such as Asma Jahangir, and Nigar Ahmed.

As Toor argues, the strategic closure of the Left through the dismantling of the PWA of Pakistan meant the co-option of Urdu intellectual tradition by the state to authenticate its credibility and sovereignty in times of crisis. She suggests that deep state politics compromised the positionality of writers. Within this larger framework, Toor sets out the context of Urdu poetry and how it has been an 'important site of women's dissent and the contestation of the politics of Islamization'. She notes that radical women poets such as Kishwar Naheed and Fahmida Riaz 'appropriated a long tradition of political poetry in South Asia to articulate a unique vision of self and society' in order to critique the state and its version of Islam. Toor's reading offers a different inflection to the association of Urdu with ashraf culture and her inclusion of feminist literary voices presents a counterhegemonic narrative through women's writing. I wish to extend Toor's argument by incorporating literary analysis and literary history in an attempt to deconstruct the hierarchies of language and gender and how they contribute to ideological representations of culture over time. Reflecting on nationalist mobilization in the pre-independence period, I consider the post-Partition phase and Pakistani women's poetry as an alternative sphere where the representation of self and subjectivity signalled the entry of a new Pakistani woman who didn't conform to a traditional cultural norm. It is at this juncture that women's poetry also shifts from a liberal elite aesthetic to an organic multivocal formation. Faiz and poets such as Ahmad Faraz and Habib Jalib were supporters and influencers of resistance poetry that embraced the values of egalitarianism and took Urdu literary culture in a new direction. They were interconnected with the women's movement as it opened up an avenue of dissent in a militarized state. The women's movement, which had started off as disparate groups with different agendas, became a more organized and integrated force in the 1980s in response to the Sharia-led Hudood Ordinances. Their dissenting voices and the Progressive journeys of Faiz and Jalib influenced the formation of a global and local feminist self-consciousness amongst women poets such as Kishwar Naheed and Fahmida Riaz. Questions of gender justice re-emerged through the women's movement as the official Left was closed down as a result of Cold War politics.[62]

Riaz and Naheed became prominent voices when they joined forces with the women's movement in Pakistan in the 1980s, but their poetry and politics remain lesser known than the voices of major Urdu poets such as Faiz Ahmed Faiz or Habib Jalib, who are associated with a resistance Urdu literary culture. As writers they experienced the shifting landscape of Urdu literary culture in the 1960s, witnessing the highs and lows of a military-led state bureaucracy and, like their male counterparts, reflected these experiences in their poetry, most prominently the seclusion of women during General Zia-ul Haq's military rule and his adoption of right-wing Islamism through legislature. In this book, I illustrate the connectivity of Faiz and Jalib to the women's movement and women poets in order to demonstrate the intertwined gendered project of the secular and sacred as it played out in verse. Women poets quietly continued the legacy of Progressive resistance, manipulating a national language to articulate personal and political trajectories of the sacred and secular by initially incorporating a transnational feminist consciousness. Fahmida Riaz, who was committed to a Marxist outlook and radical politics, became increasingly dejected with liberal patriarchies and found it impossible to maintain an alliance with the state. Kishwar Naheed, on the other hand, stayed within a liberal circle, maintained a civil service profile despite setbacks and stuck to a feminist stance with women's empowerment as her main goal. Parvin Shakir died in a tragic car crash, Sara Shagufta committed suicide, Zehra Nigah and others continue to thrive.

Form and Performativity: The Ghazal and the Mushaira

A form that is central to the theme of mystical and romantic unrequited love is the *ghazal* love lyric. As an artistic expression, its origins can be traced to the pre-Islamic Arabic ode in the seventh century and its later development in Persia in the thirteenth and fourteenth centuries and subsequent vernacular renditions in North India. In the Persian canon, the Sufi poet Jalaluddin Rumi (d. 1273) of Konya is an enduring influence, as is the more stylized Hafiz of Shiraz (d. 1399). They enriched the love lyric with themes of mysticism, philosophy and human emotion. Described as a necklace of pearls, each ghazal can consist of at least five rhyming couplets that are linked together as a sequence but can be interpreted separately. The first couplet is distinctive, with its double rhyme featuring a refrain in the second line that is repeated in the second line of subsequent verses. These connected couplets have a changing rhyme (*qafia*) and a fixed end rhyme (*radif*), and include a reference to the poet's pen name (*takhallus*) in the last verse.⁶³ The Urdu ghazal consists of free-standing couplets tied to particular metres borrowed from Perso-Arabic prosody. Metaphorically, the ghazal in its various manifestations incorporates both spiritual and secular themes. It has been argued that the Urdu ghazal came to prominence in the Mughal court, where classical ghazals were performed in poetry symposia known as the *mushaira* and at salons by tawaifs, whereas mystical ghazals were recited at Sufi shrines.⁶⁴ Thus the story of the Indian Urdu ghazal is linked to elite Persianate and non-elite Sufi formations associated with the language of the royal exalted camp, *zabaan-e Urdu-e mualla*, in North India and devotional shrine culture. Most importantly, the ghazal and Urdu poetry more generally is a performative medium that is recited in the public space of the mushaira and this phenomenon has an effect on women's relationship to it in the twentieth century. In South Asia, the ghazal was earmarked for change from sixteenth-century expressions of pre-modern love to nineteenth-century reform as the Mughal Empire gave way to the British Empire. I explore how and why the ghazal's themes of love came under scrutiny, its self-conscious separation from the courtesan quarters and the language of the bazaar, and its changing outlook in the post-national period as romantic love gave way to national affiliation.

The nineteenth-century poet Altaf Husain Hali, under the modernizing influence of the Muslim reformist Sayyid Ahmad Khan's Aligarh school of thought, pioneered '*naicharal shairi*' (natural poetry). As part of his drive for newness, he argued for a new poetic idiom that was reflective of the real world and human conditions rather than a metaphysical universe and decadent erotica. Working in the Government Book Depot from 1870 to 1874/75, editing books translated from English to Urdu, he 'described how through this process he developed a relationship with English literature, and how the prestige of Eastern literature, and especially Persian literature, "declined in my heart"'.⁶⁵ This can also be read as a response to the civilizational change wrought by a colonial education policy that brought Indians closer to the 'superior' cultural values of the English at the expense of local literature and culture.⁶⁶ If we look at his major critical work *Muqaddama sher-o shairi*, first published in 1893, it aimed at the reform of classical Urdu poetry and the need for a modern necharal material approach. In his *Muqaddama*, Hali took on board the form of the ghazal love lyric for reform. He influenced some of the new turns the ghazal would take in the twentieth century, particularly modern experimentations with social realism. Analysing Hali through the lens of comparative literature, Javed Majeed argues that 'Hali attempted to replace the lyrical world of the ghazal, and its self-conscious sense of artifice and symbol, with mimetic realist literature'.⁶⁷ Part of this transition was Hali's desire for the ghazal poet to utilize the masculine gender in the grammatical representation of the beloved, and while doing so avoid cloaking this grammatical beloved in a symbolic female form, as he thought it would lead to interpretations of the beloved as a hermaphrodite hijra.[68] Hali was very conscious of the respectability of women in purdah and therefore urged poets to preserve its sanctity. He instructed poets to refrain from mentioning the gender of the beloved and also to abstain from using words which would intimate whether it was a man or a woman, such as *qaba* (tunic), *kula* (turban), *arsi* (ring with mirror worn by women), *mehndi* (henna), *jhumar* (a group of dancing women or a piece of jewellery worn in women's hair), *churian* (bangles), *choti* (plaited hair).[69] In his review of Hali's reformist legacy, Safdar Ahmed has observed that Hali's representation of love 'desexualised the figure of the beloved' and that he 'invested the quotidian realm of the family, society, and nation-state with a sacral, extramundane importance'.[70] This reform of the representation of the beloved in the ghazal underlined Hali's commitment to the social and moral reform of Muslim society, particularly its women. And it highlighted the careful control over expressions of sexual desire indicative of a new cultural politics that effectively desexualized the body.

Hali and his contemporary Muhammad Husain Azad, both significant literary figures, were influenced by the colonial British administration through their respective jobs in the Anjuman-e Punjab (Punjab Society) and the Government Book Depot. Their reform of the ghazal was partly an endeavour to connect with the world of English literature and its Victorian aspirations, mediated by Colonel Holroyd and the English books that were brought into India, and partly an attempt to please their new patrons.[71] These two critics, who were well versed in the classical tradition and also its practitioners, therefore became the harbingers of a modern *necharal* style.

Urdu poetry has traditionally been disseminated in a public forum called the mushaira – a literary gathering which may or may not be open to the public where poets mainly recite ghazals, although it is not exclusive of other forms. The mushaira is thus the public space where Urdu poetry becomes performative, and the listening audience has an opportunity to convey their verbal appreciation or disapproval directly to the poet. There are two kinds of audience and two kinds of mushaira: the public and the private. It has been argued that the mushaira is the 'product of a princely age' because the classical period was prone to private mushairas frequented by an aristocratic class.[72] The atmosphere of the mushaira was formal and it followed certain rituals like the placing of a candle in front of the poet who was reciting and an ascending order of appearance, with the most senior poet reciting last. Poets were also known to recite ghazals in *tarannum* (melody) during a mushaira. The mushaira was a test of a poet's ability to extemporize verses in accordance with a given rhyme and metre as well as the development of metaphor creation.[73] The modern public mushaira usually has a host who is responsible for introducing each poet and organizing the appropriate order of appearance. In the post-Partition arena of an Islamic Republic, the mushaira and the ghazal form together have presented challenges to established patterns of gender when it comes to the private lives of women and performativity in public male spaces. We see this tension played out when women poets begin to perform alongside male poets in public mushairas.

A final aspect of the ghazal that is a hallmark of the modern period is the nation as beloved. This is something that Afsaneh Najmabadi writes about with reference to the changing sensibilities of the Persian ghazal and expressions of love in twentieth-century poetry. Najmabadi makes the case that the ghazal form is appropriated to re-present the 'erotic vatan' as the patriotic land, helping to construct the idea of a singular Iran.[74] In Urdu poetry we see the nation as beloved in the writing of Faiz Ahmed Faiz who infused the lyric form with a modern sensibility that absorbed the crisis of self to signal a new national culture. In doing so, he absorbed the romantic form as a quintessential part of modern experience, expressing it through a secular humanism.[75] This journey begins with his iconic poem 'Mujh se pehli si mohabbat meri mahbub na mang' (My Love, Do Not Ask of Me a Love Like Before) which transports the beloved to a modern setting of alienation and loss.

Islam and the West: Community and Nation

The secular has a long and complex history in the study of Islam and has been studied in depth by scholars of Islam as well as those wishing to understand Pakistan historically and politically. Islam has many different historical and geographical contexts. The narrative includes the Qur'an, the Prophet, the importance of ritual and obligation, and an ethical–moral spiritual formation that is in dialogue with other cultures and civilizations. *Adab* (etiquette), *akhlaq* (ethics) and *fiqh* (law) are entwined across Muslim nations, underlining the influence of Islamic philosophy on Western civilization and its interactions with Sharia. It is not within the scope of this book to provide a detailed synopsis of those positions, but it is important to acknowledge that within the Islamic community itself there is diversity and difference, from orthodox Sunni Islam to the heterodox Twelver Shi'ism. From the Crusades to the European colonial period of the seventeenth to nineteenth centuries, the Islamic community has been framed as traditional and illiberal, unable to adjust to the tenets of European modernity. This positioning is often projected through the woman question in Islam.[76] With the rise of nationalism, anticolonial movements and the dissolution of the Ottoman

Empire, the notion of a unified Islamic nationalism has struggled despite the intervention of leaders such as Mustafa Kemal Ataturk in Turkey and Gamal Abdel Nasser in Egypt.[77] In South Asia, Islam has travelled through Sufi shrines, Mughal kings and trade routes. Scholars from Muzaffar Alam to Sanjay Subrahmanyam, Richard Eaton to Barbara Metcalf have looked at the pluralities of how ideas of community have evolved over time through lived experience, madrassa education, court patronage and the rule of law. South Asian Islam is part of a cosmopolitan Islamicate civilization that connects Africa to Europe to Asia, incorporating a diversity that is difficult to imagine in a singular community, encompassing multiple languages, arts, architecture and music. The religion coexists in conjunction with these contexts. According to Bruce Lawrence, 'beyond the cultural specifier of any language or culture looms the adaptable, permeable quality of Islamicate civilization'. For him, the learning objective of such a viewpoint has to be 'that Islamicate civilisation need not "confront" multiculturalism or adapt to it, for it is, of its essence, multicultural'.[78] The spectre that confronts South Asia politically beyond a philosophic multicultural cosmopolitanism is that of jihad and terror. In her book *Partisans of Allah*, Ayesha Jalal critiques an ethical and political exploration of jihad in South Asia. Incorporating the humanism of Ghalib, Islamic hellenic philosophers, the *falsafa* of Al-Ghazali and Jalaluddin Rumi's mystical poetry, she argues that the common shared ideal in these writings is an inner jihad underwriting good deeds. She identifies secularism with Enlightenment ideals and the civilizing mission of a European modernity separate from a previously dialogic process of secularization. Jalal argues that when jihad is appropriated as a galvanizing force of a former expansionist community experiencing the loss of sovereignty, the multiple layers of jihad as an ethical idea get transmuted into an idea of religion as a marker of identity rather than a belief system. For Jalal, the turning point when the idea of jihad turns to warfare is demarcated by the teachings and influence of the eighteenth-century Delhi scholar Shah Waliullah and his reform of Islamic thought to its fundamentals. She recognizes this type of leadership and intervention as an intra-Islamic politics that has led to greater divisions amongst the Muslim community. Jalal argues that Waliullah's activist leadership gives greater authority to the *ulema* who are relied upon in Pakistan for an authentication of Islamic credentials. Thus Jalal understands jihad to be a signifier of divisions within the Muslim community rather than an all-out war against ideas of Western modernity.[79] The poet Muhammad Iqbal was influenced by Shah Waliullah's teachings yet his poetry and philosophic writings show a mixture of ideas including that of Islamic cosmopolitanism, the pursuit of a perfect community and an activism that sought an inner philosophic jihad between Sufi quietism and political activism. Elsewhere I have argued that Iqbal's poetry looks beyond the particularity of community to rethink how Islamic societies operate outside the power of local ulema networks and communitarian politics located in territorial belongings.[80]

In this book, my reading of the secular is concentrated on Pakistani Urdu writings by women in the twentieth century as it fleshes out the woman question that is at the heart of an East–West disagreement over modernity. I draw on postcolonial criticism, in particular the work of Aamir Mufti whose readings of Faiz Ahmed Faiz construe the contexts of modernity, minorization and Partition for the Urdu writer. His engagement with Edward Said's writing on the theme of 'secular criticism' is useful to note here. Gil Anidjar has critiqued Said for embracing a liberal secular perspective, arguing that he undermines a hermeneutical study of religion.[81] Mufti suggests that Said's use of the secular is 'a meaningful and productive misuse' because it sets up the groundwork for a re-examination of the term 'secular' and its association with modern progress.[82] In order to contextualize this for the purposes of this study, it is useful to note that in the colonial period we see a deliberate separation between religion and the colonial state, where the religious is demarcated as part of the private sphere and the secular as public. However, religion continued to be deployed by the colonial state in political representations across multiple communities in South Asia, underlining a communalist approach toward the recognition of social groups. At the same time, Western secularism was upheld as a model of rational thinking independent of religious values. Talal Asad analyses the secular as a series of historical formations deeply intertwined with religion, in particular Christianity, and argues that the nation-state is not separate from the religious sphere, suggesting that 'modernity is a project – or rather a series of interlinked projects – that certain people in power seek to achieve'.[83] In the case of the Indian Muslim reformists, modernity was certainly a plan that people in power aspired to work with, as can be seen in Sayyid Ahmad Khan's reformist project of education and enlightenment that sought to bring the Muslim community closer to the colonial state and helped to safeguard Muslim interests by maintaining elite interests. Eventually, the growing deliberate and self-conscious separation of the secular and the religious amongst the two political groupings of Aligarh and Deoband meant a culturalist appropriation of language that targeted the zenana in a bid to modernize it.[84] These intricate shifts inform my chapter readings, offset against a critical understanding of the concepts of community, nation and family as they have evolved in the Indian subcontinent in the twentieth century from pre-Partition India to postcolonial Pakistan.

Pakistan: Secular Sacred Ideologies

The Partition-led status of an Islamic state for India's Muslim minorities remains Pakistan's key difference with its neighbour and rival, India. I have shown that historically and politically there has been an ongoing conflict between projected modern secular and religious ideologies with Islam and the West in South Asia. This is played out in Pakistan through the respective legacies of Mohammad Ali Jinnah, the founding father and first governor general, and Muhammad Iqbal, the poet philosopher, who offer ideals of nationalism and Muslim community that have been ideologically interpreted, appropriated and represented over time. The state will from time to time make a claim to secularism, noted in the often quoted lines by Mohammad Ali Jinnah in his founding address to the constituent assembly of Pakistan on 11 August 1947:

> You are free; you are free to go to your temples, you are free to go to your mosques or to any other places of worship in this State of Pakistan. You may belong to any religion or caste or creed – that has nothing to do with the business of the State. [...] We are starting in the days when there is no discrimination, no distinction between one community and another, between one caste or creed and another. We are starting with this fundamental principle that we are all citizens and equal citizens of one State.[85]

Its structural implementation has remained fuzzy with liberal politicians and autocrats such as Field Marshal Ayub Khan, who got rid of civilian governance in 1958 and succumbed to political gain through adherence to Islamic ideology despite the liberalization of family laws and opposition to the ulema. Omar Noman has argued how the demand for Pakistan was really a demand for the protection of elite interests and property for landlords and not particularly built around majoritarian politics. However, this changed after the formation of Pakistan and especially after the Ayub period during which secularism was seen as a Western influence that was exclusivist and American led. It paved the way for the successful mobilization of the Jamaat-e Islami under the leadership of Maulana Maududi. Noman notes that Maududi 'distrusted [...] westernised political leaders and the other theologians, with whom he had long-standing doctrinal quarrels. He emphasised the incongruity of creating a secular state in Pakistan'.[86] As a term, 'secular' is not present in Pakistan's Constitution, but secularism influenced state policies before the rise of General Zia and returned again under General Pervez Musharraf's enlightened moderation programme in the 2000s. Thus post-Partition national politics have time and again appeased the religious Right to gain a majority vote and have led to a political divide between the secular and sacred as two separate entities, one a manifestation of the West and the other an authentic expression of Islam. The politics of Islamism has been played out constitutionally since the anti-Ahmadi riots of the 1950s and the rise of right-wing politics over the establishment of a true Islamic state.[87]

At the end of the 1950s and into the 1960s, the PWA in Pakistan was one of the casualties of Field Marshal Ayub's international commitment to America's Cold War agenda. He closed off avenues for resistance-led Left writers and introduced state support for ideological patriotic writing through the introduction of prize culture. With the closure of the Progressives as an association, the idea of the secular and sacred as separate spheres of modernity and tradition became further enshrined and the Left was framed as an antinational group that threatened the security of the nation. While manipulating modern secular style legislation through state policies, most notably in the overhaul of family laws, Ayub courted an Islamist agenda to secure his position of power.[88] Gender relations were therefore central to Pakistan's political formations in the 1960s and made a long-lasting impact on how the secular modern/traditional Islam divide would play out. The point of interest for women's groups during the Ayub regime was the liberalization of family laws in 1961 that led to progressive legislation for the rights of married women.[89] Ayub's 'paternalistic' martial law regime guided women toward social assistance and directed their energies toward urban welfare programmes.

Zulfiqar Ali Bhutto's democracy in the 1970s heralded an improvement in the status of women's rights. In 1972 women were accorded equal opportunities in the civil service including the appointment of Begum Rana Liaqat Ali as governor of Sindh and Begum Kaneez Yousaf as vice-chancellor of the Quaid-e-Azam University. The civil service was also a place where women could apply for posts connected to foreign and district management.[90] The Constitution of 1973, articles 25 and 27, pronounced the end of gender discrimination. Events such as the International Women's Year became part of the national consciousness. There were other measures such as the formation of a national commission that operated as a watchdog for political parties who denied the right of representation to women. While women's rights were increasingly on the government agenda, Bhutto's rise to power had relied on an alliance with the army, a collusion that would lead to his demise. Bhutto, despite his appeal to a people's politics, was equally imbricated in the structures of power that relied on authoritarianism and appeasement of the right wing.

A watershed moment for women as symbolic representatives of the Islamic state came in the 1980s under the military regime of General Zia-ul Haq, who implemented Sharia laws making sex a public matter mediated by religious law. Zia also deployed the media-led Nizam-e Mustafa (The law of

Muhammad) campaign for an Islamic way of life, targeting women's bodies through an Islamic dress code, segregation policies and separate women's universities in order to implement his particular vision of a singular Muslim community through visible identifications.[91] The juridical legislation in the Hudood Ordinance on Zina (literally 'illegitimate sex') was a direct means of controlling sexual behaviour. Zina included adultery and fornication as well as *zina-bil jabr* (rape). Perpetrators of zina were severely punished by public lashes and were also liable to stoning to death depending on the severity of the case. For women, the situation was clearly inequitable as their charge of rape had to be accompanied by the witness of four pious adult males.[92] Thus the Hudood Ordinance passed in 1979 succeeded in policing adultery and fornication as crimes against the state, and was followed by the Law of Evidence in 1984 which firmly halved women's legal status.[93] Together they formed the backbone of Zia's Islamic renaissance along with later laws on *qisas* and *diyat* (retribution and murder) that gave precedence to religious law over state law. The articulation of his renaissance took place on a national scale through the visible campaign of *chadar* and *chardivari* (veil and seclusion), targeting women as the carriers of the Islamic nation. Women in Pakistan came to embody the purity of the nation, and nation-builders of the Islamic state relied on the lives of exemplary women such as the Prophet Muhammad's mother, wives and daughters – who were amongst the first practitioners of the Islamic moral code for women – to give agency to their own prescriptions for women.[94]

Since then, state narratives have continued to engage with women's issues, including the repeal of the Hudood Ordinances and the Bill for the Protection of Women's Rights at Work in the twenty-first century, under the alternating military and civilian leaderships of General Musharraf and Nawaz Sharif of Pakistan Muslim League-Nawaz group (PML-N), followed by Imran Khan's Tehreek-e Insaf party. In the wrangle over sovereignty, the modern nation-state with a narrative of equal rights and secular citizenship has been at odds with its ideological formation as a singular sacred Islamic state appeasing religious parties and relying on the army for the security of its precarious borders.

In a related Indian context, Rajeswari Sunder Rajan argues that 'the women's movement ends by both forming alliances with the state – typically in the form of seeking the recourse of its laws in instituting legal reform or enacting new laws on behalf of women – as well as resisting the state'.[95] This 'uneven' development can be traced in the rise and fall of women's activism over a period of time, and in Pakistan we can see this quite starkly as power changes hands across individuals and parties, military dictatorships and democratic alliances. Scholars have noted how the targeting of women's bodies and sexualities through religious legislation led to a new politics of resistance in the form of the women's movement of the 1980s.[96] This movement had deep cultural connections to the arts ranging from theatre to poetry in fighting for gender justice. The groups articulated a secular stance that separated the discourse of rights from religion while working with an interpretation of Islamic law in tandem with other groups. While the secular wasn't projected as an either/or representation, they were perceived as agents of Westernization by right-wing groups.

I will take cognizance of some of these contexts in later chapters to see how women responded to state-led narratives in their imaginative representations of gender identities across secular and religious divides. What emerges from these conversations is the co-option and inclusion of women into sacred nation and state-led discourses that mythologize and symbolize ideas of honour and shame. Key political moments, from Partition to the Cold War and 9/11, are important to note as they have a bearing on women's changing relationship to the nation.[97] Amrita Chhachhi, writing about secular identity politics and women in India, argues that women have been 'crucial markers of identity – of the nation, community, caste group and religious group. They have been objects as well as agents.'[98] Drawing on Benedict Anderson's work on nationalism, she focuses on how nations utilize the 'language of kinship or the home' to further their ideology. As an example, she refers to 'the merging of the nation/community with the selfless mother/devout wife' and makes the observation that discourses of communalism, nationalism and fundamentalism include 'notions of revenge for the "violation of our mothers and sisters"'.[99] This underlines the bind women are in as symbolic representatives of the nation who are subject to sexual violence. It shows why women in both India and Pakistan are not always independent agents when it comes to the business of nation formation, and their role in nationalist campaigns also makes them vulnerable to accusations of inauthenticity as religious subjects. While there are solidarities for women that come out of transnational and global contexts, there are also specific home-led identity and communal politics that can disrupt.[100]

In this book, I work out the woman question in relation to feminism with reference to how specific notions of secular and sacred get translated in the field of Urdu literary studies over time, by women as well as men, in Pakistan. While there is no agreement over the term 'feminism' in Pakistan, there have been scholarly representations from activists in the humanities and social sciences that call for a secular approach and others who advocate for a post-secular position. Margot Badran argues that 'feminism in Islam has long been presumed non-existent by most in the West, who have insisted that "feminism and Islam" is an oxymoron'.[101] She notes the work of Islamic scholars such as Amina Wadud, Asma Barlas and Riffat Husain, who are part of a growing post-secular response mostly understood through the writing of Saba Mahmood on the grassroots women's piety movement in Egypt. But there are quite a lot of differences in how these scholars approach Islam and it is important to recognize that Wadud and Barlas are working with particular aspects of scripture and jurisprudence, whereas Mahmood's is an ethnographic study of how piety is attached to the performativity of the veil and an inner transformation in the Egyptian women's mosque movement, building on the work of Judith Butler.[102] In Badran's reading, the secular and religious affect women differently in Muslim majority countries in that 'women have acquired greater equality in secular space than in religious space'.[103] This understanding can also be found in the work of Pakistani social science scholars such as Afiya Zia, who provides a useful trajectory of activist feminism in Pakistan although her liberal versus post-secular outlook is at times didactic in its vision of what feminism can and should do.[104] This is in direct contrast to Sadaf Ahmad's study of Pakistan's growing religious piety movement amongst urban middle-class women represented through Farhat Hashmi's Al-Huda group.[105] She argues that this woman-centric formation enables the performative politics of women's piety in the form of the *dars* (religious sermon), transforming it into a shared space in which women experience empowerment through shared conversations about everyday problems and Islamic solutions in the domestic sphere. In doing so, she builds on Saba Mahmood's performative model of agency for pious women. Amina Jamal reasons that a nuanced understanding of the women's movement in Pakistan is necessary in order to shift it beyond a monolithic representation of elite women's universalist liberal feminist activism which is dismissive of religion, drawing on her study of the right-wing Islamic party Jamaat-e Islami and its women as an alternative example.[106] Her recommendation is for a transnational feminism that destabilizes notions of home, family and nation to develop a more informed reading, as those are the categories around which notions of gender have acquired a fixity of values within national discourse.[107] Jamal's critique of the secular as an elite space suggests that women are not always independent agents and vested interests play a part in the campaigns that are championed, and this is where her study of Jamaat-e Islami and its women is poised. Thus the post-secular turn mostly comes up with reference to nations where religion plays a big part in the identification of women: it is not, as Afiya Zia understands it, a confusion over women's agency by anthropologists but a different way of reading and understanding agency that looks at the possibility of a future dialogue across women's activism. For Zia, rights can only be achieved through a liberal feminist model, but it is unclear how this will work in an Islamic nation across different groups of women. In Zia's model, secular women emerge as enlightened and empowered.[108] These gendered scholarly interventions offer shifting perspectives on the secular and sacred, interpreting how changing modernities have affected women's everyday lives. In doing so they rely on the national as a defining space for women's identities, which remains a contested place both within the nation and beyond its territorial borders. Women's access to education in public spaces introduced a new secular model, but it remained uneven without equal opportunity for all. Through a global religious and secular activism, a stake in local and cross-border Progressive politics, women poets have played a transformative role in developing new dialogues across different spheres. This does not reproduce either/or positionalities and neither is it entirely trusting of existing cultural hegemonies about women.

In the chapters that follow, I scrutinize the literary history of women's representation in twentieth-century literature, arguing that the politics of gender cannot be separated from the aesthetics of the canonical Urdu literary tradition. This includes intertextual influences ranging from the classical *ghazal* (love lyric), *masnavi* (narrative poem), *dastan* (story) to the modern *nazm* (poem), *afsana* (short story) and novel. Embedded in these shifts of form are the narratives of appropriation of the feminine voice by reformists, anticolonial resistance movements and the increasing presence of women in the public sphere, and ideological interpretations of gender in post-Partition Pakistan. The story that emerges is one that demands a reinterpretation of gender in a literary tradition that has in the process of modernity conceptualized women as the softer sex in need of protection and honour bound within the heteronormative family. There is a shift in class identification from an aristocratic Urdu literary culture in the eighteenth to mid-nineteenth centuries, to a new urban middle class in the late nineteenth and twentieth centuries. After Partition we see an emphasis on the trope of the national family in women's writing and a distancing from the colonial/patriarchal family narrative.[109]

In the next chapter, I study the form of *rekhti* and the development of a gendered voice in canonical Urdu texts that reflected a crisis of masculinity after 1857. I consider the tensions in the Aligarh- and Deoband-led writings over the woman question. As reform gave way to anticolonialism with a new nationalist uprising agitating for the decolonization of India, women once again became the centre of an authenticity discourse.[110] By and large, romantic love became increasingly bound to the household, its economy and the outward piety of women in the reformist and anticolonial period.[111] Subsequently, late nineteenth- and early twentieth-century ideas of women and the family as nurturers and carers came to inform women's heteronormative position in the new Pakistani nation. Of particular note is the poetry of Altaf Husain Hali who appealed to Muslim women to protect their *qaum* (the Muslim family and community) as mothers, daughters and wives. This familial representation found a new place in prose through the legacy of Nazir Ahmad's magnum opus *Mirat-ul Arus*. The moral tone of the novel ensured women's worth was measured by their ability to successfully manage household accounts through turbulent times and periods of economic crisis.[112] I contrast Ahmad's sharif fictional daughters Akbari and Asghari with literary imaginings of the tawaif Umrao Jan at the turn of the twentieth century through a close reading of Mirza Hadi Rusva's *Umrao Jan Ada*. Alongside these novels I examine the gender politics of Maulana Ashraf Ali Thanawi's *Bihishti Zewar*, a religious manual aimed at educating women. I conclude by exploring the diary of Muhammadi Begum, a Muslim woman traveller from Hyderabad and a descendant of Nazir Ahmad, whose real-life diary provides a fitting postscript to the fictional story imagined by her great-grandfather. Through analysing these works I demonstrate how the gendering of language takes place in the late nineteenth to early twentieth centuries.

Chapter 3 considers the Progressive Writers' movement and outlines themes of gender and sexuality that are central to Progressive women poets, delineating how Progressive and later modernist sensibilities contributed to changing subjectivities for women. It provides an overview of women poets, namely Ada Jafri, Zehra Nigah and Parvin Shakir, showing the emerging presence of sharif women in public life and the challenges they encountered. Also included in the analysis is the poet Sara Shagufta, who disrupted the social order of middle-class respectability with her poetry and her social background. These poets are important figures in Pakistan's Progressive legacy.

My study of Fahmida Riaz forms the argument for Chapter 4, which details her sexual politics that drew censure from the Progressives. Fahmida Riaz is a major Marxist poet and activist and this chapter is dedicated to her representations of gender, her migrant identity as a Muhajir and her class politics. I argue that a secular sacred voice is evident in her verse, reflecting her philosophic relationship to the language of poetry. Chapter 5 is a reading of Kishwar Naheed who actively challenged gender perception in the symbolic order of nation and family. I present close readings from her personal and public life to interrogate the feminist question and her legacy as a Progressive poet. In amplifying Fahmida Riaz and Kishwar Naheed, I put across two different types of Progressive writers whose aesthetics and agency have been felt by both on-the-ground women's movements and the gatekeepers of Urdu. Their work reconciles the secular and the sacred, not as two separate categories but as shared spaces in women's everyday lives. They have come into conflict with the state in their professional lives and, in the case of Fahmida Riaz, fled the country to seek refuge. This book seeks to tell their stories. In her anthropological study, Ammara Maqsood notes the changes in the middle class after the period of Field Marshal Ayub Khan. Maqsood argues that in the 1950s and 1960s, 'national culture in Pakistan was inflected with *ashraf* etiquette and progressive sensibilities of the upper echelons of the middle class. The sense of progressivism within this class converged with the ideals of modernization theories, which enjoyed international support at the time, to produce a particular vision of modern urban life'; as micropolitical interludes that get forsaken in the mapping of high politics and canonized literary formations.[113] My analysis is informed by scholarly research as well as formal and informal interviews with many Urdu poets, writers and intellectuals including Iftikhar Arif, Asif Furrukhi, Zehra Nigah, Fahmida Riaz, Kishwar Naheed, Fatema Hasan, Yasmeen Hameed, Ahmad Nadeem Qasimi, Aamer Hussein and Intizar Husain. These interviews have taken place over the past 20 years. In the notes, formal interviews are referenced as personal communications.

Notes

1. Historians of South Asia have noted specific categorizations of the term 'sharif' (pl. *ashraf*) used as a general marker of noble descent from the Prophet in the eighteenth century. Under colonial rule this lineage was specified as four classes representative of Sayyids, Shaikhs, Mughals and Pathans. This categorization excluded those on the lower rungs of the social order such as peasants and converts, who were lumped together as ajlaf. In Urdu literary culture the quality of *sharafat* came to embody a particular kind of respectability and urbanity reflective of an Islamicate cosmopolitanism and the high culture of Mughal India. See David Lelyveld, '*Ashraf*', in *Keywords in South Asian Studies*, ed. Rachel Dwyer, SOAS South Asia Institute [online resource], accessed 12 December 2020, https://www.soas.ac.uk/south-asia-institute/keywords/file24 799.pdf. Also see his *Aligarh's First Generation: Muslim Solidarity in British India* (Princeton, NJ: Princeton University Press, 1996).
2. On intersectionality, see Kimberlé Williams Crenshaw. 'Demarginalizing the Intersection of Race and Sex: A Black Feminist Critique of Antidiscrimination Doctrine, Feminist Theory and Antiracist Politics'. University of Chicago Legal Forum 1989: 139–67; Catherine A. MacKinnon. 'Intersectionality as Method: A Note', *Signs* 38, no. 4 (2013): 1019–30, accessed 20 September 2021, https://www.jstor.org/stable/10.1086/669570 (). As my book does not engage with race, I use the term intersectional as a way of exploring differences in women's narratives across class, culture and nation.
3. Nosheen Ali, 'From Hallaj to Heer: Poetic Knowledge and the Muslim Tradition', *Journal of Narrative Politics* 3, no. 1 (2016): 2–26.
4. Ayesha Jalal, 'Forging a Muslim Community: Press, Poetry and Politics in the Late Nineteenth-Century', in *Self and Sovereignty: Individual and Community in South Asian Islam Since 1850* (Lahore: Sang-e meel, 2001), 43–101.
5. Marshall G. S. Hodgson coined the term Islamicate, based on an ethical and cultural understanding of civilizational Islam linking trade routes and imperial powers, in his *The Venture of Islam: Conscience and History in a World Civilization*, 3 vols (Chicago: University of Chicago Press, 1974). This framework has been extended by Bruce B. Lawrence in 'Islamicate Civilization: The View from Asia', in *Teaching Islam*, ed. Brannon M. Wheeler (New York: Oxford University Press, 2003), 61–76, and Shahab Ahmed offers an important critique of this categorization because it divides *adab* from *fiqh*

whereas he sees the two as interrelated in modern Islam. See Shahab Ahmed, *What Is Islam? The Importance of Being Islamic* (Princeton, NJ and Oxford: Princeton University Press, 2016), 157–75.

6   Susie Tharu and K. Lalita's two-volume study *Women Writing in India* was first published by the Feminist Press at CUNY in the United States and later adopted by Oxford University Press. It traces a grand chronology of 26 centuries of the trials and tribulations of women's writing ending with women 'writing the nation' for a global readership. Tharu and Lalita came under fire for their somewhat eclectic feminist methodology that borrows from Kate Millett's *Sexual Politics*, Sandra Gilbert and Susan Gubar's *The Madwoman in the Attic* and Elaine Showalter's gynocritics to recover Indian women's voices for a Western audience. Leela Gandhi's review in *Manushi* questions the claim of radicalism linked to the anthology, re-presenting the introductory framework of the editors as 'antihistorical and profoundly questionable'; Leela Gandhi in *Manushi* 81 (March/April 1994): 31–33 (32). However, the important work that was done by the editors of *Women Writing in India* cannot be ignored.

7   I'm very grateful to Nosheen Ali for her insights about regional poetry by women.

8   See the excellent introduction by Ania Loomba and Ritty A. Lukose, eds, *South Asian Feminisms* (Durham, NC: Duke University Press, 2012), which sets out the changing narratives of South Asian feminisms as they move from rights-based activism to equality in the workplace.

9   See Rubina Saigol, 'The Past, Present and Future of Feminist Activism in Pakistan', *Herald*, 15 July 2019, https://herald.dawn.com/news/1398878. Accessed 1 March 2021.

10 Malaqa Bai Chanda, *Divan*, ed. Shafqat Rizvi (Lahore: Majlis-e taraqqi-e Urdu, [1798] 1990). For a sample of Mah Laqa's verse in English translation, see Susie Tharu and K. Lalita, eds, *Women Writing in India: 600 BC to the Present*, vol. 1 (New York: Feminist Press, 1991), 122. This section is borrowed from my article '"*Badan darida*" (The Body Torn): Gender and Sexuality in Pakistani Women's Poetry', *Pakistan Journal of Women's Studies (Alam-e Niswan)* 13, no. 1 (2006): 45–66; republished in *The Body and The Book: Writings on Poetry and Sexuality*, ed. Glennis Byron and Andrew J. Sneddon (Amsterdam: Rodopi, 2008), 235–52.

11 For an insight into the life of Mah Laqa Bai Chanda, see Scott Kugle, *When Sun Meets Moon: Gender, Eros, and Ecstasy in Urdu Poetry* (Chapel Hill: University of North Carolina Press, 2016), 141–253.

12 Kugle, 'Mah Laqa Bai's Men', in *When Sun Meets Moon*, 166–84.

13 See Malaqa Bai Chanda, *Divan*, ed. Rizvi.

14 On *sringara rasa*, see William Reddy, *The Making of Romantic Love: Longing and Sexuality in Europe* (Chicago: University of Chicago Press, 2012), chapter 4.

15 Hir Ranjha is based on an oral tradition and a patchwork of influences. Farina Mir refers to Damodar's composition of Hir in the early seventeenth century as an early text, but she argues that the text was going around orally in Mughal India during Akbar's reign in the sixteenth century. See Farina Mir, *The Social Space of Language* (Berkeley: University of California Press, 2010).

16 It is a story about hierarchies between Jatt families in north-western Punjab. Hir's family force her to marry into a suitable clan after discovering that she is in love with the cowherd Ranjha, originally Dhidho from a landed family, in order to preserve their social status. If we follow the popular version of the story as told by Varis Shah, there are some twists and turns as Ranjha takes on the guise of a yogi and comes back

into Hir's life. Hir is not quite the conventional heroine and the romance ends tragically, with Hir poisoned by her family and Ranjha dying from shock. Farina Mir, in her analysis of the Punjabi *qissa*, offers a close reading of gender dynamics in eighteenth- and nineteenth-century versions of *Hir Ranjha*, to argue that the role of women is at odds with prescribed gender norms for women in the period, given that agency is attached to Hir. Her voice is shown to have non-realist elements of Sufi devotion and her pursuit of love a godliness that is otherworldly. For Mir, she represents a nostalgic symbol of Punjabi syncretic culture that includes multiple religious registers including Hinduism, Sikhism and Islam. On the other hand, Jeevan Deol, in his close reading of one of the most popular renditions of Hir by Varis Shah in the nineteenth century, reiterates the ambivalences in the characterization of Hir that show her to be both an active agent of resistance and a passive recipient of the expression of patriarchal love. He argues that, while Varis Shah embeds an allegorical Sufi reading through his ending of the story, it is his representation of the erotic encounters between Hir and Ranjha that offers a social critique of how sexualities are controlled. For Deol, the genius of Varis lies in his reformulation of Hir as an erotic rather than a conventional romantic heroine. See Jeevan Deol, 'Sex, Social Critique and the Female Figure in Premodern Punjabi', *Modern Asian Studies* 36, no. 1 (2002): 141–71.

17 My use of the devotional here is connected to feminist readings on the sacred and the feminine, in particular the edited collection *The Sacred and the Feminine: Imagination and Sexual Difference*, edited by Griselda Pollock and Victoria Turvey Sauron (New York: I.B. Tauris, 2007), responding to Julia Kristeva and Catherine Clément's epistolary conversation on the same theme. The essay by Ananya Jahanara Kabir, 'The Feminine, the Sacred and the Shared: The Ecumenical Space of the Sufi Dargah', with its discussion of the *dargah* as a space of sacred feminine performativity, is useful to consider with reference to public spaces and gender divisions influenced by colonial modernities (pp. 75–87). Also see Kelly Pemberton's participant-observation study of Sufism and the role of women as agents, *Women Mystics and Sufi Shrines in India* (Columbia: University of South Carolina Press, 2013).

18 Anemarie Schimmel, *My Soul Is a Woman: The Feminine in Islam* (New York: Continuum, 2003), 20. See also Heidi A. Ford. 'Hierarchical Inversions, Divine Subversions: The Miracles of Rabia al-Adawiya', *Journal of Feminist Studies in Religion* 15, no. 2 (1999): 5–24, https://www.jstor.org/stable/25002363.

19 Tariq Ali, 'The Story of Kashmir', in *Kashmir: The Case for Freedom*, ed. Tariq Ali, Hilal Bhatt, Angana P. Chatterjee, Habbah Khatun, Pankaj Mishra and Arundhati Roy (London: Verso, 2011), 12.

20 Rosalind O'Hanlon, 'Manliness and Imperial Service in Mughal North India', *Journal of the Economic and Social History of the Orient* 42, no. 1 (1999): 47–93 (52), https://www.jstor.org/stable/3632298.

21 Ibid., 53.

22 See Ruth Vanita, 'The Lady of Love – The Life and Work of Habba Khatun', *Manushi* 38 (1987): 25–28. Vanita's article draws on S. L. Sadhu's biography and essays by Akhtar Mohi-ud-Din and Ghulam Nabi Khayal.

23 Habba Khatun, *The Way of the Swan: Poems of Kashmir*, trans. Nilla Cram Crook (Bombay: Asia Publishing House, 1958).

24 For Islamicate, see Hodgson, *The Venture of Islam*.

25 See Fahmida Hussain's discussion of folk heroines in *Image of 'Woman' in the Poetry of Shah Abdul Latif*, trans. Amjad Siraj Memon (Karachi: University of Karachi, 2001).

26. For an extended discussion of the impact of reform on women's lives, see Gail Minault, *Secluded Scholars: Women's Education and Muslim Social Reform in Colonial India* (New Delhi: Oxford University Press, 1998).
27. This has been argued by Susie Tharu in her article 'Tracing Savitri's Pedigree: Victorian Racism and the Image of Women in Indo-Anglian Literature', in *Recasting Women: Essays in Colonial History*, ed. Kumkum Sangari and Sudesh Vaid (New Delhi: Kali, 1999), 254–68.
28. In a revisionist reading, the historian Antoinette Burton has analysed the domestic history of the women's sphere in the zenana through women's memoirs, diaries, travelogues and letters as an alternative archive to normative histories of colonial modernity. Engaging in an analysis of three turn of the twentieth-century elite women, Januki Majumdar, Cornelia Sorabji and Attia Hosain, she puts forward their responses to the discomfort of imperial and anticolonial projects as an archive through which a new critical history of home can be understood. Methodologically informed by a gendered and feminist lens, Burton argues that the three women's narratives come at a time that the '"Indian home" had become a well-established archive'. See Antoinette Burton, *Dwelling in the Archive: Writing House, Home and History in Late Colonial India* (New York: Oxford University Press, 2003), 25.
29. See Tharu, 'Tracing Savitri's Pedigree'. Also see Ann Laura Stoler, *Race and the Education of Desire: Foucault's History of Sexuality and the Colonial Order of Things* (Durham, NC: Duke University Press, 1995).
30. Gayatri Chakravorty Spivak, 'Can the Subaltern Speak?', in *Colonial Discourse and Postcolonial Theory*, ed. Patrick Williams and Laura Chrisman (Hemel Hempstead: Harvester Wheatsheaf, 1994), 66–111. Also see Lata Mani, *Contentious Traditions: The Debate on Sati in Colonial India* (Berkeley: University of California Press, 1998).
31. Partha Chatterjee, 'The Nationalist Resolution of the Women's Question', in *Recasting Women: Essays in Colonial History*, ed. Kumkum Sangari and Sudesh Vaid (New Delhi: Kali, 1999), 233–53.
32. Partha Chatterjee, *The Nation and Its Fragments: Colonial and Postcolonial Histories* (Princeton, NJ: Princeton University Press, 1993), 120.
33. Susie Tharu, and K. Lalita, eds, *Women Writing in India: The Twentieth Century*, vol. 2 (London: Pandora Press, 1993), 84–90. Also see Geraldine Forbes, 'The Emergence of Women's Organizations', in *Women in Modern India* (Cambridge: Cambridge University Press, 1996), 64–91.
34. Sarojini Naidu, Speeches 188–89, quoted in Sheshalatha Reddy, 'The Cosmopolitan Nationalism of Sarojini Naidu, Nightingale of India', *Victorian Literature and Culture* 38, no. 2 (2010): 571–89 (577), http://www.jstor.org/stable/25733492.
35. I borrow this phrase from Gauri Viswanathan's *Masks of Conquest* (1989) which critiques the project of English education in India, how it aimed to create mimic men and the ambivalences that it encountered both ideologically and formatively in the colony. According to Sheshalatha Reddy, while the female self projected in Naidu's poetry was reflective of the reformist vision for women as maternal figures devoted to the national project, her 'embodied voice, both poetic and political', with its juxtaposition between community and the self, is torn by her own persona as a politician/activist and a poet.
36. See Chandani Lokuge, 'Dialoguing with Empire: The Literary and Political Rhetoric of Sarojini Naidu', in Susheila Nasta, ed., *India in Britain: South Asian Networks and Connections, 1858–1950* (Houndmills: Palgrave Macmillan, 2013), 115–33.

37 Ibid., 124.
38 On patterns of religious beliefs, patriarchal values and the female devotional voice, see Kumkum Sangari, 'Mirabai and the Spiritual Economy of Bhakti', *Economic and Political Weekly* 25, no. 27 (1990): 1464–75, http://www.jstor.org/stable/4396474. Naidu's predecessor, the Christian Indian Toru Dutt, and her contemporary, the Parsi Christian Cornelia Sorabji, left lasting impressions on English poetry, inflecting it with Indian and cosmopolitan views.
39 Quoted in Antoinette Burton, 'Tourism in the Archives: Colonial Modernity and the Zenana in Cornelia Sorabji's Memoirs', in her *Dwelling in the Archive*, 65–100 (66).
40 See Burton, 'Tourism in the Archives'.
41 The daughter of Nawab Mohammad Muzammilullah Khan (1865–1938), a loyal servant of the British Empire, who was given the titles of Bahadur and Sir, and Vice Chancellor of Aligarh Muslim University. He was a follower of Sayyid Ahmad Khan and an old party leader of the Muslim League. Ze Khe Shin, whose mother died young, grew up in a politically informed and active household and was obedient to her father's restrictions as far as her respectability as a sharif woman was concerned. She wrote poems for the reformist women's journals on topics such as education, women's rights, the Swadeshi movement and Hindu Muslim unity. See Francis Robinson, *Separatism among Indian Muslims: The Politics of the United Provinces Muslims, 1860–1923* (Cambridge: Cambridge University Press, 1974); (Dr) Fatema Hasan, *Ze Khe Shin: hayat-o shairi ka tahqiqi aur tanqidi jaiza* (Karachi: Anjuman Taraqqi-e Urdu Pakistan, 2007); Gail Minault, ' "Tahzibi Bahin": Four Early Indian Muslim Women Writers', keynote address for the workshop 'Women's Autobiographies in Islamic Societies: Context and Construction', Delhi 2010, partial text accessed 6 March 2018, http://www.columbia.edu/itc/mealac/pritchett/00urduhindilinks/srffest/txt_minault_zaykaysheen.pdf. I'm grateful to Aamer Hussein and Fatema Hasan for their valuable advice.
42 Ze Khe Shin, *Aina-e Haram* (Lahore: Dar-ul ishat, 1921), 22, accessed 20 March 2018, https://www.rekhta.org/ebooks/aaina-e-haram-ebooks-1, (my translation).
43 For a selection of her poetry, see Fatema Hasan, ed., *Zahida Khatun Sherwania: intikhab kalam* (Karachi: Oxford University Press, 2015). Hasan also provides a critical overview of her work in her 2007 monograph *Ze Khe Shin: hayat-e shairi ka tahqiqi aur tanqidi jaiza*. Karachi: Anjuman-e taraqqi-e Urdu. 2007.
44 Translation from M. A. R. Barker, S. A. Salam and M. A. Siddiqi, eds, *A Reader of Classical Urdu Poetry*, 3 vols (Ithaca, NY: Spoken Language Services, 1977), vol. 2, 400.
45 Ibid., 395.
46 Ashis Nandy, *The Intimate Enemy: Loss and Recovery of Self under Colonialism* (New Delhi: Oxford University Press, 1988); Rosalind O'Hanlon, 'Issues of Masculinity in North Indian History: The Bangash Nawabs of Farrukhabad', *Indian Journal of Gender Studies* 4, no. 1 (1997): 1–10.
47 Rokeya Sakhawat Hossain, *Sultana's Dream and Padmarag: Two Feminist Utopias*, trans. Barnita Bagchi (New Delhi: Penguin, 2005). The publication notes that 'Sultana's Dream' was originally published in *The Indian Ladies Magazine*, Madras, India in 1905, in English. It is available to read on the University of Pennsylvania digital library website: http://digital.library.upenn.edu/women/sultana/dream/dream.html.
48 Geraldine Forbes, in her comprehensive history of *Women in Modern India*, has observed that Begum Rokeya was 'accused of being both pro-Christian and a Europhile', courting 'hostility' by endorsing Katherine Mayo's *Mother India*. See Forbes, *Women in Modern India*, 57.

49. Gail Minault, 'Making Invisible Women Visible: Studying the History of Muslim Women in South Asia', *Journal of South Asian Studies* 9, no. 1 (1986): 1–14 (1).
50. Ibid, 3.
51. Farzana Shaikh, *Community and Consensus in Islam: Muslim Representation in Colonial India 1860–1967* (Cambridge: Cambridge University Press, 1989), 226, 279.
52. See Farida Jamal, 'Fatema Sughra Haya: She Dwelt among the Untrodden', *Lucknow Observer*, 5 June 2015. Also see Damini Kulkarni's 'An Urdu Poet, Her Activist Niece, and Two Faces of Rebellion at Lucknow's Farangi Mahal', *Scroll.in*, 18 September 2017, https://scroll.in/reel/850967/an-urdu-poet-her-activist-niece-and-two-faces-of-rebellion-at-lucknows-farangi-mahal.
53. Personal communication with Mahmood Jamal (nephew of Haya). She died in 1948, the same year her collected poems, *Kalaam-e Sughra*, were published by Hamdam Press, Lucknow, with a second edition published from Karachi in 1967 by Khatoon Press.
54. Iqbalunnisa Hussain, *Changing India: A Muslim Woman Speaks* (Karachi: Oxford University Press, 2015), 117.
55. Iqbalunnisa Hussain's book *Purdah and Polygamy* was reprinted as an annotated edition edited by Jessica Berman and published by Oxford University Press, Karachi in 2019.
56. See Anemarie Schimmel's reading of the Western woman in *Javidnama*, in *Islam in the Indian Subcontinent* (Leiden: E. J. Brill, 1980); my reading of the poem refers to A. J. Arberry's translation, *Javid-nama* (London: Allen and Unwin, 1966).
57. Jahan Ara Shahnawaz, *Father and Daughter: A Political Autobiography* (Lahore: Nigarisht, 1971).
58. Kumkum Sangari and Sudesh Vaid, 'Recasting Women: An Introduction', in *Recasting Women: Essays in Colonial History* (New Delhi: Kali, 1999), 19.
59. Ibid., 189–97.
60. See Saadia Toor, 'Post-Partition Literary Politics: The Progressives versus the Nationalists', in *The State of Islam: Culture and Cold War Politics in Pakistan* (London: Pluto Press, 2011), 52–79.
61. See Toor, *The State of Islam*, 89–106. Subsequent quotes are from pp. 139 and 140.
62. This understanding comes from a reading of Hamza Alavi's influential argument about the state in postcolonial societies; 'The State in Post-Colonial Societies: Pakistan and Bangladesh', *New Left Review* 1, no. 74 (July/August 1972): 59–81.
63. See C. M. Naim, '*Ghazal* and *taghazzul*: The Lyric, Personal and Social', in *The Literatures of India: An Introduction*, ed. Edward C. Dimock, Edwin Gerow, C. M. Naim, A. K. Ramanujan, Gordon Roadarmel and J. A. B. van Buitenen (Chicago: University of Chicago Press, 1974), 181–97; Ralph Russell, 'The Pursuit of the Urdu Ghazal', *Journal of Asian Studies* 29L (1969): 107–24; R. Blachère and A. Bausani, 'Ghazal', in *Encyclopaedia of Islam*, ed. P. Bearman, Th. Bianquis, C. E. Bosworth, E. van Donzel and W. P. Heinrichs, 2nd ed., online (Leiden: Brill, 2012), accessed 18 February 2021, http://dx.doi.org/10.1163/1573-3912_islam_COM_0232.
64. See Christopher Shackle, 'Ghazal', in *South Asian Keywords*, ed. Rachel Dwyer, SOAS South Asia Institute [online resource], accessed 23 December 2020, https://www.soas.ac.uk/south-asia-institute/keywords/file24804.pdf.
65. Quoted in Christopher Shackle and Javed Majeed's introduction to *Hali's Musaddas: The Ebb and Flow of Islam*, ed. Christopher Shackle and Javed Majeed (Delhi: Oxford University Press, 1997), 6.

66 See Thomas Babington Macaulay, *Speeches by Lord Macaulay with His Minute on Indian Education*, selected with an introduction and notes by G. M. Young (Oxford: Oxford University Press, [1835] 1979).
67 Javed Majeed, 'Nature, Hyperbole, and the Colonial State: Some Muslim Appropriations of European Modernity in Late Nineteenth-Century Urdu Literature', in *Islam and Modernity: Muslim Intellectuals Respond*, ed. John Cooper, Ronald L. Nettler and Mohamed Mahmoud (London: I.B. Tauris, 1998), 10–37 (17).
68 An important characteristic of the ghazal is its ambivalent use of gender, a tradition it borrows from Persian which does not possess grammatical gender. Since Urdu is a gendered language, as a general rule ghazal poets use adjectives and verbs in the masculine form, while retaining the masculine gender for the lover and the feminine gender for the beloved. This gendering is merely formulaic and is supposed to maintain the enigmatic world of the Persian ghazal. According to Naim, the anonymity of gender allows the interpretation of amorous love as divine love, illicit love, homosexual love – 'even the women poets use the masculine gender for themselves and for the beloved, to maintain the tradition'; Naim, '*Ghazal* and *taghazzul*', 192. See also Tariq Rahman, 'Boy-Love in the Urdu Ghazal', *Annual of Urdu Studies* 7 (1990): 1–20. However, it is also worth taking into consideration M. Kaleem Raza Khan's argument that the construction of gender in Urdu language is structured around norms of masculinity/patriarchy. He observes that 'everything that is small, weak, flimsy, exquisite, beautiful or ephemeral is feminine in Urdu'; M. Kaleem Raza Khan, 'Anti-feminism in Urdu: A Study in Linguistics and Gender', *Pakistan Journal of Women's Studies* 1, no. 2 (1994): 64–72 (72). Thus the form has infinite possibilities and its metaphoric meaning can be determined by the social history of the time it is written in, capturing linguistic associations and social identity formations.
69 Altaf Husain Hali, *Muqaddama-e sher-o shairi* (The Poetics of Poetry) (Lahore: Sartaj Book Depot, [1893] 1950), 124.
70 Safdar Ahmed, 'Literary Romanticism and Islamic Modernity: The Case of Urdu Poetry', *South Asia: Journal of South Asian Studies* 35, no. 2 (2012): 434–55 (449).
71 On the circulation of English fiction in mid- to late nineteenth-century India, see Priya Joshi, *In Another Country: Colonialism, Culture and the English Novel in India* (New York: Columbia University Press, 2002).
72 Munibur Rahman, 'The Mushairah', *Annual of Urdu Studies* 3 (1983): 74–83 (75).
73 C. M. Naim, 'Poet–Audience Interaction at Urdu Musha'iras', in *Urdu and Muslim South Asia: Studies in Honour of Ralph Russell*, ed. Christopher Shackle (London: SOAS, 1989), 167–73. Also see his '*Ghazal* and *taghazzul*'.
74 Afsaneh Najmabadi, 'The Erotic Vatan [Homeland] as Beloved and Mother: To Love, To Possess, and To Protect', *Comparative Studies in Society and History* 39, no. 3 (1997): 442–67.
75 Aamir Mufti has argued that Faiz's poetic aesthetic illustrates the unique relationship of Urdu literary production to the crisis of national culture that is 'marked by the figure of the Muslim'. He reads Faiz's use of the lyric form as a refusal to accept communal identities, deploying a metaphorical form to express a self that is immersed in Indic Sufi thought and practice. See his 'Towards a Lyric History of India', *boundary 2* 31, no. 2 (2004): 245–74. Faiz's identification as Pakistan's unofficial poet laureate presents some problems for Mufti's reading. See my introduction to the *Pakistaniaat* special issue: Amina Yaqin, 'Faiz Ahmad Faiz: The Worlding of a Lyric Poet', *Pakistaniaat* 5, no. 1 (2013): i–ix, http://pakistaniaat.org/index.php/pak/issue/view/12.

76 See Abul A'la Maududi, *Purdah and the Status of Women in Islam* (Lahore: Islamic Publications, 1972).
77 See Hodgson, *The Venture of Islam*.
78 Lawrence, 'Islamicate Civilization', 73.
79 Ayesha Jalal, *Partisans of Allah: Jihad in South Asia* (Cambridge, MA: Harvard University Press, 2008).
80 See '*La Convivencia, La Mezquita* and Al-Andalus: An Iqbalian Vision', *Journal of Postcolonial Writing* 52, no. 2 (2016): 136–52. DOI: 10.1080/17449855.2016.1164972.
81 Gil Anidjar, 'Secularism', *Critical Enquiry* 33, no. 1 (2006): 52–57.
82 Aamir R. Mufti, 'Auerbach in Istanbul: Edward Said, Secular Criticism, and the Question of Minority Culture', *Critical Inquiry* 25, no. 1 (1998): 95–125 (107).
83 Talal Asad, *Formations of the Secular: Christianity, Islam, Modernity* (Stanford, CA: Stanford University Press, 2003), 13.
84 See Aziz Ahmad, 'Sayyid Ahmad Khan, Jamal Al Din Afghani and Muslim India', *Studia Islamica* 13 (1960): 55–78.
85 Muhammed Ali Jinnah, *Speeches and Writings of Mr Jinnah*, ed. Jamil-ud-din Ahmad, 2 vols (Lahore: M. Ashraf, 1942), vol. 2, 399–404. Extracted in *Sources of Indian Tradition, Volume Two: Modern India and Pakistan*, ed. Stephen Hay, 2nd ed. (New Delhi: Penguin, 1992), 387.
86 Omar Noman, *The Political Economy of Pakistan 1947–85* (London: KPI, 1988), 6.
87 After the anti-Ahmadi riots in 1953, a commission chaired by Justice Munir was set up to look into the cause of the riots and, as part of the inquiry into the rights of citizens, they investigated the concept of an Islamic state. The question arises of a liberal secular model in which the church and state are separate or an Islamic one in which Islam is recognized as a religio-political system, one that is envisaged by the ulema (the judiciary). It all comes to a head around the Ahmadi question and the rights of minorities. In the end the judiciary argue that the question of sovereignty is confused in Pakistan as it is not understood as a modern state amongst the populace and for as long as there isn't a consensus between the ulema and the leaders of the state the confusion will remain. See Asad Ahmed, 'Advocating a Secular Pakistan: The Munir Report of 1954', in *Islam in South Asia in Practice*, ed. Barbara Daly Metcalf (Princeton, NJ: Princeton University Press, 2009), 424–37.
88 See Ayesha Jalal, *The Struggle for Pakistan: A Muslim Homeland and Global Politics* (Cambridge, MA: Harvard University Press, 2014), 98–117.
89 A. Haroon, 'The Women's Movement in Pakistan', in *Unveiling the Issues: Pakistani Women's Perspectives on Social, Political and Ideological Issues*, ed. Nighat Said Khan and Afiya Sheherbano Zia (Lahore: ASR, 1995), 178–86 (180).
90 Ibid.
91 Asma Jahangir and Hina Jilani, *The Hudood Ordinances: A Divine Sanction?* (Lahore: Rhotas Books, 1990).
92 See F. Gardezi, 'Islam, Feminism and the Women's Movement in Pakistan: 1981–91', in *Against All Odds: Essays on Women, Religion and Development from India and Pakistan*, ed. K. Bhasin, Ritu Menon and Nighat Said Khan (New Delhi: Kali, 1994), 51–58.
93 Shahnaz Khan, in her seminal work on the Zina Ordinances and women's incarceration in prisons, has also noted the pressure on 'domestic family structures to absorb the power dynamics of state led sexual politics'. Her research offers valuable insights on how familial structures perpetuate poverty for women and exposes a morally corrupt state that, through Zina Ordinances, has contributed to the vulnerability and

destitution of poor women. See Shahnaz Khan, *Zina, Transnational Feminism, and the Moral Regulation of Pakistani Women* (Chicago: University of Chicago Press, 2006).
94 See Yaqin, '"*Badan Darida*" (The Body Torn)'.
95 Rajeswari Sunder Rajan, *Real and Imagined Women: Gender, Culture and Postcolonialism* (London: Routledge, 1993), 6.
96 Ayesha Khan, *The Women's Movement in Pakistan: Activism, Islam and Democracy* (London: I.B. Tauris, 2018).
97 See Rubina Saigol, *Feminism and the Women's Movement in Pakistan: Actors, Debates and Struggles*, Country Study (Islamabad: Friedrich-Eburt-Stiftung, 2016).
98 Amrita Chhachhi, 'Identity Politics, Secularism and Women: A South Asian Perspective', in *Forging Identities: Gender, Communities and the State*, ed. Zoya Hasan (New Delhi: Kali, 1994), 74–95 (86).
99 Amrita Chhachhi, 'Forced Identities: The State, Communalism, Fundamentalism and Women in India', in *Writing the Women's Movement*, ed. Mala Khullar (New Delhi: Zubaan, 2005), 218–42 (232).
100 Nivedita Menon, in her critique of heteronormativity in the Indian nation and the family, argues that the 'heterosexual patriarchal family' is tied to modern citizenship that relies on 'purity' of identities to project 'a particular form of the family'. See 'Outing Heteronormativity: Nation, Citizen, Feminist Disruptions', in *Sexualities: Issues in Contemporary Indian Feminism*, ed. Nivedita Menon (New Delhi: Kali for Women, 2007), 3–51 (30).
101 Margot Badran, *Feminism in Islam: Secular and Religious Convergences* (Oxford: Oneworld, 2009), 1.
102 For a more detailed discussion of Islamic feminism, see my chapter on 'Islamic Feminism in a Time of Islamophobia: The Muslim Heroines of Leila Aboulela's *Minaret* and Elif Shafak's *Forty Rules of Love*', in *Contesting Islamophobia: Anti-Muslim Prejudice in Media, Culture, Politics*, ed. Peter Morey, Amina Yaqin and Alaya Forte (London: Bloomsbury/I.B. Tauris, 2019), 123–46.
103 Margot Badran, *Feminism Beyond East and West: New Gender Talk and Practice in Global Islam* (New Delhi: Global Media, 2007), 40.
104 Afiya Zia, *Faith and Feminism: Religious Agency or Secular Autonomy* (Brighton: Sussex Academic Press, 2018).
105 Sadaf Ahmad, *Transforming Faith: The Story of Al-Huda and Islamic Revivalism Among Urban Pakistani Women* (Syracuse, NY: Syracuse University Press, 2009).
106 Amina Jamal, 'Transnational Feminism as Critical Practice: A Reading of Feminist Discourses in Pakistan', *Meridians: Feminism, Race, Transnationalism* 5, no. 2 (2005): 57–82.
107 Here Anne McClintock's reading of the family as a 'natural figure for sanctioning social hierarchy within a [...] organic unity of interests' can be extended to the nation as family. See her article 'Family Feuds: Gender, Nationalism and the Family', *Feminist Review* 44 (Summer 1993): 61–80 (63).
108 See Amina Jamal, *Jamaat-e Islami Women in Pakistan: Vanguard of a New Modernity?* (Syracuse, NY: Syracuse University Press, 2013). Scholars such as Humeira Iqtidar and Ammara Maqsood have noted that pietist movements and affiliations bring new kinds of agencies for women into the mix.
109 On the colonial appropriation of family, see Anne McClintock, *Imperial Leather: Race, Gender and Sexuality in the Colonial Conquest* (New York: Routledge, 1995).

110 Deniz Kandiyoti refers to shared ideals of nineteenth-century reform in the Muslim world of 'education, seclusion, veiling and polygyny' that aided a 'broader agenda about "progress" and the compatibility between Islam and modernity' in her *Women, Islam and the State* (Basingstoke: Macmillan, 1991), 3.

111 Afsaneh Najmabadi speaks of the shift in the conceptual idea of *vatan* (homeland) from Perso-Islamic to modern over time, and how this signalled a distinct change from a religiously defined nation to an imagined community in the nineteenth century. She refers to the project of modernity as one that was centred around romantic heteroerotic love influenced by a European gaze in the nineteenth century. However, she argues that 'cultural hybridisation' in Iran was also a meshing of 'interactions' that took place between Iran, the Ottoman Empire and the Indian subcontinent. She speaks of the way in which the 'rearticulation of classical literature of love into patriotic poetics' was translated through the female body. Emphasizing the gendering that took place around women and notions of family depicting the nation as a motherland, while reiterating the responsibility of men as protectors, providers and possessors of women and as carers, Najmabadi underlines how this was reflected in the change of the allegorical Sufi concept of mother Earth to a beloved Iran. She traces this move in her close reading of prose and patriotic poetry, arguing that classical forms such as the *qasida* and the *ghazal* were also used to 'eulogize *vatan*'. Increasingly, as the modern state built itself around a militaristic and prophetic model in the early twentieth century, it began to project a hypermasculine state. Najmabadi, 'The Erotic Vatan [Homeland] as Beloved and Mother'.

112 I am grateful to Samreen Kazmi for sharing her insights.

113 My use of the term micropolitics here is influenced by Chandra Mohanty's emphasis on the need for cross-cultural feminism to focus on an activist micropolitics of context, subjectivity and struggle in conversation with the macropolitics of global economies and political systems. See Chandra Mohanty, *Feminism without Borders: Decolonizing Theory, Practicing Solidarity* (Durham, NC: Duke University Press, 2003) and 'Under Western Eyes: Revisited', *Signs* 28, no. 2 (Winter 2003): 499–535. Also see Loomba and Lukose, *South Asian Feminisms*.

Chapter 2

FORM, EDUCATION AND WOMEN: REKHTI, REFORM AND THE ZENANA

In this chapter, I analyse the construction of voice and form deployed in a variety of Urdu texts about women at the turn of the century. In particular, I examine the social contexts, linguistic registers and literary form of the Urdu novel to assess the kind of middle-class values that were normalized at the time. Form is a necessary consideration when it comes to late nineteenth-century representations of gender, as both fiction and prescriptive texts played an influential role in depictions of sharif Muslim women as heroines at a time of reform and changing reading publics.[1] I explore the centrality of women's moral and ethical behaviour, *sharafat*, in selected texts, elucidating the colonial project of women's education and reform of the zenana mediated by the modernizing forces of two schools of thought, Aligarh and Deoband. The reformists set out a narrow vision of gender in cultural narratives enshrining the heteronormative Muslim family as an ideal nation. This is something that has been explored in detail by historians and literary scholars looking at this period.[2] However, what is sometimes overlooked is the hybridity of voice in these forms. Given Urdu's links to an Islamicate and Indic heritage, it is relevant to note Maria Rosa Menocal's observations about Islamicate cultural narratives in medieval Spain and how they influenced new European languages in the twelfth century.[3] Urdu is a hybrid language that developed as a spoken lingua franca in the subcontinent with a Perso-Arabic vocabulary and an Indo-Aryan linguistic background. It has been variously known as the Persian rekhta (mixed), Turkish Urdu (camp) and Indo-Aryan Hindi. As a literary language, the classical canon was established in the Deccan, a centre of Dravidian languages, which came under the influence of Muslim dynasties in Golconda and Bijapur. Dakani Urdu incorporated the local idiom in its poetic diction and rekhti is attached to this organic relationship. Delhi and Lucknow as the centres of literary Urdu became synonymous with the writings of the poets Mir Taqi Mir, Mirza Muhammad Rafi Sauda and Mirza Asadullah Khan Ghalib.[4] Experimentations with form in the nineteenth century were part of the shifting dynamics of language and power and the standardization of Urdu as a modern language. Thus a variety of texts, including popular manuals and moral guidebooks for women with male voices ventriloquizing women through the use of idiomatic *begamati zaban*, imagined women as the reading public while determining their moral and ethical subjectivities. A muted ventriloquized genteel *nisvani zaban* (feminine voice) that preserved an ideal notion of the zenana as an inner cultural temple of piety became the carrier of progressivism and education, casting a lasting mould for women. The women of the zenana were to become suitably learned wives for their modern educated husbands, creating harmony at home, and responsibly progressive mothers. This social reform extended to the purification of literary forms that were deemed regressive, such as the ghazal love lyric, and extended to the playful and transgressive form of rekhti, associated with female voice experimentations in Urdu's poetic language. Rekhti was a deliberate gendering of the poetic voice as female, unlike the normative mode of rekhta poetry in which the speaker was male. In their drive to articulate a sober nisvani zaban for Muslim women, the reformists cleansed poetic language of rekhti, articulating a demure and elegant Urdu. Through this project of cultural purification, reformists worked in tandem with the British colonizers determined to modernize the zenana in accordance with Enlightenment ideals.[5]

My analysis of linguistic variations and cross-cultural influences over time reviews how strategic modernizing and gendered interventions were adapted into the Urdu literary sphere in the late nineteenth century. Commercial textual representations competed with oral cultural forms as well as the manuscript tradition, incorporating the colonial project of educating the zenana.[6] Urdu was also being transformed by the rise of a commercialized print culture, especially by those invested in it.[7] Increased production of Urdu books from 1868 to 1895 contributed to a growth in ideological representations of the secular and religious as two opposing forces, particularly as Urdu narratives became tied to Muslim identification.[8] I argue that it is only by considering the dialogicality of voice contained within textual representations themselves that we can begin to understand the religious and secular as linked moral and ethical constructs that influenced a community of Urdu writers, who would separate into religious and secular camps over time.

Over the course of the twentieth century, works that had aimed at modernizing traditional Urdu literature became canonical themselves. In order to investigate form and voice in these interventions, I offer selected close readings from three texts. My first example is the prize-winning novel *Mirat-ul Arus*, by Nazir Ahmad, about a sharif family and two daughters who bring shame and honour upon their menfolk.[9] I contrast the form of this fictional text with a short extract from a popular religious text *Bihishti Zewar*, by the Deoband leader Maulana Ashraf Ali Thanawi, produced as an instruction manual for women. It utilized a woman's voice for the purposes of religious education. The third text that informs my discussion is the novel *Umrao Jan Ada*, by Mirza Hadi Rusva, which depicts the redemptive story of a fallen woman at the turn of the century. I explore how the novel shifts attention from the performance of dance by the tawaif to the genteel poetic idiom of the metaphorical ghazal, contextualizing her as a noble woman instead of a fallen woman. Rusva's novel is reminiscent of representations by nineteenth-century French novelists allegorizing 'social upheaval and change' and can be read as a product of hybrid influences on the Urdu prose tradition during the colonial period, although we don't have concrete evidence that any borrowing took place.[10] By contrasting these different forms and voices, I illustrate the significance of understanding sociolinguistic contexts in relation to form and storytelling and why deterministic readings over time have led to a fixity of positions on gender. I argue that Urdu's gendered hybridities can be understood through its cultural exchange and transformation across regions. The dynamics of its moral and ethical landscape are embedded in a mixed Islamicate and Indic heritage, making it difficult to separate the secular from the religious. However, the religious is gradually mapped on to the secular through the piety of women. This gender politics utilizes feminine voice to maintain the moral credentials of an authentic Islam but it varies across Deoband and Aligarh, Lucknow and Delhi. By tracing the variation of voice and form we can see how gender dynamics were influenced by different contact zones in a time of change.[11] As a concluding point I refer to the diary of Muhammadi Begum, the granddaughter of Nazir Ahmad.

Linguistic Cross-Dressing and the Otherness of Rekhti

In this section, I look at the contact zones across rekhti that are contained within Urdu to provide the context to my close readings. By setting out these diversities at the outset I make the case for how the gendered self gets constructed in canonical Urdu texts and also uncover the tensions that are present within textual representations. Rekhti was generally associated with a low linguistic register so it is unsurprising, given late nineteenth- and twentieth-century Urdu scholarship's emphasis on canonicity, high culture and the aspirations of a new middle class, that it became an expendable genre. When it comes to gender and voice, the background to rekhti as a genre shows how Urdu connected across class and sexuality.

Historically, the difference between the language used by the courtesan-poet Mah Laqa from the south and the fictive prosaic Umrao Jan imagined from Lucknow in the north shows a comparatively distinct tone and style.[12] The attribution of feminine frivolity as part of the northern Lucknow poetic aesthetic can be read as a nod to a southern Dakani Urdu that has been shown to contain Indic terms for conceptualizing ideas of love, *sringara* and the beloved in poetry attached to the persona of Mah Laqa.[13] Scott Kugle draws attention to the gendered linguistic intricacies of rekhti and rekhta by considering the routes and roots of Urdu across North and South India. Borrowing from Jamila Nishat's study of Dakani Urdu as a vehicle for social expression, he homes in on the fusion period of the independent Deccan Muslim kingdom, the Bahmani Sultunate (1347–1518) in the fifteenth century. Of particular note, he says, are the intermarriages between Persian-speaking Muslim men and Marathi-, Telugu- and Kannada-speaking Hindu women that were seen to be formative in the development of a unique Dakani Urdu: 'It was for centuries the language of the bedroom and kitchen, of trade and household chores.'[14] It is this history that is seen to give Dakani Urdu its particular feminine flavour. While Petievich makes a case for a north–south divide, Kugle argues otherwise, emphasizing cultural exchange and resting his argument on a cosmopolitan Islamicate conceptualization that collapses differences.[15] The critic Meenakshi Mukherjee also notes the differential impacts of reform on inland and coastal communities, noting the insularity of Lucknow.[16] Digging deeper into the origins of rekhti underlines the significance of place and community – in this instance, South India, a Shi'i influence and multiple 'contact zones' – revealing how place, group dynamics and linguistic variations affect gender construction in Urdu verse.[17] Thus in the genre of rekhti we see geographical and linguistic connections contributing to an evolving landscape of Urdu poetry that reflected multiple voices.[18]

There are several canonical Urdu texts that note the shift of reference from a woman's dialect, notably the historical treatise of Lucknow lifestyles entitled *Guzashtah Lakhnau* (The Past of Lucknow), written by the novelist Abdul Halim Sharar (1860–1926), and the recognition of the rekhti form in Insha Allah Khan's Grammar entitled *Darya-i Latafat* (The Sea of Elegance).[19] Typically, Insha credits Rangin with the invention of rekhti: 'Because he is an avid patron of prostitutes [*randi*], Rangin's mind has taken to vulgarity and lewdness [*shuhudpun*]. Consequently putting aside *rekhta*, he has invented *rekhti*, hoping that young women of good families would read his verses and fall for him and that he would then "blacken his face" with them.'[20] In this particular instance, Insha separates rekhta from rekhti, emphasizing his friend's penchant for prostitution and his dangerous allure for respectable women, and spelling out an association that begins the task of moral cleansing. C. M. Naim questions Insha's attribution of Rangin as the creator of rekhti, suggesting that a similar kind of verse was in circulation in Bijapur and Hyderabad. He argues that rekhti verse was usually performed by a male poet in a public setting, and deliberately played with notions of cross-dressing, blurring the boundaries of gender while requiring a degree of performativity from both poet and audience. Naim's representation of rekhti as transvestic verse presents the case of a form punctuated by otherness, showcasing sexual desire and pleasure in its use of feminine voice but reiterating a hypermasculinity in the closing couplet.[21] Naim suggests that the speech and idioms of women in rekhti have latterly been read by critics such as Jamil Jalibi as a shameful sign of a soft feminized society that contributed to the eventual decline of Muslim culture in North India, especially Lucknow. To place Jalibi's reading, we need to recognize his location in Pakistan and his identification as a Muhajir migrant from Aligarh to Karachi. For the Urdu critic Ali Jawad Zaidi, rekhti 'never attained respectability and often sunk into vulgarity, catering for those who sought decadent pleasure'.[22] Zaidi's twentieth-century critical lens is a moral one, which seeks to rescue Urdu from articulations of sexuality that take it away from the aspirations of an ashraf class.

To illustrate the moral objections to rekhti, the following example of rekhti verse from Insha can be read as an example of the 'vulgar' sensibility that sexualized the female body and narrativized cross-dressing:

> This silly over-embroidered bodice is pricking me. Someone bring me a plain kind of bodice.
> Golden thread, frills, spangled ribbons, silver leaf, and sequins – what do I want with them? All they do is make this wretched bodice vulgar!
> Yesterday, when I tossed a ball, she became shy and daintily adjusted her bodice.
> The bodice that the sempstress sewed for her was not to her liking. So her ladyship just threw it back at her head.
> When we exchange our shawls, my sister, give me the heaviest bodice you have as well.
> How clever must have been the one who embroidered these flowers! Well done! My bodice has become a flower garden.[23]

The voice and pronoun appropriated by the male poet are feminine, depicting the body through an emphasis on adornment – 'golden thread, frills, spangled ribbons' –and fetishizing the bodice. Notably, the rekhti verse expresses titillation and double entendre in relation to women's clothing and mixes women from different social backgrounds. The form was performed in gatherings and was seen to reinforce the debauchery of men in the late nineteenth century.

In a different vein to how rekhti verse was read and understood, Ruth Vanita identifies the hybridity of rekhti and the 'mixing' that comes with eighteenth-century manifestations of urban life, including travel, class, gender and genre, as a key to reading it.[24] She pays close attention to linguistic registers, the mixing of Indic and Persianate traditions, medieval romances and erotic devotional poetry. Her suggestion is that rekhti 'emerges as the figure of an indigenous modernity' because the woman is shown to claim her 'pleasures and predilections'.[25] In selected examples, she underlines its Indic rather than Persianate influence, which borrowed from medieval Hindu erotic poetry and romance narratives. Her critique of rekhti emphasizes its doubleness by bringing into focus same-sex desire, the woman speaker and her narrative of sexual pleasure that is erotic and explicit. This is noted in the following example from Rangin by Carla Pietevich:

> Dil tarpi hai tujh bin mera ai jan dogana
> Rah ja mere ghar aj tu mehman dogana
> Ghar valon ke khatre se tere milne ka hi hai
> Reh ja'e mere dil men na arman dogana
> Jab bandhti hai apne kamar se tu sabura
> Ur jati hain tab bandi ke ausan dogana
> Buta sa qad aur us tere ankhil bane par
> Ho kyun na dogana tere qurban dogana
> Deti hai jo ragar to zara niche kehak kar
> Vari teri men ab meri nadan dogana
> Do din men teri sab ye pech ja'engi kali
> Rangin se mila kar tu na ai jan dogana

> [Darling dogana, without you
> My heart just throbs;
> Stay and be a guest in my house today,
> Darling dogana.

> If I try to see you there's danger
> From others in the house:
> But how to let go of this heart's desire,
> Darling dogana?

> Darling when you strap that dildo to your waist
> This poor slave's patience and peace of mind
> Just fly right out the window.

> With your delicate stature
> And your straightforward ways

Why wouldn't your sweetheart sacrifice
Herself for you, darling dogana?

As you let out a cry and rub me
A little lower
I become your slave, my foolish dogana.
Soon your budding freshness will be jaded, sweetheart
Especially if you keep meeting that Rangin!]²⁶

Rangin's verse represents an intimate and explicit conversation between two lovers. It draws attention to the domestic space of the house as a dangerous one for two female lovers who can be discovered at any time. The ending is suggestive, with its reference to the male persona of Rangin the poet intimating a bisexual love triangle, and also performs the ghazal convention by including the poet's nom de plume in the last couplet.²⁷ Vanita's argument about doubleness in rekhti verse is emphasized through her reading and translation of the term *du-gana* as one that carries a double meaning. It is glossed from Rangin as 'two women who split and eat a doubled (literal meaning of *du-gana*) fruit or nut, with the "masculine" and "feminine" roles being arbitrarily assigned to each depending on the part each happens to get' and the act of female–female sex.²⁸ Her emphasis is on how pleasure for women and men was vocalized in rekhti. Vanita's twenty-first-century argument reclaims the urban culture of rekhti and its mixing of low and high linguistic registers, reflecting both the zenana women of nobility and the *kotha* (brothel) courtesans.

In contrast to Vanita's reading is C. M. Naim's interpretation of rekhti as transvestic verse where he interprets rekhti as trans identification by male poets performing their identity as women. The linkage of rekhti with trans can be thought of in different ways ranging from the courtly associations in Islamicate cultures of 'eunuchs' or '*khwaja siras*' in empowered positions to lower-class '*hijras*' in Indian history. Both categories were collapsed during colonial rule and criminalized under section 377 of the Indian Penal Code in 1871.²⁹ The Indian elites colluded with the British colonial state to establish a heteronormative sexuality, casting out those with effeminate mannerisms and taboo sexualities. Therefore the cleansing of rekhti from Urdu verse is something that is part of an evolving colonial influence hinting at the growing anxiety over sexualities. Vanita's reading of rekhti as an articulation of pleasure and doubleness offers an alternative argument, suggesting the transformative potential of rekhti without the restrictions of reform. These evolving interpretations of rekhti as a premodern form reiterate the influence of religious sensibilities and political formations in Urdu verse and the flattening of sexualized articulations in the nineteenth century. Urdu was being transformed into a genteel and heteronormative language with strong North Indian roots and by the twentieth century rekhti had become a shameful secret in Urdu's past.

Educating Women: Reforming the Zenana

The reformists' aspiration toward a Western-style modernity is best exemplified in their relationship to women's education. A seminal role for Muslim women's education is attached to the reformist and aristocratic Begums of Bhopal in late nineteenth century. They worked in close collaboration with the British government and the Christian missionaries to increase literacy amongst women.[30] By colluding with the colonial state after the Rebellion of 1857, the Begums opened up channels of support for their princely state of Bhopal and literally came out from behind the veil to lead the state as sovereigns. But, as Siobhan Lambert-Hurley points out, it would be a misrepresentation to read their activism as a communal sisterhood.[31] Inspired by her grandmother, Nawab Sikander Begam, who founded the Victoria School for girls in Bhopal and challenged Sayyid Ahmad Khan's ideals of seclusion for women, Sultan Jahan Begam developed her own particular style of reform and writing that incorporated hybrid influences from Aligarh, Deoband and Ahl-e hadith traditions. Continuing her grandmother's legacy for girls' education, she left a lasting imprint on the development, administration, funding and curriculum development for girls' schools in the region, establishing herself as a progressive and pious leader.[32]

The poet Altaf Hussain Hali's poem *Chup ki dad* (Homage to the Silent) (1905), written at the request of Shaikh Abdullah, the editor of the Urdu women's journal *Khatun*, paid tribute to the patronage of Sultan Jahan, attributing her investment in women's education to the spirit of a 'divine collaboration'. Ironically, in his poem Hali eulogized women's status in caring roles as 'mothers, sisters, and daughters' rather than leaders, and at the same time entrusted them with the moral responsibility of acting as custodians of faith:

Naiki ki tum tasvir ho, iffat ki tum tadbir ho
Ho din ki tum pasban, iman salamat tum se hai

[You are the Picture of piety,
The counselor of chastity,
Of religion the guarantee.
Protection of the faith
Comes from you][33]

Thus Hali's praise of Muslim women's domestic lives was not designed to rock the boat but to transmit the value of what Anne McClintock in another context refers to as a 'national fetish', echoing the spirit of the Aligarh 'Delhi Muslim renaissance men' eager to raise modernized women in the zenana.[34] In this poem he reiterated some of the ideas from his earlier prose work *Majalis-un Nisa*, emphasizing the uplift of the Muslim community through sharif women's education. The price that women had to pay was subservience to a colonial project of modernity mimicking the moral values prevalent in Victorian England.[35] However, we can see from the examples of the Begums of Bhopal that there were challenges and upheavals from women as activists and participants in the process of reform. Hali's poem ensured that the message of reform was contained in a form available to and patronized by a large listening public and, most importantly, its endorsement by the Begums sent out a strong message to literate sharif women in the zenana of the power of education and public life. Thus this relationship played out satisfactorily for the colonial project of uplift of women in the zenana.[36]

In the meantime, an internal war over educating the zenana was raging between Muslim reformist men. There were disagreements over what women could and couldn't do, revealing conflicting tensions across two schools of reform, Aligarh and Deoband; the former was led by a liberal viewpoint and the other by a more orthodox Islamic ethics. A leading Muslim reformer, Sayyid Ahmad Khan, founder of the Aligarh movement and the Aligarh school for boys who embraced colonial values of progress and rationalism, was openly disapproving of women's education in schools outside the zenana.[37] In an address to women in Punjab, Khan advised: 'Educating your boys is the strategy for the restoration of your rights. Once they are educated you will naturally get back your usurped rights without any demands.'[38] He was adamant that women's place was in the home and their key role was to restore the status of Muslim nobility that had been lost in 1857. They could be domestic goddesses, princesses in their own homes, but were not expected to participate in public activities. In her reading of Sayyid Ahmad Khan's address, Tahera Aftab is of the view that his resistance to women in the public sphere was partly a reaction to the work of the Christian missionary women of the Zenana Bible missions, who were accessing the inner sanctity of Muslim households for teaching purposes. Therefore, it is no surprise to learn that when he read Sayyid Mumtaz Ali's manuscript of *Huquq un-Niswan* (The Rights of Women), a manual on women's rights, he was shocked and tore it up, determined to keep the inner sanctum intact beyond the reach of Christian missionaries. Ali published the manual in 1898 after the death of Sayyid Ahmad Khan. Gail Minault has traced Ali's intervention as a product of interactions with Aligarh, Deoband and Christian missionary influences.[39]

According to Minault, Ali's family were linked to the founders of the Deoband school and influenced by the political thought of the eighteenth-century religious scholar Shah Waliullah. These connections show internal variations within the Islamic community that were linked to progressive thought. The Deobandis were stakeholders in women's education as they wished to reform some of the 'Sufi' customs that were practised by women. In the following sections I look at how the two representatives of Aligarh and Deoband appropriated women's voices in their work and how women's education became a matter of disagreement over secular and sacred values.

Akbari and Asghari

The secret of the success of the Urdu novel in its early days was its female readership. Gail Minault's scholarship on *nisvani* or *begamati zaban* translates its stylistic and ideological adaptation in the linguistic narration of novels, short stories and poems.[40] This sharif *nisvani* language was successfully appropriated by Nazir Ahmad, a deputy collector in the revenue service of the British Raj, who rose to fame with a bestselling novel of manners for young women entitled *Mirat-ul Arus* (The Bride's Mirror), published in 1869. The book first gained popularity through precirculation amongst his local female readers as separate published stories of Akbari and Asghari. Ahmad went on to publish this in novel form to critical acclaim, educating his readers in the etiquette of being good wives, mothers and daughters and leading virtuous, purposeful lives. He was awarded a prize in 1870 by the government of the North West Frontier Provinces for writing a book suitable for the women of India and *Mirat-ul Arus* was recommended as a text for inclusion in school curricula. The book reached three editions by 1874. Its circulation in 20 years increased to over a hundred thousand copies and it still remains in print. Ahmad went on to publish another two novels on connected themes, *Banat-un nash* (1873) and *Taubat-un nasuh* (1874), both of which also won prizes. *Mirat-ul Arus* was translated into other Indian languages, including English in 1903, and is a part of the Urdu canon.[41] It remains a popular text to this day, inspiring the heroines scripted by women digest writers, television drama adaptations and school curricula.[42]

In a sociological study, Shenila Khoja-Moolji examines classic literary and cultural texts including *Mirat-ul Arus* to study the formation of modern subjects and girls' education in Pakistan. She argues that ideals about girls' education set out by Muslim reformists and ulema are reproduced in various contemporary cultural forms in the present, from schools to instructive television dramas.[43] While Khoja-Moolji's argument focuses on identity and identification in the novel to complement her sociological analysis, I argue that despite their didactic purposes, novels from this earlier period can also be read through their dialogism, refracting a monological worldview. In the process of contributing to a reformist agenda about women's education, authors were also connecting with a longer prose tradition and the aesthetics of storytelling.

Ahmad's *Mirat-ul Arus* depicts a formulaic story of two sisters, the good and kind-hearted Asghari and the frivolous and badly behaved Akbari.[44] They are ideological and exaggerated representations of the 'good' and 'evil' that Nazir Ahmad saw in zenana life.[45] Akbari and Asghari's father is a *tehsildar* (tax officer) for the Raj who marries off his girls to two brothers, Mohammad Aaqil and Mohammad Kamil, sons of Maulvi Muhammad Fazil. The main source of income for both families is employment in the lower courts by the colonial state. The *tamizdar bahu* (well-mannered daughter-in-law) Asghari leads her family toward prosperity and good fortune through the logic of capital by encouraging her husband to seek employment as a British colonial subject. She establishes her own school and gets the better of the devious Mama Azmat who had usurped the household finances. Thus Asghari is an active agent who saves her marital home from spiralling into debt and rescues her philandering husband from a nawabi lifestyle to a utilitarian outlook. She traverses the private and public spheres of a changing family structure to get household finances in order and plan for the future.

The novelist sets out the benefit of literacy for women at the start. In the introduction, he makes the case that women are men's equals when it comes to 'intelligence, thought, memory' but it is their lack of interest in studying and affinity with 'playing with dolls' that affects their 'ignorance'. Taking care to list elite and global women leaders, such as the Mughal emperor Jahangir's wife Nur Jahan, Aurangzeb's daughter Zebunnisa, Navab Sikander Begam and Queen Victoria, he keeps returning to 'ignorant women', who are the projected reading public for his prose and the theme of literacy:[46]

> I do not deny that too much learning is unnecessary for a woman, but how many women are there who acquire even so much as is absolutely necessary? It is of the greatest importance to them, at the very least, to be able to read and write the vernacular. [...] Writing is certainly a little difficult in comparison with reading, but any person who will make a practice of copying out four lines a day from a book, and of writing that amount over again from memory – getting the exercise corrected – in a few months, at the outside, will have learnt to write. [...] But suppose you never are able to write quite so well as boys; without a doubt you will at least be able to write sufficiently well to meet your own requirements, and you will no longer be put to the inconvenience of having to get up and draw lines on the wall, or make little heaps of gravel or pebbles, in

order to check the clothes you sent to wash, or the reckonings of the woman who grinds your corn. To keep all the accounts of the house – what there is to receive, and what there is to pay – entirely by rote is a very difficult matter, and it is a way with some husbands to ask for an account every now and then of the different sums they have paid towards the household expenses. If the wife cannot remember the items pat, the husband gets suspicious and asks to himself: 'Where has all that money gone?' [...] If women would only learn so much writing as would enable them to be accurate in their own accounts, what a good thing it would be!⁴⁷

What is interesting to note is that the pursuit of literacy is directly linked to the management of accounts and household capital. From the outset Ahmad sets out the criteria by which his heroine will be measured. Asghari fulfils her creator's vision by saving the family finances from the machinations of Mama Azmat, the old family servant who assists with the running of her in-laws' household and 'has been plundering the family', bringing it to the 'verge of ruin'.⁴⁸ Azmat makes the family vulnerable to the moneylender Hazari Mal. It is Asghari's diligent management of finances and housekeeping accounts that discovers the fraudulent Mama Azmat, and she embarks on a mission to get her dismissed, but first she has to win over her mother-in-law and her husband. She writes a letter to her brother to enlist his support and cleverly outwits Azmat with her family's support. After her success, she visits her parents' home and, when questioned by her father about the management of the house, replies with confidence, 'now I will look after everything myself'.⁴⁹ Therefore the novel first tests and then confirms her competency and management skills, showing her to be a householder who understands the power of economy in the household and by extension the community. By working hard and contributing to the immediate needs of her family (ensuring job success for her husband, a good marriage proposal for her sister-in-law) and her community, she demonstrates that moral rewards are attached to education and materially she benefits with better circumstances as well.

In her role as educator in the community, she runs a school for girls in her *mohalla* (neighbourhood). When a mother, Safihan, entrusts her 10-year-old daughter Fazilat to Asghari because she doesn't help her with household chores, she is shocked to discover her daughter playing with dolls on a visit to the school. 'My word, madam! You are a fine school-mistress, bringing these girls to ruin! All the times I have come to see Fazilat I have never once found her reading. Call this a school! It is a regular playing-house! That is why the girls are all so eager to come here!' (ibid., p. 130). Asghari patiently explains to Safihan that her daughter has made greater progress in reading with her than she had at her previous school. Once she has settled the disagreement she says:

> Your anxiety was not unnatural. But it is in these very amusements that I teach the girls things of real use. In their games of cooking the children learn the way of preparing every kind of dish. They get to know the proportion of spices, to judge the amount of salt, and to test things by their flavour and odour. Eh, Fazilat! [...].

> '... Sister Safihan, Sister Safihan, it is but a few days since your daughter began coming here, but the girls who have been with me for some time [...] I say it in all humility: if the management of some big, well-appointed household were committed to them at once, they could discharge it as well as the most practised and experienced woman could do. It is not only their reading which I insist upon: I try to make them useful for the business of the world, which will fall upon their heads before many days are over.[50]

Asghari is a problem-solver, a communicator and she is entrepreneurial, all essential qualities for a new woman challenging the orientalist perception of the zenana and firmly positioning herself as the leader of a modern Muslim community, along the lines of a Sikander Begum but from a modest background.

The last chapter of the novel is articulated as a letter written to Asghari by her father. Asghari has by now lost several children and, upon news of the latest bereavement, he writes her a note of condolence. He encourages her not to lose hope and to live for the higher moral cause of godliness over worldliness. The use of the epistolary form is suggestive and it is here that we might look for an alternative reading of Asghari beyond that of a ventriloquized sharif woman. By narrating the despair of a father trying to console his daughter over the loss of another child, the novel conveys the intimacy of family. But his emotions are held in check in this communication as he relies on spirituality to convey his grief over the tragedy of death and philosophically prepare her for the afterlife where only deeds matter and not human relationships.

Ahmad's development of dialogue to narrate his story and abstinence from the fantastical romance language of the dastan put forward an 'imagined community' over space and time that made it more than just a moral fable.[51] By deploying the novel form, Ahmad mixed existing oral prose forms such as the *dastan* and *qissa* traditions, which predate the arrival of the novel in English, with monologues, dialogues, third-person narrative and letters. His didactic monologues are broken by incursions into the zenana and contrasting conversational representations of a *mizajdar* and *tamizdar bahu* (daughter-in-law). Through these juxtapositions, he represents the declining economic worth of a traditional sharif Muslim household.

However, Ahmad's book was seen in a negative light by Maulana Ashraf Ali Thanawi, who advised his readers to stay away from both *Mirat-ul Arus* and *Banat-un nash* as they had sections that 'weaken faith'. C. M. Naim offers some 'speculative' reasons for the difference of opinion between Thanawi and Ahmad. He argues that Thanawi's critique of Ahmad was about the threat to religious values, the close association with missionaries and 'his portrayal of highly capable and dynamic women, who tower over the men around them'.[52] Ahmad's modernizing vision of the two central characters, Akbari and Asghari, in *Mirat-ul Arus*, and how he envisages Asghari as someone who can traverse private and public worlds was opposed to Thanawi's idea for pious women.

Maulana Ashraf Ali Thanawi's *Bihishti Zewar* (Heavenly Ornaments), an educational manual for women, underlined reformist ideology from Deobandi writings. The book, in 10 parts, prescribes a Muslim woman's private and public role in society according to the Qur'an and Hadith, educating her in simplified Urdu prose style. It gained popularity for its simplicity of style and ease of access as a moral compendium for Muslim women. Thanawi's conduct book instructed women on how to behave with piety and decorum and was designed to preserve authentic Muslim values in the zenana. *Bihishti Zewar* benefitted from the commercialization of print culture, interest in women's education and the blurred lines of private and public in the evolving zenana. Considered as one of the 'most influential' books of twentieth-century Muslim South Asia, it found an audience amongst a burgeoning female readership and remains in circulation to this day as a religious handbook for women in India and Pakistan.[53] Barbara Daly Metcalf has commented on the potentially liberal discourse of Thanawi's conduct book, as it puts women on an equal plane with men in its explanation of Sharia and disrupts the orientalized notion of women's position as second-class citizens in Islam. She argues that *Bihishti Zewar* 'gives evidence of important roles for women in exercising moral leadership, creating social alliances, and managing economic resources in the society it represents'.[54] Pitching his book to young women, Thanawi encouraged them to value intellect over adornment, reason over emotion. His use of form in the manual, deploying both prose and verse to deliver his message, is not that different to experimentations with voice that were taking place in the novel. Using simplified Urdu, he educated women about the burden of dowry and their moral obligations. The message of the true jewellery of humanity is conveyed through the form of a poem. Appropriating the voice of a mother speaking to her daughter, his message is not dissimilar to that of Nazir Ahmad:

Jewelry of silver, gold, is only a thing to see.
Four days of silvery light, and then dark night will be.

It is required of you the kind of jewelry to want
From which good faith and life, my dear, may never want.

Good sense, dear, always be the head fringe you put on;
Sense is the means by which your work gets done.[55]

However, that is where the similarity ends. The difference between Ahmad and Thanawi lies in their representation of family and the function of women within it. Ahmad did not shy away from taking his imaginary heroines into public spaces: for instance, Asghari's engagement with the world outside is a key part of her character. Thanawi, on the other hand, advises women to stay within the confines of their homes through his moral compendium. Usamah Ansari makes a case for 'shariatic modernity' in his interpretation of *Bihishti Zewar*, by which he means the family is modern but 'patriarchal, nuclear and conjugal'.[56] He bases this interpretation on a comparison with the conjugal household in classic *fiqh* sources, which do not emphasize household management for women in the same way. Crucially, *Bihishti Zewar* was focused on training women how to negotiate moral responsibility within the home in a way that was suited to modern living. Ansari's reading elaborates on how the liberalizing force of education clashed with the inner sanctity of the zenana and the way in which *Bihishti Zewar*'s strategic capitalization of the project of educating women incorporated limited modernities.

In many ways both books complemented the linguistic reform of poetry and the reconstruction of gender into distinct feminine and masculine categories reflective of the cultural politics of a new urban elite. But Thanawi took the additional step of speaking out against Ahmad's book. He was making a very specific recommendation over what he considered *halal* and *haram* options according to *din* (religion). *Bihishti Zewar* made it clear that women had to behave according to the principles of Sharia translated by Thanawi. He structurally controlled women readers through a scriptural relationship, establishing himself as the moral authority and his vision as an all-encompassing one. In this bond, a Nazir Ahmad-style literacy for women was a dangerous thing.

While Thanawi encouraged women's education in *Bihishti Zewar*, he was careful to note his reservations about women writing, in an essay in 1913:

Writing is needful for domestic life. But if there is any fear of impropriety [on the part of the girl], it is more important to protect yourself from iniquity than to seek a thing that may be useful but is not in fact obligatory. Under such circumstances, do not let the girl be instructed in the art of writing, and do not let her write on her own either.[57]

He recognized that women's literacy was useful for the home but at the same time it could make them vulnerable to vice. To be a good Muslim woman in Thanawi's world required complete submission to familial obligation, duty and community. In other words, the world of writing could lead to a weakening of faith.

Umrao Jan Ada: The Courtesan Poet and the Hybrid Urdu Novel

Different to the story of *Mirat-ul Arus* is Mirza Hadi Rusva's experimental, turn-of-the-century Urdu novel, *Umrao Jan Ada*. The nostalgic tale of a late eighteenth- and early nineteenth-century Lucknow courtesan-poet, Umrao Jan, it captured the imagination of twentieth- and twenty-first-century writers of Urdu prose, Hindi film and Urdu television drama. It is the seedling for the Lollywood film directed by Hassan Tariq (1972), the Bollywood film directed by Muzaffar Ali (1981), the Pakistani Geo television adaptation in 2003 and the Bollywood film of the same name directed by J. P. Dutta in 2006. The film and television narratives are coloured by a nostalgia for the past and how indigenous Indian courtly culture gave way to a utilitarian European modernity. These multiple representations of Umrao Jan translate a traditional aristocratic culture in North India that was at the brink of collapse at the fag end of the nineteenth century, juxtaposing it against the life story and moral universe of a strong female character who had climbed her way to the top of her profession. In the visual narratives, the culture of dance and song is paramount whereas in the novel it is hardly mentioned. The novelist Rusva as a self-conscious artist believed his novels to be a 'history of our times', independent of a social message. However, there is a moral tone to his story of a courtesan who is at heart a kind and likeable character. His narration of Umrao Jan's story relies on a hybrid mix of storytelling devices borrowing from the dastan, the picaresque and the episodic.[58] On the surface it is the life story of a Lakhnavi courtesan retold by the author/narrator Rusva, who is selected for his integrity and his command over verse. We are given colourful snapshots of courtesans' lives, contrasting with and complementing the debauchery of nawabi culture against the backdrop of the historical period of the 1857 Rebellion. At a deeper level, the novel offers a dialogic engagement with the aesthetics of love and sexuality amongst an elite Muslim class in Lucknow, marking the loss of a traditional lifestyle.

At an initial glance, *Umrao Jan Ada* can be read as a fictional adaptation of Mah Laqa's story from the southern region of Hyderabad Deccan and transformation to the nawabi culture of Lucknow in the north. While Mah Laqa's presence is acknowledged in historical biographies of the period, she is understandably not a celebrated icon amongst twentieth-century Urdu women poets. Her pioneering contribution to the literary history of women's poetry publications remains overshadowed by her profession and her class. Like her late nineteenth-century literary counterpart Umrao Jan Ada, she is deeply associated with the excesses of the aristocracy and her poetry is understood within the frame of her performativity as a courtesan inhabiting the traditionally male sphere of the private mushaira.[59] Frances Pritchett, who has undertaken an archival analysis of the novel, disproves through her research that Umrao Jan is a 'real' character, citing the 'inconsistencies' in the novel that invalidate its claim as a biography. She identifies the inaccuracy of Umrao Jan's father working as a *jamedar* at Bahu Begum's tomb in Faizabad as a key historical discrepancy. This research helps to underline differences between the fictional story and the actual life of the courtesan Mah Laqa while illustrating intertextual references that have fed into the characterization by Rusva. However, Pritchett's reading places an emphasis on Rusva's novel as a form of representational realism and this has been contested through analyses of the central characterization of Amiran, who dons the mask of Umrao Jan.[60]

On the front cover of the 1899 edition, published by Munshi Gulab Singh and Sons Press, Lucknow, we are given a short paragraph illustrating the content of the novel, telling us that it is the *savane umri* (autobiography) of a tawaif. The class of the tawaif is similar to that of the hetaira in Ancient Greece and public censure was directed more at the lower randis (prostitutes).[61] Rusva, in his introduction to the novel, makes a clear distinction between the preferable lifestyle of the elegant tawaif who lives next door to his friend's house and the randis, who perform services at a lower level. In the novel, Umrao Jan often refers to herself and her female counterparts as randis although she takes care to distinguish herself as a tawaif rather than a randi because of a respectable background at birth. In turn, Rusva the narrator establishes Umrao Jan as a tawaif through his interactions with her, a status he does not accord to randis. As the novel progresses to its end the moral message of redemption is reinforced as Umrao Jan finds solace in religious spirituality.

Umrao Jan's introspections to her biographer take place in dialogue and verse forms, playfully juxtaposing the bawdiness of rekhti and the traditional aesthetic form of the love lyric. Her fictional characterization provides a foil to her real-life counterpart, Mah Laqa, whose *Divan* resorts to more conventional representations.[62] Umrao Jan's voice is mediated by the unreliable narrator called Rusva in the text of the novel, who is a conceit of the omniscient author Rusva, the author of the novel and an unknown editor.[63] The mixing of genres such as the love lyric, biography and autobiography, dialogue and introspective narrative makes *Umrao Jan Ada* a novel of many possibilities. It reflects the morality of a good courtesan, her unreliable and untrustworthy clients and an ironic retelling by the narrator. The frequent use of the lyric form brings digressive moments into the novel and breaks the narrative flow.[64] Rusva establishes himself as a trustworthy person with whom Umrao Jan can share the intrigues of her life in the kotha. She also wants him to know that she was not born but sold into the profession as a young girl. The linguistic tone deployed by the narrator is fairly informal, although the dialogue is peppered with conventional *matlas* (opening couplets) and short ghazals, as the two protagonists are shown to share a love of poetry. The inclusion of a mushaira at the start of the novel gives a formal metrical setting to the informal dialogic narration that is to follow. It complicates the 'realist' narration of the novel and frames a performative and metaphorical element from the start.

Umrao Jan articulates her desires and experiences as a professional courtesan who plays the game of love, as well as acquainting us with her inner feelings and frustrations. As the story unfolds, the introspective narrative shifts from the third person of Rusva to the first person of Umrao Jan, intersecting a slipperiness of narrative voices. At times, Rusva the listener interrupts the narrative flow with his observations, interpreting and translating Umrao Jan's actions. For instance, when she is trying to explain why she left her benefactor Khanum's kotha, he pre-empts her and says, 'Living at Khanum's house was not a good deed. I've understood from our conversation that you always understood adultery to be a bad deed. Although your circumstances forced you into that situation. It must have seemed far better to give yourself up to one man than to continue to stay at Khanum's house'.[65] He ends by noting that despite being a fallen woman she was not wise to the actions of a *daku* (highway robber) and a rogue like Faiz Ali, the man who professed to love and save her from her existence in the kotha. His interruptions, although small, are significant as they reinforce the moral stance of the novel. It is worth pointing out that when the dialogue between Umrao Jan and Rusva takes place the characters are named as Umrao and Rusva but when action is taking place amongst different characters Umrao is referred to in the first person singular as '*main*' (I). This personification allows a slippage between the voice of the kidnapped girl Amiran and her professional voice as Umrao. As her chosen companion/collaborator for the narration of her story, Rusva adds another dissociation of voice. At times, Rusva seems to be the ventriloquist, controlling Umrao Jan with his occasional commentary. The differential gender power dynamic between the two means that as readers we cannot take at face value that which is attributed to Umrao Jan. Her couplet that is presented at the beginning of her story encapsulates this framing: 'Lutf hai kaunsi kahani men / Ap biti kahun ke jag biti' (Which story will entertain? Which story should I tell you? Mine or the story of the times?).[66] Here, the author uses the device of the historical novel to emplot a cultural myth about the courtesan. In representing history as fiction and projecting the courtesan as protagonist, the novel offers an alternative chronicle to educating narratives that popularized women's changing status in late nineteenth-century India.[67]

Toward the end of the novel we are told that, although Umrao Jan finds herself increasingly drawn to religion in later life, she did not have an awareness of it at the start of her working life as a courtesan. There is a fairly lengthy monologue by Umrao Jan leading to the conclusion that '*randis* should beware that anyone will truly love them [...] a *bazari* woman cannot be blessed by God in the pursuit of love'.[68] The appeal to redemption through a pious transformation of character is not unusual in a turn of the century novel as it reflects the high moral ground of an Indian authenticity that was used to resist the colonial power of the British Raj.[69] As far as the ambivalence of gender is concerned in the novel, women are firmly brought out of the world of metaphor, performance and bawdiness to live a pious life.

What is different about this novel in contrast to the didacticism of Nazir Ahmad's *Mirat-ul Arus* is its articulation of 'female' desire and sexuality through a tawaif. As the social period was in flux, the novel charts those changing intersections of religion, politics and ethics, representing altered attitudes toward morality and sexual behaviour in Indian Muslim society. The ironic dialogue between Umrao Jan and Rusva highlights the distinction between the 'old' and the 'new' morality that was coming into play and it also articulates the perceived feminine frivolity of a Lakhnavi Urdu culture. Umrao Jan conveys a premodern sexuality for courtesans that is comfortable in the company of both men and women.[70] She entertains her readers with 'real events' from her life against the backdrop of the changing fortunes of Lucknow. However, the novel is conscious of the need for Umrao Jan to reform to a more conventional sexuality and ultimately this concern is what drives the narrative forward.

A key contextual difference between *Umrao Jan Ada*, *Mirat-ul Arus* and *Bihishti Zewar* is the nawabi lifestyle and Lucknow culture encapsulated in the narration of Umrao Jan. This sets it apart as a novel that reflects the changing fabric of a city in flux, reiterating the patronage of courtly culture and to some extent its influence on a syncretic Urdu cultural environment attuned to an Islamicate culture. In contrast, *Bihishti Zewar*, a popular manual for women, sets out new Islamic ethics for women and *Mirat-ul Arus* fictionalizes the kind of girl who is required to be the subject of a new Muslim modernity. Novels such as *Umrao Jan Ada* and *Mirat-ul Arus* illustrate the complex negotiations between form and ideology that marked the development of Urdu and the limits of sharif behaviour for women while working within the paradigm of the colonial civilizing mission. They show the variations of the secular and the sacred as they were dialogized by an ashraf class constantly negotiating and renegotiating the private and the public in relation to modernity and Islamic values. There are ambivalences to be found in voice and register, class and morality. The commonality across these texts is a female readership in Urdu. These key developments in the late nineteenth and early twentieth centuries set the scene for the subsequent expansion of women's participation in literature as reform gave way to modernity.

After Nazir Ahmad's award-winning tale and Rusva's nostalgic *Umrao Jan* is the example of Muhammadi Begum, the first Urdu woman novelist whose novel *Sharif Beti* (The Noble Daughter) was published circa 1902.[71] She was followed by the novelist Nazar Sajjad Hyder, whose most well-known contribution on women remains her essay on 'Purdah' (seclusion). In all, ashraf women such as Muhammadi Begum, Bibi Ashraf, Nazar Sajjad Hyder and others through the project of writing extended the reformist framework in which to express new and modern selves for women. Begum Atiya Fyzee, a regular contributor to the women's magazine *Tehzib-un niswan* in the first decade of the twentieth century, presents a cosmopolitan persona in the publication of her letters in diary form, *Zamana-e tehsil* (A Time of Education), recording her cross-cultural encounters in London. A woman from Bombay, she traversed boundaries of class and caste in London and it is perhaps Atiya Fyzee who is referred to in Muhammad Iqbal's *Javidnama* as someone who was vulnerable to the influence of suffragettes in a modern atmosphere without sharif distinctions between the public and the private.[72]

A recent travelogue has come to light of another Muhammadi Begum from the South Indian state of Hyderabad, who was a direct descendant of Nazir Ahmad. She studied at Osmania University and gained a scholarship from the Nizam of Hyderabad to study at St Hugh's College, Oxford University, in 1934. Muhammadi Begum was 24 years old and came with her husband, Jamil Husain, a graduate of Aligarh University. He was employed by the Nizam as a civil servant and took leave of absence to accompany his wife. Her diary is a pragmatic account of her life as a student at Oxford, making friends, worrying about scholarship administration, food, the state of women's dress and philosophic concerns. Some of her letters sent to her mother, Qaiseri Begam, the granddaughter of Maulvi Nazir Ahmad and author of *Kitab-e zindagi* (The Book of Life), were published in *Tehzib-un niswan*. Notably, in response to a question about 'how modern women feel about the purdah system', Muhammadi Begum replies that, in her opinion, 'women did not want to remain in *purdah* and it would disappear in time' (p. 56).[73] She is also passionate about women's full participation in the Oxford Student Union and frustrated by some of the restrictions for women at Oxford. For her, the motherland and family are part of the same equation: 'Whatever my feelings, I would never disown my country nor disparage its image in the eyes of the world nor cast aspersions on my kith and kin. I am utterly devoted to family and its welfare and I see that as my sacred duty' (p. 115). In the diary she also lets slip that, on a visit to see their friend Fazal-ur-Rahman, she and Jameel are told that 'Deputy' Nazir Ahmad went through a period of 'no belief in God at all' (p. 167).[74] This revelation is one of the many new things she learns as part of her life at Oxford, from visits to the British Museum to watching Paul Robeson perform live at Oxford. She talks about the weakness that comes from '"feeling obliged" and unable to "refuse" out of politeness' creating problems for her (p. 38). There are breakfasts, lunches, teas and dinners, telling us of the social life and food habits of the migrant family alongside a regular routine of *namaz, duas* and reading of the Qur'an and *wazifas*. Some interesting discoveries are made in the process, such as people in the British Isles spending an 'enormous amount of time' on four daily meals and all not being as it seems in 'England's green and pleasant land' (pp. 55–6, 60). A baby is born; intellectual conversations about freedom, rights, taxation and women's position in society abound. Overall in the travelogue of Muhammadi Begum we see an anthropological study of her own life and that of her surroundings, taking the story of women's voices in new directions, conveying the challenges of pregnancy, reading *The Forsyte Saga* and learning French (pp. 18, 23, 35, 48, 52, 53, 67, 113 (Forsyte Saga); References to French learning are present throughout the text). Her experiences of sending and writing letters home from Oxford make her reflect on a cosmopolitan life that has been made possible through a scholarship. It makes her conscious of how much she is beholden to others. She feels the burden to prove 'how serious I am', especially as she is expecting her first child and there are rumours, she says, about her ability to cope with her studies (p. 57).

In conclusion, by juxtaposing representations of family, gender and education in Urdu literary culture through the genre of rekhti, the novel form, a religious manual by male writers and the diary/travelogue by a woman writer, I have argued how creative imaginings and religious texts present us with variations of voice and a crisis of masculinity during the period of reform. Feminine voice was strategically deployed by reformists and coloured by different ideologies over time. The diary of the travelling scholar Muhammadi Begum demonstrates how women's personal experiences were changing through travel and cosmopolitan interactions and the intersectional dilemmas of education and scholarship. Urdu literary culture at the turn of the twentieth century was a site of conflicting emotions and intellectual differences. Modernizers and reformers had sought to make it more utilitarian and in the process of representation flattened the multiplicity of gendered voices.

Notes

1. On the form of the English novel in the eighteenth century, see Ian Watt's *The Rise of the Novel*, 2nd ed. (Berkeley: University of California Press, 2001). This has useful insights for Urdu literary studies given the influence of English education in India and its impact on local literatures. Also see Meenakshi Mukherjee's insightful study of *Realism and Reality: The Novel and Society in India* (Delhi: Oxford University Press, 1985). Mukherjee discusses the relevance of the eighteenth-century English novel to the nineteenth-century Indian novel, underlining some shared concerns for women's moral improvement, for instance, *Pamela* by Samuel Richardson. My analysis in this chapter is also influenced by Bakhtin's conceptualisation of dialogicality and the discourse of language interactions. See M. M. Bakhtin, *The Dialogic Imagination: Four Essays*, trans. M. Holquist and C. Emerson (Austin: University of Texas Press, 1981).
2. See David Lelyveld, '*Ashraf*', in *Keywords in South Asian Studies*, ed. Rachel Dwyer, SOAS South Asia Institute [online resource], accessed 25 June 2020, https://www.soas.ac.uk/south-asiainstitute/keywords/file24799.pdf.
3. Her close reading of Petrus Alfonsi's *Priestly Tales* accounts for the vast cultural exchange that took place through translations between Arabic and Latin. She argues that the 'basic plotlines' that are contained in *Priestly Tales* are a model for the modern narrative and she sees it as a book that bridged the oral and written forms between Latin and Arabic. Maria Rosa Menocal, *The Ornament of the World: How Muslims, Jews, and Christians Created a Culture of Tolerance in Medieval Spain* (New York: Black Bay Books, Little Brown, 2002), 152–55.
4. Christopher Shackle and Rupert Snell, *Hindi and Urdu since 1800: A Common Reader* (London: SOAS, University of London, 1990).
5. See Edward Said, *Orientalism: Western Conceptions of the Orient* (London: Routledge and Kegan Paul, 1978); Rana Kabbani, *Europe's Myths of Orient* (London: Pandora Press, 1988); Reina Lewis, *Rethinking Orientalism: Women, Travel and the Ottoman Harem* (London: I.B. Tauris, 2004).
6. Anindita Ghosh, writing on print cultures in North India, notes how printing presses, European missionaries and administrators, and oral cultures in Bengal added tensions in the modernity narrative. Anindita Ghosh, 'An Uncertain "Coming of the Book": Early Print Cultures in Colonial India', *Book History* 6 (2003): 23–55.
7. On commercialization in the nineteenth century and the impact of capitalism on a Macaulay-educated class of Indian Muslim service gentry, see Chris Bayly, *Rulers, Townsmen and Bazaars: North Indian Society in the Age of British Expansion 1770–1870* (Cambridge: Cambridge University Press, 1983).
8. Ulrike Starke, *An Empire of Books: The Naval Kishore Press and the Diffusion of the Printed Word in Colonial India* (Delhi: Permanent Black, 2007).
9. See Frances W. Pritchett, 'Afterword: The First Urdu Bestseller', in Maulvi Nazir Ahmad, *The Bride's Mirror: A Tale of Life in Delhi a Hundred Years Ago*, trans. G. E. Ward (London: Henry Frowde, 1903; Delhi: Permanent Black, 2001), 204–21, http://www.columbia.edu/itc/mealac/pritchett/00fwp/published/txt_mirat_intro.html.
10. Michèle Roberts, 'The Fallen Woman: Prostitution in Literature', *The Guardian*, 14 April 2017, https://www.theguardian.com/books/2017/apr/14/the-fallen-woman-prostitution-in-literature. The ambivalence of the courtesan has been evocatively captured in a novel that brings together English literature and Urdu literature, Anita Desai's *In Custody*, creatively representing the artistic creativity of

the courtesan in a dying culture of decadence, bringing to light her passion and devotion for Urdu poetry against the revered figure of the permanently drunk and colonized poet. See my article, 'The Communalisation and Disintegration of Urdu in Anita Desai's *In Custody*', *Annual of Urdu Studies* 19 (2004): 120–41.

11 On contact zones, see Mary Louise Pratt, 'Arts of the Contact Zone', *Profession* (1991): 33–40, https://www.jstor.org/stable/25595469.

12 Scott Kugle, 'Mah Laqa Bai and Gender: The Language, Poetry and Performance of a Courtesan in Hyderabad', *Comparative Studies of South Asia, Africa, and the Middle East* 30, no. 3 (2010): 365–85, http://muse.jhu.edu/journals/cst/summary/v030/30.3.kugle.html.; Ghulam Samdani Gauhar, *Hayat-e Mah laqa* (Hyderabad: Nizam al-Matabi, 1904).

13 Kugle, 'Mah Laqa Bai and Gender', 381.

14 Ibid., 379.

15 See Carla Petievich, *Assembly of Rivals: Delhi, Lucknow and the Urdu Ghazal* (Lahore: Vanguard Books, 1992) and Bruce B. Lawrence, 'Islamicate Civilization: The View from Asia', in *Teaching Islam*, ed. Brannon M. Wheeler (New York: Oxford University Press, 2003), 61–76.

16 Mukherjee, *Realism and Reality*, 91.

17 I borrow this term from Mary Louise Pratt's seminal essay 'Arts of the Contact Zone'.

18 Shamsur Rahman Faruqi identifies Altaf Husain Hali's *Muqaddama sher-o shairi* (1893) as the key critical text that spelt out a dividing line for Urdu literary culture into a Delhi and a Lucknow school of poetry. See Shamsur Rahman Faruqi, *Early Urdu Literary Culture and History* (New Delhi: Oxford University Press, 2001).

19 Insha Allah Khan, *Darya-i Latafat* (Aurangabad: Anjuman-e taraqqi-e Urdu, 1935), 170–85.

20 Quoted in C. M. Naim, 'Transvestic Words?: The *Rekhti* in Urdu', *Annual of Urdu Studies* 16, no. 5 (2001): 3–26.

21 Naim gives the example of Ahad Ali Khan Yakta whose *tazkira* was completed in 1834, just after Rangin and Insha's appropriation of the form in Lucknow to illustrate the distinction of *rekhti* from *rekhta* as a separate world of women. According to Yakta, '[R]ēkhtī is a kind of poetry in which only the speech and idioms of women are used and only those matters are mentioned that happen between women or between a woman and a man. Further, it must not contain any word or phrase that is exclusive to men.' Yakta, *Dasturu 'l-Fasahat*, ed. Imtiaz 'Ali Khan 'Arshi (Rampur: Rampur State Library, 1943), 97, quoted in Naim, 'Transvestic Words', 7.

22 A. J. Zaidi, *A History of Urdu Literature* (Delhi: Sahitya Akademi, 1993), 137.

23 Translation by D. J. Matthews and Christopher Shackle in *An Anthology of Classical Urdu Love Lyrics*, ed. D. J. Matthews and Christopher Shackle (London: Oxford University Press, 1972), 94. For a selection of Insha's rekhti verse, see Syed Sibt Mohammad Naqvi (ed.), *Intikhab rekhti* (Lucknow: Uttar Pradesh Urdu Academy, 1983), 22–28.

24 Ruth Vanita, *Gender, Sex and the City: Urdu Rekhti Poetry 1780–1870* (New Delhi: Orient Blackswan, 2012).

25 Ibid., 38.

26 Translation by Carla Petievich in her *When Men Speak as Women: Vocal Masquerade in Indo-Muslim Poetry* (Delhi: Oxford University Press, 2007), 304–5.

27 Vanita's critical position relies on a complementary reading of *rekhta* and *rekhti*, putting the *ghazal, masnavi, mukhammas* side by side with *rekhti* and looking at similarities of theme, language and tone to develop a hybrid reading.

28 Vanita, *Gender, Sex and the City*, 139, 142.
29 See Shahnaz Khan, 'What Is in a Name? Khwaja Sira, Hijras and Eunuchs in Pakistan', *Indian Journal of Gender Studies* 23, no. 2 (2016): 218–42. DOI: 10.1177/0971521516635327.
30 In his *Maqalat*, the Islamic scholar Shibli Naumani acknowledges the debt owed by Hindustani Muslim society to their women, who played a key role in setting up centres of Islamic learning, dedicated to the teachings of the Qur'an and Hadith; M. Shibli, *Maqalat-e Shibli* [Shibli's Letters], vol. 4 (Lahore: Majlis-e traqqi-e adab, 1956), 86–88.
31 Focusing on Sultan Jahan Begam, the last of the Begums of Bhopal, who reigned from 1901 to 1926 and served as president of the All-India Ladies Association, Lambert-Hurley describes her as a pioneering intermediary across groups and generations advocating women's education. Siobhan Lambert-Hurley, 'Fostering Sisterhood: Muslim Women and the All-India Ladies' Association', *Journal of Women's History* 16, no. 2 (2004): 40–65. Also see her monograph *Muslim Women, Reform and Princely Patronage: Nawab Sultan Jahan Begam of Bhopal* (New York: Routledge, 2007).
32 Lambert-Hurley's archival research has shown that the Begums of Bhopal drew on a range of 'reformist models' including the colonial state, Aligarh, Maria Montessori and Deobandi ulema, but she notes that they were 'certainly not contained by them'; *Muslim Women, Reform and Princely Patronage*, 99.
33 Hali, *Voices of Silence: English Translation of Hali's Majalis-un-nissa and Chup ki dad*, trans. Gail Minault (Delhi: Chanakya, 1986), 141.
34 On the idea of the national 'fetish', see Anne McClintock, '"No Longer in a Future Heaven": Gender, Race and Nationalism', in *Dangerous Liaisons: Gender, Nation and Postcolonial Perspectives*, ed. Anne McClintock, Aamir Mufti and Ella Shohat (Minneapolis: University of Minneapolis Press, 2004), 89–112; the term 'Delhi renaissance men' is borrowed from David Lelyveld, *Aligarh's First Generation: Muslim Solidarity in British India* (Princeton, NJ: Princeton University Press, 1996).
35 As Susie Tharu notes, 'the Victorians laid great stress on sexual restraint and moral uprightness in women, for without systematic control, women's sexual powers and appetites were considered dangerous to 'civic' society as a whole'; Susie Tharu, 'Tracing Savitri's Pedigree: Victorian Racism and the Image of Women in Indo-Anglian Literature', in *Recasting Women: Essays in Colonial History*, ed. Kumkum Sangari and Sudesh Vaid (New Delhi: Kali, 1999), 254–68 (260).
36 Notably, Nawab Sikander Begum has left a lasting and pioneering legacy in print through her travelogue about her pilgrimage to Makkah in 1870 that reiterates both her economic and social power as a woman. In detailing the journey, she articulates her personal experiences of performing the Haj. See Siobhan Lambert-Hurley's introduction to her edited book, *A Princess's Pilgrimage: Nawab Sikander Begum's 'A Pilgrimage to Mecca'* (Bloomington: Indiana University Press, 2008). Also see Nawab Sikander Begum of Bhopal, *A Pilgrimage to Mecca*, trans. Mrs Willoughby Osborne (London: W. H. Allen, 1870).
37 See Lelyveld, *Aligarh's First Generation*; Mushirul Hasan, 'Aligarh's "Notre Eminent Contemporain": Assessing Syed Ahmad Khan's Reformist Agenda', *Economic and Political Weekly* 33, no. 19 (9–15 May 1998): 1077–81, https://www.jstor.org/stable/4406749.
38 Tahera Aftab, 'Negotiating with Patriarchy: South Asian Muslim Women and the Appeal to Sir Syed Ahmed Khan', *Women's History Review* 14, no. 1 (2005): 75–98 (86).
39 Gail Minault, 'Sayyid Mumtaz Ali and "Huquq un-Niswan": An Advocate of Women's Rights in Islam in the Late Nineteenth Century', *Modern Asian Studies* 24, no. 1 (1990): 147–72 (149).

40   Minault, 'Begamati Zuban: Women's Language and Culture in Nineteenth Century Delhi', *India International Centre Quarterly* 11, no. 2 (1984): 155–70 (157–70); *Secluded Scholars: Women's Education and Muslim Social Reform in Colonial India* (New Delhi: Oxford University Press, 1998), 37.
41   See Pritchett, 'Afterword: The First Urdu Bestseller'.
42   *Mirat-ul Aroos* was adapted for the Pakistan television network in the 1990s by Haq Nawaz, and as television dramas *Maat* (2011) adapted by Umera Ahmed for Hum TV, *Akbari Asghari* (2011) adapted by Faiza Iftikhar for Hum TV, *Mirat ul Aroos* (2012) adapted by Umera Ahmed for Geo TV.
43   Shenila Khoja-Moolji, *Forging the Ideal Educated Girl: The Production of Desirable Subjects in Muslim South Asia* (Oakland: University of California Press, 2018). As part of her critical framework, she represents the construction of the ideal educated girl at the turn of the century to develop contemporary case studies of Pakistani girls/women and education. Her project contributes to ongoing research on ashraf middle-class values and their impact on a new urban middle class, studying religious piety as part of nation building, linking gender and education to economic growth and modernity.
44   Mohammad Sadiq, *A History of Urdu Literature* (Lahore: Sang-e meel, 1995), 409; S. A. Qadir, *The New School of Urdu Literature: A Critical Study of Hali, Azad, Nazir Ahmad, Rattan Nath Sarshar and Abdul Halim Sharar* (Lahore: Shaikh Mubarak Ali, 1932), 48–58.
45   Minault, *Secluded Scholars*, 37–38.
46   We have the true story of Bibi Ashraf whose entry into public life was enabled by the colonial state. She came from a *sharif* family, was widowed and orphaned at a young age, learned to support herself as a seamstress and later as a school teacher. (See Ruby Lal, *Coming of Age in Nineteenth-Century India: The Girl-Child and the Art of Playfulness* (Cambridge: Cambridge University Press, 2013), 172: her reading of Bibi Ashraf's story is derived from an interaction with the original text *Hayat-e Ashraf* [The Lifestory of Ashraf], a compilation of Bibi Ashraf's essays and conversations edited by Muhammadi Begum.) Bibi Ashraf's initial desire for acquiring Urdu literacy was kindled during the 40-day observation period of *Muharram* in the separate majalis held for men and women every day, where matters of faith were discussed from books. Various female elders dismissed her desire to learn as inconsequential and unnecessary. Feeling sidelined, she decided to teach herself how to write. Her story was published in the women's magazine *Tehzib-un niswan* in 1899. See C. M. Naim, 'How Bibi Ashraf Learned to Read and Write', *Annual of Urdu Studies* 6 (1987): 99–115.
47   Nazir Ahmad, 'Introduction', in *The Bride's Mirror: A Tale of Life in Delhi a Hundred Years Ago*, trans. G. E. Ward (London: Henry Frowde, 1903; Delhi: Permanent Black, 2001), 8–10.
48   Ahmad, *The Bride's Mirror*, 84.
49   Ibid., 105.
50   Ibid., 131, 36.
51   If we consider Ahmad's broader intertextual references, then, according to Mohammad Asaduddin, he was influenced by Thomas Day's *History of Sandford and Merton* and Daniel Defoe's *Family Instructor* for his second and third books, while his prose style owes its simplicity to the colonial Fort William College with its emphasis on a clear and lucid textuality, prioritized in order to assist with the training of English officers in indigenous languages. For a longer discussion, see my article 'Truth, Fiction and Autobiography in the Modern Urdu Narrative Tradition', *Comparative Critical Studies* 4, no. 3 (2007): 379–402. For a reading of the dastan and Nazir Ahmad's

fiction, see Christina Oesterheld, 'Nazir Ahmad and the Early Urdu Novel: Some Observations', *Annual of Urdu Studies* 16 (2001): 27–42.
52   See C. M. Naim, 'Prize-Winning *Adab*: A Study of Five Books Written in Response to the Allahabad Government Gazette Notification', in *Moral Conduct and Authority: The Place of Adab in South Asian Islam*, ed. Barbara Daly Metcalf (Berkeley: University of California Press, 1984), 290–314 (quoted in Pritchett, 'Afterword: The First Urdu Bestseller').
53   Francis Robinson, 'Religious Change and the Self in Muslim South Asia since 1800', *Journal of South Asian Studies* 20, no. 1 (1997): 1–15.
54   Barbara Daly Metcalf, *Perfecting Women: Maulana Ashraf Ali Thanavi's Bihishti Zewar: A Partial Translation with Commentary* (Berkeley: University of California Press, 1990), 6.
55   Ibid., 51–52.
56   Usamah Ansari, 'Producing the Conjugal Patriarchal Family in Maulana Thanavi's Heavenly Ornaments: Biopolitics, "Shariatic Modernity" and Managing Women', *Comparative Islamic Studies* 5, no. 1 (2009): 93–110 (104–6).
57   Quoted in Naim, 'How Bibi Ashraf Learned to Read and Write', 113.
58   See Mukherjee, *Realism and Reality*; Alison Safadi, 'The "Fallen" Woman in Two Colonial Novels: *Umrao Jan Ada* and *Bazaar-e Husn/Sevasadan*', *Annual of Urdu Studies* 24 (2009): 16–53; Yaqin, 'Truth, Fiction and Autobiography'.
59   Mirza Muhammad Hadi Rusva, *Umrao Jan Ada*, ed. Zahir Fatehpuri (Lahore: Majlis-e taraqqi-e adab, [1899] 1988). For an English translation, see *Umrao Jan Ada*, trans. David Matthews (Calcutta: Rupa, 1996).
60   Sharon Pillai, '"Tell … the Truth but Tell it Slant": Form and Fiction in Rusva's *Umrao Jan Ada*', *Journal of Commonwealth Literature* 50, no. 2 (June 2015): 110–26.
61   In the Encyclopedia Britannica the hetaira is described as: 'One of a class of professional independent courtesans of Ancient Greece who, besides developing physical beauty, cultivated their minds and talents to a degree far beyond that allowed to the Average Attic woman […] the hetairai enjoyed an enviable and respected position of wealth and were protected and taxed by the state'; accessed 29 November 2013, https://www.britannica.com/topic/hetaira.
62   See Scott Kugle's analysis of Mah Laqa's life, personality, poetry and dance including translations of her poetry in his book *When Sun Meets Moon: Gender, Eros and Ecstasy in Urdu Poetry* (Chapel Hill: University of North Carolina Press, 2016), 147–234.
63   See Frances Pritchett's *Umrao Jan Ada: A Study Site*, accessed 29 November 2013, http://www.columbia.edu/itc/mealac/pritchett/00urdu/umraojan/. This is an incredibly well-resourced website that provides access to the original novel and includes an introduction by Frances Pritchett. It also has a link to the inconsistencies in the novel. There are links to articles on the novel, the films and translations.
64   Sharon Pillai has argued that *Umrao Jan Ada* is 'double-voiced: there is the *rekhta* narration of Umrao Jan and the *rekhti* narrative of Ruswa', closely analysing the opening mushaira as a stylistic device and centrepiece of the novel; Pillai, '"Tell … the Truth but Tell it Slant"'. However, this does not reflect the doubleness of *rekhti* as noted by Ruth Vanita earlier in this chapter.
65   Rusva, *Umrao Jan Ada*, 93 (my translation).
66   Ibid., 1.
67   On history as fiction and emplotment, see Hayden White, *Tropics of Discourse: Essays in Cultural Criticism* (Baltimore, MD: Johns Hopkins University Press, 1978), 51–80.
68   Rusva, *Umrao Jan Ada*, 185.

69 See Partha Chatterjee, *The Nation and Its Fragments: Colonial and Postcolonial Histories* (Princeton, NJ: Princeton University Press, 1993), 120.
70 Here it is worth noting Veena Oldenburg's analysis of Lucknow courtesans, in which she puts forward her observation that the courtesans' sexual behaviour does not fit heteronormative patterns and they are comfortable with both men and women, some preferring the company of women; Veena Talwar Oldenburg, *The Making of Colonial Lucknow 1856–1877* (Princeton, NJ: Princeton University Press, 1984). Also see Kokila Dang, 'Prostitutes, Patrons and the State: Nineteenth Century Awadh', *Social Scientist* 21, no. 9/11 (September–October 1993): 173–96.
71 For an estimation of Muhammadi Begum's stature in the progress of the Urdu novel, see Aamer Hussein, 'Forcing Silence to Speak: Muhammadi Begum, *Mir'atu'l-'Arus*, and the Urdu Novel', *Annual of Urdu Studies* 11 (1996): 71–86.
72 On Atiya Fyzee, see Siobhan Lambert-Hurley, 'Forging Global Networks in the Imperial Era: Atiya Fyzee in Imperial London', in *India in Britain: South Asian Networks and Connections, 1858–1950*, ed. Susheila Nasta (Basingstoke: Palgrave Macmillan, 2013), 64–79.
73 I am grateful to Amena Husein Saiyid and Kulsoom Husein Saiyid for sharing with me the manuscript in preparation of Muhammadi Begum entitled '*A Long Way from Hyderabad: Scholarly Dreams and a Modern Dilemma for a Young Muslim Woman*', trans. Zehra Ahmad and Zainab Masud, ed. Kulsoom Husein (Primus Press), in press.
74 Ibid.

Chapter 3

PROGRESSIVE ASPIRATIONS: SEXUAL POLITICS AND WOMEN'S WRITING

In this chapter, I explore women's activism and the Progressive Writers' movement in the first half of the twentieth century to see where the fault lines lie between secular modernity and religious affiliations. Poetry as a medium for change also inspired Progressive women poets, who initially started off in the inner sanctum of the zenana under the watchful gaze of a religious community that placed its visible Islamic representation on the shoulders of women, and subsequently found themselves in the public spaces of the post-Partition nation actively taking part in national and political culture. It is their story that is lesser known and important to contextualize as the community transformed into nation. The poet Faiz Ahmed Faiz played an important role in the nurture of women poets as he imbued the lyric form with a progressive modernity. His linkages to women poets and female music artists, along with an emphasis on a secular Urdu aesthetic, facilitated an opening up of gender borders that had been tightly drawn into sacred spaces in the lead-up to Partition.

In the post-Partition nation, sharif women's performative poetry inhabited the public sphere at a time when iconic women's voices in the associated world of music and song ruled the sound waves – notably, the flamboyant Madam Noor Jehan and the restrained Malika Pukhraj. Both sang Faiz Ahmed Faiz's verse, immortalizing his poems through electronic media. Their presence as musicians in Pakistan highlighted both the enduring popularity of the craft and heritage of a long-standing Indic music tradition, as well as the new urban middle class's historical distancing of itself from the musical *gharana* family in order to represent respectable values.[1] The modernizers sought to spiritualize, standardize and eventually nurture a new middle-class taste in music. These bifurcating affiliations with the performing arts for women in the postcolonial nation had been ideologically framed in reformist texts. For instance, Mirza Rusva avoids any reference to the *mujra* dance in *Umrao Jan Ada*, although it features heavily in film adaptations of the novel. The *mujra* is used as a reminder of a decadent past and one of the causes of the downfall of Muslim rule in

India, while in Hindi films it serves as a nostalgic reference to the Muslim other. The contemporary Pakistani dancer and activist Sheema Kermani, in her bid to preserve an Indic cultural heritage in the performing arts, speaks of a 'theatre of vulgar jokes and loud humour and filmi dance in the *mujra* style [...] encouraged at an official level' that belittles her efforts.[2] These were and are major public barriers of perception for women when they perform in the public sphere. The Urdu poet who became a sensation in her teen years, Zehra Nigah, speaks of the anxiety of sharif men around her who wished to protect her from being affiliated with performative courtesan culture when she started reciting her ghazals in public. Claire Pamment, writing on Punjabi theatre in Pakistan, interrogates the role of the female dancer in popular theatre, looking at the shift in state narrative from the 1980s to the 2000s as the liberalization of media transported sexually explicit dance performances from the stage consumption of lower-middle-class audiences to upper-middle-class and elite drawing-rooms through VCD and DVD recordings. Pamment argues that this triggered a 'moral debate in the public domain that condemned both the vulgar comedian and dancer'.[3] These examples highlight the titillation for middle-class audiences of courtesan quarters and the voyeuristic appeal of looking from the outside in.[4] The 'moral debate', Pamment reminds us, goes back to the colonial period when the British imposed bans on theatre performances through the 1876 Dramatic Performance Act, citing obscenity and disloyalty to the Raj. Projecting themselves as moral guardians, the colonizers made a clear distinction between lower-caste immoral depictions, including the presence on stage of actresses from 'prostitute backgrounds', and the nobility of the civilizing mission.[5] The colonial forces deflected their own tyrannies by coercing an upper-class Brahman and Indian elite to support the theatre ban in the interest of the civilizing mission for the Indian public and the policy that started in Bengal was applied to the rest of India. This ban resonates with another embargo during the colonial period that led to the censorship of a book of short stories, *Angare*, in United Provinces under Section 295A of the Indian Penal Code. The book had offended the feelings of certain sections of the religious community with its provocative representation of sexual misconduct.[6] The British retained a higher moral authority by banning the book, but in doing so they created further resentment against colonial rule among a rising middle class. This act of censorship led to the formation of the Progressive Writers' Association (PWA) in 1935 with strong links to the Communist Party and the International Association of Writers for the Defence of Culture. This Association was formed in London, starting out as an informal reading group in 1934 drawing its members from student communities in London, Oxford and Cambridge as well as expatriate Indians. The first formal All India PWA meeting took place in Lucknow in 1936. As part of the resistance struggle, Urdu literature became a channel for political dissent as it gave voice to a left-leaning Progressive Writers' movement. One of the key areas that the Progressives targeted for change was the controlled depiction of sexualities that had flourished under reform. This led to censorship, moral outrage and a clear demarcation between a perceived progressive Western and conservative Eastern way of thinking. Over time, differences developed amongst the Progressives themselves regarding the moral tone of their writing and these became more pronounced with Partition.[7]

In the first half of this chapter, I highlight the movement's secular identifications and the controversies over sexually open representations in the *Angare* collection. Two subsequent writers who took on the challenge of writing about sexualities and taboo topics, Ismat Chughtai and Saadat Hasan Manto, found that their work too was held up to the censorship register and the ensuing controversies underlined a rift within the Progressives over the limits of representation in Urdu writing and state censure. Interestingly, the radicalism of their open writing about sexualities was interpreted as too risky to be associated with the broader group by Progressive gatekeepers. Their gritty stories did not gain the universal appeal enjoyed by the Progressive poet Faiz Ahmed Faiz, whose poetry deployed metaphor and symbol coded in the language of the romantic lyric form.

The second half of this chapter looks at the lesser-known story of Progressive women poets as it took shape in the zenana and its transformation after Partition. I chart their inspirations and their challenges as they quietly continued the legacy of a radical movement at a time of political conservatism and censorship. Early to mid-twentieth-century Progressive women poets first wrote exclusively from within the zenana and after Partition stepped outside secluded homes to narrate and perform their poetry in public places. I argue that poets such as Ada Jafri and Zehra Nigah, who as married women put their families before their careers, have had more acceptability and respect afforded to them as inheritors and representatives of sharif culture. The popular poet Parvin Shakir, a single mother and a civil servant who died young in a car accident, is celebrated for her romantic poetry and yearned for as the literal unattainable beloved of the Urdu ghazal. On the other end of the spectrum are poets such as Sara Shagufta, whose class background and nonconformist relationships meant that she was generally perceived as an outcaste; her tragic death by suicide adds to the censure. Thus the story of Progressive women poets is both in dialogue with and critical of a national discourse in which there is little agency for women as speaking subjects. Women were, in the pre-Partition phase, part of a power dynamic in which 'white men saved brown women from brown men', with education high on the agenda in the zenana, and, in the post-Partition phase, a corollary to the nation.[8] The Progressives, on the other hand, sought to give women agency by empowering them to represent themselves but the project was not as straightforward as they thought and disagreements over representations of sexualities became a dividing line within the group itself. This chapter sets out the tensions of radical politics and national limitations experienced by writers writing against the grain, especially when it comes to the open expression of sexualities, and sets the context for the following chapters on Fahmida Riaz and Kishwar Naheed.

Resistance and the Rise of the Left: The Progressive Writers' Movement

The control and censorship of creative writing that caused moral offence was a legacy of colonial state politics that sought to appease religious sensibilities. It was subsequently adopted by the postcolonial state as a measure to placate religious communities. The anticolonial resistance movement, looking to redefine conventional notions of sexuality and by extension love and the family, was led by a group of Muslim radical thinkers and intellectuals who mobilized under the banner of the PWA. The Progressives became known for their rejection of institutionalized practices of religion, influenced by an international left culture of writers and intellectuals responding to a fascist agenda in Europe. This cosmopolitan coterie left a lasting influence on Urdu literary culture, projecting a new sense of self and subjectivity for men and women and articulating a modern consciousness for the nation in the making. They demanded a change to existing social hierarchies of gender, religio-cultural and political attitudes through both their activism and their writing. As Marxists, they had, at times, an instrumental understanding of literature as a means for social change and they demanded a concentration on themes of realism and reality.[9] According to one of their benefactors, the writer Dhanpat Rai, popularly known by his pen name Munshi Premchand, their challenge was to transform traditional perceptions of beauty in Indian literature with a view to reflecting societal conditions and humanity.[10] To understand the emergence of this new literary culture, I turn to the controversial Urdu short story collection *Angare*, which triggered the initial self-conscious and reactive formation of a new aesthetics that became the backbone of the Progressive literary agenda. Aziz Ahmad referred to *Angare* as a declaration of war by the middle class that put family and sexuality on the agenda, coloured by a Communist consciousness. However, he was dismissive of the treatment of religion by this group of writers and he felt that their attack on religious values was uncalled for and extremist in its articulation. For that reason he felt that the Progressives alienated a large section of society.[11] In this section, I investigate the politics of *Angare* to briefly trace the Progressive controversy over sexuality in the 1930s.

The next two writers who came under scrutiny were Ismat Chughtai and Saadat Hasan Manto, whose writings were identified as problematic and in need of state censure. Both Manto and Chughtai offended orthodox morality with their exploration of taboo topics.

Angare was published as a slim volume from Lucknow in 1932 and was subsequently banned by the Uttar Pradesh state government in 1933. In particular, the book upset Muslim religious groups, which gave the state sanction to ban it under the Indian Penal Code Section 295A for its perceived 'vulgarity' and 'moral depravity'. Less discussed for its literary merit, it gained notoriety for being offensive. One particular story by Sajjad Zaheer, 'Jannat ki basharat' (Vision of Heaven), caused umbrage with its explicit narration of a Maulana's wet dream of houris.[12] To counter the negative publicity, the *Angare* collective published a statement from Delhi, five months after the book was published, entitled 'In Defence of *Angarey*: Shall We Submit to Gagging?' in *The Leader*, an Allahabad journal. They unapologetically made their case for freedom of speech, defending their position on women and sexuality as part of a larger struggle for equal citizenship and opining: 'it is matter of fact that our women are oppressed and our sexual practices are out of harmony with the requirements of our social life. Yet these opinions and the revelation of these facts must remain sealed.'[13] In the public realm, the focus on women's sexual freedoms did not get as much attention as the provocative treatment of religion, which generated institutional responses from the 'government of UP' and 'the Central Standing Committee of the All-India Shia conference' that were publicized in the print media. The perceived act of offence was further exacerbated by the coverage in the Urdu press at the time, which portrayed them as a group who were disrespectful of the Prophet and Islamic rituals.[14] For instance, an editorial in *Sarguzasht* gave out incendiary advice to its readers by suggesting, 'It is a primary duty of those who are offended by this dirty literature to become real examples of true Islam,' framing the *Angare* writers outside the boundaries of true faith.[15] An important observation that emerges from these positionalities is that a divide between secular as Western and religion as Eastern was being crystallized through intracommunity politics. After the obscenity trial of *Angare*, the Progressives chose to strike a balance between writing that caused offence and a genuine desire to inflect a radical realism that opened up class representations and allowed for a critical secular response to the moral landscape.[16]

In Geeta Patel's assessment, the colonial state's decision to ban the book and foray into a 'community's private affairs' was indicative of their desire to control matters that presented a potential civil threat, and, in manifesting this power, they fanned the flames of conservative religious values under the appeasing cloak of 'principles of tolerance'. She reads the *Angare* collection as an example of 'vehemently *secular*' literature that challenged socioreligious reformers, while also bringing about a change in literary culture that, in turn, inspired an equally strong response by civil society, highlighting a rejection of religion.[17] The authors were targeted as 'anti-God' and 'anti-Muslim', much as a later state-led ideology manipulated patriotic loyalties in Pakistan by branding secular writing as antinationalist and treasonous.[18] Patel's reading of a purposefully secular Urdu aesthetic contained within *Angare* is insightful and suggestive. She sees the irreverent 'secularized politics' of an international liberal left echoed in the atheism of the Progressives that was perceived as a direct threat by Muslim religious groups in Lucknow and Aligarh.[19] The legal intervention by the colonial state of proscription using Section 295A of the Indian Penal Code thus helped to cement an exaggerated and reactionary anti-West response by local religious groups in order to return to the fundamentals of an Islamic society. The tolerance that the Progressives offer through the lens of Sufism has been translated by poets such as Faiz and Ali Sardar Jafri but that too remains a contested field. Imagining a utopian egalitarian community, the Muslim Progressives were unable to sell their vision of a united India and a plural Muslim community. Rakshanda Jalil has noted that Lucknow and Aligarh hosted 'festive book burnings' that drew both community and government attention to social divisions. The language of *Angare* was labelled as deeply offensive and out of sync with sharafat by scholars and journalists who wrote it off as blasphemous. What these events also underlined were the class differences behind attacks on privileged members of the *Angare* group such as Sajjad Zaheer and Rashid Jahan.[20]

Priyamvada Gopal has studied the Progressive Writers' movement as a project that was invested in the ideals of resistance as nationalism yet also critical of it, building her argument on Frantz Fanon's critique of an 'anti-colonial national culture' that starts with a return to nativism and ends with a violent struggle against occupation.[21] She concludes that the body of work produced under the banner of the PWA was 'uneven' and should be read as a 'broader cultural project', transformative in its engagements with modernity, nationalism and humanism rather than a mimetic undertaking.[22] Gopal's analysis focuses on a radical Marxist anticolonial project, while Patel's critique offers a sideways engagement with how gender identities and sexualities came to inform hierarchies within the movement itself. Patel observes that, in PWA criticism of the 1940s, discussions on sexuality were used as a measure of exclusion: 'Naming a literary piece "excessively sexual" was a way of devalorizing it as well as labelling it deviant.'[23] She argues that the demarcation of sexuality as 'deviant' placed it outside discourses of normalized behaviour and was a phenomenon that drew from Raj politics, in which a clear line of hierarchical control was maintained through a strict social management of sexuality.

For instance, sex for British soldiers with local Indian women was overseen through 'lock hospitals', to ensure a safe space beyond the brothel where venereal disease could be kept in check.[24] Patel views this management of the public sphere through racialized notions of purity and danger as something that was later reproduced in post-Partition Progressive politics and attitudes toward sexuality.[25]

Meanwhile the only woman writer in the *Angare* collection was Rashid Jahan. Known as 'Urdu literature's first angry young woman', she presented an insurmountable cultural problem, cohabiting space with men who were *namehram* (strangers) and, as a practising doctor, intervening in taboo matters connected to women's health.[26] She was both an active member of the Indian People's Theatre Association (IPTA), who wrote for theatre performances and radio, and a member of the Communist Party of India (CPI).[27] Her fictions including 'Parde ke piche' (Behind the Veil), a one-act play, and 'Dilli ki sair' (A Tour of Delhi) convey the spirit of scientific knowledge and belief in modern medicine, empowering women to embrace change through rational associations. Although Jahan's narratives were part of the *Angare* collection, they did not become the target of contempt in the same way as Zaheer's, her lifestyle, persona and activism added to the perception of Westernization as an alien force that seduced women away from the zenana. While 'Dilli ki sair' recounted the powerlessness of a woman trapped by her burqa and at the mercy of her husband, 'Parde ke piche' addressed the taboo topic of birth control.[28] Emboldened by her class and networked into an elite literary group, Rashid Jahan's instrumentalist writing took on the injustices of society against women, encouraging them to take control of their sexualities and to explore public spaces.[29] An observer of society, she loved going to fairs, exhibitions and religious festivals. Her literary influences ranged from the classics of English, Russian and French literatures to local literary figures such as Rabindranath Tagore and Bankim Chandra Chattopadhyay.[30]

Hamida Saiduzzafar, Rashid Jahan's aunt, comments that 'Rashida felt more at home with simple people than with the upper classes [...] She could sit for hours and chat with some of the purdah-observing women just as easily as she could with women who were not in purdah'.[31] Through her close interaction with a hybrid group of women, she rejected the class bias of her social group, but her knowledge of medicine and gynaecology came into conflict with local practices. This family insight conveys a deeper understanding of how Rashid Jahan fulfilled her activist commitment to dialogue across class borders, answering the remit of the Progressive project to redress the plight of the working classes.[32] Jahan's stories also turned a scientific lens on women's health, transforming the moral reformist model of women's education toward a reflective ethical stance. But despite the outreach to non-elite women, the challenge of transforming a wider audience beyond an elite middle class through Urdu writing remained. Rashid Jahan was at the vanguard of women's public participation in the Progressive project and set the standard for others who followed her. However, over time, writings that addressed sexualities increasingly invited censorship and began to encroach on the private lives of women.

Ismat Chughtai was an immediate successor to Rashid Jahan as someone who was modern, Western, secular and critical of conservative moral values. Chughtai's association with the Progressives began whilst she was an undergraduate at Lucknow University. In an interview with *Mahfil*, she expressed her open admiration for Rashid Jahan and the role she played as a mentor, advising her how to approach writing as something that should be 'expressed' rather than suppressed, regardless of whether it caused shame. 'She said that if you feel a thing in your mind and heart and cannot express it, then thinking it is worse and speaking it better, because you can get it out into the open with words'.[33]

According to the Progressive writer Krishan Chander, 'as soon as Ismat's name is mentioned, male short-story writers get hysterical, they are embarrassed, they experience mortification'.[34] Saadat Hasan Manto felt it was her unique feminine sensibility that shaped the stories 'Bhul bhulaiyan' (The Maze), 'Til' (The Mole), 'Lihaf' (The Cover) and 'Gainda' (The Marigold).[35] He saw in Chughtai a kindred spirit writing objectively and critically of the society she lived in and its double standards. It is very interesting to see the kinds of feminist labels attached to her work as they reflect the different attitudes toward her writing and how she was and is read.

Chughtai became known for her short story 'Lihaf', which earned her notoriety for its narration of a lesbian encounter between a maid, Rabbu, and her employer, the affluent and sex-starved Begum Jan who is married to a boy-loving nawabi husband. The twist in the tale is provided by a young girl relative who comes to stay with Begum Jan and her observations of the relationship between Begum Jan and Rabbu.[36] We are told by the narrator that Begum Jan and Rabbu are the cause of much amusement amongst Begum Jan's social circle. Begum Jan herself is in her forties, tall and beautifully fair, with dark oiled hair and facial features that resemble those of a young boy. In contrast, Rabbu is described as dark, her face scarred with smallpox, with big swollen lips, quick hands and a strong body odour. The Begum has a constantly itchy body and requires Rabbu to scratch her in the right places to ease her discomfort. She frequently massages the Begum and generally looks after her personal needs. This intimacy is set up for the reader before the narration of a disturbance in the night that wakes up the little girl visitor staying in Begum Jan's room. She fears she has seen an elephant-like creature underneath the duvet casting its shadows on the wall. She is terrified by the spectacle but is reassured by the Begum to return to sleep. After a few days, when this happens a second time, the heaving duvet is accompanied by sounds of smacking lips, leaving little to the imagination. In the meanwhile, the reader learns of a lovers' tiff between Rabbu and the Begum, followed by a reconciliation coinciding with the night of the second disturbance. The story shocks with its exposé of a middle-aged elite woman's pleasures in the zenana. It crosses the borders of respectability with its frank representation of erotic desire between two women observed by a young child. There is no getting away from the fact that the story details a homoerotic relationship between two women, Rabbu and Begum Jan. The Urdu register in those moments is informal and sensuous, reflective of the mood of rekhti.

Aziz Ahmad, reacting to the story, adopted a moral tone by opining that Chughtai was straying from educational and character-building topics for women and focusing her energies on self-indulgent experimental and sensational writing. In her memoir, *Kaghazi hai pairahan,* Ismat Chughtai writes about the negative family and public reactions she faced for 'Lihaf', following the court summons for an obscenity lawsuit from the Crown in December 1944. She says that the only support she had was from Saadat Hasan Manto, who also had an obscenity case filed against him for his short story 'Bu' (The Stink). He told her to be proud of her work because 'it's the only great story you've written'. Chughtai's personal life was invaded by 'filthy letters [...] filled with such invective and convoluted obscenities that had they been uttered before a corpse, it would have got up and run for cover'.[37] She became distraught by the personal attacks made on her entire family. When her husband, Shahid, saw the letters he threatened her with divorce. She decided to keep a low profile, burning the correspondence and maintaining silence over newspaper reportage and public gatherings that discussed her story. But the damage was done and she confesses that married life became a 'battlefield'. Although she won the court case, Chughtai felt she had lost, as 'Lihaf' became the defining feature of her career as a writer and everything that she wrote was always measured against it.[38] We will never know how strongly Chughtai felt about the story but it was clear that she was looking beyond the measure of an obscenity trial to define her career as a writer. In his review of Chughtai's short stories, the writer and critic Aamer Hussein observes that 'Lihaf' is a 'weak effort' and 'mildly homophobic', making the case instead for her semi-autobiographical novel *Terhi lakir* (The Crooked Line), set in the all-female environment of a boarding school, as a much better exposition of 'homoerotic subtexts'. Chughtai's stereotypical characterisation and representation of what happens under the duvet covers is possibly what Hussein is referring to as a homophobic description. He argues that her appeal lay in her ability to combine humour, romance, satire and social transgressions with a unique aesthetic style that made her an artist and not just a chronicler of her times.[39]

Terhi lakir, published in 1944, is set in the turbulent pre-independence period of the 1940s. It narrates the story of the female protagonist, Shaman, growing up and coming to terms with her sexuality.[40] She comes to understand herself initially through the structures of the family, her experiences as a college student and finally her life as a working professional in the capacity of a school headmistress. Gopal reads *Terhi lakir* as a chronicle that encapsulates the 'conflicted perspective' of women whose lived experience was tied to the unfolding history of modernity in India. She argues that the novel articulates those contradictory experiences which 'were nowhere more apparent than in the realm of desire and sexuality, which reveal themselves to be profoundly shaped by social imperatives'.[41] Beset by contradictions, Shaman's values shift from those defined by a family tradition to public life, including her involvement in the nationalist movement. The novel illustrates her search for the 'ideal Indian woman', a quest Chughtai describes in *Kaghazi hai pairahan*, including considerations of mythical and historical female figures such as Sita, Mira Bai, Savitri and Razia Sultana, that left her with only two options: prostitution or modesty.[42] Ismat Chughtai's unique rendition of Shaman transports the reader from Aligarh to Lucknow to Bareilly, sharing the emotional journey of a privileged girl and her changing relationship to family and home. Yet it is in 'Lihaf' that we find an exposure of the sanctimoniousness of middle-class life, the starkness of class and caste difference, and the representation of sexual intimacy and desire. It is no wonder that Manto admired this particular example of her integrity as a writer and was disappointed by the reticence in her later writings.

Complementing Chughtai's secular middle-class heroines were the women populating Manto's writing. He drew censure for his stark writing that laid bare the brutality of women's sexual encounters and the crisis of masculinities. Aamir Mufti argues that, as far as Manto's heroines were concerned, the subjectivities of impoverished and exploited prostitutes displaced the high cultural figure of the tawaif through which narratives of a distinct 'Muslim' cultural experience had so often been mediated in modern Indian culture.[43] In devalorizing the cultural mythology of women as obedient mothers, daughters and tawaifs, Manto and Chughtai both wrote against the grain, challenging nationalist nostalgia and mythmaking in Pakistan and India about women and class-based attitudes toward sexuality. Manto's stories are grittier, without the gloss of Chughtai's diction, and lay bare the inequalities of Indian society.

In Manto's controversial short story 'Bu', the main focus is on the strong sexual desire that the protagonist Randhir feels for the *Ghatan laundiya* (Marathi girl) and this attraction is highlighted as one that offended sharif sensibilities because of class connotations.[44] The story is about a middle-class boy and his social aspirations. He desires whiteness, represented through his attraction to the Christian girls recruited in the Women's Auxiliary Corps (WAC) and his fair wife, but his body betrays him through its sexual yearning for the earthy, dark *Ghatan*. The narration in intimate detail of Randhir's lack of attraction to his middle-class fair wife's naked body was considered by Sajjad Zaheer as an unnecessary and self-indulgent representation of the sharif middle class.[45] The erotic descriptions of the female body and women's state of dress and undress led to accusations of obscenity. Sarah Waheed argues that the publication and banning of 'Bu' in the journal *Adb-e Latif* was because Manto's short story didn't go down well with military officials in Punjab, who were unhappy with the link in the story between the WAC of the British army and prostitution.[46] They felt it would impact recruitment and give the army a negative image at a time when the British Raj was at a low ebb, facing rebellions, strikes and demonstrations. After the case was transferred to the Home Office, the story was, on review, placed under 'obscenity' law, Section 292 of the Indian Penal Code. Waheed maps how the moral censure over offensive representations of sexuality became a useful cover for the colonial state to protect its own interests, both military and racial. Thus the colonial state's obscenity law helps to showcase how the state absorbed mob sentiments of offence to divert attention and assert power. In the postcolonial state this has become an effective strategy of collusion between the state and the elite to control dissenting literary voices.

Overall, the censorship of 'Lihaf', 'Bu' and other stories cannot be seen independently from the initial reception that was accorded to *Angare*.[47] Ironically, it set a pattern for literary exclusions by the very same PWA at the heart of vanguardism when they 'wanted to criticize, condemn, and expel poets like the modernist Miraji, and short-story writers such as Manto and Ismat Chughtai from the movement'.[48] This exclusion identified sexuality as a forbidden topic for good literature and an association that had been founded under the banner of a radical collection of stories, addressing sexuality and religious double standards, retreated into politically motivated conservative liberalism when it came to aesthetics that challenged the status quo of sharif sensibilities. It reflected the split between the founding members of the Progressive group themselves, some of whom saw it as a purely radical platform (for instance, Sajjad Zaheer) and others (such as Ahmed Ali) who were motivated by the opportunity it provided for artistic experimentation. The change that was brought about by the Progressives was further displaced by an intellectual rebellion within the group against a prescriptive manifesto-led approach that privileged polemical writing over literary aesthetics. This division was further complicated by nationalist affiliations in the post-Partition period.

In the case of Manto, while he was supported in the publication of the short story 'Bu' in *Adb-e Latif* by the notable writer and journalist Ahmad Nadeem Qasimi, he was ostracized by Sajjad Zaheer for not staying true to a Progressive spirit by centring his story around the sentiments of a satisfied member of the middle class.[49] Manto, whose pre-Partition differences with the Progressive administration had been over the issue of a lack of morality in his writing, found that post-Partition these differences escalated into a full-scale parting of the ways.[50] He blamed the Progressives for disowning him over his open collection of Partition sketches, *Siyah hashiye* (Black Margins), and for his alliance with Muhammad Hasan Askari, a candid sceptic of the Progressive Writers' movement.[51] He was subsequently adopted by the Halqa-e arbab-e zauq, a group devoted to modernist aesthetics, but by then he was disillusioned with self-appointed gatekeepers of literary values and saw himself as a lone wolf whose writing spoke for itself. *Jadidiyat* (modernity) was the defining feature of the work produced by the Halqa and they saw themselves as an aesthetic alternative to the polemical Progressives.[52] Ismat Chughtai comments in *Kaghazi hai pairahan* that, 'Manto was driven mad to the extent that he became a wreck. The Progressives did not come to his rescue. [...] Manto became a pauper in Pakistan'.[53] What is clear in Manto's case is that the historical context of offending sexualities was used as a measure to exclude him, capitalizing on a colonial strategy of a liberal politics of tolerance revitalized for the purposes of an ideological Islamic state.

The Middle Ground of Faiz Ahmed Faiz: Bridging Sexual and Progressive Politics

In contrast to the offending Manto and Chughtai was the Progressive writer and intellectual who remained firmly in the Progressive camp, the lyric poet par excellence Faiz Ahmed Faiz. He was close to the Progressive activists Mahmuduzzafar and Rashid Jahan and known to be a 'sympathiser of the Communist Party India'.[54] Speaking as a journalist and a writer, he says that he was 'very much part of the great controversies that developed around the Progressive Writers' Movement' and, as editor of *Adb-e Latif*, aware of the rivalries between the Halqa and the Progressives and a witness to the explosive debates that took place.[55] As a poet, he excelled in interweaving the classical ornamental style of an aristocratic stylized Urdu rhyme and metre with the modern functionality of social realism. In his work, we see the shift from the public to the private, as ideas of morality were consigned to the private domain, while the public sphere was shaped by matters of citizenship, equal opportunities and a good life.[56] Faiz adapted the classical imagery of the lover and the beloved, the literal and metaphorical desolate desert of their separation and the hopeful metaphor of the morning breeze to form a new aesthetic that was similar to the Persian reconfiguration of the erotic love lyric, developing new interpretations of *ishq* (love) that extended it to ideals of nation, home and belonging.[57] There is no better example of this than the nazm that launched his career as a poet, 'Mujh se pehli si mohabbat meri mahbub na mang' (Beloved Do Not Ask of Me a Love Like Before), a poem which he gifted to Noor Jehan, the singer known as *Malika-e tarannum* (the queen of melody) in Pakistan:

> Mujh se pehli si mohabbat meri mahbub na mang
> Main ne samjha tha tu hai to darakshan hai hayat
> Tera gham hai to gham dahr ka jhagra kya hai
> Teri surat se hai alam men baharon ko sabat
> Teri ankhon ke siva dunya men rakha kya hai
> Tu jo mil jaye to taqdir nigun ho jaye
>
> Yun na tha, main ne faqat chaha tha yun ho jaye
> Aur bhi dukh hain zamane men mohabbat ke siva
> Rahaten aur bhi hain vasl ki rahat ke siva
> An-gint sadiyon ke tarik bahimana tilism
> Resham-o atlas-o kamkhab men bunwae hue
> Ja baja bikte hue kucha-o bazar men jism
> Khak men lithre hue khun men nehlaye hue
>
> Jism nikle hue amraz ke tannuron se
> Pip bahti hui galte hue nasuron se
> Lot jati hai udhar ko bhi nazar kya kije
> Ab bhi dilkash hai tera husn, magar kya kije
> Aur bhi dukh hain zamane men mohabbat ke siva
>
> Rahaten aur bhi hain vasl ki rahat ke siva
> Mujh se pehli si mohabbat meri mahbub na mang

[Do not ask from me, my beloved, love like that former one.
I had believed that you are, therefore life is shining;
There is anguish over you, so what wrangle is there over the sorrow of
    the age?
From your aspect springtimes on earth have permanence;
What does the world hold except your eyes?
If you were to become mine, fate would be humbled.
– It was not so, I had only wished that it should be so.
There are other sufferings of the time (world) besides love,
There are other pleasures besides the pleasures of union.
This dark beastly spell of countless centuries.

Woven into silk and satin and brocade
Bodies sold everywhere in alley and market,
Smeared with dust, washed in blood,
Bodies that have emerged from the ovens of diseases,
Pus flowing from rotten ulcers –
My glance comes back that way too: what is to be done?
Your beauty is still charming, but what is to be done?
There are other sufferings of the time (world) besides love,
There are other pleasures besides the pleasures of union;
Do not ask from me, my beloved, love like that former one.][58]

This poem changed the perception and representation of the classical beloved for twentieth-century poets. It marked a farewell to the old beloved and ushered in harsh images of modern reality, which could no longer be ignored nor give precedence to an undying love for the beloved. The poem also shifted the philosophic trajectory of *ilm o ishq* (knowledge and love) that had been the hallmark of Iqbal's Urdu poetry; instead Faiz transformed Iqbal's metaphysical world into an organic earthly place, imagined through the body, its separation and pain. Though the Progressive manifesto had warned against the use of classical representations of sexuality as they were 'furtive and sentimental', Faiz fermented his new wine from the substance in those very old bottles.[59] In these verses, Faiz was replacing the desire for a sacred beloved with a new hunger for nationalist mobilization seeking social justice.[60]

Faiz's politics and his prominent role as an activist Progressive poet with an affiliation to the Communist Party placed him in a vulnerable position and he became a target of the proxy Cold War politics in Pakistan. For his leftist activism, he paid a heavy price with incarceration and the label of antinationalism. He was charged with the criminal offence of conspiracy to overthrow the government of Liaquat Ali Khan. It was alleged that he and fellow conspirators had assisted Major General Akbar Khan in this endeavour backed by the Soviets in 1951. Faiz continued to write inspirational verse while in prison, sending out a message of hope to his followers. In 1954, the Communist Party of Pakistan was banned by the state and this also signalled an end for the PWA, which was shut down in 1958 by Field Marshal Ayub Khan.[61] Ayub's regime supported the formation of the Pakistan Writers' Guild in 1959, an association dedicated to the promotion of new Urdu writing, giving out annual prizes and stipends to promising new writers.[62] As the editor of the *Urdu Digest*, Altaf Husain Qureshi, and the writer and scholar Mashkur Husain Yad recall, 'The Writers Guild with its close ties to the authorities in power limited the freedom of expression in literature. The writers had money in their pockets but it came at the price of censoring their own writing'.[63] The funding for the Progressive papers dried up and there was no financial support structure.

The state's deliberate intrusion into cultural politics and control over the press was a watershed moment for Urdu literary culture as it led to the birth of a new category, 'the establishment writer'.[64] The subsequent culture war that was unleashed in Pakistan meant that Urdu literature became a platform for patriotism led by a liberal authoritarian state courting American Cold War politics. Saadia Toor argues that the patriotic stance of a respected critic such as Muhammad Hasan Askari came across as anti-Progressive because he deliberately singled out the Communist association as separatist and an enemy within the ideological Muslim state of Pakistan.[65] Askari's intervention as a critic is important to consider when it comes to the distinction between a hard Left and a liberal Left. It is also worth noting that in Askari's criticism across the board he was never sympathetic to reactionary Marxist posturing in Progressive writing before or after Partition.[66] In his 1948 essay 'Musalman adib aur musalman qaum' (Muslim Writers and Muslim Nation), he writes emotionally and patriotically as a Pakistani who believed that the national community had been created to preserve an old way of life and was therefore not a new *qaum* (nation). He had no qualms about expressing his reservations regarding the Communists as a negative influence on Pakistan because he felt they were responsible for creating differences between groups in the country, and he pinpointed the controversy over Urdu and Bengali in former East Pakistan as a legacy of their politics.[67] Toor identifies Askari as a liberal, arguing that his stance typifies the fracturing of the Progressives into two factions, one committed to a hardcore left nationalism and the other made up of liberals increasingly affiliated to a conservative and patriotic state. However, Faiz's poetry passed the test of Askari's literary criticism for its quality of authenticity and newness. His stance on Faiz complicates Toor's reading somewhat.[68] It is worth noting that he speaks of Faiz in the same breath as the modernists

Noon Meem Rashed and Miraji, referring to their successful experimentation with form and content, raising the banner of *nai shairi* (new poetry). He wrote in defence of Faiz and his contemporaries when they were categorized as pornographic writers by critics because they worshipped women and the body. This perception, he argued, was based on literalist textual readings that didn't pay attention to the deeper psychological processes that were at work.[69]

Thus Faiz's poetry represents a middle ground that could be appropriated by the liberals and the Left. His treatment of sexuality in verse didn't attract moral censure in the same way as Chughtai's and Manto's prose writings and, on the rare occasions it did, he had the support of influential centrist critics such as Askari. In this way, Faiz's pioneering legacy paved the way for a new conceptualization of modernity that would find its translation in Pakistani women's poetry. His changing style and lyricism appealed to the 'new Pakistani woman' and his experimentation with form connected him across literary groups.[70] Rashid Jahan had left a lasting impression on Faiz and her influence is visible in his writings and endorsements of a new generation of women poets. Faiz's poetry marks a turning point from cosmopolitan universalisms to specific lived experiences that set the stage for a twentieth-century feminist expression in verse that was unique to Pakistan. As far as middle-class women poets were concerned, they could at long last take part in the public sphere without the same degree of guardianship that had inhibited them in the pre-colonial period. Faiz's advocacy for women as public intellectuals bridges left politics and controversies over sexuality in earlier writing. His use of the Sufi idiom made him more palatable as a Progressive who appealed to different kinds of publics.

Ada Jafri and Zehra Nigah

In contrast to the fiery and radical transformations in women's writing in prose, the change in women's diction in poetry would take some time to evolve. The story of Progressive women's Urdu poetry begins with Ada Jafri, who was born in 1926 in pre-Partition India and died in post-Partition Pakistan in 2015. In a special volume dedicated to her work, Farman Fatehpuri and Umrao Tariq reiterate her status as the 'first lady of Urdu poetry' in the twentieth century.[71] In their view, what she did for raising the profile of women's poetry is equivalent to the influence on ghazal poetry in the eighteenth century by poet Vali Dakhini.[72] Their estimation indicates the power of Jafri's ghazal writing, which captured the hearts of many. Her popularity rose from the musical rendition of her intensely romantic ghazal 'Honton pe kabhi un ke mera nam hi aae' (I Wish My Name Would Come on Their Lips sometime) by the late Ustad Amanat Ali Khan on Pakistan Television and Radio

Pakistan. The collection of essays in Fatehpuri and Tariq's book is a testimony to the recognition given to Ada Jafri by a majority of male critics with a minimal inclusion of female voices.

Jafri came from a conventional family in Badaun, Uttar Pradesh, India, who migrated to Pakistan after Partition. In her memoir, entitled *Jo rahi so bekhabri rahi* (An Innocence That Remained), she speaks of the constricted culture for girls' education in which she grew up and the exceptional experience of home-schooling that she and her sisters received thanks to her mother's progressive attitude. She composed poetry in an environment where women faced increased restrictions when it came to public life, especially if they hailed from sharif families. Developing confidence from reading female voices in verse, such as Haya Lakhnavi, Safiya Shamim Malihabadi and Najma Tassaduque Hussain, in journals, Jafri's inspiration was 'silenced lips that dared to write in verse'.[73] Supported by her mother, she completed her first manuscript, 'Main saz dhundhti rahi' (I Kept Looking for Harmony), in 1947 before getting married. Her husband, Nur-ul Hasan Jafri, was a high-ranking civil servant, a columnist for Urdu and English newspapers and served as the president of the Anjuman-e Taraqqi-e Urdu in Karachi. Jafri's volume of poetry was published three years later in 1950. Influenced by the Progressive Writers' movement, she was excited by the modern developments of form that affected Urdu poetry, such as the *azad nazm* (free verse poem) and *nazm-e muarra* (blank verse poem). For her this marked a major shift from Persian to English literary influences in Urdu poetry. Alongside the distinctive voices and styles of Miraji, N. M. Rashed and Faiz Ahmed Faiz, Jafri made a unique place for herself with an understated style and heartfelt content. Asif Furrukhi credits her poetry with introducing a new mood that was different to her predecessors and that distinguished her as a poet of merit.[74]

There was a gap of 17 years between Jafri's first and second collections of poetry. She would go on to publish several collections: *Shahr-e dard* (The City of Pain) in 1967 followed by *Ghazalan tum to vaqif ho* (Gazelle, At Least You Are Familiar) in 1972 and *Saz-e sukhan bahana hai* (The Music of Poetry Is the Reason) in 1982. With five collections of poetry and glowing tributes from male contemporaries, Jafri won a lifetime achievement award for her poetry in 2004, the first woman poet in Pakistan to receive this recognition. Her literary contributions had already been recognized through other prestigious literature prizes such as the Adamjee Award in 1965 and the Tamgha-e Imtiaz in 1981.

In her autobiography, written as a series of reflections in flashback form, she starts from her secluded life in Badaun before moving across several cities in Pakistan and becoming an international traveller with her husband. Throughout the book, Jafri assesses herself, her poetry and that of her peers, and her relationships. She describes her second book as 'a second life for the poetess […] this book was very dear to me. This became a verification of my self.'[75] While she expresses some of the inner dissatisfaction she felt on giving up her poetry for 17 years after marriage, she also justifies it as a natural progression in a woman poet's life, because writing for her was a luxury in comparison with the necessity of raising a family.[76] In her poem 'Milad-e Bahar' (The Festival of Spring) she articulates the idea of herself as a nurturer and a mother who finds attachment in the garden and plantation as she adjusts to a life of temporary abodes with her civil servant husband's regular relocations. She writes: 'I will not forget you / Because I am a mother by nature'.[77] The nature/nurture imagery identifies a fairly conventional and safe place for women in her poetry that, along with her life choices, gave her voice a particular legitimacy and acceptance amongst her peers. The 'conscious' self that she constructs in her narrative was in accordance with the values of new Pakistani middle-class women. At the same time, home for this new middle class was a constantly evolving idea that was influenced by *hijrat* (migration), travel and transnational connections. In her verse, Ada is the proverbial mother who comes to symbolize Pakistan as the motherland for her children who migrate to other countries. Her autobiography narrates the pain of parting and loss, marked by nostalgia, which comes with experiences of migration and separations including Partition. Poetry becomes a confessional space to express the intensity of her emotions based on everyday life. Writing as wife and mother, her prose narrative is interwoven with her lengthy poem 'Us ko nazdik aane na do' (Do Not Let Him/Her Come Near), dedicated to her children and the children of the next generation who go abroad to earn a living. In this poem she projects the voice of the sacrificing mother, an extension of the motherland, rooted in her soil, preserving the sanctity of their home.[78] In her poem 'Barhte hue sae' (Lengthening Shadows) the mother begs her children to return from foreign lands and claim their homeland before it becomes an alien place.

اب لوٹ آؤ
دیکھو کہ تمہارے نقشِ قدم
بھیگی ہوئی گھاس کے سینے پر
اس وقت نمایاں ہیں
دیکھو کہ گلوں کے چہرے بھی
کرنوں کی تپش سے ترساں ہیں
سوچو کہ نسیمِ دوراں کو
آخر تو چال بدلنا ہے
سوچو کہ ابھی دن ڈھلتا ہے
ایسا نہ ہو مڑ کر دیکھو تو
خود اپنی جگہ انجان لگے
اک نقشِ قدم رہبر نہ بنے

ایسا نہ ہو گر کی راہوں میں
یادوں کے ہزاروں ڈھیر ملیں
اس ڈھیر میں اپنے کوچے کو
تم جان نہ پاؤ
لوٹ آؤ
ایسا نہ ہو آنسو دھول بنے
اس دھول میں گھر کے آنگن کو
پہچان نہ پاؤ
لوٹ آؤ
ہاں اس کا بھی امکان تو ہے
جب رات پڑے
کھلائے ہوئے دیوٹ پہ دیا
جلتا نہ ملے!

Ab laut aao
Dekho ke tumhare naqsh-e qadam
Bhigi hui ghas ke sine par
Is waqt numayan hain
Dekho ke gulon ke chehre bhi
Kirnon ki taphish se tarsan hain
Socho ke nasim-e dauran ko

Akhir to chal badalna hai
Socho ke abhi din dhalna hai
Aisa na ho mur kar dekho to
Khud apni nigah anjan lage
Ik naqsh-e qadam rahbar na bane

Aisa na ho
Ghar ki rahon men
Yadon ke hazaron dher milen
Is dher men apne kuche ko
Tum jan no pao
Laut aao
Aisa na ho aansu dhul bane
Is dhul men ghar ke aangan ko
Pehchan na pao
Laut aao
Han is ka bhi imkan to hai

Jab rat pare
Kujlaye hue devat pe diya
Jalta na mile!

[Come back now
See your footprints
Visible right now
On the wet grass
See also the contours of the flowers
Hungering for the warmth of [the sun's] rays
Imagine, the breeze of time
Will at some point change its direction
Imagine that the day has yet to pass
Let it not be, when you turn back to look
You are a stranger to yourself
Your footprints don't guide you
Let it not be that on your way home
Your mind becomes foggy with thousands of
    memories
In this jumble you don't recognize your place
Come home

Let it not be that tears turn to dust
And with that dust in your eyes, you fail to recognize the front yard of your home
Come home]⁷⁹

This poem is narrated as part of a chapter in her memoir entitled 'Stories of Months and Years' and bears witness to her children's migrations for better opportunities abroad. She extends the story of her children's move to the Global North with the deteriorating state of the city of Karachi, shrouded in fear, which makes her sorrowful for 'the city of lights'. Both nostalgia and loss mark her poetic voice. Her poems have an ethereal quality about them, populated with dreams, landscapes and flowers, imagining metaphorical places driven by her strong attachment to the love lyric. They echo a longing for home through filiation to family and reject an affiliation to social constructed homes that are not rooted in emotional bonds.⁸⁰ This concept of home, emotions and connections is also evident in the ghazal 'Phul sehraon men khilte hon ge' from her signature edition, *Ghazalan tum to vaqif ho*:

پھول صحراؤں میں کھلتے ہوں گے
آ کے بچھڑے ہوئے ملتے ہوں گے

کتنی ویران گزر گاہوں سے
سلسلے خواب کے ملتے ہوں گے

آ کس زنے گی : جی سنبھلے گا
چاک دل بھی کہیں سلتے ہوں گے

صبح زنداں میں بھی ہوتی ہو گی
پھول مقتل میں بھی کھلتے ہوں گے

ہم بھی خوشبو ہیں' صبا سے کہیئے
ہم نفس روز نہ ملتے ہوں گے

اجنبی شہر میں اپنوں سے اذا
اتفاقاً بھی تو ملتے ہوں گے

۱۹۹۸

Phul sehraon men khilte hon ge
Aa ke bhichre hue milte hon ge

Kitni viran guzargahon se
Silsile khvab ke milte hon ge

Aas tute gi na ji sambhle ga
Chak-e dil bhi kahin silte hon ge

Subh zindan men bhi hoti ho gi
Phul maqtal men bhi khilte hon ge

Hum bhi khushbu hain, saba se kehyo
Hum nafs roz na milte hon ge

Ajnabi shahr men apnon se Ada
Itefaqann bhi to milte hon ge

[Flowers may bloom in deserts
They who have been separated may meet again

How many barren landscapes
Resemble fields of dreams

Neither hope will be lost, nor the heart calmed
Somewhere torn hearts may be mended again

Morning must break in prison too
Flowers must bloom behind bars too

Let the wind know, we too are like perfume
Kindred spirits who don't meet every day

Ada, in an unknown city those who are a part of them
May meet by coincidence][81]

There is a search for familiarity in alien places and for those who are known. The poet is looking for union after separation but 'barren landscapes' and the 'alien city' disturb the traditional ghazal garden. Like Faiz, she too is confronted by a change of perspective but her reaction to it is more personal.

Jafri is both genteel and gentle; she is laidback as a Progressive poet, focusing on questions of form and experience. The language of Progressivism is tempered with romance, softening her critical stance. She retreats into the world of metaphors and symbolism in the lines below:

کس کس نے ساتھ چھوڑ دیا دھوپ چھاؤں میں
ذکرِ وفا نہیں ہے ہماری خطاؤں میں

موجِ ہوا بھی ریت کی دیوار بن گئی
ہم نے خدا تلاش کیا نا خداؤں میں

شاید ادھر سے قافلہ رنگ و بو گیا
خوشبو کی سسکیاں ہیں ابھی تک ہواؤں میں

اب کے صبا کی نرم مزاجی کو کیا ہوا
بکھرے پڑے ہیں تازہ شگوفے ہواؤں میں

مقدور بھر سرِ رہ گزر کا پتھر بنے سبھے
وہ لوگ یاد آتے ہیں اکثر دعاؤں میں

ویرانیاں دلوں کی بھی کچھ کم نہ تھیں آدا
کیا ڈھونڈنے گئے ہیں مسافر خلاؤں میں

Kis kis ne sath chor diya dhup chaon men
Zikr-e vafa nahin hai hamari khataon men

Mauj-e hawa bhi rait ki divar ban gayi
Ham ne khuda talash kiya na khudaon men

Shaid idhar se qafila-e rang-o bu gaya
Khushbu ki siskian hain abhi tak hawaon men

Ab ke saba ki narm mizaji ko kya hua
Bikhare pare hain taza shagufe hawaon men

Maqdur bhar jo rah ka pathar bane rahe
Voh log yad aaen hai aksar duaon men

Viranian dilon ki bhi kuch kam na thin Ada
Kya dhundhne gai hain musafir khalaon men

[How many deserted us in times of shade
Our repertoire does not boast the mistake of faithfulness

The gust of wind transformed into a wall of sand too
We tried to find God amongst unbelievers

Perhaps the caravan full of colour and fragrance passed through here
Pockets of perfume are permeating the wind still

What happened to the soft temperament of the morning breeze this time
Fresh buds are scattered in the wind

Those in power who created obstacles all along
I have often remembered those people in my prayers

The emptiness of hearts was no less Ada
Than that which travellers look for in space][82]

Marking the journey of migration and the life of travellers, Ada Jafri's verse engages with classic metaphors of the morning breeze and the caravan, signifying the migrant experience of the Umma. Her message is one of survival through loss. This is envisaged through a figurative journey to godliness often disrupted by the experience of those 'who created obstacles all along'. These absent figures are included in the poet persona's prayers as her path of resistance relies on forgiveness.

Her nom de plume, Ada, present in the last couplet of each ghazal according to convention, infused a distinctive female voice in the ghazal and, as a Progressive, she's fairly conventional, unlike her prose counterparts. However, if we look at the dominance of male presence in Urdu poetry circles, it was only a Progressive woman who could have crossed the threshold of the zenana and joined the public sphere of performative poetry. Progressivism influenced her ideas and her spirit, and she paved the way for her successor, the young sensation who shook Urdu circles with her electric live performances: Zehra Nigah.[83]

A young Zehra Nigah began composing poetry in 1950 at about 13 years of age. She was an instant success as a pretty girl with a melodious voice reciting Urdu poetry in *tarannum* in mushairas in the cultural heartlands of Karachi and Lahore. A recipient of the prestigious Tamgha-e husn-e karkardagi (Pride of Performance Award) by the government of Pakistan, she (along with Ada Jafri) changed the outlook of Urdu poetry from a public space occupied by men to one in which women were actively present.[84] In a tribute to Zehra Nigah, Asif Furrukhi has credited her as the steadfast star of Urdu poetry and a 'living classic' whose nazm, with its distinctive style of rendition, has 'broken new ground'.[85] However, early on in her career, her writing was not always considered her own. It was during her time in London, when she came under the influence of Faiz Ahmed Faiz, that her poetry became increasingly inflected with the principles of social realism, class consciousness and equal rights. Faiz wrote the foreword for her first poetry collection, *Sham ka pehla tara* (The First Star of Evening), acknowledging the challenges she had faced in establishing herself as a poet of substance and noting her self-recognition as a representative of *sinf-e nazuk ki shairi* (poetry from the gentle sex) advocating for women's respect, protection and honour.[86] As a poet she takes pride in her craft and is of the opinion that one should first master the technique of the *radif* (end rhyme) in the ghazal before progressing to free verse and prose poetry. She says the best place for mastering the ghazal technique is the mushaira.[87] In Faiz's overview, Zehra Nigah is much more than just a ghazal poet, with a distinctive realist style that was neither romantic nor modernist. The unpretentious candour of her poetic voice appealed to him and set her apart from her peers.

Her first mushaira, at the behest of her schoolteacher, was for the All Pakistan Women's Association. She has spoken candidly about the difficulties of being a woman poet performing in public and being advised about what to wear and the culture of alcoholic excess amongst poets.[88] Recollecting her first mushaira, she says: 'it was wonderful, a very strange type of *mushaira*, you won't believe it', and carefully describes the setting of a marquee with a walled-off square in the centre. The strangeness, she says, was that it was the male poets who were seated inside the covered area, while the women sat outside either listening or participating on stage. To this day, the incident has the power to amuse her with its absurdity of men reciting ghazals from behind a veil. She admits that since childhood she has been conscious of the link between the tawaif and Urdu poetry, always aware of the potential threat to her identity as a sharif woman. One of the ways in which she initially separated herself from it, on the advice of a senior male poet, was by rejecting the mannerism of raising her hand to her forehead in the traditional gesture of greetings (*adab*) to her audience.[89] This disjuncture between the performativity of poetry and the preservation of an ashraf culture enacted through the bodies of women reflects how literary culture was not a neutral space for women. In an interview at the Karachi Literature Festival, Zehra Nigah recounts a mushaira in Islamabad where she, along with Habib Jalib and several male poets, was performing. She says, 'all the male poets except for Habib Jalib walked out' because they were threatened by her popularity. Her melodic voice coupled with mastery of the lyric form gave her instant success. Kishwar Naheed, who attended Nigah's mushairas as a young girl, witnessed this type of reaction and notes that men would comment negatively on the authorship of the verse by insinuating that her lyrics were not her own: 'Who writes her lyrics for her? (the insinuation was another man)'.[90]

Despite the challenges, Zehra Nigah developed her unique style. Her poem 'Samjhota' (Compromise) best captures what Faiz is referring to when he articulates the category of *sinf-e nazuk*, attributing to Nigah's quality of writing a unique *nisvani* style:

ُملائم گرم سمجھوتے کی چادر
یہ چادر میں نے برسوں میں بُنی ہے
کہیں بھی سچ کے گل بُوٹے نہیں ہیں
کسی بھی جھوٹ کا ٹانکا نہیں ہے

اِسی سے میں بھی تن ڈھک لوں گی اپنا
اِسی سے تم بھی آسودہ رہو گے !
نہ خوش ہوگے، نہ پژمردہ رہو گے

اس کو تان کر بن جائے گا گھر
بچھا لیں گے تو کھل اٹھے گا آنگن
اٹھا لیں گے تو گر جائے گی چلمن

Mulaim garm samjhote ki chadar
Ye chadar men ne barson men buni hai
Kahin bhi such ke gul bute nahin hain
Kisi bhi jhut ka tanka nahin hai

Isi se men bhi tan dhuk lun gi apna
Isi se tum bhi asuda raho ge!
Na khush ho ge, na pazmurda raho ge

Isi ko tan kar ban jae ga ghar
Bicha len ge to khil uthe ga aangan
Utha len ge to gir jae gi chilman

[Oh soft warm cover of compromise
Over many years I have knitted this cover
There are no flowers or sprigs of honesty
There is not a dishonest stitch

I too will wrap my body in this cover
You too will remain calm because of it
It will not make you happy or sad

By stretching it a house will be made
If we spread it out our home will prosper
If we remove it the curtain will fall][91]

The poet-narrator, speaking to herself, addresses the chadar that she has knitted as opposed to the one that is placed upon her by family or society. Inflecting it with the power of women's labour and the softness of the female body, she offers the cultural interpretation of the chadar as both a metaphorical and a literal cover that protects the home. Deploying the term *samjhota* as her title, she embeds the story of compromise as her message. The last stanza of the poem can be read ironically as an illustration of what women face if they let go of the notion of compromise that defines their relationships in society.

Her poem 'Jurm vada' (Criminal Promise) encapsulates the Progressive aesthetic of reforming women's lives through knowledge and self-awareness. The subject of 'Jurm vada' is a 'tired, exhausted' woman faced with the criminal charge of reneging on a promise she made to her child.

میرے بچے ہزاروں بار میں نے تم کو اک قصّہ سنایا ہے
کبھی لوری کے آنچل میں
کبھی باتوں کے جھُولے میں تمہیں بہلا کے لپٹا کے سُلایا ہے
تمہارے گرم رخساروں کو اپنے سرد ہونٹوں سے چھُوا ہے
تم سے اک وعدہ کیا ہے
وہی وعدہ' جو انسانوں کی تقدیروں میں لکھا ہے
تحفظ کا' تمہاری آبرو کا' سربلندی کا
میرے بچے!
کہانی میں تھکی ہاری جو لڑکی تھی
وہ شہزادی نہیں،'میں' تھی
وہ جادو کا محل جو ایک پل میں جل کے صحرا ہو گیا تھا' وہ مرا گھر تھا
جہاں آنکھوں کی سُوئیاں رہ گئیں تھیں
خواب میرے تھے
وہ جن میں گھر گئی تھی
غیر کیا سب میرے اپنے تھے
جہاں اس کا فسانہ تھا
وہیں میری حقیقت تھی
جہاں وہ مُڑ کے پتھر ہو گئی
میری محبّت تھی
ہزاروں آگ کے میدان تھے
بارش لہو کی تھی
یہ سب کچھ میرا قصّہ تھا
یہ سب کچھ مجھ پہ گزری تھی
میرے بچے کہانی میں
تھکی ہاری جو لڑکی تھی
وہ شہزادی نہیں،'میں' تھی

PROGRESSIVE ASPIRATIONS

جہاں قصے کا آخر تھا
مرے بچے!
وہاں تم تھے
خوشی کی زندگانی کی علامت
تمناؤں کا اک خوابِ مسلسل
رفاقت کی صداقت کی ضمانت
جہاں پر صرف خوش انجام تھا، ہر ایک افسانہ
مرے بچے! وہاں تم تھے، وہاں تم تھے
مری آنکھیں کسی پیماں کے زخموں سے بوجھل تھیں
تمہارا عکس ان زخموں کا مرہم تھا
ادھورے عہد کے رشتے سے میرے ہاتھ لرزاں تھے
تمہارا ساتھ اک تسکینِ پیہم تھا
مجھے اقرار تھا
میں خاک ہوں
تم حسن و زیبائش
مجھے احساس تھا
میں خوف ہوں
تم امن و آسائش
میں ماضی ہوں
مگر تم صورتِ فردا فروزاں ہو
میں مشکل ہوں
مگر تم صورتِ امید آساں ہو
مرے بچے!
مرا احساس اور اقرار دونوں آج مجرم ہیں
میں اپنا سر جھکائے اپنی فردِ جرم سنتی ہوں
بجائے گُل ردائے آرزو سے خار چنتی ہوں
تمہیں معلوم ہے
الزام کیا ہے
وہی وعدہ جو انسانوں کی تقدیروں میں لکھا ہے
تحفظ کا، تمہاری آبرو کا، سربلندی کا

Mere bache hazaron bar main ne tum ko ik qissa sunaya hai
Kabhi lori ke aanchal men
Kabhi baton ke jhule men tumhe behla ke lipta ke sulaya hai
Tumhare garm rukhsaron ko apne sard honton se chuua hai
Tum se ik vada kiya hai
Vohi vada, jo insanon ki taqdiron men likha hai
Tahafuz ka, tumhari aabru ka, sar bulandi ka
[…]
Mere bache!
Mera ehsas aur iqrar donon aaj mujrim hain
Main apna sar jhukae apni fard-e jurm sunti hun
Bajae gul rida-e aarzu se khar chunti hun
Tumhe malum hai
Ilzam kya hai
Vohi vada jo insanon ke taqidron men likha hai
Tahafuz ka, tumhari aabru ka, sar bulandi ka

[My child a thousand times have I told you this story
Sometimes in a lullaby
Sometimes lulled you to sleep cradled and cuddled with words
I have touched your warm cheeks with my cold lips
I have made a promise to you
That which has been written as divine decree for human beings, that same promise
Of your honour, of safety, of success
[…]
My child!
Today both my faith and my conscience are guilty
I hear my criminal offence with my head bowed
Plucking thorns instead of flowers from my field of dreams
Do you know
What the allegation is
That same promise which has been written as divine decree for all human beings
Of safety, of your honour, of success][92]

The full poem narrates the story of a mythical fairy-tale princess who has everything and wants for nothing until one day when things go wrong. In the selected stanzas above from the beginning and the end of the poem, this princess is confronted with harsh realities where dreams don't come true, endings are unhappy and sorrow plentiful. In fact, the princess is made of clay and her 'real' story is the tragic fairy tale the child has listened to in her/his mother's lullabies. As a mother, she is unable to ascertain her own child's future and shroud it in the security of 'safety, honour and success'. The poem ends on a dramatic note with the mother being charged with the criminal offence of neglecting her duties toward her child. She is guilty of betraying the same child who restored her own faith in humanity. By imbuing the mood and the myth of the fairy tale in her poem, she reiterates the stereotype of motherhood and there is a degree of Progressive didacticism in some of the lines that are 'educating women'.

Of women she says, 'the real downtrodden woman is the one who belongs to the lower middle class'.[93] Through her poems 'Meri saheli' (My Girlfriend) and 'Ek larki' (The Girl) she gives voice to these women.[94] 'Meri saheli' is a free verse poem of varying-length stanzas with an irregular rhyme sequence. Its subject is a friend with a bookish face, intelligent eyes, wheatish complexion and the poem works with a rich girl/poor girl stereotype. The poor girl occupies the fringes of the poem, a silent listener to her rich friend's exotic travelling tales. As the poem progresses, the social status of the narrator and her friend becomes more obvious: the narrator is from an elite background and her friend is a member of an underprivileged class. The nameless subaltern friend, who is voiceless until the penultimate stanza of the poem, pushes the narrator to question the rules of friendship: 'On the forehead of [your] convenience shine my tears, you know, / in the blood of [your] reality churn my dreams, you admit'.[95] It is, in fact, her difference, her status as a servant that has sealed the bond of their friendship; her slavery has silenced her own dreams and facilitated those of her mistress. The poem ends enigmatically: 'who can see, who can learn, if she won or if she lost'.[96] These last lines and the first stanza are shrouded in an aura of ambiguity, reflecting the 'other' girl as a guilty secret. With its socially aware critique of an elite class, the poem reflects a cautious Progressive outlook in Nigah's poetry.

In contrast, 'Ek larki' is set to the pattern of rhyming couplets narrating the story of a sex worker, based on a real meeting at a bus stop in London. The first half of the poem focuses on the stormy weather, the poet caught wandering aimlessly in the storm, and her chance encounter with a woman leaning against a lamp post waiting for a potential customer.[97] The sensibility of the poem is informed by a respectable woman feeling the trauma of the prostitute. Like the rich girl of the previous poem, she too feels the need to save the prostitute from her destiny. She is like a mother face-to-face with a long-lost daughter, wishing to protect her in a motherly embrace and build a nest around her. Nigah's tone is slightly stilted, as in the previous poem, broaching the subject of the downtrodden woman from the eyes of an elite benefactor. As a Progressive, she takes on the task of representing the other, creating a space for subaltern voices, but in the act of representation she is constrained by her own class position and status within Pakistan.

Zehra Nigah's poetic voice is distinctive in 'Gul chandni' (The Moonflower Tree), a poem that articulates superstition and hauntings.[98] In this poem, Nigah breaks out of a prescriptive mode by depicting dream-like illusion and reality:

کل شام یاد آیا مجھے !
ایسے کہ جیسے خواب تھا
کونے میں آنگن کے ہمرے
گل چاندنی کا پیڑ تھا

میں ساری ساری دوپہر
سائے میں اس کے کھیلتی
پھولوں کو چھو کر بھاگتی
شاخوں سے مل کر جھولتی
اس کے تنے میں بیسیوں !
لوہے کی کیلیں تھیں جڑی

کیلوں کو مت چھونا کبھی
تاکید تھی مجھ کو یہی !
یہ راز مجھ پہ فاش تھا
اُس پیڑ پر آسیب تھا !
اک مردِ کامل نے مگر
ایسا عمل اُس پر کیا
باہر وہ آ سکتا نہیں!!
کیلوں میں اس کو جڑ دیا
ہاں کوئی کیلوں کو اگر
کھینچے گا اوپر کی طرف !
آسیب بھی چھٹ جائے گا
پھولوں کو بھی کھا جائے گا
پتّوں پہ بھی منڈلائے گا
پھر دیکھتے ہی دیکھتے
یہ گھر کا گھر جل جائے گا

اِس صحن جسم و جاں میں بھی
گل چاندنی کا پیڑ ہے !
سب پھول میرے ساتھ ہیں
پتے مرے ہم راز ہیں
اِس پیڑ کا سایہ مجھے !
اب بھی بہت محبوب ہے
اس کے تنے میں آج تک
آسیب وہ محصور ہے
یہ سوچتی ہوں آج بھی !
کیلوں کو گر چھیڑا کبھی
آسیب بھی چھٹ جائے گا
کیلوں سے کیا لینا اسے
پھولوں سے کیا مطلب اسے
بس گھر مرا جل جائے گا
کیا گھر مرا جل جائے گا ؟

Kal sham yad aya mujhe!
Aise ke jaise khvab tha
Kone men aangan ke mere
Gul chandni ka per tha
Main sari sari dopahr
Sae men us se khelti
Phulon ko chu kar bhagti
Shakhon se mil kar jhulti
Is ke tane men bisiyon!
Lohe ki kilen thi jari

Kilon ko mat chuna kabhi
Taqid thi mujh ko yehi!
Ye raz mujh pe fash tha
Us per par aseb tha!
Ik mard-e kamil ne magar
Aisa amal us par kiya
Bahir voh aa sakta nahin!
Kilon men us ko jar diya
Han koi kilon ko agar
Khenche ga upar ki taraf!
Aasaib bhi chut jaye ga
Phulon ko bhi kha jaye ga

Patton pe bhi mandlaye ga
Phir dekhte hi dekhte
Ye ghar ka ghar jal jae ga
Is sahn jism-o jan men bhi
Gul Chandni ka per hai!
Sab phul mere sath hain
Patte mere hum raz hain
Is per ka saya mujhe!
Ab bhi bohat mahbub hai
Is ke tane men aaj tak
Aaseb voh mahsur hai
Ye sochti hun aaj bhi!
Kilon ko gar chehra kabhi
Aasaib bhi chut jae ga
Patton se kya lena ise
Phulon se kya matlab ise
Bas ghar mera jal jaye ga
Kya ghar mera jal jaye ga?

[Yesterday evening I remembered
As if it were a dream
In a corner of my house
There was a Moonflower tree

Long afternoons I
Would play beneath its shadow
Touching the flowers and running
Swinging and hanging off its branches
In the tree trunk hundreds of
Iron nails had been driven in
Don't ever touch the nails
I had been warned
This secret was known to me
That the tree was haunted
But a holy man had
Performed such a right over it
The spirit could not come out!
Crucified on the nails
Yes if someone would pull out the nails!
The spirit would be freed
It would eat the flowers too
Looming over the leaves too

And in front of your eyes
This house, the whole house would burn

In the body and heart's verandah too
There is a Moonflower tree!
All flowers are with me
The leaves my confidants
To me, the shade of this tree
Is very dear, even now
Until today, in its bark
Is still trapped the haunted spirit
Even today I think
If I ever touch those nails
The spirit will be freed
It wants nothing from the leaves
It has no business with the flowers
But my house will burn
Will my house burn?]⁹⁹

The narrative poem builds on the theme of possession. She says this is a common experience which occurs consistently across different provinces in Pakistan: 'Our society, our laws, our systems nail a woman's mind, her first love, her thought, they think these are all a source of *fitna* [chaos]'.¹⁰⁰ The most that a woman who has been possessed can do is to think tentatively, as in the last two lines of the poem. Nigah explains: 'the traditional exorcism relies on an *amil* [exorcist] to perform the holy rites which would free the girl from possession and perform the symbolic act of trapping the *bhoot*, *aseb* [spirit] by fixing a nail in the wall. The process of exorcism for the girl can be violent and abusive'.¹⁰¹ The use of voice in this poem is subtle: the narrating voice in the first stanza establishes a traditional practice and the second stanza reverses the perspective by reflecting its internalization by the same woman. The 'holy man' who influences the girl's thoughts is the type of exorcist figure that Ashraf Ali Thanawi's Deobandi reformers were fighting off in order to develop a rational and authentic relationship through purity of religious ritual. Zehra Nigah's poem thus works on two levels: an imaginative one that shows the challenges for women if they step beyond accepted moral codes of conduct and how, from an early age, girls are familiarized with the idea of spiritual possession through exposure to 'fake' holy men. This poem straddles a sacred–secular stance in its narration of ghosts that haunt women's everyday experiences through totems and taboos.¹⁰²

A contrasting poem that narrates the silences in her own life and is knowingly confessional compared with the rest of the collection is 'Zehra ne bohat din se kuch bhi nahin likha hai' (Zehra Has Not Written Anything for Many Days):

زہرا نے بہت دن سے کچھ بھی نہیں لکھا ہے
حالانکہ درائیں اتنا کیا کچھ نہیں دیکھا ہے
پر لکھے تو کیا لکھے؟ اور سوچے تو کیا سوچے؟
کچھ فکر بھی مبہم ہے، کچھ ہاتھ لرزتا ہے

زہرا نے بہت دن سے کچھ بھی نہیں لکھا ہے!

دیوانی نہیں اِتنی، جو منہ میں ہو بک جائے
چُپ شاہ کا روزہ بھی یونہی نہیں رکھا ہے
بوڑھی بھی نہیں اِتنی، اس طرح وہ تھک جائے
اب جان کے اس نے یہ انداز بنایا ہے
ہر چیز بُھلاوے کے صندوق میں رکھ دی ہے
آسانی سے جینے کا اچھا یہ طریقہ ہے

زہرا نے بہت دن سے کچھ بھی نہیں لکھا ہے!

گھر بار، سمجھتی تھی، قلعہ ہے حفاظت کا
دیکھا کہ گرہستی بھی مٹی کا کھلونا ہے
مٹی ہو کہ پتھر ہو، ہیرا ہو کہ موتی ہو
گھربار کے مالک کا گھر بار پہ قبضہ ہے
احساسِ حکومت کے اظہار کا کیا کہنا!
انعام ہے مذہب کا، جو ہاتھ میں کوڑا ہے

زہرا نے بہت دن سے کچھ بھی نہیں لکھا ہے!

دیوار پہ ٹانگا تھا فرمان رفاقت کا
کیا وقت کے دریا نے دیوار کو ڈھایا ہے
فرمانِ رفاقت کی تقدیس بس اِتنی ہے
اک جنبشِ لب پر ہے، رشتہ جو ازل کا ہے

زہرا نے بہت دن سے کچھ بھی نہیں لکھا ہے!

دو بیٹوں کو کیا پالا، ناداں یہ سمجھتی تھی
اِس دولتِ دنیا کی مالک وہی تنہا ہے
پر وقت نے آئینہ کچھ ایسا دکھایا ہے
تصویر کا یہ پہلو اب سامنے آیا ہے
بڑھتے ہوئے بچّوں پر کھلتی ہوئی دنیا ہے
کھلتی ہوئی دنیا کا ہر باب تماشہ ہے
ماں باپ کی صورت تو دیکھا ہوا نقشہ ہے
دیکھے ہوئے نقشے کا ہر رنگ پرانا ہے
زہرا نے بہت دن سے کچھ بھی نہیں لکھا ہے!

سوچا تھا بہن بھائی دریا ہیں محبّت کے
دیکھا کہ کبھی دریا رستہ بھی بدلتا ہے
بھائی بھی گرفتارِ مجبوری خدمت ہیں
بہنوں پہ بھی طاری ہے قسمت کا جو لکھا ہے
اک ماں ہے جو پیڑوں سے باتیں کیے جاتی ہے
کہنے کو ہیں دس بچّے، اور پھر بھی وہ تنہا ہے
زہرا نے بہت دن سے کچھ بھی نہیں لکھا ہے!

Zehra ne bohat din se kuch bhi nahin likha hai
Halanke darin asna kya kuch nahin dekha hai
Par likhe to kya likhe? Aur soche to kya soche?
Kuch fikr bhi mubham hai, kuch hath larzta hai
    Zehra ne bohat din se kuch bhi nahin likha hai!
Diwani nahin itni, jo mun men ho bak jae
Chup shah ka roza bhi yunhi nahin rakha hai
Burhi bhi nahin itni, is tarah voh thak jae
Ab jan ke us ne ye andaz banaya hai
Har chiz bhulawe ke sanduq men rakh di hai
Aasani se jine ka accha ye tariqa hai
    Zehra ne bohat din se kuch bhi nahin likha hai!

Ghar bar, samajhti thi, qila hai hifazat ka
Dekha ke girhasti bhi mitti ka khilona hai
Mitti ho ke pathar ho, hira ho ke moti ho
Ghar bar ke malik ka ghar bar pe qabza hai
Ehsas-e hakumat ke izhar ka kya kehna!
Inam hai mazhab ka, jo hath men kora hai
   Zehra ne bohat din se kuch bhi nahin likha hai!

Divar pe tanga tha farman rafaqat ka
Kya vaqt ke darya ne divar ko dhaya hai
Farman-e rafaqat ki taqdis bas itni hai
Ik jumbish lab par hai, rishta jo azal ka hai
   Zehra ne bohat din se kuch bhi nahin likha hai!

Do beton ko kya pala, nadan ye samajhti thi
Is daulat-e dunya ki malik vohi tanha hai
Par vaqt ne aaina kuch aisa dikhaya hai
Tasvir ka ye pehlu ab samne aaya hai
Barhte hue bachon par khulti hui dunya hai
Khulti hui dunya ka har bab tamasha hai
Ma bap ki surat to dekha hua naqsha hai
Dekhe hue naqshe ka har rang purana hai
   Zehra ne bohat din se kuch bhi nahin likha hai!

Socha tha behn bhai darya hain mohabbat ke
Dekha ke kabhi darya rasta bhi badalta hai
Bhai bhi giraftar-e majburi-e khidmat hain
Bhenon pe bhi tari hai qismat ka jo likha hai
Ik man hai jo peron se baten kiye jati hai
Kehne ko hain das bache, aur phi bhi vo tanha hai
   Zehra ne bohat din se kuch bhi nahin likha hai!

[Zehra has not written anything for many days
Although during that time what is it that she has not seen
But if she writes, what should she write? and if she thinks, what
 should she think?
Thought has dimmed a little, the hand trembles a little
Zehra has not written anything for many days!

Not so simple to say anything that comes to mind
Nor is her silence without reason
Nor is she so old, that she will tire from this

She has deliberately appropriated this style now
Stored everything in a trunk of memories
This is a good way of living at ease
Zehra has not written anything for many days!

She thought the house and its effects were a fortress of protection
Observed that the housekeeper was made of clay
Be it diamond or pearl, be it clay or stone
The owner of the house is the one with rights over the house
What to say of the feeling which comes from being governed
The rubbish in hand is a reward of religion
Zehra has not written anything for many days!

The mandate of friendship was hung on the wall
Has the river of time broken down the wall
The sanctity of love's mandate is just this
A quivering of the lips, a relationship from birth
Zehra has not written anything for many days!

This naive woman thought by raising two sons
She alone owned the wealth of this world
But time has shown her a mirror such
The perspective is now front to back
For children growing up the world is a discovery
And every chapter exciting
While the faces of mothers and fathers are well travelled maps
And every contour of the map is worn
Zehra has not written anything for many days!

I had thought brothers and sisters to be rivers of love
I saw that sometimes the river changed its course
Brothers are trapped in obligatory caretaking too
Sisters too undergo that which fate decrees
The mother is left chatting to the trees
Though a mother of ten children, she stands alone
Zehra has not written anything for many days!][103]

As an opening poem to her second collection, it articulates the long gap between her first two publications. On being questioned about why she stopped writing after her marriage, she says that it was domestic life that caught up with her.[104] According to the poet Fatema Hasan, Zehra Nigah had to contend with a challenging domestic life and a patriarchal home environment that did not give her the freedom to write.[105] In the poem, the poet-narrator, addressing herself, takes us on a journey of her life as a wife, a mother and a sister. This woman has lived her life for others in her family and has come to the realization that she stands alone despite her many familial connections. The poem breaks down on many levels when it comes to family, signifying both sacred duty and national loyalty. Ironically, it is the writing she locked away in a forgotten suitcase, gathering dust, that revives her self. On a surface level, Nigah can be seen to be actively responding to those critics who felt her silence after her marriage signalled a premature end to an illustrious career.[106] At a deeper level she is reflecting on the hollowness of her life as a nurturer, reiterating the assessment offered by Fatema Hasan of a difficult life. Zehra Nigah's personal circumstances allowed her to return to the world of writing after a long gap and reclaim the position that she had relinquished as a young woman with powerful poems about female infanticide, a national conscience looking at Bangladesh and Afghanistan and natural disasters in Azad Kashmir.

Parvin Shakir, the poet and critic who questioned delays in Zehra Nigah's writing, spoke from within the profession as a woman poet resigned to such occurrences. Younger than Zehra Nigah and more outspoken, her poetic journey took on a different hue. Shakir was a civil servant employed by the Customs Office in Islamabad as a tax officer. Prior to that she had taught English as a second language for nine years.[107] With two postgraduate taught masters degrees in English and linguistics, she was a recipient of an American Fulbright scholarship and held a PhD in banking.[108] She made a substantial contribution to the archives of Urdu poetry during her life. Her skill in the art and craft of both the ghazal and the nazm are evident in four collections of poetry, published over a period of 23 years.[109] She published her first collection, entitled *Khushbu* (Fragrance), in 1977, *Sadbarg* (Marigold) in 1980, *Khud Kalami* (Soliloquy) in 1985 and *Inkar* (Refusal) in 1990. *Khushbu* was awarded the Adamjee Literary Prize for being the book of the year. The first printed edition sold out in six months and went into a second printing – 'a rare honor for any book in Urdu'.[110] Yasmeen Hameed's memorial, featured in *The News* on 7 January 1996, bears witness to Shakir's long-lasting appeal and why critics were quick to judge her as just another pretty face:

> When she lived as one of the most popular poets of her time, Perveen Shakir's contemporaries liked to label her poetry as an outburst of youthful emotions and a verbalisation of teenage sentimentality. Although she was often projected by the media as a symbol of glamour, she had made her mark in literature at a very early age as one of the important poets of the post-Faiz era.[111]

Hameed's reference here is to the reception of *Khushbu* by critics as an outpouring of femininity and adolescent emotions, branding her a confessional poet.[112] C. M. Naim opines that it is a misrepresentation to call her confessional because she did not write about deep psychological problems.[113] In her edited collection of feminist Urdu poetry, Rukhsana Ahmad purposefully excluded Shakir from her selection because she thought that her writing was 'apolitical, sentimental and conformist'.[114] The light-hearted tone of her poetry and her distance from Faiz kept her out of the Progressive camp. Like her predecessors, Parvin was also influenced by American and English poets and canonical male writers informed her repertoire. The subject of her poem 'Wasteland' (inspired by T. S. Eliot's *The Waste Land*) is the wilting canon of Urdu poetry in need of inspiration from outside sources.[115] She used frivolity to express an absurdist angle – for instance, her translation of Shakespeare's *Othello* took the form of a modern tale of jealousy conveyed by the lover's misgivings over the beloved's constantly engaged telephone line.[116] Shakir was fully aware of how she was read and her poem 'Tanqid aur takhliq' (Writing and Criticism) captures the confidence of her voice and self-belief as she defends herself against the criticism of superficiality:

"آپ کی شاعری صرف خوشبو ہے
دل میں اُترتی ہوئی
روح پر شبنمی ہاتھ رکھتی ہوئی
یہ مگر۔۔۔ ذہن کو صرف پلکے سے چھو کر گزر جائے گی
آپ اسے رنگ کا پیرہن دیجیے
کوئی آورش اُدینا، انوکھا عقیدہ، کوئی گنجلک فلسفہ
سخت ناقابل فہم الفاظ میں پیش کرنے کی کوشش کریں
آپ کی سوچ میں کچھ تو گہرائی ہو۔۔۔ !"
آپ سچ کہہ رہے ہیں
مگر۔۔۔ دیکھیے نا۔۔۔ ابھی میرا فن کئی عمروں میں ہے
(آپ اسے خواب ہی دیکھنے دیجیے)
اتنی گمبھیر دانشوری میں نہ اُلجھائیے)
میں نہیں چاہتی۔۔۔ کہ میرا فن
جواں ہونے سے قبل ہی بوڑھا ہو جائے
اور فلسفے کا عصا لے کے چلنے لگے !

'Aap ki shairi sirf khushbu hai
Dil men utarti hui
Ruh par shabnami hath rakhti hui
Ye magar – zehn ko sirf halke se chu kar guzar jae gi
Aap ise rang ka perahan dijye
Koi adarsh uncha, anokha aqida, koi gunjalak falsafa
Sakht naqabil-e fahm alfaz men pesh karne ki koshish karen
Aap ki soch men kuch to gehrai ho –!'

Aap such keh rahen hain
Magar – dekhye na – abhi mera fun kucchi umron men hai
(aap ise khvab hi dekhne dijiye)
(itni ghambir danishwari men na uljhaye)
Main nahin chahti – ke mera fun
Jawan hone se qabl hi burha ho jae
Aur falsafe ka asa le ke chalne lage!

['Your poetry is only *Khushbu*
Pleasing to the heart
Touching the spirit with a dewy hand
But this – will only touch the mind lightly
Please will you clothe it in colour
Project it as a high ideal, a unique creed, dense philosophy
Try and present it in unfathomable words
There should be some depth to your thought –!'

You are telling the truth
But – see – my craft is in its infancy
(Please allow it to dream)
(Please do not confuse it in complex intelligence)
I do not desire – that my craft
Should grow old before its youth
And lean on the staff of philosophy!][117]

In contrast to the light-hearted ghazals are lesser-known unique poems, such as 'Istenografer' (The Stenographer) from the *Sadbarg* collection, which conveys the routine and insignificant role of the automaton-like female worker. It is a tribute to the contribution made by women to public working life beyond their role as mothers and daughters. Most hard-hitting is the poem 'Tomato Ketchup' in *Inkar*, narrating the beleaguered life of her contemporary, the poet Sara Shagufta, and how her work was belittled through sexual advances and accusations that she was a loose woman. The poet-narrator expresses the frustration of a woman whose verse was continually interpreted very personally by her male contemporaries: 'har mard khud ko us ka mukhatib samajhta hai / aur chunke haqiqat men aisa nahin hota / is liye us ka dushman ho jata hai' (Every man imagined himself to be her addressee / And when disappointed by the reality / Became her enemy instead).[118] Using the medium of the prose poem, Shakir writes in defence of Sara Shagufta, expressing her dismay that 'Ek se ek gae guzre likhne vale ka dawa tha / ke voh us ke sath so chuki hai' (Every mediocre writer who fancied himself / Would claim that she had slept with him). The poet-narrator tells us that, oblivious to mundane but key household tasks such as paying the bills or buying medicines for women and children, the literati would spend hours pontificating on literature and philosophy. We learn that Shagufta succumbed to flattery doled out by intellectuals who would call her the Amrita Pritam of Pakistan. Eventually she learnt of their hypocrisy and fled, and in doing so 'left the jungle altogether!' This line refers to Sara's suicide. The poet-narrator's anger toward the male writers who undermined Sara is palpable and her power lies in her truth-telling as she exposes the two-facedness of the inner circle of Urdu poetry. Using sarcasm, she uses tomato ketchup as a metaphor for their representation of Sara after her death, bringing her back into literary conversations to add a lively flavour for the purpose of titillation.

In narrating Sara's story, Shakir brings biographical narrative to the Urdu poem, underlining the ordinary life of a woman poet who fell victim to Urdu poetry's double standards of patriarchy, class bias and elitism. Kamran Asdar Ali has argued that, in trying to unearth the life story of Sara Shagufta, he came across the usual reflections of a hypersexual woman, who was easy to cast aside because she came from the 'wrong side of the tracks' as a lower-middle-class woman from 1960s Karachi.[119] He argues that her attempt to transform her class through her participation in elite Urdu literary circles was restricted because of the strict gatekeeping of sexualities in those groups. His assessment is that Shagufta experienced a similar fate to Manto because she went against the grain. Ali makes an interesting case for a comparison between the two because of the nonconformity to middle-class values enacted through their writings. I would like to extend that to argue that their gendered experiences tell different tales. In Sara's case, her life experiences add another layer to the story.

The Indian Punjabi writer Amrita Pritam, Shagufta's muse, has published her poetry and letters, projecting a harrowing account of a girl from Gujranwala married at 17 years of age. Shagufta gave birth to three children in rapid succession, suffered abusive relationships, terminated a pregnancy and fell out of favour with her in-laws. Married three times, mistreated and misrepresented by jealous husbands, her mental health deteriorated and she was put in an asylum. In 1984, at 29 years old, she committed suicide. Her story bears testimony to the framed narrative of 'possession' for girls/women in Zehra Nigah's poem 'Gul Chandni' and in this case we learn about treatment through electric shocks and isolation. She writes poems in her letters to her friend Pritam, articulating a body in pain. The theme of honour is writ large in some of the compositions; the subject of her poetry is the shamed 'whore' who speaks of giving birth and being abandoned. In her letter to Pritam dated 22 September 1981, she pens the following verse during a time she was undergoing electric shock treatment at Karachi's Liaquat hospital. The chapter from which this is taken, entitled 'Masjid ki int' (The Brick of a Mosque), articulates Shagufta's frustration with societal hypocrisy that relies on performative acts of religiosity from donning a dupatta to reading namaz. She complains about constantly being judged by other women and male contemporaries for her lack of modesty. In her rebuttal of these character assessments she writes of her integrity and honesty when it comes to her moral values, which is greater than those who would steal bricks from a broken down mosque. The only people who sustain her in Pakistan are Ahmed Salim and Amrita Pritam, the addressee of her letters:

> Abhi to men ne qalam ko pakarna bhi nahin sikha tha, meri takhti par likh dena
> Mujhe kori ankhon ke didar likhne hain…
> Mujhe insanon se khauf aata hai
> Main lambe safar ko nikal jaun to?
> Insani sahifa kahan hai?
> Dhundhna, puchna aur mujhe chap dena[120]

> [I have yet to learn how to hold the pen
> [D]o write on the writing-board
> I have to draw a picture of the blank eyes
> I'm afraid of men
> I set out on a long journey
> In search of the Holy Book
> Go in search of it and publish it for me][121]

There is no solace for Shagufta in sacred or secular spaces. She describes herself as a victim of sexual violence and societal prejudices. Unable to continue living, she finds relief in suicide. Her poetry expresses her modernist aspirations and her broken spirit and, while she is cited by her female peers, male poets maintain a silence over a female persona who breaks all the rules of sharafat.

Sara Shagufta's and Parvin Shakir's interventions, experiences and presence as poets alter the sedate middle-class subjectivity of early Progressive Urdu women poets, who came from sharif backgrounds and avoided conversations about sexuality. Although Zehra Nigah speaks about her experiences as a performer of poetry in interviews, the chapter of her married life remains firmly closed to the public and the explanation she gives of her long silence in 'Zehra ne bohat din se kuch bhi nahin likha hai' is measured. With her later collections she projects a Progressive national conscience that is critical of social injustices against women and society at large. Most importantly she doesn't break the codes of sharif moral values in her own life and neither does Ada Jafri. It is interesting to note that neither Shakir nor Sara Shagufta are included in the Progressive poets repertoire and that is telling in itself. They demonstrate how poetry was developing beyond the tight-knit circle of a Progressive group of poets. Their commitment to modernity and modernism is evident in their poems and this demands recognition beyond their biographies.

In conclusion, women were ready to step beyond their comfort zone as Progressive poets; however, class played a big part in the reception and circulation of their work, as did their personal lives. While Ada Jafri and Zehra Nigah enjoy a national presence, Parvin Shakir is loved as a romantic poet but judged for her personal life, and Sara Shagufta was never admitted into the inner circle. Thus, in this chapter, I have shown that Progressivism is a closely guarded space in Urdu circles and those on the margins are often left out rather than let in. Women poets have to negotiate performativity with respectability and observe social norms pertaining to sexual behaviour and those who don't conform run the risk of reputational damage and ostracization both by the literary community and Pakistani society. In the next chapter I look in greater depth at a poet, Fahmida Riaz, who was a contemporary and a revolutionary to see how women's Progressive poetry continued to evolve and respond to women artists who were also activists. The stories of Ada Jafri, Zehra Nigah, Parvin Shakir and Sara Shagufta set the context for the distinctive legacies of both Fahmida Riaz and Kishwar Naheed (the subject of Chapter 5). The writing and biographies of these two major poets are informed by an activist-led vision of what secular and sacred came to mean for women as the ideology of Islam tightened its grip in Pakistan.

Notes

1. See Katherine Schofield, 'Reviving the Golden Age Again: "Classicisation", Hindustani Music, and the Mughals', *Ethnomusicology* 54, no. 3 (2010): 484–517.
2. Sheema Kermani, 'Tehrik-e-Niswan's Tilismati Tees Aur Aik Saal' (Magical Thirty and One Years), in *Gender, Politics, and Performance in South Asia*, ed. Sheema Kermani,

Asif Furrukhi and Kamran Asdar Ali (Karachi: Oxford University Press, 2015), 3–34 (25).

3   Claire Pamment, 'A Split Discourse: Body Politics in Pakistan's Popular Punjabi Theatre', in *Gender, Politics and Performance in South Asia*, ed. Sheema Kermani, Asif Farrukhi and Kamran Asdar Ali (Karachi: Oxford University Press, 2015), 203–34 (214).

4   For a measured reading of tawaifs as performers, see Regula B. Qureshi, 'Female Agency and Patrilineal Constraints: Situating Courtesans in Twentieth-Century India', in *The Courtesan's Arts: Cross-Cultural Perspectives*, ed. Martha Feldman and Bonnie Gordon (Oxford: Oxford University Press, 2006), 312–31.

5   See Claire Pamment, '*Police of Pig and Sheep*: Representations of the White Sahib and the Construction of Theatre Censorship in Colonial India', *South Asian Popular Culture* 7, no. 3 (2009): 233–45 (241). Pamment argues that the Raj's tactics of taking the moral high ground drew attention away from plays such as *Surendra-Binodini*, *Gajadananda and the Prince* and *Police of Pig and Sheep*, written and directed by Upendra Nath Das, which depicted the rape of local women as a critique of the Raj.

6   See Priyamvada Gopal, *Literary Radicalism in India: Gender, Nation and the Transition to Independence* (London: Routledge, 2005), 13–38.

7   Carlo Coppola, 'Urdu Poetry: The Progressive episode' (PhD thesis, University of Chicago, 1975); Carlo Coppola, ed., *Marxist Influences and South Asian Literature* (New Delhi: Oxford University Press, 1988); Hafeez Malik, 'The Marxist Literary Movement in India and Pakistan', *Journal of Asian Studies* 26, no. 4 (1967): 649–64; Ahmed Ali and N. M. Rashed, 'The Progressive Writers' Movement in Its Historical Perspective', *Journal of South Asian Literature* 13, no. 1/4 (1977–78): 91–97; Shabana Mahmud, '*Angare* and the Founding of the Progressive Writers' Association', *Modern Asian Studies* 30, no. 2 (1996): 447–67.

8   Gayatri Chakravorty Spivak, 'Can the Subaltern Speak?', in *Colonial Discourse and Postcolonial Theory*, ed. Patrick Williams and Laura Chrisman (Hemel Hempstead: Harvester Wheatsheaf, 1994), 66–111.

9   Shamsur Rahman Faruqi is deeply critical of the Progressives' practice of a literary social realism, arguing that while their primary theoretical influences were from Marx and Engels their literary knowledge was limited to Ralph Fox and Caudwell. 'Sajjad Zahir and 'Abdul 'Alim did say that socialist realism did not mean kissing literary values goodbye. But how one could manage to serve both ideals at the same time was a question that they answered with inane generalities, if at all'; Shamsur Rahman Faruqi, 'Images in a Darkened Mirror: Issues and Ideas in Modern Urdu Literature', *Annual of Urdu Studies* 6 (1987): 43–54 (50).

10   See Carlo Coppola, 'Premchand's Address to the First Meeting of the All-India Progressive Writers Association: Some Speculations', *Journal of South Asian Literature* 21, no. 2 (1986): 21–39. Also, see Amrit Rai, *Premchand: His Life and Times* (Delhi: Oxford University Press, 2004).

11   Aziz Ahmad, 'Urdu adab ki jadid tehrik' [Urdu Literature's New Movement], in his *Taraqqi Pasand Adab* (Delhi: Chaman Book Depot, 1945), 43–59. See pp. 57–60 on *Angare*.

12   Syed Sajjad Zaheer, 'Jannat ki Basharat', in *Angare*, ed. Dr Khalid Alvi (Delhi: Educational Publishing House, 2013), 115–123. Rakshanda Jalil gives a detailed summary and close reading of all the stories in the *Angare* collection in her chapter 'Analysing *Angarey*', in *Liking Progress, Loving Change: A Literary History of the Progressive*

Writers' Movement in Urdu (New Delhi: Oxford University Press, 2014), 108–45. Also see Geeta Patel, 'The Terms of the Encounter: Miraji and the Progressive Writers' Association', in *Lyrical Movements, Historical Hauntings: On Gender, Colonialism and Desire in Miraji's Urdu Poetry* (Stanford, CA: Stanford University Press, 2001; reprint, New Delhi: Manohar, 2005), 83–128.

13 Quoted in Patel, *Lyrical Movements, Historical Hauntings*, 93–94. The article is also referenced in Rakshanda Jalil's *A Rebel and Her Cause: The Life and Work of Rashid Jahan* (Karachi: Oxford University Press, 2015). Jalil says that she found the original typed copy of the article in Ahmad Ali's collection of papers in Karachi (pp. 58, 65).

14 Through access to Ahmed Ali's personal archive, Shabana Mahmud has recovered clippings from that time that illustrate the negative reaction to the book. See Mahmud, '*Angare* and the Founding of the Progressive Writers' Association'.

15 'Aag dekhi, pani dekha aur angare dekhe' (We Saw Fire, Water and Embers), *Sarguzasht*, 24 February 1933. Quoted in Mahmud, '*Angare* and the Founding of the Progressive Writers' Association', 449. Also see Ali and Rashed, 'The Progressive Writers Movement in Its Historical Perspective'; Rakshanda Jalil's chapter on 'The Furore over the Publication of *Angarey*', in *Liking Progress, Loving Change*, 146–89.

16 The Pakistani British writer Kamila Shamsie has argued that 'offence' is an intra-Muslim affair that has interesting and important moments in Islam's history with the west and in the case of India with the British. Kamila Shamsie, *Offence: The Muslim Case* (Calcutta: Seagull Books, 2009).

17 Patel, *Lyrical Movements, Historical Hauntings*, 96.

18 Carlo Coppola, 'The Angare Group: The Enfants Terribles of Urdu Literature', *Annual of Urdu Studies* 1 (1981): 57–69 (63). For a detailed history of the Progressives, see Coppola's dissertation, 'Urdu Poetry, 1935–1970'.

19 I borrow this term from Timothy Brennan in his overview of Salman Rushdie's work and its relationship to religion in his book *Wars of Position: The Cultural Politics of Left and Right* (New York: Columbia University Press, 2006), 73.

20 Jalil, *Liking Progress, Loving Change*, 164–81.

21 Frantz Fanon, 'On National Culture', in his *The Wretched of the Earth*, trans. Constance Farrington (London: Penguin, 1967), 166–99.

22 Gopal, *Literary Radicalism in India*, 4–10.

23 Patel, *Lyrical Movements, Historical Hauntings*, 103.

24 Patel notes that 'regulating sexuality by regulating sexual interactions and disease produced a vision of normal sexuality that could be cleaned up and brought under the medical and legal supervision of a colonial state'; ibid., 104.

25 Through a consideration of the modernist poet Miraji, she illustrates how a writer who openly experimented with sexual themes in his writing was subject to the limits of the colonial state. According to Patel, Miraji constructed an alternative literary vision of colonial progress and modernity across a project of translation signifying 'new literary affiliations'. After completing translations and close readings of European writers from Sappho to D. H. Lawrence, he began re-presenting Urdu terminologies associated with modernity, such as '*jadidiyat, tabdili* and *taraqqi*' (Patel, *Lyrical Movements, Historical Hauntings*, 155).

26 Carlo Coppola and S. Zubair, 'Rashid Jahan: Urdu Literature's First "Angry Young Woman"', *Journal of South Asian Literature* 22, no. 1 (1987): 166–83 (166).

27 See Jalil, *A Rebel and Her Cause*.

28 Gopal's analysis of her fictional work underlines an articulation of a cautious modernity through an emphasis on female body crossings into public spaces and subjectivities, which embraced the secular as a dialogic process. See her chapter, 'Gender, Modernity and the Politics of Space: Rashid Jahan, "Angareywali"', in *Literary Radicalism in India*, 39–64.
29 S. M. Poulos, 'Feminine Sense and Sensibility: A Comparative Study of Six Modern Women Short Fiction Writers in Hindi and Urdu: Rashid Jahan, Ismat Chughtai, Qurratulain Hyder, Mannu Bhandari, Usha Priyamvada, Vijay Chauhan' (PhD thesis, University of Chicago, 1975), 267.
30 Ibid.
31 Hamida Saiduzzafar, quoted in 'My sister Rashid Jahan 1905–1952', in *A Woman of Substance: The Memoirs of Begum Khurshid Mirza*, ed. Lubna Kazim (Delhi: Zubaan, 2005), 86–104 (94). Also see 'JSAL Interviews Dr Hamida Saiduzzafar: A Conversation with Rashid Jahan's Sister-in-Law, Aligarh, 1973', *Journal of South Asian Literature* 22, no. 1 (Winter/Spring 1987): 158–65.
32 Through these gendered cultural and class confluences, Gopal suggests that Rashid Jahan's work offers an alternative reading of modernity as a one-sided derivative discourse of colonialism; *Literary Radicalism*, 39–63. Gopal is responding to Partha Chatterjee's thesis on modernity as a derivative discourse of colonialism. See Partha Chatterjee, *Nationalist Thought and the Colonial World: A Derivative Discourse* (Minneapolis: University of Minnesota Press, 1993).
33 Ismat Chughtai, '*Mahfil* Interviews Ismat Chughtai', *Mahfil* 8, no. 2/3 (1972): 169–88 (172).
34 Ismat Chughtai, *The Quilt and Other Stories*, trans. and ed. Tahira Naqvi and S. S. Hameed (New Delhi: Kali, 1990), vii.
35 Chughtai, *The Quilt and Other Stories*, 110–26; Saadat Hasan Manto, *Mantonama* (Lahore: Sang-e Meel, 1999), 102; Tahira Naqvi, 'Introduction', in Chughtai, *The Quilt and Other Stories*, vii–ix (viii).
36 Ismat Chughtai. *Choten* (Delhi: M. Azad Mirza Malik Book Depot, 1953), 82–92.
37 Ismat Chughtai, *A Life in Words: Memoirs*, trans. from the original Urdu *Kaghazi Hai Pairahan* by M. Asaduddin (India: Penguin Books, 2012), 25.
38 Ibid., 40.
39 Aamer Hussein, 'Aamer Hussein Reviews Ismat Chughtai's Short Stories', *Asymptote*, accessed 1 December 2020, https://www.asymptotejournal.com/criticism/ismat-chughtais-short-stories/#.WJhP4mHenQg.facebook.
40 Ismat Chughtai, *Terhi Lakir* in *Kulliyat Ismat Chughtai (Navil)*, ed. Asif Nawaz (Lahore: Maktaba-e sher-o adab. n.d.), 135–556.
41 Gopal, *Literary Radicalism in India*, 76.
42 Chughtai, *A Life in Words*, 42.
43 Aamir R. Mufti, *Enlightenment in the Colony: The Jewish Question and the Crisis of Postcolonial Culture* (Princeton, NJ: Princeton University Press, 2007), 179.
44 See Saadat Hasan Manto, 'Bu', in *Mantonama* (Collected Short Stories) (Lahore: Sang-e meel, 1995), 621–28.
45 See the introduction by Ali Mir and Saadia Toor to their edited volume *Saadat Hasan Manto: The Armchair Revolutionary and Other Sketches*, trans. Khalid Hasan (New Delhi: Leftword Books, 2016).
46 Sarah Waheed, 'Anatomy of an Obscenity Trial', *Himal SouthAsian*, 1 July 2013. https://www.himalmag.com/anatomy-obscenity-trial/.

47 The Urdu literary critic Mohammad Sadiq, in his history of Urdu literature, hesitantly acknowledges Manto's prowess as a successful short story writer but takes him to task over moral values, reiterating the vulgarity label because he disapproved of what he thought was Manto's voyeuristic preoccupation with themes of sex; Mohammad Sadiq, *Twentieth Century Urdu Literature* (Karachi: Royal Book, 1983), 306.
48 Patel, *Lyrical Movements, Historical Hauntings*, 102.
49 Manto, *The Armchair Revolutionary*, 'Introduction'.
50 Safdar M. Mir, *Modern Urdu Prose: Essays in Literary History* (Lahore: Azad, 1998), 100.
51 Leslie A. Flemming, *Another Lonely Voice: The Urdu Short Stories of Saadat Hasan Manto* (Berkeley: University of California, Center for South and Southeast Asia Studies, 1979), 22–30; Muhammad Umar Memon, 'Preamble', in *My Name Is Radha: The Essential Manto*, trans. Muhammad Umar Memon (Gurgaon, Haryana: Penguin Books India, 2016), ix–xxv.
52 Muhammad Hasan Askari, *Jadidiyat ya maghribi gumrahiyon ki tarikh ka khaka* [Modernism or a Sketch of Western Ignorance] (Lahore: Iffat Hasan, 1979); A. H. Madni, *Jadid Urdu shairi* [Modern Urdu Poetry] (Karachi: Anjuman-e taraqqi-e Urdu, 1990).
53 Chughtai, *A Life in Words*, 40. For a family history of Manto, see Ayesha Jalal, *The Pity of Partition: Manto's Life, Times and Work across the India–Pakistan Divide* (Princeton, NJ: Princeton University Press, 2013).
54 See Ali Madeeh Hashmi, *Love and Revolution: Faiz Ahmed Faiz: The Authorized Biography* (New Delhi: Rupa, 2016).
55 *The Unicorn and the Dancing Girl: Poems of Faiz Ahmad Faiz*, trans. Daud Kamal, ed. Khalid Hasan (London: Independent, 1988), xxvii.
56 See discussion of Faiz's essays on Pakistani culture in my 'Variants of Cultural Nationalism in Pakistan: A Reading of Faiz Ahmad Faiz, Jamil Jalibi and Fahmida Riaz', in *Shared Idioms, Sacred Symbols and the Articulation of Identities in South Asia*, ed. Kelly Pemberton and Michael Nijhawan (London: Routledge, 2009), 115–42.
57 See Afsaneh Najmabadi, 'The Erotic Vatan [Homeland] as Beloved and Mother: To Love, To Possess, and To Protect', *Comparative Studies in Society and History* 39, no. 3 (1997), 442–67; Gopi Chand Narang, 'Tradition and Innovation in Urdu Poetry', in *Poetry and Renaissance: Kumaran Asan Birth Centenary Volume*, ed. M. Govindan (Madras: Sameeksha, 1974), 415–34.
58 Faiz Ahmad Faiz, *Poems by Faiz*, trans. V. G. Kiernan (Lahore: Vanguard Books, 1971), 65.
59 See A. Sean Pue's article 'Rethinking Modernism and Progressivism in Urdu Poetry: Faiz Ahmad Faiz and N. M. Rashed', *Pakistaniaat: A Journal of Pakistan Studies* 5, no. 1 (2013), in which he refers to Rashed's description of Faiz's early work as an example of romantic realism. Available at https://pakistaniaat.org/index.php/pak/article/view/184.
60 For a longer discussion on Faiz, see Amina Yaqin, 'Faiz Ahmad Faiz: The Worlding of a Lyric Poet', *Pakistaniaat* 5, no. 1 (2013): i–ix, http://pakistaniaat.org/index.php/pak/issue/view/12.
61 In 1959, Ayub's regime took away ownership of The Progressive Papers Limited (PPL), which included the *Pakistan Times*, the *Imroze* and the weekly *Lail-o-Nahar*, from the Left leaving them without a platform in West Pakistan.
62 Their mission statement acknowledged them as writers of Pakistani literatures dedicating themselves to the development of the nation and international peace,

identifying with human rights standards set by the United Nations (UN) council; Pakistan Writers Guild, ed., *Muraqqa musanafin* (Book of Authors) (Sukkur: Pakistan Writers Guild, [ca.1966]), 2.

63 Altaf Husain Qureshi and Mashkur Husain Yad, personal communication, 9 April 2000.

64 Saadia Toor, *The State of Islam: Culture and Cold War Politics in Pakistan* (London: Pluto, 2011), 90–91.

65 Toor, *The State of Islam*, 63–65. On Muhammad Hasan Askari's intellectual development as a literary critic in a time of crisis from Indo-Muslim to Pakistan contexts, see Mehr Afshan Faruqi's *Urdu Literary Culture: Vernacular Modernity in the Writing of Muhammad Hasan Askari* (New York: Palgrave Macmillan, 2012).

66 It is true that after Partition he felt that Sajjad Zaheer in particular was aligning himself with the interests of the Communist Party of India rather than national interests in Pakistan with reference to the Kashmir issue.

67 Muhammad Hasan Askari, 'Musalman adib aur musalman qaum', in *Majmu'a Muhammad Hassan Askari* (Lahore: Sang-e meel, 2008), 1111–19 (on the Kashmir issue, 1116; on the Urdu/Bengali controversy, 1119).

68 See Toor, *The State of Islam*, 63–79.

69 Askari, 'Jadid shairi 2' (Modern Poetry), in *Majmu'a Muhammad Hassan Askari*, 848.

70 I borrow this term from Rajeswari Sunder Rajan and her discussion of the new Indian woman.

71 Farman Fatehpuri and Umrao Tariq, eds, *Ada Jafri: fan-o shakhsiat* (Karachi: Halqa-e niaz-o nigar, 1998).

72 Known as the 'father of the ghazal', he influenced the literary elite culture of the North with his distinctive southern style. See entry on 'ghazal', in Amaresh Datta, ed., *Encyclopaedia of Indian Literature, Volume 2: Devraj to Jyoti* (New Delhi: Sahitya Akademi, 1988), 1396.

73 Ada Jafri, *Jo rahi so bekhabri rahi* [An Ignorance That Remained] (Karachi: Maktaba-e Daniyaal, 1995), 61.

74 Asif Furrukhi, 'Kis ada ke sath', in Fatehpuri and Tariq, eds, *Ada Jafri*, 163–85 (165).

75 Jafri, *Jo rahi so bekhabri rahi*, 26.

76 Ibid., 320–21.

77 Ibid., 214.

78 Ibid., 321.

79 Ibid., 321–22.

80 In an essay elsewhere, I've engaged with Rosemary Marangoly George's discussion of homes as places that are not open and welcoming in the sense that Jafri constructs them in her poem. There seems to be a generational gap between her need for a family to define a home and that of the next generation. In my essay I also contextualize Edward Said's connections between filiation and affiliation where he describes the former as being made out of natural bonds and the latter as a social construct. See Amina Yaqin, 'Family and Gender in Rushdie's Writing', in *The Cambridge Companion to Salman Rushdie*, ed. Abdulrazak Gurnah (Cambridge: Cambridge University Press, 2007), 61–74.

81 Ada Jafri, 'Phul sehraon men khilte hon ge' [Flowers May Bloom in Deserts], in *Ghazalan tum to vaqif ho* [Ghazalan You Know], 2nd ed. (Lahore: Ghalib, 1982).

82 Jafri, *Ghazalan tum to vaqif ho*, 91–92.

83 Kishwar Naheed, 'Likhne valiyon ki tanhai' [The Loneliness of Women Writers], in *Apni nigah: auraton ki likhi takhliqat aur tanqidi jaize* [A Lens of Their Own: Women's Writing and Critical Surveys], ed. Javeria Khalid and Samina Rehman (Lahore: ASR, 1995), 72–75 (72–73).
84 Ibid.
85 Asif Furrukhi, 'Nazm-i Nigah', *Dawn*, 12 January 2014.
86 Faiz Ahmed Faiz, 'Dibacha' (Foreword) to *Shama ka pehla tara* [The First Star of Evening] in Zehra Nigah, *Majmua-e Kalaam* (Lahore: Sang-e meel, 2012), 9–12.
87 Zehra Nigah, personal communication, 30 March 1997.
88 See Asim Akhtar's interview with Zehra Nigah, *Baithak*, 1 November 2005, http://baithak.blogspot.co.uk/2005/11/zehra-nigah-aasim-akhtar.html.
89 Personal communication, 25 March 1998.
90 Karachi Literature Festival, '*Adab kay sitaray*: Zehra Nigah, Kishwar Naheed, Masood Ashar, Mustansar Hussain Tarar', 10 February 2017, https://www.youtube.com/watch?v=YiaC6fQtXX4.
91 Zehra Nigah, *Sham ka pehla tara* [The First Star of Evening] (Lahore: Asatir, 1998), 68.
92 Ibid., 30–33.
93 Personal communication, 25 March 1998.
94 Translation by Rukhsana Ahmad in her *We Sinful Women: Contemporary Urdu Feminist Poetry Including the Original Urdu* (New Delhi: Rupa, 1994), 124–35; Nigah, *Sham ka pehla tara*, 96–99, 117–20.
95 Nigah, *Sham ka pehla tara*, 99.
96 Ibid.
97 Nigah, personal communication, 25 March 1998
98 On superstitions, see Sabiha Hafeez, 'Social Discrimination of Women in Folk Literature and Culture', in *Women: Myth and Realities*, ed. Kishwar Naheed (Lahore: Sang-e meel, [ca.1993]), 286–98.
99 Nigah, *Sham ka pehla tara*, 54–56.
100 Personal communication, 25 March 1998.
101 Personal communication, 25 March 1998.
102 I borrow the term from Sigmund Freud's classic psychoanalytic study *Totem and Taboo*, trans. James Strachey (1913; London: Routledge and Kegan Paul, 1950).
103 Zehra Nigah, *Varq* (Lahore: Asatir, 1998), 17–19.
104 Personal communication, 25 March 1998.
105 Personal communication, 8 July 2018.
106 'She became silent at the seminal stage of her career: her marriage consumed her totally and her readers were left absolutely clueless as to what was going on in her mind'. Parvin Shakir, 'Women Poets of Pakistan' [reproduced from the *News International*, 9 October 1994], *Pakistan Journal of Women's Studies* 2, no. 1 (1995): 22–30 (23).
107 Pakistan Academy of Letters, 'Special Issue on Women's Writing', *Pakistani Literature* 3, no. 2 (1994): 231–34 (327); Rafaqat Javed, *Parvin Shakir jaisa main ne dekha* [Parvin Shakir as I Saw Her] (Islamabad: Parvin Shakir Trust, 2014).
108 Three years after her death her verse was immortalized in an edited collection entitled *Sukhan ki shahzadi: Parvin Shakir* (Princess of Verse), ed. Rifat Haider (Islamabad: Dost Pablikeshanz, 1997).
109 C. M. Naim, 'Parveen Shakir: A Note and Twelve Poems', *Annual of Urdu Studies* 7 (1990): 181–91.
110 Naim, 'Parveen Shakir', 182.

111 Yasmeen Hameed, 'Beyond the Glamorous Façade', *News International*, 7 January 1996: 9.
112 See S. Baksh, ed., *Pakistani adbiyat men khavatin ka kirdar* [The Role of Women in Pakistani Literature] (Islamabad: Allama Iqbal Open University, 1996), 117.
113 Naim, 'Parveen Shakir', 185.
114 Rukhsana Ahmad, in her introduction to *We Sinful Women*, 6.
115 Parvin Shakir, *Mah-e tammam: kulliyat* [The Full Moon: Collected Works] (Islamabad: Murad Publications, n.d.), bk 1, 87–89. Also see T. S. Eliot, *The Waste Land and Other Poems* (London: Faber and Faber, 1971); Rainer Emig, *Modernism in Poetry: Motivations, Structures and Limits* (London: Longman, 1995), 61–87.
116 Shakir, *Mah-e tammam*, bk 1, 181.
117 Shakir, 'Khushbu', in *Mah-e tammam*, bk 1, 180.
118 Shakir, 'Tomato Ketchup' from *Inkar*, in *Mah-e tammam*, bk 4, 159–61. Also see Attiya Dawood's 'Sara meri dost' [My Friend Sara] in *Apni Nigah: auraton ki likhi taakhliqat aur tanqidi jaize*, ed. Javeria Khalid and Samina Rahman (Lahore: ASR, 1995), 76–89. See also, 'Tomato Ketchup' in *Defiance of the Rose: Selected Poems by Perveen Shakir* (translated from Urdu by Naima Rashid). (Karachi: Oxford University Press, 2019), 56–57.
119 Kamran Asdar Ali, 'The Other Side of the "Tracks": Sara Shagufta and the Politics of Gender and Class', in *Gender, Politics and Performance in South Asia*, ed. Sheema Kermani, Asif Farrukhi and Kamran Asdar Ali (Karachi: Oxford University Press, 2015), 431–62.
120 Amrita Pritam, *Ek thi Sara: Sara Shagufta ka zindagi nama* [There Was a Sara: Sara Shagufta's Life Writings] (Lahore: Fiction House, 1994), 47–53.
121 Sara Shagufta, quoted in Amrita Pritam, *Life and Poetry of Sara Shagufta*, trans. Gurdev Chauhan (New Delhi: B. R. Publishing, 1994), 32.

Chapter 4

FAHMIDA RIAZ: A WOMAN IMPURE

کاغذ، تیرا رنگ فق کیوں ہو گیا؟
"شاعر، تیرے تیور دیکھ کر"
کاغذ، تیرے رخسار پر یہ داغ کیسے ہیں
"شاعر، میں تیرے آنسو پی نہ سکا"
کاغذ، میں تجھ سے سچ کہوں......
"شاعر! میرا دل پھٹ جائے گا"

Kaghaz, tera rang faq kyun ho gaya?
'Shair, tere tewar dekh kar'
Kaghaz, tere rukhsar par ye dagh kaise hain
'shair, main tere aansu pi na saka'
Kaghaz, main tujh se sach kahun.....
'Shair! Mera dil phat jaye ga'

[Paper, why has your complexion faded?
'Poet, from watching your deeds'
Paper, what are these blemishes upon your cheek?
'Poet, I could not drink your tears'
Paper, shall I tell you the truth.....?
'Poet! my heart will burst'][1]

Born in 1945 in Meerut, attached to an urban Uttar Pradesh household, Fahmida Riaz grew up in the heartland of Urdu.[2] After the untimely death of her father, Riazuddin Ahmad, in 1950, it was Riaz's mother who took over the role of provider for her family. She provided financial stability and a learning environment at home for her daughters. At school, Riaz became interested in Progressive literature and before long was composing her own verse. As she grew up, she increasingly felt the generational divide between her mother and herself widen, compounded by societal restrictions imposed upon women.[3] In 1963, her first year at Government College for Girls, Hyderabad, she began contributing poems to the literary journal *Funun*, edited by the eminent writer Ahmad Nadeem Qasimi. While studying for her postgraduate degree programme at Sindh University, she came into close contact with members of the banned Communist Party, fuelling her leftist inclinations in politics. This was a comradeship she had flirted with during her undergraduate years as a member of the Student Union. In 1967 Riaz's marriage was arranged and her academic life abandoned. She moved to England and found herself adopting the role of a housewife. Soon she got pregnant and became a mother. Afterwards she joined the London Film School but her heart remained in Pakistan: 'I was very deeply involved with the dream of making a social change in Pakistan and becoming a socialist.'[4] Her marriage ended in divorce and she returned to Karachi in 1973 with her daughter and published a controversial poetry collection entitled *Badan darida* (The Body Torn) which she had composed in London. Riaz's second marriage was to the political activist Zafar Ali Ujjan in 1976 and coincided with her third publication, *Dhup* (Sunshine). Subsequently she became editor and publisher of a new monthly news and literary magazine, *Awaz*.[5] Her journalism witnessed turbulent times as the political climate in Pakistan changed from Zulfiqar Ali Bhutto's 'people's democracy' to General Zia's rule of martial law. As editor of *Awaz* magazine, with an allegiance to Bhutto's Pakistan's People's Party (PPP), Riaz continued to publish critical commentaries on state practices and was put under continual surveillance. The Zia regime's censorship policy of the national press maintained strict surveillance of dissent. She received regular notices, culminating in a charge of sedition. This injunction, with its threat of capital punishment, was instrumental in her decision to leave Pakistan. Riaz escaped to India and it is rumoured that the Punjabi poet Amrita Pritam helped her to make that journey into exile across the border.[6] In Delhi, she took up academic affiliations: first as poet-in-residence at the Jamia Millia Islamia, and second as senior research fellow at Jawaharlal Nehru University. Here she lived in exile until 1987, producing another two volumes of poetry and her vision in prose of a new Pakistani literary culture, entitled *Pakistan: Literature and Society*, in 1986.[7] This thought-provoking study focused on the marginalized provincial literary traditions of Sindhi, Punjabi, Balochi and Pashto in Pakistan. The book critiqued the idea of a singular national literature and community by drawing attention to the plural tradition of regional literatures.[8] A strong believer in a global and local woman's movement, in 1987 she also started a women's publishing house as an NGO by the name of Wada (Women and Development Association) in Karachi.[9] On her return to Karachi, the political tide had turned, with Benazir Bhutto's first government in power, and she joined the editorial team of the national English daily the *Frontier Post*. She would go on to serve as the director for the National Book Council of Pakistan in Islamabad for a year. Her prose work entitled *Zinda bahar: ek safarnama – ek naval* (Living Spring: A Travelogue – A Novel), a travel narrative based on her trip to Bangladesh, was published in 1996 and the novel *Karachi* in 1998.[10] From 2009 to 2011 she was the chief editor for the Urdu Dictionary Board, an official project of the Ministry of Education.

Riaz's body of work ranges across different forms incorporating ghazals, prose poems, novels, essays and columns, displaying concerns beyond state and nation, as well as women-only politics. She was a supporter of secularism, a critic of neoliberalism and guided in her philosophic thinking by socialist beliefs as well as an Islamic ethics. Her literary influences drew on a worldly heritage, from the philosophy of Taoism to the teachings of Hafiz to Neruda. Her short fiction ranges from stories of magical mythical women such as Akhit Jadoo to ethnographic tales of her encounters with Balochi protagonists.[11] She forayed into the genre of the novella with *Godavri*, a multilayered text influenced by Dharmananda Damodar Kosambi's study of Indian society. Set at the time of the Bombay riots in 1992, the novel offers insights into the politics of the subaltern Adivasi community interspersed with the story of a married couple.[12] Strong multilingual Indic and Islamicate attachments are hallmarks of her philosophic outlook and aesthetic style. Across her Urdu volumes of poetry there is a noticeable shift from the lyrical romance-laden language of a hopeful young girl who thinks 'dunya kitni hasin hai' (the world is beautiful) to the stripped-down prose poem in which she articulates her commitment to writing 'barud ka git' (a song of explosives), marked by her desperation and isolation after fleeing Pakistan because of sedition charges by the state. Later her love of poetry revives with a return to the spiritual world of Rumi and Shams of Tabriz through her book of translation, *Ye Khana-e Aab-o gil* (The House of Water and Clay).[13] In 2007, a major life-changing incident was the tragic and accidental death by drowning of her young son Kabeer, while he was studying for an MA in the United States.[14] His death drew her back to poetry and she published a collection of poems entitled *Tum Kabir…* in his memory.[15] Her final creative endeavour was a philosophic novel, *Qila-e Faramoshi*, dedicated to the story of Mazdak, a revolutionary figure in fifth-century Persia whose interpretation of Zoroastrianism has been described as communistic.¹⁶ More recently, she joined the world of social media through her Facebook account and was active on it until 2017 when her health began to deteriorate. She died in 2019.

Her poetry manifests conflicted national formations during a period of neoliberal economic growth in the 1980s and an Islamic socialist agenda in 1960s and 1970s Pakistan. Writing and publishing as a Marxist in conflict-ridden times, her poetry and prose documented the increased polarization of gender identities under neoliberalism and Islamism, seeking social justice. Although a self-proclaimed atheist, she was empathetic to religion and looked to the Sufi tradition to enhance her understanding of the universe. Riaz's life as a divorced woman who married again may have raised a few eyebrows but the real challenge came from the content of her writing, her political affiliations and representations of women in sacred discourse. Her poetic voice upset the conformity expected from women in poetry circles. The journalist Raza Rumi describes her as a 'woman who has always been true to herself, fearless and outspoken with cavil' whose life was full of contradictions, from living a middle-class life to working with landless peasants in Sindh.¹⁷

In this chapter, I wish to argue that Fahmida Riaz's writing inspires a new secular–sacred perspective that draws on feminist and Marxist thought, tempered by a spiritual outlook. She articulates a gendered identity that is rooted in imaginations of culture and language beyond the nation. The multi-ethnic city of Karachi is a place that is central to her work and her sensibility. Its cultural and natural environment, class and sectarian differences are part of her oeuvre. Speaking truth to power as an editor of a political Urdu magazine in Karachi, she was forced into exile by the Pakistani deep state's surveillance of her journalistic endeavours. Her passage to India in the 1980s attracted labels of antinationalism but it has always been her writing about women's sexual desire that has earned her the greatest notoriety. Her gender politics structure the poems in her controversial collection *Badan darida*. She speaks vehemently about a personal and collective desire to transform social norms, and the deep need to actively challenge the perception that her writing is merely obscene and shocking. In other words, penning a radical poem such as 'Zabanon ka bosa' (The Tongues That Kissed) was a necessary act, signalling integrity both personal and political. She courted controversy amongst an elite Urdu literati by projecting the voice of a sexually liberated, individual poet-narrator, determined to prove that women's self-esteem as creative artists or as citizens need not be reliant on social constructions of gender enshrined in linguistic tropes of honour and shame. Through her prose she attempted to demystify perceptions attached to her as a woman poet, a political activist and a working professional. But her reputation as a rebel meant that the gatekeepers of a polite Urdu literary culture kept her at arm's length. Both her public and personal life presented stark differences to the domesticated ashraf family ideal for women. Her poetry pushed the limits of a genteel language, inflecting it with earthy organic expressions and experiences unique to women. Mohammad Khalid Akhtar predicted in 1966 that Riaz would in time become a renowned national poet but despite multiple awards it is still questionable whether she has achieved this status.[18] She was awarded the Hellman-Hammet grant for her resistance writing from Human Rights Watch in 1987 in recognition of her political persecution by the Zia regime. The Qatari Al-Muftah Award gave her recognition for her poetry in 2009. In 2010, she received the Sheikh Ayaz Literary Award from the Sindh government and the Sitara-e imtiaz (Pride of Performance) award from the government of Pakistan.

Despite the scope and range of her work, Riaz confessed that she never felt accepted in Pakistan because of how certain labels were attached to her persona, such as 'whorish' and 'a striptease'.[19] Anita Anantharam has analysed the 'erotics and poetics of the body' as a means of decoding Fahmida Riaz's poetry alongside her contemporaries in Urdu and Hindi.[20] In contrast, through selected readings of her biography, poetry and critical responses to her work, this chapter considers how she disrupted Urdu poetry's safe passage on sexualities in Pakistan. In Riaz's oeuvre, there is no room for the quietist sharif middle-class woman. Throughout her career, given a volatile reception from her peers, Riaz often looked for inspiration beyond national borders and she found it in global and Islamicate connections – for instance, the Iranian poet Forough Farrokhzad whose poetry outraged the Iranian establishment with its 'unorthodox convictions',[21] and at other times the poets Fariduddin Attar, Jalaluddin Rumi, Shah Abdul Latif Bhitai, Shaikh Ayaz, Naguib Mahfouz and Attiya Dawood. They were her favoured muses, some of whom she translated. Her exploration with the formal structures of Urdu is noticeable in her early poetry, which is attuned to the ghazal and autobiographical expression, both reviving a nostalgic mood of metaphorical storytelling and a global Islamic feminist aesthetic reflected in an altered metrical form and new symbolism. She chose to emphasize the *azad nazm* (free verse) and *nazm-e muarra* (blank verse) styles, attaching herself to modernity through her deployment of form.[22] Her poetic voice retains a lyricality that is reminiscent of Faiz and, similar to his trajectory, she remains a deeply political poet. Over time, she came to feel that the form of the ghazal was no longer an appropriate medium, given how long it took to compose. This disengagement can be seen in the noticeable shift toward prose in the latter half of her career, indicating a preference for a quicker means of production and communication.[23] It also reflects her desire to write realist prose fiction as a microcosm of a conflict-ridden city and nation, wearily retreating from the metaphorical world of ghazal poetry.

Protest, Activism and Radical Writing

During her exile in India, Fahmida Riaz wrote a letter to the prime minister of Pakistan on 27 July 1987, protesting against the heavy-handed treatment that had led to her and her husband's forced exile:

> Our case is a classic example of the unabashed victimisation and vindictiveness [of army rule]. I am a poet, committed to my people. The journal *Awaz* that I edited and published had no affiliation with any political party. My husband, Zafar Ali Ujjan, is a devoted political cadre of Pakistan People's Party; since 1978 he has been working for the ideals of his party. However, *Awaz* always provided a forum for all shades of opinions representing the democratic struggle, and we are genuinely proud of having done our duty in face of extreme hardships.
>
> The Home Department of Sindh Government, at the instance [sic] of the rulers in Islamabad, made every effort to suppress and stifle our journal. Notices imposing fines to the tune of thousands of rupees were issued frequently, and Ferozabad police station officials conducted house search on several occasions to harass and intimidate us. […] After failing in these attempts, the regime then implicated me in false cases, one of them under Section 124-A (Sedition) of Criminal Procedure Code in the court of the District Magistrate South, Karachi, and another, under 116 Press and Publication Maintenance Order of 1962 in the court of Assistant Commissioner, South Karachi. To avoid arrest under Section 124-A, I had to bail myself prior to arrest. For the whole year of 1980, and for three months of 1981, the undersigned was made to face the miserable drama of being continuously summoned to the court where no hearing would ever be held. Officials in the court only smiled and told me quietly that since it was a fake case, the question of a hearing

does not arise, and if I 'behave' myself and seek audience with some military official in Islamabad, the files of my cases would be quietly 'buried', and the police would not harass me any longer; otherwise my bail would be cancelled at any time. [...] After the proclamation of the PCO that completely suppressed the judiciary, we had no choice but to seek shelter elsewhere. The Sindh Government reportedly declared me a fugitive. In the last five years, wild and unfounded allegations against me and my husband have been deliberately spread through a section of the press.[24]

Riaz's letter documents a close link with the People's Party of Pakistan and altercations with the military. It is testimony to how the deep state responded to critical journalistic interventions that challenged an authoritarian political infrastructure, and the imbrication of the justice system and the media in its power networks. She voices the lack of freedom of speech and how the forces of civil society were deployed by the military state to curb criticism and differences of opinion. In doing so, she gave evidence of how much the military regime feared opposition. Riaz also notes how the press worked in collusion with the state to frame a particular narrative about her, compounded by inefficiencies in the justice system, ensuring the supremacy of the army over civil society. The letter is a protest, noting how censorship and the law are brought together by the state to close down civil liberties, and a critique of the state.

Riaz's key inspiration for radical writing was the Progressive Writers' movement yet, while she was an admirer of the Progressives for opening up the secluded sphere for women, she was also aware of the peripheral role accorded to them within the movement and her writing directly confronted their conservative stance concerning sexualities. This detachment is important to note given her political affiliation as an activist in the Democratic Women's Federation, the Women's Wing of the Communist Party of Pakistan. The experience of Communist activism with a women-only group was marked by frustration because, in her words, 'women's organizations do not support women writers'.[25] Her feeling as an outsider was compounded by exclusions in creative writing circles. Reflecting on her personal experience of being othered, she says that the rejection made her question whether Progressivism had any commitment to gender equality: 'Politically progressive people had no understanding of women's situation, and I decided that if they don't accept me, I don't accept them. I wrote a poem entitled *Raj singhasan* (The Ruling Throne) as my response to them.'[26]

راج سنگھاسن

انقلاب کی راج سنگھاسن پر براجتے گنوانو......
تم کیا دو گے گیان مجھے!
مجھ کو سیدھی راہ دکھانے والو
اتنا پہچانو
تم کرسی پر بیٹھے ہو
اور مَیں دھرتی پر کھڑی ہوئی ہوں

اپنے راجیہ مندر کی چوکھٹ سے مجھ کو لوٹاتے ہو؟
میری تھالی میں تو میرے گرم لہو کا دیپ جلا ہے
دل کو کوری مٹی سے جو پھوٹا ہے وہ پھول کھلا ہے
تم کیا دو گے گیان
سنبھالو اپنے شوالے
شاستروں کو رٹ رٹ کر جو تم نے جیون بھر میں نہ سیکھا
وہ اِک ناری نے اپنے گھائل تن میں محسوس کیا ہے

Inqilab ke raj singhasan par barajte gunwano…
Tum kya do ge gyan mujhe!
Mujh ko sidhi rah dikhane valo
Itna pehchano
Tum kursi par bethe ho
Aur men dharti par khari hui hun

Apne rajia mandir ki chokhat se mujh ko lotate ho?
Meri thali men to mere garam lahu ka dip jala hai

Dil ki kori mitti se jo phuta hai voh phul khila hai
Tum kya do ge gyan
Sambhalo apne shivale
Shastron ko rat rat kar jo tum ne jeevan bhar men na sikha
Vo ik nari ne apne ghayal tun me mehsus kiya hai

[O beneficiaries residing on the ruling throne of revolution …
What intelligence will you bestow upon me
You who lead me on the righteous path

Know this
You are seated on the chair
And I am stood on the ground

Now you turn me away as I stand poised on the threshold of your
   temple's kingdom?
My body has burned with the hot blood of revolution
Resistance has blossomed into a flower erupting from the ashes of
   my heart

What intelligence will you bestow upon me
Take care of your Shiva's temple

That which you could not learn by reciting scriptures all your life
That a woman has felt in her stricken body][27]

In this poem, Riaz dons the classical mantle of a lover spurned by his beloved and, contrary to the love lyric's theme of the lover's annihilation upon rejection, she subverts the poetic mood by returning the beloved's rejection with interest and by voicing her dissatisfaction. The abundant use of classical metaphors (such as the candle, rose, temple) and reference to Indic scriptures is deliberate and ironic, critiquing the double standards in poetry circles that celebrate male revolutionary poets and their attachment to socialism, but don't extend the same recognition to women. She echoes the language of Faiz in her transformative representation of the classical beloved, and at the same time she exposes the failure of that language to accommodate a free expression of desire. Fahmida accuses the Progressives of harbouring a hypermasculinity that is Shiva-like in its destructive power and without the love of Parvati. To fully appreciate her response, it is important to mention that the Progressives were excluding her because one of her poems, entitled 'Zabanon ka bosa', stepped beyond the limits of sharafat with its erotic expression of romance through the act of intimate kissing and personification of a female voice:

زبانوں کا بوسہ

زبانوں کے رس میں یہ کیسی مہک ہے!
یہ بوسہ کہ جس سے محبت کی صہبا کی اڑتی ہے خوشبو
یہ بدمست خوشبو جو گہرا غنودہ نشہ لا رہی ہے
یہ کیسا نشہ ہے!
مرے ذہن کے ریزے ریزے میں ایک آنکھ سی کھل گئی ہے
تم اپنی زباں مرے منہ میں رکھے جیسے پاتال سے میری جاں کھینچتے ہو
یہ بھیگا ہوا گرم و تاریک بوسہ
اماوس کی کالی برستی ہوئی رات جیسے اُمڈتی چلی آ رہی ہے
کہیں کوئی ساعت ازل سے رمیدہ
مری روح کے دشت میں اُڑ رہی تھی
وہ ساعت قریں تر چلی آ رہی ہے
مجھے ایسا لگتا ہے
تاریکیوں کے
لرزتے ہوئے پل کو
میں پار کرتی چلی جا رہی ہوں
یہ پل ختم ہونے کو ہے
اور اب
اُس کے آگے
کہیں روشنی ہے

Tum apni zabaan mere mun men rakhe jaise pataal se meri jaan khenchte ho
Ye bhiga hua garm-o tarik bosa
Amawas ki kali barasti hui rat jaise umadti chali a rahi hai
Kahin koi saat azl se rasida
Meri ruh ke dasht men ur rahi thi
Voh saat qarin tar chali aa rahi hai

[When you put your tongue in my mouth, it is as if you're dragging my soul from an abyss
This warm wet and bleak kiss
Feels like the rapid advance of a black night before a full moon

As if a moment before the beginning of time
Was floating free in the jungle of my soul]²⁸

Her explicit description of sexual desire has a shocking quality, articulating desire in a tone that is considered vulgar, expressing content that is taboo in literary representations. In the unspoken code of ethics observed by the gatekeepers of Urdu literary culture in Pakistan, normative representations of sharif women in the national archive were paramount and Riaz's intervention was a provocation in the face of convention. The Progressives, who had an oppositional relationship with the state because of left politics at the time of Partition, found little advantage in including such voices in their altered liberal and patriotic positionalities. There was no official body to support Riaz's radical representation and instead her poem rekindled a historic disassociation from taboo topics with its expression of women's sexual pleasure. For the poet, there was more to the poem than just an expression of the body. This can be gauged from the ending of the poem that hints at a journey beyond sensuality.

Mujhe aisa lagta hai
Tarikion ke
Larazte hue pul ko
main par karti chali ja rahi hun
Ye pul khatm hone ko hai
Aur ab
Us ke age
Kahin roshni hai

[It seems as if
I am crossing the rickety bridge of desolation
And am nearly at the end
And now
Ahead of it
Somewhere there is light]²⁹

The ending of the poem is punctuated by darkness and loneliness and the poet-narrator expresses a desire for hope and light at the end of the tunnel. It is useful to contrast the frank mood of this poem with 'Jhijhak' (Hesitation), an understated example from her first volume of poetry, a collection that was characterized by a romantic tone and a young self hidden in silences. 'Jhijhak' is a precursor to her later, more explicit enunciations of the body:

یہ میری سوچ کی اَن جان، کنواری لڑکی
غیر کے سامنے کچھ کہنے سے شرماتی ہے
اپنی مبہم سی عبارت کے دوپٹے میں چھپی
سر جھکائے ہوئے، کترا کے نکل جاتی ہے

Ye meri soch ki anjan kanwari larki
Ghair ke samne kuch kahne se sharmati hai
Apni mabham si ibarat ke dopatte men chupi
Sar jhukae hue, katra ke nikl jati hai

[This unaware unmarried girl, a figment of my imagination
Shies away from speaking in front of strangers
Hiding in the foggy narrative of her veil
Head bowed, she recoils and slips out][30]

The poet-narrator writes about a girl who hesitates to speak. This 'unaware unmarried girl' is a key and recurring figure, who can be read as a symbolic representation of an experiential part of girls' lives in the subcontinent – they are rewarded for being silent and demure while being nurtured for arranged marriages and very rigid ideas of femininity. She is a shadowy preoccupation on the fringes of the poet-narrator's consciousness, but unable to be represented through language. The poet writes about her as an absent presence, visible through her body but absent in speech. Through this representation, Riaz can be seen to be critically responding to the social gaze, evident in linguistic and textual monologues shaping public opinion, that positions women in cameo roles and imagines their 'reality' for them.[31] Her use of language to express silences and absence of the girl from discourse is a declaration of her philosophy at this early stage where truth is not hidden in transcendental meaning and silences convey alternative possibilities. The journey between the two poems shows a mind in distress, conflicted by alienation and looking for connections through the body as well as broader hermeneutic meanings.

Dissent and Intimacy in *Badan Darida* (The Body Torn)

Badan darida was published in 1973 and the poems were written over a period spanning the years 1968 to 1973, including the war of independence between

East Pakistan and West Pakistan that ended with the cessation of East Pakistan and the creation of an independent new nation, Bangladesh, in 1971. In her foreword to *Badan darida*, she shares the inspiration that guides her poetic journey:

> Darasal shair ek divar se apna sar phorta hua khud kalami karta hai. Is aml men sirf us ka apna mukammal wajud shamil hai. Us ka damaghi aur jazbati wajud, jise us ki ruh ne aisa ghera hai jaise samundar ka pani kisi jazeere ko gherta hai. Us ki nazm parhne ya sunne vale is aml men kahin sharik nahin hote. Agar hote hain to sirf is had tak ke us ki ruh ki irtiqa men sare muashre ki akhlaqi iqdar hissa leti hen aur us ke uljhave in iqdar ke baham takrao aur tazad ka natija hote hain.

> [Actually the poet by banging her/his head against the wall is speaking to himself [*sic*]. This action involves her/his entire being only. Her/his mental and emotional state is dominated by her/his spirit like the sea which surrounds an island. Those reading or listening to the poet's *nazm* are in no way shareholders of her/his thoughts. If they are present then only to the extent in which all of society's behavioural characteristics contribute to the poet's spiritual ascendancy, and her/his enigmas result from the clash and opposition of wills.][32]

She speaks of the drive that motivates her as a creative artist, a quest for finding the self. The listener, she argues, cannot experience that struggle and can only be a witness to the stories narrated. External forces in the form of society are reflected in the poet's ethical stance, which is arrived at by a constant clash and opposition of ideas. For Riaz, questions of context are important and she confirms that 'meri shairi men metaphysical notions nahin hain' (there are no metaphysical notions in my poetry).[33] There is instead an existential dialogue with the permanent unbridgeable gap between the self that is known and the self that is unknown. Writing openly and frankly, she acknowledges that 'some people are very opposed to some of the topics included, they are of the opinion that these are obscene and have been written with the aim to offend'.[34]

To justify her stance, Riaz deliberately interjects a poet persona that is the antithesis of the sharif woman with poems such as 'Mere aur tumhare bich' (Between You and Me), 'Bakira' (Virgin), 'Lao hath apna lao zara' (Come, Please Give Me Your Hand), 'Kab tak' (Until When), 'Badan darida' (The Body Torn), 'Zabanon ka bosa' (The Kissing of Tongues), 'Rajam' (Stoning), 'Aqlima' and 'Voh ek zan-e napak hai' (She Is an Impure Woman).[35] Emphasizing female sexuality and spirituality, she offers a new aesthetics of the female body that appears to combine the *jouissance* of French feminism with historical materialism tempered by folk influences and global connections.[36] The compilation inspired tributes from her fellow feminist activists in Pakistan.[37]

If we consider the opening poem of *Badan darida*, 'Tasvir' (Image), it takes us back to the 'unaware girl' of her first volume, *Pathar ki zaban*. It is clear that a transformation has taken place culturally and linguistically in how the female form is imagined and represented in this collection. The 'unaware girl' of *Pathar ki zaban* now has a sense of that 'foggy' inner self that does not correspond to societal conventions and bears little resemblance to the persona that is recognized by friends:

تصویر

مرے دل کے نہاں خانے میں اک تصویر ہے میری
خدا جانے اُسے کس نے بنایا، کب بنایا تھا
یہ پوشیدہ ہے میرے دوستوں سے اور مجھ سے بھی
کبھی بھولے سے لیکن میں اُسے گر دیکھ لیتی ہوں
اُسے خود سے ملاؤں تو مرا دل کانپ جاتا ہے

Mere dil ke nihan khane men ik tasvir hai meri
Khuda jane use kis ne banaya, kab banaya tha
Ye poshida hai mere doston se aur mujh se bhi
Kabhi bhule se lekin men use gar dekh leti hun
Use khud se milaon to mera dil kamp jata hai

[Buried deep in my heart is a picture of myself
God knows who made it and when it was made
It is hidden from my friends and from me too
Sometimes, but absentmindedly if I do manage to see it
And compare it with my self then my heart shivers][38]

On being questioned about the meaning of the poem, Riaz confesses that the image which the poet-narrator's heart holds of herself is very different from her actual self – she has been unable to reach her inner soul.[39] As a result, the self she projects is inauthentic. The bearer of the false identity is made conscious of her duplicity when her guard slips and the knowledge of this split persona makes her uncomfortable and is disquieting for the reader. What the poet-narrator intimates is that, as a woman, she is playing a double role, performing a conformist identity to family and friends, yet inside is a silent visual wasteland that is buried in the unknown depths of her soul.[40] The poem raises many unanswered questions with its articulation of a hidden othered self, suggestive of the directions that Riaz's poetry would take over time, deploying traditional form and radical content to make known the subjectivities of the unknown self. Similar to her Progressive contemporaries, this was an expression of modernism but inflected with a woman's perspective.

As the volume progresses, a distinctive voice begins to emerge, reflecting a new dialogue between feminist-led Marxist thinking and Islamic ethics. The poem 'Bakira' (Virgin) sets the tone for this. It renders in verse the ritual of animal sacrifice from Islamic theology, and uses it as a satirical yet metaphoric reference to the religio-cultural community's investment in women's virginity:

باکرہ

آسماں تپتے ہوئے لوہے کی مانند سفید
ریگ سوکھی ہوئی پیاسے کی زباں کے مانند
پیاس حلقوم میں ہے، جسم میں ہے، جان میں ہے

سر بہ زانو ہوں، جھلستے ہوئے ریگستاں میں
تیری سرکار میں لے آئی ہوں یہ وحشِ ذبیح!
مجھ پہ لازم تھی جو قربانی وہ مَیں نے کر دی

اُس کی اُبلی ہوئی آنکھوں میں ابھی تک ہے چمک
اور سیہ بال ہیں بھیگے ہوئے خوں سے اب تک
تیرا فرمان یہ تھا اس پہ کوئی داغ نہ ہو
سو یہ بے عیب اچھوتا بھی تھا ان دیکھا بھی
بے کراں ریگ میں سب گرم لہو جذب ہوا
دیکھ چادر پہ مری ثبت ہے اس کا دھبا
اے خداوندِ کبیر
اے جبار!
متکبر و جلیل!
ہاں ترے نام پڑھے اور کیا ذبح اسے

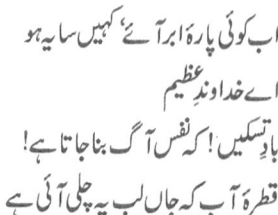

Aasman, tapte lohe ki manind safaid
Raig sukhi hui pyase ki zaban ke manind
Pyas halqum men hai, jism men hai, jan men hai

Sar bezanu hun, jhulste hue registan men
Teri Sarkar men le ai hun ye vahsh zabih!
Mujh pe lazim thi jo qurbani voh main ne kar di

Us ki ubli hui ankhon men abhi tak hai
    chamak
Aur siyah bal hain bhige hue khun se ab tak
Tera farman ye tha is pe koi dagh na ho
So ye be-aib achuta bhi tha un dekha bhi
Bekaran reg main sab garm lahu jazb hua
Dekh chador pe meri sabt hai us ka dhabba
Ae khudavand Kabir
Ae Jabbar!
Mutakabbir o jalil!
Han tere nam parhe aur kiya zibah ise
Ab koi para-e abr ae, kahin saya ho
Ae khudavand-e azim
Bad-e taskin! Ke nafs aag bana jata hai!
Qatra-e ab ke jan lab pe chali ai hai

[Sky white, like overheated iron
Sand like parched thirsty tongue
Thirst is in the throat, in the body, in the soul

In this burning desert, my head is bowed
I have brought this frightful slaughter in your service!
That sacrifice to which I was bound, I have done

There is still a sparkle in those bulging eyes
And even now the black hair is soaked in blood
Your command was that there be no stain on it
Therefore this innocent was untouched too and unseen too
Endless sand absorbed all pulsating blood
Look my veil carries the seal of its stain
O *Khudavand-e kabir* (Great God)
O *Jabbar* (Omnipotent)!
Mutakabbir-o jalil (Proud and illustrious)!
Yes I recited your names and slit its throat
Now if only a cloudy fragment would appear, shade be found somewhere
O *Khudavand-e azim* (Almighty God)
The breeze of fulfilment! the soul is on fire!
A drop of water for my heart is in my mouth][41]

With its citation of several of the 99 names of God and its enactment of the ritual of sacrifice, this poem sarcastically renders the story of Abrahamic sacrifice through a female voice. The gender of the story's protagonist is made evident to the reader/listener in the second line of the second stanza with its feminine verb endings in Urdu: 'teri sarkar men le **ai** hun ye vahsh zabih!' (I have brought this frightful slaughter in your service!). Similarly the victim is given a male voice: 'so ye beaib achhuta bhi **tha** undekha bhi' (therefore this innocent was untouched too and unseen too). These are deliberate inversions of gender, deploying the ritual of animal sacrifice in religious tradition as metaphor. The Qur'anic story of sacrificial slaughter in the way of God is reimagined with the protagonist as a woman who has made the necessary sacrifice of her body. If we substitute the father with the mother in the poem's inference of the ritual then the person who has led her daughter to slaughter is the mother. But in this case, there is no godly intervention that rescues her daughter from the butchery of her virginal body. Instead, she counters the wrath of the beast who attacks her by slaughtering him in turn. The feral wild beast is visualized through his piercing bulging eyeballs that gleam and his black hair, we are told, is soaked in wet blood. As readers we don't know whose blood this refers to. The woman who has committed the sacrifice to attain social approval gives her evidence to God by showing the bloodstain on her veil, a classic sign of virginal penetration on the wedding night. She now seeks forgiveness from God for her act of slaughter to save her own life.

The imagery of the poem – the intense heat of the desert, the body ravaged by physical and spiritual thirst – mimics the landscape of Hijaz, Arabia and the deserts of Sindh in Pakistan. Readers of the classical Urdu *marsiya* may also note the similarities between the mood of martyrdom in this poem and the sensibility of the elegiac form.[42] The lone woman wandering the desert with a slaughtered virgin can be read as a representation from the historical incident at Karbala, recalling the strong-willed daughter of Muhammad, Fatima, and her martyred son, Husain, the Prophet's grandson.[43] In the poem, the protagonist confirms that she is the co-conspirator in her daughter's limited fate as virgin and looks for solace in sacred duty as the moral reason for her act of betrayal.

The latter half of the poem unfolds as an awakening of the conscience. It is a scenario that takes place after the sacrifice has been performed between God and the slayer of the virgin. This recalls the questioning stance of Muhammad Iqbal, and his Miltonic equivocation between man and God in his controversial poem *Shikwa* (Complaint).[44] We can detect a similar yet extremely divergent search between duty and selfhood in Fahmida's poetic voice for women. The last two lines of the poem – 'The breeze of fulfilment! the soul is on fire! / A drop of water for my heart is in my mouth' – rest with the subjective persona of the virgin-slayer, whom we first met in the second stanza with her bowed head and sacrificial offering. The female protagonist of her poem, who has performed the duty of sacrifice and submission that is usually undertaken by men, is questioning the lack of spiritual relief she feels from enacting this merciless obligation.[45] Riaz's style is purposely constructed using Qur'anic references and mixing them with her own commentary. This critical voice sometimes questions the absolutism of faith and at other times expounds it. Altogether she is creating a space for self-criticism and self-analysis for female subjectivities in her poetry.

Another reading of the poem that lends itself is the context of a national allegory.[46] 'Bakira' can be read similarly to the way in which Mahasweta Devi's 'Douloti the Bountiful' is sacrificed on the altar of Indian nationalism as a victim of sexual violence. The comparison also allows for a deeper analysis of class and indigeneity when it comes to the unnamed woman, reflective of Riaz's interest in anthropology.[47] Given that *Badan darida* was published in 1973 and the poems were written over a period spanning the years 1968 to 1973, we can also read 'Bakira' as a symbolic poem giving voice to victims of the sexual violence that took place during East Pakistan's war of independence against the incursions by the West Pakistani army. The seal of blood on the veil can be read as a metaphorical reference to the bloodshed and rape experienced by civilians in East Pakistan, now Bangladesh, and its untold story in West Pakistan.

From sexual violence, sacrifice and duty, Riaz draws the reader's focus to the theme of women's difference in the forceful poem that addresses the topic of women's unequal representation in religious discourse, 'Aqlima'. This poem protests against gender discrimination based on biological sexual difference:

اقلیما
جو ہابیل کی قابیل کی ماں جائی ہے
ماں جائی
مگر مختلف
مختلف بیچ میں رانوں کے
اور پستانوں کے اُبھار میں
اور اپنے پیٹ کے اندر
اپنی کوکھ میں
ان سب کی قسمت کیوں ہے
اِک فربہ بھیڑ کے بچے کی قربانی

وہ اپنے بدن کی قیدی
تپتی ہوئی دھوپ میں جلتے
ٹیلے پر کھڑی ہوئی ہے
پتھر پر نقش بنی ہے
اس نقش کو غور سے دیکھو
لمبی رانوں سے اُوپر
اُبھرے پستانوں سے اُوپر
پیچیدہ کوکھ سے اُوپر
اقلیما کا سر بھی ہے
اللہ کبھی اقلیما سے بھی کلام کرے
اور کچھ پوچھے !

Aqlima
Jo habil ki qabil ki ma jai hai
ma jai
magar mukhtalif

mukhtalif bich men ranon ke
aur pustanon ke ubhar men
aur apne pet ke andar
apni kukh men
in sab ki qismat kyun hai
ik farba bher ke bache ki qurbani
voh apne badan ki qaidi
tapti hui dhup men jalte
tile par khari hui hai
pathar par naqsh bani hai
is naqsh ko ghor se dekho
lambi ranon se upar
ubharte pustanon se upar
pechida kukh se upar
Aqlima ka sar bhi hai
Allah kabhi Aqlima se bhi kalam kare
aur kuch puche!

[Aqlima
Who is the sister of Cain and Abel
Their sister
But different

Different in the middle of her thighs
And in the swell of her breasts
And inside her stomach
In her womb
Why is the fate of all these
The sacrifice of one stout lamb

She is the prisoner of her body
Burning in the scorching sun
Standing on a mound
Etched in rock
Look carefully at this sculpture

Above the long thighs
Above the protruding breasts
Above the ravelled womb
Aqlima has a head as well
Sometimes Aqlima too should be spoken to by Allah
And asked something!]⁴⁸

Riaz uses a prosaic style to introduce the subject of her oral history, Aqlima. Deploying the third-person voice, the poet narrates Aqlima's history as one that is marked by difference. This difference is visibly noted in the 'swell of her breasts', her 'ravelled womb' and her long thighs, with the narrator protesting at those bodily differences as markers of her imprisonment. The inference is that these parts of Aqlima's body mark her as the second sex, whose story has to take a back seat to that of Cain and Abel because her persona is only constructed in and around her body and not through her intellect. In the poem, she makes a direct plea to God to address Aqlima as someone who thinks rather than just feels. It is an important inversion of body politics in Urdu literature that puts women at the centre of the narrative. Her plea is contained within the landscape of a burning desert, reconstructing the homeland of Islam and offering a different ideal, that of an alternate Hijaz with a woman at its centre. For the poet, Aqlima is the unclaimed sister of Cain and Abel. The story of the two brothers, a part of Hebrew mythology, is common to the Abrahamic faiths – Judaism, Christianity and Islam.[49] Adding Aqlima's story to the sacred story of Cain and Abel establishes the importance and necessity of women's herstories to sacred narratives.[50]

Staying with the sacred theme but speaking biographically is her poem 'Sura-e yasin'. It is a reflection from Riaz's life in London, an unfamiliar city with a spatial geography that unnerves her in the dark. She draws on a sacred theme of security and safety from the Qur'an to protect herself from danger. Is home an imagined place in her mind? And will she ever find it? are questions that linger in the narration of her poem. It captures her mental state of unbelonging and unhappiness at the time. She bridges two worlds in this poem, a spiritual one that gives her protection and solace and the temporal one where she is located. The spiritual context connects her to the East and the material to the West. She is unable to find a position of comfort between the two. Her pessimism colours the ending of the poem, making for uncomfortable reading.

سورۂ یاسین

یہ آخر شب کا سناٹا!
اس نیم اندھیرے رستے پر
جلدی میں قدم بڑھاتی ہوئی
مَیں ایک اکیلی عورت ہوں
بڑی دیر سے میرے تعاقب میں
اک چاپ ہے جو چلی آتی ہے
گھر.....!
میرا گھر.....!
مَیں اپنے گھر کیسے پہنچوں
سوکھے حلقوم اور بیٹھتے دل سے سوچتی ہوں
شاید مَیں رستہ بھول گئی
یہ راہ تو میری راہ نہیں
اس راہ سے مَیں کب گزری تھی
سب گلیوں پر یہاں نام لکھے
اس گلی پہ کوئی نام نہیں
اور دُور دُور تک دَم سادھے
یہ سارے گھر انجانے ہیں
لو پیلے چاند کا ٹکڑا بھی

کالے پتوں میں ڈوب گیا
اب کچھ بھی نہیں
بس میرے منہ میں خوف سے بھاری اور مفلوج زباں ہے
یا
تلووں سے اُوپر چڑھتی ہوئی
میرے انگ انگ میں رچی ہوئی
اِک خنکی ہے

Ye akhir shab ka sannata!
Is nim andhere raste par
Jaldi men qadam barhati hui
Main ek akeli aurat hun
Bari der se mere taqub men
Ik chap hai jo chali ati hai
Ghar–!
Mera ghar–!
Men apne ghar kaise puhnchun
Sukhe halqum aur bethte dil se sochti hun
Shaid men rasta bhul gai
Ye rah to meri rah nahin
Is rah se men kab guzri thi
Sab galiyon par yahan nam likhe
Is gali pe koi nam nahin
Aur dur dur tak dam sadhe
Ye sare ghar anjane hain
Lo pile chand ka tukra bhi
Kale paton men dub gaya
Ab kuch bhi nahin
Bas mere mun men khauf se bhari aur mafluj zaban hai
Ya
Talon se upar charhti hui
Mere ang ang men rachi hui
Ik khunki hai.

[The eerie lull of twilight!
On this nearly dark road
Hurriedly increasing my pace
I am one lone woman
Following me for a long time
Is the sound of footsteps coming my way

Home – !

My home – !

How will I reach my home
I wonder with parched throat and sinking heart
Perhaps I forgot the way
This route is not my route
When did I pass this way
All the street names here are displayed
This street does not have its name displayed
Far and wide holding their breath
All these unknown houses
Lo, the yellow crescent moon too
Has sunk behind black leaves
Now there is nothing
Except in my mouth a fear burdened and paralysed tongue
Or
Creeping upwards from my soles
Saturated in my every pore
Is a chill.][51]

The title of the poem refers to the 36th Sura of the Qur'an and is from the Prophet Muhammad's early-middle Makki period. It is believed to contain all the essentials of revelation and is particularly recited for the dead (recalling Matthew 25:21), and also to aid the recovery of the sick.[52] Riaz has reproduced some of the imagery in this poem from the original Sura, such as the night obliterating the daylight. There is also an ominous foregrounding of death. The Sura is associated with the spiritual power of healing, and of safe passage into the next life and immortality for those who read it and for those for whom it is recited. It is about belief in the sovereignty of God, the right path offered by Prophet Muhammad and the Day of Judgement. It confronts the mockery of the Prophet by non-believers as a poet and reiterates the authenticity of his message. Although the poem never directly quotes from the Sura, the title and the mood of the poem encapsulate the period of twilight and the poet-narrator's search for home, the right path and the uncertainty of her faith that is unlikely to give her salvation. It is a material narration of an everyday spiritual connection that empowers and enables individuals to cope with worldly challenges.

Reflecting back on the poem, Riaz says that she wrote it as an expression of her feelings of alienation in foreign surroundings, when she made her way back home one night from the London Film School. It was a time of personal despair as her arranged marriage was making her deeply unhappy. The poem pessimistically reflects what death should feel like, hopeless with utter desolation, enveloped in darkness.[53] Her poet persona makes emphatic use of the first-person pronoun, *main* (I), in the third line of the poem. But this is not the ego of the poet; it is her bodily presence. She uses the imagery of twilight and darkness to emphasize the danger she feels, adding to her sense of having lost her way. Menace is exaggerated with the stealthy sound of echoing footsteps following her. Even the moonlight deserts her and the mood of the poem conveys impending doom in the last few lines with a wintry chill saturating her body. This is a poem about loss, alienation and loneliness.

While Riaz's voice conveys the existential distress of losing faith, there are other poems in the collection that express the celebration of love and desire. A poem that brought notoriety for its erotic tone and which provides a stark contrast to the spiritual theme is 'Lao, hath apna lao zara' (Come, Please Give Me Your Hand). Articulating an intimate moment between a pregnant woman and her lover, it openly expresses the need for touch and the first move comes from the female protagonist. In a culture that frowns upon women being active agents in the pursuit of love, this is a deliberate inversion that normalizes a desirous woman.

لاؤٗ ہاتھ اپنا لاؤ ذرا

لاؤٗ ہاتھ اپنا لاؤ ذرا
چھو کے میرا بدن
اپنے بچّے کے دل کا دھڑکنا سنو
ناف کے اس طرف
اس کی جنبش کو محسوس کرتے ہو تم؟
بس یہیں چھوڑ دو
تھوڑی دیر اور اس ہاتھ کو میرے ٹھنڈے بدن پر یہیں چھوڑ دو
میرے بے کل نفس کو قرار آ گیا
میرے عیسیٰ! مرے درد کے چارہ گر
میرا ہر موئے تن
اس ہتھیلی سے تسکین پانے لگا
اس ہتھیلی کے نیچے مرا لال کروٹ سی لینے لگا
انگلیوں سے بدن اس کا پہچان لو
تم اسے جان لو

چومنے دو مجھے اپنی یہ اُنگلیاں
اُن کی ہر پور کو چومنے دو مجھے
ناخنوں کو لبوں سے لگا لوں ذرا
اس ہتھیلی میں منہ تو چھپا لوں ذرا

Lao, hath apna lao zara
Chu ke mera badan
Apne bache ke dil ka dharakna suno
Naf ke is taraf
Is ki jumbish ko mehsus karte ho tum?
[…]
Tum ise jan lo
Chumne do mujhe apni ye unglian

Un ki har por ko chumne do mujhe
Nakhunon ko labon se laga lun zara
Is hatheli men mun to chupa lun zara
Phul lati hui ye hari unglian
Meri ankhon se ansu ubalte hue
In se senchun gi main
Phul lati hui unglion ki jaren. Chumne do mujhe
Apne bal, apne mathe ka chand, apne lab
Ye chamakti hui kali ankhen
Mere kampte hont, meri chalakti hui ankh ko dekh kar kitni hairan hain
Tum ko malum kya, tum ko malum kya
. . .
Tum ne andar mera is tarah bhar diya
Phutti hai mere jism se roshni
. . .
Sab muqaddas kitaben jo nazil huin
Sab payambar jo ab tak uttare gaye
. . .
Aj sab par mujhe
Aitebar aa gaya - Aitebar aa gaya

[Come, give me your hand
Touch my body
And listen to the beating of your child's heart
On that side of the navel
Can you feel it stirring?
[...]
Let your fingers know its body
Get to know it
Let me kiss these fingers of yours
Let me kiss each and every fingertip
Let me touch your nails with my lips
Let me hide my face in this palm for a bit
These green fingers which bring flowers
With the tears which bubble up in my eyes
I shall tend these
The roots of these fingers which bring flowers
Let me kiss them
The hair, the moon of your forehead, your lips
These shining black eyes,
So amazed to see my trembling lips and my brimming eye][54]

This poem was a cause of great controversy amongst her critics with its frank expression of desire. It led to her being ostracized as a writer who lacked quality and wrote for the purposes of titillation and shock.[55]

Riaz was actively changing the language of love in Urdu poetry and bringing women's sexual experiences to the forefront. The hierarchical world of Urdu poetry didn't quite know how to deal with this other than to write it off as attention-seeking. She confesses that Faiz too was shocked when she recited her poems to him. Her writing was influenced by transnational and worldly links and interests – for example, her open admiration for the feminist poetry of Forough Farrokhzad, the sensual verse of Pablo Neruda and the politics of D. H. Lawrence's *Sons and Lovers*. She was determined to communicate that no woman liked to write about sex for the sake of sex. Through her poems, she tries to convey an organic connection between lovers so that women and men feel emancipated and confident with intimacy, instead of having their sexual lives dictated by societal codes inhibiting and controlling sexual behaviour. Embedded in her poetry is a disregard for class aspirations.

This dissidence is present most noticeably and vehemently in the poem entitled 'Voh ek zan-e napak hai' (She Is a Woman Impure). This poem addresses the biological determination of gender – the physical process of menstruation marking puberty and the reproductive order of a woman's body. Riaz uses the Persian word *zan* with an *izafat* to emphasize her subject: the impure woman. The word *zan* contains a double meaning of 'woman' and 'being hit'.[56] This accentuates the duality of the imagery in the poem concerning the female body being hit by the monthly cycle of menstruation. In the poem, she highlights the taboo of purity and pollution in religious discourse, which excludes women during their menstrual period because of the shame attached to it. Riaz inscribes the menstruating impure female body into the sacred, making it critical to her intervention when it comes to the status of women in conventional Islamic discourse. Women's social alienation is one that takes place alongside impurity, defilement, as expressed by the word *napak* (impure) in the title. This is not just specific to Muslim societies, the anthropologist Mary Douglas has argued; when it comes to social constructions, 'purity is the enemy of change, of ambiguity and compromise' and dirt is conceptualized through material and symbolic associations, setting up a binary divide with cleanliness.[57] Drawing on African and Maori contexts, Douglas speaks of the associations of danger that are linked to menstrual blood. Douglas's broader distinction between ritual and disorder emphasizes social control in religious societies.[58] She contrasts how power operates in both secular and sacred contexts and how social structures respond to threats of disorder. It is Douglas's idea of social control that I'd like to draw on for my argument. Riaz is challenging this 'social control' through her representation of the 'uncontrolled' female body. Playing on the unknowability of the danger that is associated with such bodies, she demonstrates through her poem how religious discourse is used to disempower women.

Riaz's poem is also important as a social commentary on menstruation and women's bodies in a culture where there is mostly silence surrounding it. By speaking openly about it, she creates familiarity with a taboo topic and establishes a space for women to connect materially with their bodies. It is useful to compare her poetic intervention with an academic study by Patricia Jeffery, *Frogs in a Well*, that as part of its ethnography looks at the material effects of menstruation amongst the Pirzada women in India. Despite the stereotypical title of the book, Jeffery's work helps to illustrate the association of pollution with menstruation as a structural aspect of a specific Muslim group and how it also influences the further seclusion of women as secondary to men.[59] She remarks:

> Menstrual pollutions may be symbolic statements, of which two types seem particularly worth bearing in mind in relation to the *pirzada* women. On the one hand, they may assert male superiority, through the association of women with dirt and impurity. Secondly, menstrual pollutions may emphasize the separateness of male and female spheres, by limiting the intrusion of women into the affairs of men [...]. Degradation and separation both figure in the menstrual and post-partum pollutions of the *pirzada* women, and form an important part of their subordination.[60]

In contrast, Riaz, who does not mention a particular ethnic group, identifies a universal 'napak' woman using the symbolic language of Islamic purity. This more universalist 'napak' woman in the poem takes ownership of her independent sexual body that is oblivious to sacred constraints and openly expressive of desire. What Jeffery has observed with regard to one small group of Muslim women in India is a microcosm of the phenomenon that affects women across classes and ethnicities. In writing this poem, Riaz undertakes representation at a larger level, bringing into the limelight an issue that is absent in Urdu literature. She acknowledges that when she wrote 'Voh ek zan-e napak hai' or any of the other poems in this collection, she did not deliberate about what the public reaction to her poem would be. Riaz gives her physical distance from Pakistan at the time of writing as one of the reasons why she forgot to anticipate the hostility that followed in the wake of *Badan darida*'s publication in Pakistan, as well as among the expatriate community abroad.[61]

In Urdu, the word 'napak' connects sacred discourse to concepts of purity and pollution.[62] Riaz's poem challenges this separation:

وہ اِک زنِ ناپاک ہے

وہ اِک زنِ ناپاک ہے
بہتے لہو کی قید میں
گردش میں ماہ و سال کی
دہکی ہوس کی آگ میں
اپنی طلب کی چاہ میں
زائیدۂ ابلیس تھی
چل دی اسی کی راہ میں
اس منزلِ موہوم کو
جس کا نشاں پیدا نہیں
سنگم وہ نور و نار کا
جس کا پتہ ملتا نہیں
اُبلے لہو کے جوش سے
پستان اس کے پھٹ چکے
ہر نوکِ خارِ راہ سے
بندِ لحم سب کٹ چکے
اس کے بدن کی شرم پر
تقدیس کا سایہ نہیں

Voh ek zan-e napak hai
Behte lahu ki qaid men
Gardish men mah-o sal ki
Dahki havis ki aag men
Apni talab ki chah men
Zaida-e iblis thi
Chal di us ki rah men

Is manzil-e mohom ko
Jis ka nishan paida nahin
Sangam voh nur-o nar ka
Jis ka pata milta nahin
Uble lahu ki josh se
Pustan us ke phat chuke
Har nok-e khar-e rah se
Band-e lahm sab kat chuke
Is ke badan ki sharm par
Taqdis ka saya nahin
Lekin khuda-e bahr-o bar
Aisa kabhi dekha nahin
Farman tere sab rava
Han is zan-e napak ke
Lab par nahin koi dua
Sar men koi sajda nahin

[She is a woman impure
Inside a prison of flowing blood
In a rotation of month and year
Burning in the greedy fire of lust
In pursuit of her desire
She was Satan's progeny
Took to his path
Of an unknown destination
No sign of which has been born
A union of light and fire
That is untraceable
From the bubbling boiling blood
Her breasts have spilled out
From every thorn-tipped passage
All bodily flesh was slashed
On her body's shame
No shade of sanctity
But God of land and ocean
Such has never been seen
All your worthy commands
Yes, this impure woman
On her lips there is no prayer
From her head no prostration][63]

Attempting to normalize the impure woman and challenge her exclusion from the sacred sphere, Riaz makes her a central protagonist of the poem. Her strategy of normalization relies on the borrowing of a Sufi aesthetic. She mockingly defines this 'abnormal' woman undergoing her menstrual period as 'Satan's procreation', referencing the Qur'anic Satan, or Iblis, who was exiled from the kingdom of God and seduced Adam and Eve into temptation. Her use of the word 'Iblis' rather than 'shaitan' is suggestive of a borrowing from the Sufi tradition of Urdu poetry where Iblis represents tragedy instead of evil. The association of the menstruating woman with Iblis is powerful as it connects with representations of the androgynous Qur'anic Iblis and prophetic stories. Peter J. Awn has argued that the 'generative power of Iblis is vastly different from human maleness', reflecting what he calls a 'true hermaphrodite' with the power to reproduce. Riaz engages with this characterization of Iblis, critically responding to perceptions of desirous women as seducers. Homing in on an expression of a menstruating woman's wanton desire, she associates her with those who are worshippers of Iblis, defiant and licentious.[64] The poet's frank public acclaim of the menstruating body is a deliberate rebellion against the religio-cultural community's silencing of a woman during her period. She flamboyantly parades the woman in a prison of blood on the genteel surface of Urdu verse.

The poem that comes immediately after 'Voh ek zan-e napak hai' and offsets its bristling quality of disagreement is the more sedate 'Ek aurat ki hansi' (The Laughter of a Woman). It acts as a contrasting afterword, showcasing an aspect of female behaviour that is also monitored but not taboo in representations of women. In the poem, she highlights the conventional and familiar form of the female body with long tresses, bringing her distinctive voice to a title that headlines a female trait that she wishes to celebrate, of unchecked laughter. Riaz strikes a middle ground by projecting the laughter as soft and feminine.

ایک عورت کی ہنسی

پتھریلے کوہسار کے گاتے چشموں میں
گونج رہی ہے اک عورت کی نرم ہنسی
دولت، طاقت اور شہرت، سب کچھ بھی نہیں
اس کے بدن میں چھپی ہے اس کی آزادی
دنیا کے معبد کے نئے بُت کچھ کر لیں
سُن نہیں سکتے اس کی لذت کی سسکی
اس بازار میں گوہر مال بکاؤ ہے
کوئی خرید کے لائے ذرا تسکیں اس کی
اِک سرشاری جس سے وہ ہی واقف ہے
چاہے بھی تو اس کو بیچ نہیں سکتی

وادی کی آوارہ ہواؤ! آ جاؤ
آؤ اور اس کے چہرے پر بوسے دو
اپنے لمبے لمبے بال اُڑاتی جائے
ہوا کی بیٹی ساتھ ہوا کے گاتی جائے

Pathrilay kuhsar ke gate chashmon men
Gunj rahi hai ek aurat ki narm hansi
Daulat, taqat aur shohrat, sab kuch bhi nahin
Us ke badan men chupi hai us ki azadi
Dunya ke mabad ke nae but kuch kar len
Sun nahin sakte us ki lazzat ki siski
Is bazar men go, har mal bikao hai

Koi kharid ke lae zara taskin is ki
Ik sarshari jis se voh hi vaqif hai
Chahe bhi to is ko bech nahin sakti
Vadi ki aawara hawao! Aa jao
Aao aur is ke chehre par bose do
Apne lambe lambe bal urati jae
Hawa ki beti, sath hawa ke gati jae

[In the rocky mountains, singing cataracts
Echo the soft laughter of one woman
Wealth, Power and Fame, all are nothing

Hidden in her body is her freedom
The worshippers of the world with their new idols, whatever they do
They cannot hear her cry of pleasure

Though in this bazaar, every item is for sale
Can someone just go and buy her satisfaction
An intoxication that is known only to her
Even if she wanted she cannot sell it
Wandering winds of the valley! Come
Come and plant kisses on her face
Flying her long long tresses she goes
Daughter of the wind, singing with the wind][65]

Deploying nature as a foil for her female protagonist, Riaz speaks in a language that is familiar to her Urdu readership. Her imagery and style are reminiscent of the romantic lyricism favoured by the Progressive poets Josh Malihabadi, Firaq Gorakhpuri and Faiz. However, in her description of the woman, Riaz does not use the conventional intense ghazal imagery for the beloved, nor does she refer to unrequited love as the desired goal. Instead, she chooses to personify laughter and freedom over power, fame and wealth in order to characterize independence, instilling the familiar female form represented through long tresses with a new persona.

In spite of the gentler 'Ek aurat ki hansi', the overall subject matter and tone of the poems in this collection were indeed shocking for readers of Urdu poetry, who were not used to women writing openly about sexual encounters, articulating pleasure and challenging social norms. In the past, Manto and Ismat Chughtai had paid a heavy price for writing on sexualities and now it was Riaz's turn. Unfortunately, the negative reaction to *Badan darida* meant that the collection has not enjoyed a strong readership and is only known for a few poems. This overlooks the emotional journey in the collection that eventually relinquishes the desires and pleasures of the female body for the temporality of clay, articulating the poet-narrator's equivocation between the sacred and the secular before eventually adopting a middle ground. Her poem 'Main to mitti ki murat hun' (I am Made of Clay) crystallizes this quandary in the last two lines: 'Ye mitti ghulti jae gi / ghat-ta jae ga badan mera' (This clay will keep dissolving / my body will keep receding). There is lamentation too over homelessness in Karachi in 'Sahil ki eek sham' (An Evening at the Beach); the betrayal of democracy in Rawalpindi expressed in the poem '23 March 1973', when the state's emergency powers allowed for four hours of firing against an opposition party rally; and the need to protect the motherland from *waderas* (landlords). The ghazals in the collection echo a return to spiritual love (*ishq-e haqiqi*), expressing a dissatisfaction with romantic love (*ishq-e majazi*) both as a woman and as a soul in search of greater knowledge. As an artist, Riaz remains true to the claim in her foreword to *Badan darida* that she is at war with societal approval. The cultural pressure in Pakistani society of 'what will people say' is met by verse formations that are outspoken and dissident.

From Sacred to Secular: Culminating the Journey of Resistance

Riaz's secularity comes through strongly in poems such as 'Lori' (Lullaby) that draw on values of rights and democracy through a gendered lens. 'Lori', part of her collection *Dhup* (Sunshine), is dedicated to her daughter. The title of the poem suggests a gentle rhyme to help children transition to bedtime except that this is no ordinary song that will lull a child to sleep. It is a lullaby in the form of a feminist anthem dedicated to the power of women, narrating a transformative experience that empowered the mother and changed her outlook on life from bleak to hopeful. 'Lori' is part lyrical ballad and part fairy tale; it is part of a folkloric tradition. Like an amoral fairy tale, it focuses on the assurance of success and the development of an ability to succeed.[66] An integral feature of this poem is Riaz's deliberate gendering of language; for instance, the original Urdu verb endings or pronouns in every line relating to the child underline the feminine gender. This is impossible to reproduce in an English translation. Similarly, when the wolf symbolizing danger enters the narration, the possessive nouns indicate his masculinity. The original refers to the wolf in the third person '*us*' that can be translated as either 'her' or 'his', but it is the wolf's description as lord, ruler and so on possessing masculine verb endings that lead to the use of 'his' in the translation.

اری تیرا چاند مُکھڑا

مِری جان کا یہ مُکھڑا

دیکھتی ہی جاؤں ری

نین میں بساؤں ری

تجھ کو اپنی باہنوں کا جھُولنا جھُلاؤں ری

کلیجے لگاؤں ری

سُن ری میری نین تارا

تری ماں کا جیون سارا

آنسوؤں کی بہتی دھارا

گزرتا چلا گیا

اسی تقطرے جل کا ہے یہ کٹورا بھرا ہوا

پھُول ہاتھ ، کنول پاؤں اسی سے دھُلاؤں ری

نین سے لگاؤں ری

دُکھی جیون روتے روتے ، تجھے دیکھ آنسو رُکے

کِھل کِھلا کر ہنس پڑے

مری سہمی ماں ممتا کو تجھ پہ مان ہیں بڑے

لگے کل کی بات مجھ کو

یاد ہے وہ رات مجھ کو

تُو نے جب جنم لیا

رات تھی وہ بڑی کالی
پپیہا ترپانے والی
پر تری ہنکار سُن کر دیا سا تھا جل گیا

پیارے سے پیارے انگ تیرے
تازہ تازہ ، ہرے بھرے
چُھونے نہ پاؤں ری
کانپ کانپ جاؤں ری

جانتی ہوں مرے دوار کھڑا ایک بھیڑیا
کھا رہا میری جوانی ، مرا خون پی رہا
بھیڑیا جو دھن نے پالا
جگ پہ راج کرنے والا
ہم کو جگ جگ کا شراپ

جس کی کارن اس نگر میں
سوچنا اک دوکش ٹھہرا
پیار کرنا ——— مہا پاپ

آدمی کی آتما کا خُون اس کے مُنہ سے لگا ہے
تری باٹ تک رہا ہے
نَین سو سو پاؤں ری
جاگتی ہی جاؤں ری
سُن ری میری کوکھ جائی
یہ نگر انبیائے کا ہے
گُن تجھے سکھاؤں کیا

آتی جاتی ناریوں نے
بُوٹے کاڑھے جالی جالی
پروسی تھی تھالی تھالی
کھا گیا جو بھجیڑیا

آج ہر رسوئی خالی
تجھے میَں دِکھاؤں کیا
گُن تجھے سِکھاؤں کیا——!

تجھے جب میَں گود میں لُوں
سمے کی پکار سُنوں
بڑی ہا ہا کار سُنوں
رن کی للکار سُنوں
یہی بار بار سُنوں
ترا گُن ہے 'وریتا'!

سُن مری نَنھی سی جان
یہ زمین یہ آسمان
سُکھ کی ساری آن بان
منڈیوں میں بھرا دھان

جب تلک ہمارا نہیں
چین سے گزارا نہیں
کسی کا سہارا نہیں
کوئی اور چارہ نہیں

Arri tera chand mukhra
Meri jan ka ye tukra
Dekhti hi jaun ri
Nain main basaon ri

Tujh ko apni bahon ka jhulna jhulaon ri
Kaleje lagaon ri
Sun ri meri nen tara
Teri ma ka jeevan sara
Ansuon ki behti dhara
Guzarta chala gaya
Isi nithray jal ka hai ye katora bhara hua
Phul hath, kanwal paon isi se dhulaon ri
Nen se lagaon ri

Dukhi jeevan rote rote, tujhe dekh ansu roke
Khilkhila kar hans pare
Meri sehmi mamta ko tujh pe man hen bare

Lage kal ki bat mujh ko
Yad hai voh rat mujh ko
Tu ne jab janam liya

Rat thi voh bari kali
Pira tarpane vali
Par teri hanker sun kar diya sat ha jal gaya

Pyare pyare ang tere
Taza taza, hare bhare
Chumne na paon ri
Kamp kamp jaon ri

[Dearest your countenance like the moon
You who are a part of my heart
Dearest I keep on looking
Dearest my eyes are filled with you

Dearest I rock you in my cradled arms
Holding you next to my heart

Dearest sparkle in my eye listen
Your mother's entire life,
A flowing cataract of tears
Passed by
From that clear water has this bowl been filled
Dearest let me wash in it your flowerlike hands, lotuslike feet
Hold you close to my eyes

Sorrowful existence endlessly I wept, seeing you I stopped the tears
They unfurled and blossomed into laughter
My frightened motherhood has great expectations of you

It seems like yesterday's talk to me
I can remember that night
When you were born

That night was very black
Heart tormented with pain
But upon hearing your cry a makeshift candle wick began to glow

Your beautiful beautiful limbs
Fresh, fresh, healthy and prospering,
Dearest can't seem to manage a kiss
Dearest from shuddering and shivering][67]

The mother's terms of endearment cushion the stinging tale being told and, as the story turns sinister, she communicates to her child the need to belong, to have a home where there is safety and the promise of a livelihood. The lullaby draws inspiration from the fairy tale of Red Riding Hood with its reference to the big bad wolf, except that the wolf in this case is the fat cat capitalist whose hunger for money runs the world.

Janti ho mere dovar khara ek bherya
Kha raha hai meri jawani, mera khun pi raha
Bherya jo dhan ne pala
Jag pe raj karne wala
Hum ko jug jug ka sharap

Jis ki karan is nagar men
Sochna ik dosh tehra
Pyaar karna – maha pap

Aadmi ki atma ka khun us ke mun laga hai
Teri bat tak raha hai
Ren so na paon ri
Jagti hi jaon ri

Sun ri meri kukh jai
Ye nagar anyae ka hai
Gun tujhe sikhaon kya

[Do you know a wolf stood on my doorway
Drinking my blood, consuming my youth
Wolf who was nourished by money
Who can rule the world
We with a curse from age to age

In this world for whom
Thinking is considered a crime
To love – a major sin

He has tasted the blood of a human soul
Watching your every move
Dearest cannot sleep at night
Dearest I keep constantly awake

Dearest borne of my womb listen
This world belongs to injustice
What skills shall I teach you?][68]

As the wolf enters the poem, we see digressions coming in from the narratorial voice as it changes to a philosophical and knowing tone, breaking up the intimate conversational style of the mother speaking to her daughter. This is also noticeable in the next stanza, which seeks to plot the lived experience of women piece-workers, whose stories contextualize the precarity of labour and exploitation through global neoliberal economy networks:[69]

Aati jati nariyon ne
Bute karhe jail jail
Parosi thi thali thali
Kha gaya jo bherya

Aaj har rasoi khali
Tujhe men dikhaon kiya

Gun tujhe sikhaon kya-!
Tujhe jab god men lun
Same ki pukar sunun
Bari hahakar sunun
Ran ki lalkar sunun
Yehi bar bar sunun
Tera gun hai 'veerta'!

[Women who came and went
Embroidered sprigs on net upon net
Put food on platter upon platter
That the wolf ate

Today every kitchen is empty
What shall I show you
What skill shall I teach you!

Whenever I take you in my arms
Listening to the call of time
Listening to great battlecries
Listening to the beckoning of war
Listening to that again and again
Your skill is 'bravery' Veerta!][70]

The message the poet-narrator puts out for her daughter in real life, Veerta, named in the poem, is bravery, the quality that will guide her through the trials that life will present. She reminds her that her shared history is with women, who have been providers, whose unacknowledged labour has been usurped by the wolf's greed. The lyrical voice promotes a sense of empowerment through the reclamation of history and a fight against capitalism. The purpose of the poem is political and as readers we can see the poem working at two levels, the personal and the collective.

Sun meri nanhi si jan
Ye zamin ye asman
Sukh ki sari an ban
Mandion men bhara dhan

Jab talak hamara nahin
Chen se guzara nahin

Kisi ka sahara nahin
Koi aur chara nahin

Bherye se nahin darna
Meri jan! jam ke larna
Kabhi mat hona niras

Veerta sikhaon tujh ko
Sherni banaon tujh ko
Dar na phatke aas pas

Sun meri nanhi naveli
Nahin hogi tu akeli
Sang hon ge banh beli

Teri sangi, tere mit
Tere sath sath hon ge
Hath men kai hath hon ge
Yehi meri ek aas!

[Listen my dear little one
This earth, this sky all the grandeur of peace
The markets full of grain

Until that does not belong to us
We cannot exist in harmony
No support from anyone
There is no other option

Do not fear the wolf
Dear heart! fight with conviction
Do not ever despair

I will teach you bravery
Make you into a lioness
Fear will not come near you

Listen my dear new little one
Never will you be alone
With you arm in arm will be your friends

Your companions, your friends
Will together accompany you
Many hands will be linked together
This is my one wish]⁷¹

The voice of the mother is overlaid with the voice of the activist poet and we see the shifts in the mother's character over the course of the poem. By the end of the poem, the poet-narrator and the mother merge into one voice. The lullaby has been transformed into a feminist song for survival and hope. It is an anthem for working women who don't have access to class privilege and a good life.

In contrast to this poem is the more sarcastic 'Chadar aur divari' (The Wall and Seclusion), part of her *Hamrikab* (Poems of Exile) collection composed from March 1981 to 1987. Her distance from Pakistan gives her the freedom to be openly critical about the status of women under General Zia's dictatorship in the 1980s. She mocks the law that puts the onus of modesty on women as proof of their innocence. Her sensibility as a feminist is at its height in her strongly worded protest against Hudood Ordinances, targeting the higher court of justice as part of the mockery that marked women as the living dead. The chadar that had been a haven in Zehra Nigah's poetry comes back to bite in this poem as a symbol of women's national oppression. With a symbolic reference to a black veil, she also intertextually alludes to the Iranian Revolution of 1979, a movement that led to the unseating of the Shah of Iran and marked the start of an Islamist era with the introduction of compulsory veiling for women.

چادر اور چار دیواری

حضور میں اس سیاہ چادر کا کیا کروں گی
یہ آپ کیوں مجھ کو بخشتے ہیں بصد عنایت!

نہ سوگ میں ہوں کہ اس کو اوڑھوں
غم والم خلق کو دکھاؤں
نہ روگ ہوں میں کہ اس کی تاریکیوں میں خفت سے ڈوب جاؤں
نہ میں گنہ گار ہوں نہ مجرم
کہ اس سیاہی کی مہر اپنی جبیں پہ ہر حال میں لگاؤں
اگر نہ گستاخ مجھ کو سمجھیں
گر میں جاں کی امان پاؤں
تو دست بستہ کروں گزارش
کہ بندہ پرور!
حضور کے حجرۂ معطر میں ایک لاشہ پڑا ہوا ہے
نہ جانے کب کا گلا سڑا ہے
یہ آپ سے رحم چاہتا ہے
حضورا اتنا کرم تو کیجئے
سیاہ چادر مجھے نہ دیجئے
سیاہ چادر سے اپنے حجرہ کی بے کفن لاش ڈھانپ دیجئے

کہ اس سے پھوٹی ہے جو عفونت
وہ کوچے کوچے میں ہانپتی ہے
وہ سر پٹکتی ہے چوکھٹوں پر
برہنگی تن کی ڈھانپتی ہے
سنیں ذرا دلخراش چیخیں
بنا رہی ہیں عجب ہیولے
جو چادروں میں بھی ہیں برہنہ

یہ کون ہیں؟ جانتے تو ہوں گے
حضور پہچانتے تو ہوں گے!

یہ لونڈیاں ہیں!
کہ یرغمالی حلالِ شب بھر ہیں
دمِ صبح در بدر ہیں
یہ باندیاں ہیں!
حضور کے نطفۂ مبارک کے نصف ورثہ سے بے معتبر ہیں

یہ بیبیاں ہیں!
کہ زوجگی کا خراج دینے
قطار اندر قطار باری کی منتظر ہیں

یہ بچیاں ہیں!
کہ جن کے سر پر پھر جو حضرت کا دستِ شفقت
تو کم سنی کے لہو سے ریشِ سپید رنگین ہو گئی ہے

حضور کے حجلۂ معطر میں زندگی خون رو گئی ہے
پڑا ہوا ہے جہاں یہ لاشہ
طویل صدیوں سے قتلِ انسانیت کا یہ خوں چکاں تماشہ
اب اس تماشہ کو ختم کیجئے
حضور اب اس کو ڈھانپ دیجئے!

سیاہ چادر تو بن چکی ہے مری نہیں آپ کی ضرورت
کہ اس زمیں پر وجود میرا نہیں فقط اک نشانِ شہوت
حیات کی شاہراہ پر جگمگا رہی ہے مری ذہانت
زمین کے رخ پر جو ہے پسینہ تو جھلملاتی ہے میری محنت

یہ چار دیواریاں، یہ چادر، گلی سڑی لاش کو مبارک
کھل فضاؤں میں بادباں کھول کر بڑھے گا مرا سفینہ
میں آدمِ نو کی ہم سفر ہوں
کہ جس نے جیتی مری بھروسہ بھری رفاقت!

Hazur main is siyah chadar ka kya karun gi
Ye aap kyun mujhe bakshte hain, basd Inayat!

Na sog men hun ke is ko orhun
Gham-o alam khalq ko dikhaon
Na rog hun main ke is ki tarikion men khaft se dub jaon
Na main gunahgar hun na mujrim
Ke is siyahi ki muhr apni jabin pe har hal men lagaon
Agar na gustakh mujh ko samjhen
Gar main jan ki aman paon
To dast basta karun guzarish
Ke banda parwar!
Huzoor ke hujra-e muatar men ek lasha para hua hai
Na jane kab ka gala sara hai
Ye aap se rahm chahta hai
Hazur itna karm to kijye
Siyah chadar mujhe na dijye
Siyah chador se apne hujre ki be-kafan lash dhamp dijye
Ke is se phuti hai jo afunat
Voh kuche kuche men hampti hai
Voh sar patakti hai chokhton par
Barhengi tan ki dhampti hai
Sunen zara dil kharash cheekhen
Bana rahi hain ajib huule
Jo chadaron men bhi hain birehna

Ye kaun hain? Jante to hon ge
Huzoor pehchante to hon ge!

Ye londiyan hain!
[…]

Siyah chador to ban chuki hai meri nahin ap ki zarurat
Ke is zamin par wajud mera nahin faqat ik nishan-e shahut
Hayat ki shahra par jagmaga rahi hai meri zahanat
Zamin ke rukh par jo hai pasina to jhilmilati hai meri mehnat

Ye char divarian, ye chadar, gali sari lash ko mubarak
Khuli fizaon men badban khol kar barhe ga mera safina
Main adam no ki humsafar hun
Ke jis ne jiti meri bharosa bhari rafaqat!

[Your honour, what will I do with this black chadar
Why do you bestow it upon me as a sign of your humanity

I am not in mourning that I should wear it
Nor do I need to show grief to the world
Neither am I ill needing to drown myself in its dark depths
I am no sinner nor a criminal
And I don't need to engrave my brows in this black ink
Please don't think I'm being disrespectful
I wish to save my life as a citizen
I make this request with folded hands
O Protector!
In your honour's perfumed chamber lies a corpse
It is not known for how long it has been decomposing
This corpse wants your mercy
Your honour please perform this small act
Please don't give me this black chadar
You can use it to cover the corpse in your room that lacks a shroud
The odour that is rising from it
Spreads from street corner to street corner
She bangs her head on every threshold
Hiding her naked body
Listen to her bloodcurdling cries
Creating strange curvatures
That are naked despite the shawls

Who are they? Surely you know
Your honour surely you can recognise them!

They are young lasses!
[...]

This black shawl has become your need not mine
Because my being in this world is not determined by tokens of modesty
My intelligence dances on life's boulevard
My hard work is reflected in the perspiration of the earth

The rotting corpse is welcome to these four walls and this shawl
My ship will sail with its mast flying high in open winds
I am the companion of Adam
Who won my trustworthy friendship!][72]

Wrapped in the chadar is a woman's honour and shame, and ironically the same chadar chokes her to death. Appropriating the voice of the condemned woman, Riaz speaks out, from the suffocating folds, against injustice. In this poem Fahmida's sensibility as an Urdu poet echoes Faiz in its use of classical metaphors in modern forms and her commitment to social realism. But unlike Faiz she doesn't hold back and gives full expression to her anger. The subject of her poetry is the woman freed from the chains of an imposed national Islamic ideology that colludes with the law and governance to deliver a model of justice that discriminates against those who are powerless. At the end of the poem, she embeds the message of trust, friendship and equality as a key part of male–female relationships, returning to the sacred story of Adam and Eve to make her case. The mood of this poem is polemical, but it makes clever use of language to invert stereotypes, charting a path to a new modernity that requires those in power to relinquish control over women's bodies as an attempt to establish an authentic Islamic state.

The poem provides commentary on a justice system that has become hostage to the Hudood Ordinances. In many ways, it takes us back to the historic question of Pakistan's raison d'être that was raised by Muhammad Munir, a senior member of the judiciary, in response to the violence against the minority Ahmadi community in 1950s Lahore, disputing their membership of the wider Muslim community because of a question mark over their authenticity as Muslims. Later, they would be deemed non-Muslim and minority citizens because of the status accorded to Mirza Ghulam Ahmad, their Mahdi. Asad Ahmad argues that the report establishes a modern interpretation of Islam that can only be provided through the secular state rather than through the ulema, who continue to fuel sectarian divisions in society.[73] It is also important to note that the Ahmadis were a successful economic community who were small in number but garnered a certain degree of power. This, as Kamila Shamsie notes, was 'a dangerous combination of vulnerability and cause for envy'.[74] Comparatively, in this instance 30 years after the publication of the poem, the state has continued to court and appease demands by the religious right, often abandoning the question of human rights to exacerbate further the divide between the perception of a modern Westernized society that is a hangover of colonialism in favour of a conservative moral, religious one. Riaz's poem demonstrates the failure of the judicial system to uphold secular rights for citizens, particularly women, who she says are marked as the living dead through the implementation of Sharia laws because of the judiciary's capitulation to the demands of an authoritarian state seeking legitimacy through religious discourse.

Conclusion

Riaz's most hard-hitting poems have been written at a distance from Pakistan. Whether she would have been able to write and publish these verses from within the country is debatable given her troubled relationship with the state and curbs over freedom of expression. What becomes evident in her collections is a rite of passage from a girl to a woman, a lover to a citizen. At every step of her poetic journey, she has challenged the norms of female subjectivity in Urdu poetry, bringing Progressive realism to her experimental use of form in order to shift the nostalgic mood of the love lyric. Her use of the Urdu poetic form declined over time as her fight against social injustice looked for answers in prose ranging from travel writing to novels to short stories. Attracted to an Indian secular spirit, she felt dejected by the increasing majoritarianism across the border, writing the often quoted lines of disillusionment after the demolition of the Babri Masjid in 1992:

نیا بھارت

تم بالکل ہم جیسے نکلے
اب تک کہاں چھپے تھے بھائی؟
وہ مورکھتا، وہ گھامڑ پن
جس میں ہم نے صدی گنوائی
آخر پہنچی دوار تمہارے
ارے بدھائی، بہت بدھائی!

بھوت دھرم کا ناچ رہا ہے
قائم ہندو راج کرو گے
سارے اُلٹے کاج کرو گے
اپنا چمن تاراج کرو گے

بیٹھے بیٹھے کرو گے سوچا
پوری ہے ویسی تیاری
کون ہے ہندو، کون نہیں ہے
تم بھی کرو گے فتوے جاری

ہو گا کٹھن یہاں بھی جینا
دانتوں آ جائے گا پسینا
جیسے تیسے کٹا کرے گی
یہاں بھی سب کی سانس گھٹے گی

ماتھے پر سیندور کی ریکھا
کچھ بھی نہیں پڑوس سے سیکھا؟
کیا ہم نے دُر دَشا بنائی
کچھ بھی تم کو نظر نہ آئی؟

بھاڑ میں جائے سِکھشا وکھشا
اب جاہل پن کے گن گانا
آگے گڑھا ہے یہ مت دیکھو
واپس لاؤ گیا زمانہ!

دنیہ واد یہ گمان مٹایا
مسلمان ہے احمق جایا
جس پر ہم رویا کرتے تھے
تم نے بھی وہ بات اب کی ہی
بہت ملال ہے، ہم کو لیکن
با با با با، ہو ہو، بی ہی!

کل دکھ سے سوچا کرتی تھی
سوچ کے بہت ہنسی آج آئی

تم بالکل ہم جیسے نکلے
ہم دو قوم نہیں تھے بھائی

مشق کرو تم آ جائے گا
الٹے پاؤں چلتے جانا
دھیان نہ من میں دوجا آئے
بس پیچھے ہی نظر جمانا

ایک جاپ سا کرتے جاؤ
بارم بار یہی دہراؤ
"کتنا ویر مہان تھا بھارت!
کیسا عالی شان تھا بھارت!"
پھر تم لوگ پہنچ جاؤ گے
بس پرلوک پہنچ جاؤ گے

ہم تو ہیں پہلے سے وہاں پر
تم بھی سے نکالتے رہنا
اب جس نرک میں جاؤ وہاں سے
چٹھی وٹھی ڈالتے رہنا

Tum bilkul hum jaise nikle
Ab tak kahan chupe the bhai
[...]
Kaun he hindu, kaun nahin hai
Tum bhi karo ge fatwe jari
[...]
Tum bilkul ham jaise nikle
Hum do qaum nahin the bhai

[You too turned out just like us,
Where were you hiding until now
...
Who is a hindu, and who isn't
You too will give out fatwas
...
You too turned out like us
Sigh, we are not two separate nations][75]

Her vision for a democratic future as a Progressive writer was disrupted by witnessing the rise of Hindu majoritarianism in India. She mourns the loss of democracy, freedom and education and notes the ideological return to a glorious past that puts both nations on par. The poem is a stark reminder of how political culture in India and Pakistan will be determined by communitarian identity politics.

Critical of the state and of class hierarchies, Riaz continuously expressed her vision through a woman-centric universe, putting the onus of responsibility equally on the sacred and secular as a connected consciousness in an evolving postcolonial society. Her perspective evolves over time but she doesn't discard religion nor does she appropriate it through a post-secular lens. Through her language and poetry she tries to bridge the two separate worlds of secular and religious citizens, arguing for the necessity of a shared vision that breaks through gender and class divisions. In her book of poetry *Kya tum pura chand na dekho ge?* (Won't You See the Full Moon?) she lambasts the rise of neoliberalism and the continued nurture of capital. Her lengthy prose poem divided into five chapters borrows stylistically from the *masnavi* to narrate a tale of woe and fear set in Karachi. The protagonists in the poem are the poet's conscience and her critique of a rising neoliberal economy that has killed off any organic relation between the nation and its people. In the prologue to the poem the paper mocks the poet:

Paper, why has your complexion faded?
'Poet, from watching your deeds'
Paper, what are these blemishes upon your cheek?
'Poet, I could not drink your tears'
Paper, shall I tell you the truth.....?
'Poet! my heart will burst'[76]

The poet is unable to record truth on paper, and the story that unfolds in the prose poem seems to suggest that the poet's creative spirit has been murdered. She has no choice left but to forsake the art of metaphor creation. She writes:

آج میرے اندر کوئی استعارہ صرف تھکن سے مر گیا ہے

لفظ حیران کھڑے ہیں

اور قافیہ ہاتھ چھڑا کر چلا گیا ہے

بنجر ہو گئی ہے زمین

اور وزن ۔۔۔ منہ کے بل گر پڑا ہے

کہاں کھو گیا میرا آہنگ ؟

آدھے راستے میں ۔۔۔۔۔

کیا تو بھی ۔۔۔

میری شاعری، تو بھی ؟

منہ پھیر لے گی ؟ آنکھیں چُرائے گی ؟

Aaj mere ander koi isteara sirf thakan se mar gaya hai
Lafz heran khare hain
Aur qafiya hath chura kar chala gaya hai
Banjar ho gai hai zamin
Aur vazan – mun ke bal gir para hai […]
Kya tu bhi –
Meri shairi, tu bhi?
Mun pher le gi? Ankhen churaye gi?

[Today only exhaustion has been the cause of death of a metaphor inside of me
Words are standing surprised
And the rhyming *qafiya* has freed itself from my hand
The domain has become barren
And metre – has fallen flat on its face […]
Will you too –
My poetry, you too?
Will you turn your face away? not meet my eyes?][77]

These lines reflect the death of the love that has sustained metaphor creation and the poet's exhaustion with poetry as a form due to what she sees around her. It seems there is nothing left to sustain verse. She provides a testimony of the crowded lawless city that informs her resistance, an existence shadowed by the police, guns and bullets, trucks full of explosives driven by uniforms, national roads and structures such as the grand American Embassy.[78] She is the poet-narrator, the Muhajir migrant, the observer of what is going on. The fear of what is happening in Karachi inspires her to write a war song that will rock the foundations of injustice with its horrifying content. She determinedly asks the question, 'Kya tum pura chand na dekho ge?' (Won't you see the full picture, the whole story, the complete truth?). Plotting a narrative of fear, she describes a police state, spies in the civil service, constant surveillance, weapons, the presence of the army in their khaki uniforms. Her narration is a mixture of direct and reported speech, factual account, identity politics and historicization. As the chapters progress, her role as the poet becomes the central focus. She is the protagonist of this narrative. The mantle of honesty and authenticity is the trademark that differentiates her from the rulers and officials of the state. Her version of history becomes clear with the progression of verse.

The prose poem is symbolic of the murder of the socialist poet's dying lyric that is 'bleeding on every page' of her text. The city is shown to be a prostitute to power, contradicting the age of 'enlightenment and hope'. As a poet, she feels that she has been unfairly pressed by her benefactor to write about this hopelessly 'impenetrable darkness' of a 'petro-dollar' economy subservient to the United States and Saudi Arabia.[79] The only consolation she has is that the people who are responsible for the corruption have no attachment to the motherland, they have no investment in organic roots of their mother earth. They are the inspiration for her verse. In the end she opines that as a poet it was not her fate to write a sunny panegyric *qasida*; her job was to report the truth and she has done that.[80] She has lived a life of fear surrounded by rattlesnakes, never knowing who to trust. Breaking free from the poisonous fear of mistrust she asks for recognition from the people of her homeland. She speaks of migrancy, the anguish of exile and the need to belong and feel at home.[81] She offers her testimony as authentic proof of her love and commitment to the city and the country. But she notes her differences with the state and her commitment to social justice walking through the city of Karachi, noting its changing dynamics that are deepening social divisions in society. The poet's persona is a body torn: a Progressive rebel and a nonconformist searching for social justice.

Notes

1. Fahmida Riaz, from *Kya tum pura chand na dekho ge* [Won't You See the Full Moon] in her collection *Main mitti ki murat hun* (Lahore: Sang-e meel, 1988), 312.
2. Fahmida Riaz, personal communication, 10 March 1998.
3. Zeenat Hisam, 'Fahmida Riaz: Life and Work of a Poet', *Pakistan Journal of Women's Studies* 2, no. 1 (1995): 43–52 (43–44).
4. Fahmida Riaz, personal communication, 10 March 1998.
5. Hisam, 'Fahmida Riaz', 49.
6. I have no archival reference for this connection to Amrita Pritam. The information comes from oral conversations with those who were close to Fahmida Riaz. I am

grateful to Sara Kazmi for looking into this. We were in conversation with reference to her article 'Don't Make My Corpse Apologise: Lessons in Dissidence from Fahmida Riaz', *Dawn*, 4 December 2018.
7   She was attached as a senior research fellow to the All India Institute of Social Sciences from 1983 to 1985 and at the All India Institute of Historical Research from 1986 to 1987.
8   Fahmida Riaz, *Pakistan: Literature and Society* (New Delhi: Patriot, 1986), 11.
9   Fahmida Riaz, personal communication, 10 March 1998. Here she published books in translation building on her transnational feminist connections as well as a study of women in Urdu literature funded by UK Department for international Development (DIFID). See *Adab ki nisai radd-e tashkil* (Karachi: wada kitab ghar, 2006).
10 Fahmida Riaz, *Zinda Bahar: ek. Safarnama, ek navil* (Lahore: Dastavez matbuat, 1996); *Karachi: navil* (Lahore: Takhliqat, 1998).
11 Fahmida Riaz, 'Us ne kaha tha' [S/he Said That], *Dunyazad* 3 (2001): 146–71; 'Ek Bhuli hu'i kahani' [A Forgotten Tale], *Dunyazad* 29 (2010): 248–61; 'Akhit Jadoo', trans. Amna Zafar, *Critical Muslim* 5: *Love and Death* (2013): 183–96.
12 Fahmida Riaz, *Godavri* (Islamabad: Dost, 1995). See Dharmananda Damodar Kosambi, *The Culture and Civilisation of Ancient India in Historical Outline* (Delhi: Vikas Publications, 1970).
13 Fahmida Riaz, *Ye Khana-e Aab-o gil* (Scheherzade: Karachi, 2006).
14 'Fehmeeda Riaz's Son Drowns', *The News*, 27 October 2007, https://www.thenews.com.pk/archive/print/76606-fehmeeda-riaz%E2%80%99s-son-drowns.
15 Sanam Zeb, 'From My Bookshelf: "*Akhir-i-Shab* Haunts Me Because I was Associated with the Left"' [interview with Fahmida Riaz], *Dawn*, 22 March 2017 https://www.dawn.com/news/1321991; Fahmida Riaz, *Tum Kabir...* . (Karachi: Oxford University Press, 2017).
16 He is understood to be a heretic who modified Zoroaster's religion. See Fahmida Riaz, *Qila-e Faramoshi* (Karachi: Oxford University Press, 2017).
17 Raza Rumi, *Being Pakistani: Society, Culture and the Arts* (n.p.: HarperCollins India, 2018), 132.
18 Mohammad Khalid Akhtar, 'Fahmida Riaz', *Funun* 2, nos. 4–5 (1966): 294–95; S. Baksh, ed., *Pakistani adbiyat men khavatin ka kirdar* (Islamabad: Allama Iqbal Open University, 1996), 108–9.
19 Anita Anantharam, *Bodies That Remember: Women's Indigenous Knowledge and Cosmopolitanism in South Asian Poetry* (Syracuse, NY: Syracuse University Press, 2012), 106–7.
20 Anantharam, *Bodies That Remember*, 145. She draws on Judith Butler and Gloria Anzaldua's feminist critique to make her case for Fahmida's representation of the body as a means of reclaiming national space for women, contending that gender performativity and border politics are intrinsic to women's poetry. Anantharam argues that a 'new nation is imagined' in the writings of Fahmida Riaz and Kishwar Naheed.
21 Farzaneh Milani, 'Formation, Confrontation and Emancipation in the Poetry of Forugh Farrokhzad', in *A Rebirth: Poems by Foroogh Farrokhzaad*, trans. and ed. David Martin (Costa Mesa: Mazda, 1985), 123–33 (123). Her personal life was also viewed as stepping beyond the limits of respectability.
22 Khalida Hussain, 'Nisai khud shinasi aur Fahmida Riaz', in *Feminism or Hum: Adab ki gavahi*, ed. Fatema Hasan (Karachi: Vada Kitab Ghar, 2005), 183–94.
23 Riaz, personal communication, 10 March 1998.

24 Riaz, letter to the prime minister of Pakistan (reproduced from *Mainstream*, 11 July 1987, 30), *Annual of Urdu Studies* 6 (1987): 131–32.
25 Quoted in Anantharam, *Bodies That Remember*, 107.
26 Riaz, personal communication, 10 March 1998.
27 Riaz, *Main mitti ki murat hun*, 283–84.
28 Ibid., 151.
29 Ibid., 152.
30 Ibid., 15.
31 David Gilmartin, 'Democracy, Nationalism and the Public: A Speculation on Colonial Muslim Politics', *South Asia* 14, no. 1 (1991): 123–40.
32 Riaz, *Main mitti ki murat hun*, 91.
33 Riaz, personal communication, 10 March 1998.
34 Riaz, *Main mitti ki murat hun*, 91.
35 Ibid., 118, 120–21, 124–27, 137, 138–39, 151, 155–56, 157, 160–61.
36 See Hélène Cixous, 'The Laugh of the Medusa', *Jalibi* (1991): 182–87; Gopi Chand Narang, *Adbi tanqid aur aslubiyat* (Literary Criticism) (Lahore: Sang-e meel, 1991), 133–75, 176–215.
37 Baksh, *Pakistani adbiyat men khavatin ka kirdar*, 108–9; S. Hasan, 'Urdu shairi men jadid Pakistani aurat ki haisiyat ka izhar' [The Articulation of the Status of the Modern Pakistani Woman in Urdu Poetry], in *Apni nigah: auraton ki takhliqat aur tanqidi jaize*, ed. Javeria Khalid and Samina Rahman (Lahore: ASR, 1995), 9–26 (18–19).
38 Riaz, *Main mitti ki murat hun*, 95.
39 Riaz, personal communication, 10 March 1998.
40 See the discussion on the role of gender and performativity with reference to Muslim girls and how their interaction with dolls at an early age determines ideological behaviour in my article on 'Islamic Barbie: The Politics of Gender and Performativity', *Fashion Theory* 11, nos. 2–3 (2007): 173–288, https://doi.org/10.2752/136270407 X202736.
41 Riaz, *Main mitti ki murat hun*, 120–21.
42 C. M. Naim, 'The Art of the Urdu Marsiya', in *Islamic Society and Culture: Essays in Honour of Professor Aziz Ahmad*, ed. Milton Israel and N. K. Wagle (New Delhi: Manohar, 1983), 101–16.
43 Fatima Mernissi, *Hidden From History: Forgotten Queens of Islam* (Lahore: ASR, 1994), 125–26.
44 Muhammad Iqbal, *Shikwa and Jawab-e Shikwa (Complaint and Answer): Iqbal's Dialogue with Allah*, trans. Khushwant Singh (Delhi: Oxford University Press, 1981), 25–96. Also available in *Kulliyat-e Iqbal* [The Collected Works of Iqbal] (Lahore: Iqbal Academy and National Book Foundation, 1990).
45 R. S. Bhatnagar, *Mysticism in Urdu Poetry* (New Delhi: Dept of Islamic Studies, Jamia Hamdard, 1995), 8–9.
46 Fredric Jameson, 'Third World Literature in the Age of Multinational Capitalism', *Social Text* 15 (1986): 65–88.
47 Mahasweta Devi, 'Douloti the Bountiful', trans. Gayatri Chakravorty Spivak, in *Imaginary Maps: Three Stories by Mahasweta Devi*, trans. Gayatri Chakravorty Spivak (New York: Routledge, 1995), 19–94.
48 Riaz, *Main mitti ki murat hun*, 157–58.
49 S. M. Hooke, *Middle Eastern Mythology* (London: Penguin, 1963), 121–33.
50 The silencing of women referred to in 'Aqlima' has intertextual and dialogic resonances with some of her translated work, in particular, her translation of Attiya Dawood's poem

from Sindhi into Urdu entitled 'Sharafat ka pul sarat' [The Bridge of Honour], in *Apni Nigah: auraton ki likhi taakhliqat aur tanqidi jaize*, ed. Javeria Khalid and Samina Rahman (Lahore: ASR, 1995), 141. See Saadia Toor, 'The State, Fundamentalism and Civil Society', in *Engendering the Nation-State*, ed. Neelam Hussain, Samiya K. Mumtaz and Rubina Saigol, vol. 1 (Lahore: Simorgh, 1997), 131–34.
51 Riaz, *Main mitti ki murat hun*, 116–17 (punctuation original).
52 Cyril Glassé, *The Concise Encyclopaedia of Islam* (London: Stacey International, 1989), 424.
53 Riaz, personal communication, 10 March 1998.
54 Translation by Rukhsana Ahmad in her *We Sinful Women: Contemporary Urdu Feminist Poetry Including the Original Urdu* (New Delhi: Rupa, 1994), 73–74.
55 Amongst the censure, it is worth singling out Dr Rashid Amjad's lone positive review of *Badan darida* as he urges his readers to disregard the overwhelming perception of a rebellious poet seeking popularity by upsetting her readers; 'Pakistan ki Urdu shairat' [Women Poets of Pakistan], in *Ibarat: Pakistan men Urdu adab ke pachas sal*, ed. Nawazish Ali (Rawalpindi: Rabita, n.d.), 99–112 (110).
56 Yunus Jaffery, *History of Persian Literature* (Delhi: Triveni, 1981).
57 Mary Douglas, *Purity and Danger: An Analysis of Concepts of Pollution and Taboo* (London: Routledge and Kegan Paul, 1966), 10. See also Chapter 6, 'Powers and Dangers', 95–114.
58 Ibid., Chapter 6.
59 For Chandra Mohanty's critical reading of the Zed Press Book Series 'Women in the Third World', which Jeffery's book is a part of, see her 'Under Western Eyes: Feminist Scholarship and Colonial Discourses', *Feminist Review* 30, no. 1 (1988): 61–88.
60 Patricia Jeffery, *Frogs in a Well: Indian Women in Purdah* (London: Zed, 1979), 113–14.
61 Riaz, personal communication, 10 March 1998.
62 Jeffery, *Frogs in a Well*, 110–15.
63 Riaz, *Main mitti ki murat hun*, 160–61.
64 See Peter J. Awn, *Satan's Tragedy and Redemption: Iblis in Sufi Psychology* (Leiden: E. J. Brill, 1983), 32.
65 Riaz, *Main mitti ki murat hun*, 162–63.
66 Bruno Bettelheim, *The Uses of Enchantment: The Meaning and Importance of Fairy Tales* (Harmondsworth: Penguin, 1978), 10.
67 Riaz, *Main mitti ki murat hun*, 262–63.
68 Ibid., 264–65.
69 See Mohanty, 'Under Western Eyes'.
70 Riaz, *Main mitti ki murat hun*, 265–66.
71 Ibid., 266–67.
72 Fahmida Riaz, 'Chadar aur divari', from her collection *Hamrikab*, anthologized in *Sab Lal-o Guhar: Kulliyat 1967–2000* [All Rubies and Pearls: Collected Works 1967–2000] (Lahore: Sang-e Meel, 2011), 345–47.
73 Asad Ahmad, 'Advocating a Secular Pakistan: The Munir Report of 1954', in *Islam in South Asia in Practice*, ed. Barbara Metcalf (Princeton, NJ: Princeton University Press, 2009), 424–37. Also see M. Munir and M. R. Kayani, *Report of the Court of Inquiry Constituted Under Punjab Act 11 of 1954 to Enquire into the Punjab Disturbances of 1953* (Lahore: Government Printing, Punjab, 1954). For a recent study of the Ahmadi question with reference to the law, see Shazia Ahmad, 'A New Dispensation

in Islam: The Ahmadiyya and the Law in Colonial India, 1872–1939' (PhD thesis, SOAS, University of London, 2015).
74 Kamila Shamsie, *Offence: The Muslim Case* (Calcutta: Seagull Books, 2009), 35.
75 Fahmida Riaz, 'Naya Bharat' [The New Bharat], *Aaj* 31 (April–June 2000): 141–43.
76 Riaz, *Main mitti ki murat hun*, 312.
77 Riaz, *Main mitti ki murat hun*, 313–14.
78 This interpretation of testimony is based on a suggestion from Naiza Khan. I'm very grateful to her for sharing her work on Karachi with me.
79 Riaz, *Main mitti ki murat hun*, 359.
80 Christopher Shackle and Stefan Sperl, eds., *Qasida Poetry in Islamic Asia and Africa* (Leiden: E. J. Brill, 1996). See introduction.
81 Riaz, *Main mitti ki murat hun*, 375–88.

Chapter 5

KISHWAR NAHEED: DREAMER, STORYTELLER, CHANGEMAKER

Hum kab se kahanion ki chaton pe charhe
Ye soch rahe hain
Ke ye shahr hamara hai
Bunyad ki diwaron ki zamin beth gayi hai
Magar ab tak hum kahanion ki chaton pe charhe
Phiki dopahron ki ujri galyon ki tuti inton ki
Chauri dararon ko zindagi samajh rahe hain

[Since when are we stood on the rooftops of stories
Thinking this
That the city is ours
The ground beneath the foundation walls has collapsed
But we are still perched on the rooftops of stories
Thinking that life is
Colourless afternoons in ruined alleys with broken bricks with
    wide chasms][1]

The lines above from Kishwar Naheed's poem 'Censorship', written in the 1980s, are emblematic of the resilience that marks her poetry collections and her biography. She is a towering figure amongst her contemporaries, a pioneering self-professed feminist poet of the twentieth century, with a utopian vision for the kind of nation she wants Pakistan to be. Her writings offer an alternative gendered history that is avowedly secular. Like her contemporaries, Kishwar's progressive and secular trajectory has been strongly influenced by Faiz, but her ambition has been greater: to convince the Urdu literati that she is an equal contender as a woman. Naheed's strategy for prominence has been to shift her audience from the world of Urdu intellectuals to activists and women's groups. As a civil servant, she worked in close proximity with the state as part of the information team. This experience and connection has given her the power of influence as well as exposed her to the limits of free expression. She has used both these contexts strategically to build networks and relationships while avoiding the charge of corruption through her integrity. Thus the profile of civil service combined with feminist activism has helped to translate a groundbreaking and prolific literary output into a transformative one. In the argument that follows, I set out how Naheed has managed to navigate this tricky terrain to emerge as a key caretaker of Urdu. I consider the stumbling blocks in her career and the innovations she has brought to Urdu poetry in an attempt to transgress borders and boundaries of sharafat, respectability and patriotism.

Kishwar Naheed was born in 1940 in Bulandshahr, a township of Uttar Pradesh. In September 1949, two years after Partition, her family migrated to West Pakistan and settled in Lahore. At the time of migration to Pakistan Naheed had attended six years of primary school. She continued with her secondary and higher education in Lahore. Naheed enrolled at Government College when she was 19 years old; a year later she married Yusuf Kamran, and at 22 she was the mother of two children. Her marriage to Kamran meant a rebellion against her parents who excommunicated her from the family for marrying outside the Sayyid clan. Naheed temporarily abandoned her higher education in order to make ends meet in her conjugal home. However, she didn't stay away for long, successfully completing her MA in economics in 1961. Her home environment had exposed her to Urdu poetry and literature from an early age. The hazy childhood memory of a mushaira held at her parent's house is one of her earliest associations with Urdu poetry. She began writing poetry when she was in the last stages of her secondary education. In her first year at college, she participated in a public mushaira for the first time.

Her formative years were spent living under the military regimes of Ayub Khan and Yahya Khan. She joined the civil service after leaving university. During the 1960s, she became a broadcaster and presenter, taking part in programmes for Radio Pakistan and Lahore television. In September 1971, she was sent on an official visit to East Pakistan to write a booklet in favour of the army officials committing atrocities against the Bengali civilians. What she saw deeply affected her and left her in such an unstable condition that her friends arranged for her to go back to West Pakistan immediately. On her return, the report that she submitted was censored and discarded. She and other supporters of East Pakistan were labelled as unpatriotic traitors. Kishwar Naheed herself attracted the attention of the Central Intelligence Unit from 1977 to 1979. She has a strong memory of the atmosphere of cruelty and intolerance that pervaded the jails during the Ayub Khan, Yahya Khan and Zia years. In the 1990s she spent her energies on official duties of cultural ambassadorship in her capacity as director general of the National Council of Arts in Islamabad. She stepped down from the Arts Council directorship in 1999, after a lifetime of fighting for democratic survival in the civil service.[2] Since then she has been working on several projects including her grassroots activism supporting employment for women in Punjab villages and running her NGO, Hawwa Crafts, a cooperative for women artisans.

Naheed's profile has included editorial affiliations with Progressive Urdu literary journals such as *Adb-e Latif* and the state-funded *Mah-e nau*.[3] As an editor she was charged with many offences and acquired a reputation as a formidable force to be reckoned with. As far as the national archive of Urdu literature is concerned, she claims she has deliberately intervened in her capacity as a civil servant and magazine editor to ensure the poetry of Faiz and Riaz was published in mainstream literary magazines without drawing attention from the state censor. Her own poetic oeuvre is defined by free verse and prose poetry narrating Pakistan's political history interspersed with her own stories. Her distinctive voice places an emphasis on the everyday, contributing to Urdu's changing cultural landscape as it traverses secular and sacred territories shifting from the narrative of high politics to the lives of ordinary people. She is the recipient of many national awards and international recognition; the anthology *Nae zamane ki birhan* (A Beloved for a New Age) bears witness to her stature as a national poet.[4]

The Feminist

In an interview with Kishwar Naheed, the Urdu critic and translator Asif Furrukhi cryptically comments, 'If Albee wrote in Urdu and he had written the drama, "*Who's Afraid of Virginia Woolf?*" sitting in Pakistan then he would have called it, Who's Afraid of Kishwar Naheed? The answer to this is many people'.[5] By referring to the play, Furrukhi seems to be drawing attention to a marital home torn apart by personal conflicts between a dominant wife and a weak husband. Through this representation Furrukhi reflects an understanding of Naheed that is coated in familial topography. Focusing on the quality of her poetry, the noted Urdu writer Intizar Husain refers to Naheed's poetic voice as that of 'nae zamane ki birhan' (a woman lover for a new age). This is an important acknowledgement from an eminent Urdu authority and puts to rest questions of authenticity over her work. Husain's judgement is based on a critical review of Naheed's collection *Malamaton ke darmiyan* (Amidst Censure), written from 1978 to 1982. He argues that he first read it as a book of Hindi poetry with the voice of the *virahini* from the *Baramasa* pining for her beloved rather than that of the Urdu lyric poet but changed his mind on reflection, because this *birhan* was not singing the traditional song of separation; instead she was lamenting the loneliness of two lovers living in the same house.[6] For Husain, hers is not the nostalgic voice of the submissive Hindi *birhan* nor the nostalgic voice of the Urdu lyric poet but that of a conjugal woman confronted by the challenges of a modern life. He ends by saying, 'Kishwar Naheed appears to be dedicating herself to the job of putting an end to the worries and sorrows of all third world women'.[7] He argues that in reading her voice as that of the *birhan* translating her life experiences he is not suggesting that she should be read as a confessional poet. Instead she encompasses a worldly perspective for women.[8] Naheed has opined that 'many of our Urdu writers, including Intizar Husain, and all this crowd, have been calling me a *na-aurat*, not-woman because they feel threatened by an unconventional woman'.[9] This is an interesting observation by Naheed, noting her insecurities amongst an inner circle of male gatekeepers and absorption of gender prejudice toward women in the civil service. She claims that she was often the subject of ridicule and amusement and her own couplet was used to taunt her: 'kuch yun hi zard zard si nahid aj thi / kuch orhni ka rang bhi khulta hua na tha' (Naheed looked paler than pale today / Her dress was also dowdy and dull).[10] Intizar Husain concludes his review by emphasizing how Naheed's voice inflects newness to the *raqib* (rival) in the ghazal bringing the *sokan* (rival wife) into play. Thus there is an interesting tension between perception and reception illustrating a male bias that pigeonholes women into particular heteronormative gendered categories.

As a self-proclaimed feminist writer, Naheed has often looked beyond national borders to step outside the frame. One such example is her translation of Simone de Beauvoir's *The Second Sex* in 1982, an inspirational text for Euro-American feminist thought. Naheed reminisces that this book was her daily companion for 22 years before she undertook the translation.[11] In 1984 Columbia University honoured her with an award for best translation for this work. The book was banned for obscenity in Pakistan and she recounts that she didn't have a copy in the end herself. She blames the Jamaat-e Islami and one of its former members, Appa Nisar Fatima, who served on the Islamic Ideology Council, for the injunction:

> Three cases were instituted against me. One was that I had translated and published *The Second Sex* without government permission. Second, that I had violated the copyrights permission, and third that what I had published [*The Second Sex*] was vulgar and pornographic. [...] The case was dismissed three years later.[12]

This experience of being challenged and blocked through agitations made to the state by concerned parties was a temporary one for Naheed as she manoeuvred things to get herself reinstated. In the process she claims she was transferred 10 times because Appa Nisar Fatima had painted her in an anti-Islamic light for publishing a 'pornographic' book. However, the incident did not deter her, and she got around the censors by rewriting the book as *Aurat mard ka rishta: mazamin* (The Relationship between Women and Men: Essays) from India in 1994 instead. This book amalgamates her edited translations of Simone de Beauvoir's work and Jean-Paul Sartre's published letters and writings. The revised book was publicly less provocative than the translation of *The Second Sex* as it muted de Beauvoir by focusing more on Sartre. But it is Naheed's attachment to de Beauvoir's book that is of particular relevance as it underlines her relationship to the women's movement in Pakistan and a gender-based philosophy about the construction of femininity. De Beauvoir's philosophic legacy of how one is not born a woman but becomes one through attachments and social processes was original and transformative in reviewing the way in which women thought about themselves and were thought of, in turn.[13] De Beauvoir drew on her life experiences and her philosophic training to develop a thesis that has universal appeal. However, it has been noted that one of the things that bothered de Beauvoir was that her life was read as an 'erotic plot' through her sexual relationships rather than through her intellectual work. This is something that has disturbed Naheed as well when it comes to the reception of women intellectuals and poets in the Urdu sphere, including herself. She finds that women are always reduced to their bodies. In her autobiography, *Buri aurat ki katha* (The Story of a Shameless Woman), she writes:

Vaise adba ke ravaiye apni jaga, kisi se pucho falan khatun ki kahani suni? Jawab mile ga kahani kahan. Hum to us ki LOW NECK dekhne gae the. Kisi se pucho 'falan ki nazm suni' jawab mile ga 'nazm ka to pata nahin us ki sleeveless banhen achi lagti hain'. Kisi se pucho falan ka mazmun suna jawab mile ga bhar men gaya mazmun hamen to ye acha lagta hai ke isse vapas chorne jaen. Raste bhar muskarati rehti hai. Sharmati bohat hai mujh se. Yaqinan bat samajhti hai' sawal 'ye kisi ki biwi nahin' jawab 'han ho gi magar achi hoti to ghar se hi kyun nikalti'.

[... the behaviour of male contemporaries does not change. If you ask someone 'Did you hear that woman's story?' You are likely to get a reply that the story was unimportant, 'we had gone to see the LOW NECK she was exposing'. Ask someone 'Did you hear her poem?' and the answer will be 'can't say about the poem but I do like her bare arms'. Ask someone if they heard some woman's essay and the reply will be 'to hell with the essay, I like to escort her back to her place. She is very coy with me and smiled throughout the journey. She definitely understands the implication'. Question, 'isn't she somebody's wife?' Reply, 'yes that's possible but if she was respectable she would not have stepped out of the house'.]¹⁴

This particular extract from her life writing underlines the sexualization of women poets and the hypermasculine atmosphere of Urdu poetry circles in which women are preyed upon. Therefore the spontaneity that is required in a mushaira, the openness and vulnerability, becomes a moral question for women. Thus the crisis of modernity that was envisaged in texts by reformist intellectuals discussed in Chapter 2 comes full circle as men feel increasingly threatened by the presence of women and change to an established hierarchy. Biographically it is also important to look closely at the context of dress that is alluded to by Naheed above as it touches a deeper chord in her life but is something she doesn't show and tell in the book.¹⁵ I've understood this better from conversations both with her and with those around her such as Ayesha Siddiqa, who knew her from childhood through her mother Jamila Hashmi's friendship.¹⁶

The issue of what to wear and its moral implications is something that is close to her heart as she was subjected to severe scrutiny when she took up the office of Director of the National Centre in 1972. She tells Shahla Haeri that in those days the fashion was for sleeveless blouses with saris and, as a follower of that trend, Kishwar became a hot topic in the news media not for her intellect but for what she wore:

> [In] every newspaper, whether English or local, but particularly in the locals – and there were many of them – there would be at least one article about my clothing, the way my bare arms were showing and my sari was hanging around my body! Nobody ever talked and wrote about what I was doing, how I was managing and conducting the functions of the centre, and how I was organizing the council. I got so fed up that I called my tailor and said, 'Go and take it off. If this is the only problem of this country. I dislike it. Take all these blouses and put sleeves on them!'¹⁷

Thus as a civil servant she was expected to uphold a particular image for an Islamic nation and wearing a sari with a sleeveless blouse was a problem because it brought into focus two issues, 'bare arms' and the sari. The former was an affront to conservative moralists and the latter gave off the unwelcome vibe of an antinational dress because of associations with an Indian and Bengali past.¹⁸ During the Bhutto period, she witnessed the courtship of Islam through his Ministry of Religious Affairs and Auqaf Department, noting how religious preferences crept into cultural life through Islamic television programming, Arabic lessons and clothing. Naheed narrates the anecdote of hosting Maulana Qadir Azad of Badshahi Mosque, Lahore, for a talk and her deliberate decision to wear a sari for the occasion, which led to a reprimand from the Maulana that the sari she wore was not 'our own style of dress', which he described as the *shalwar*, *qamiz* and *dupatta*.[19] The dialogue between the Maulana and Naheed as she narrates it doesn't result in polarized positions but an agreement to disagree. This is only possible because Naheed speaks from a position of power at the time of the conversation. Had she not had the backing of the state her story would have been different. Therefore when she writes about women's bodies being read as their texts in poetry symposia and intellectual gatherings, she is also inflecting into the narrative her own experiences. In her own life, she recounts that, despite her differences with her mother over veiling and sharafat as a Sayyid Muslim, she was influenced by her mother's choice to educate her daughters and her active participation in the Muslim League campaign. In college and university life, the burqa became something of a performative piece for Naheed as she wore it to please the family and took it off to express herself.[20]

Her career trajectory as a feminist is thus directly linked to her personal life experiences. According to Naheed, the decision to marry her college sweetheart Yusuf Kamran, who was also a poet, was forced upon her by her family who found out about her association with Kamran and demanded an honourable resolution.[21] As it turned out, theirs was a rocky marriage, made so by issues of loyalty and trust. This, combined with the regular gathering at their house of male poets who were not ready to acknowledge women as equals beyond their physical appearance and attractiveness, brought home the real-life challenges women faced as creative artists. An oft-quoted couplet from Naheed voices the frustrations of a woman's life as householder, shifting the lyrical tone from the passion of unrequited love to the emptiness of performing mundane household chores: 'Ghar ke dhande ke nimatte hi nahin Naheed / main nikalna bhi agar sham ko ghar se chahun' (Naheed the chores around the house never get done / Even if I want to go out in the evening).[22] Her collections of poetry are marked by expressions of loneliness and disillusionment in love. She interprets this isolation in an article entitled 'Likhne valiyon ki tanhai' (The Loneliness of Women Writers), paying tribute to women's writing that has survived despite the overwhelming presence of male critics and their biases toward women.[23]

Speaking on a personal note, she observes that critics were kinder to her in the past because she was married to the Urdu poet Yusuf Kamran, who died in 1984 at the age of 45. She also felt the exclusions of a gendered society that recognized her as an extension of her husband rather than the independent woman she was. Before that, her father thought that she was an impostor, '"copying" other people's work'.[24] Both in her own words and in her interviews, she expresses frustration at how her writing was perceived to be inauthentic and serviced by other men. Naheed and Kamran made for an interesting couple and, despite Naheed's influence and power, it was the literary establishment that made her feel an outsider and trespasser. Given this perception, it is important to see how Kamran is represented by the bestselling author Mustansar Husain Tarar in his book *Lahore Awargi* (Gallivanting in Lahore). In his chapter on 'Lahore ke adbi salon' (Lahore's literary salons), he refers in passing to Yusuf Kamran as 'apne kashmiri husn pe nazan, cigret phunkta, ek playboy jo Apa Hijab se baqaeda flirt karta […] ek kamina shakhs tha' (someone who was cocky about his Kashmiri lure, a playboy puffing cigarettes, who took pleasure in flirting with Hijab [Imtiaz Ali] Apa […] he was a cruel person).[25] Thus he characterizes and indirectly confirms the accusations of Kamran's infidelities, listed by Naheed in her poetry and in her interview to Haeri, observing his flirtatious manner with women of all ages, including the renowned writer of romance fiction Hijab Imtiaz Ali. Through his selected incursions into Lahore's literary salons, he confirms the reputation that Naheed spells out of a handsome womanizer who regularly tormented his wife. Tarar's book is not an exposé of people, but gossipy inclusions, such as the one on Kamran. He notes the glittering literary gatherings held at Naheed's residences, first in her old house in Krishan Nagar and later in Iqbal town, which accommodated literary celebrities while she was married to Kamran. He points out that Naheed was the primary owner of the marital home, hinting at the economic power she held in the household. Naheed confesses to Haeri that she felt both 'pain' and 'relief' when she was given the news of Kamran's sudden death over the telephone.[26]

As far as her writing was concerned, Naheed revealed in an interview with the writer Harris Khalique that 'Yousuf Kamran – who was my friend before being my husband – would discourage me from writing bold poems. Ghazals were fine but my nazms would make him nervous.'[27] Naheed's poem 'Yousaf Kamran', dedicated to her husband, voices her feelings of loss and abandonment over a love affair gone wrong. Her public confession of a troubled personal relationship disrupts the sharif construct of the family unit as a space for women's discretion and silence. By making personal experiences central to both her craft and her professional life Naheed decentres the exclusions of national culture that privilege the storytelling of male public intellectuals and state bureaucracy.[28] It is a poem that would have made Kamran extremely nervous.

وہ تو مجرم تھا محبت کا
میں اُسے جانتی تھی
میں تو اُس شخص کے ہر نقص کو پہچانتی تھی
میں اُسے چاہتی تھی ۔

وہ شفق رنگ ، حیا جس کو کہیں
تھی یہی میری دف کی تعبیر
وہ بہانہ جسے چشمک سمجھیں
تھی مرے تیرے تعلق کی نظیر ۔

تو کہ محبوب مجھے تھا ، مجھے معلوم ہے یہ

تو کہ مجرم تھا ، مرے پیار
مری چاہت کا
تو کہ دیوانۂ مخفئ محبت تھا سدا
تجھ کو کیا سوجھی
کہ قدموں کے نشاں اُلجھا کر
چہرۂ زرد دیے
میری ہتھیلی پہ لگی مہندی کو دُھند لانے لگا
جیل کی گرم سلاخوں سے
مرے بچوں کو تڑپانے لگا
تو کہ مجرم تھا محبت کا
زمانے کو خبر کیسے ہوئی یا!

Tu ke mahbub mujhe tha, mujhe malum hai ye
Tu ke mujrim tha, mere pyar
Meri chahat ka
Tu ke diwana makhfi-e muhabbat tha sada
Tujh ko kya sujhi
Ke qadmon ke nishan uljha kar
Chehra-e zard liye
Meri hatheli pe lagi mehndi ko dhundhlane laga
Jail ki garam sulakhon se
Mere bachon ko tarpane laga
Tu ke mujrim tha muhabbat ka
Zamane ko khabar kaise hui!!

[You were dear to me, I know
You were my love's captive,
My desire you were forever love's mad secret
What struck you
That you confused your footprints
With your pale face
You misted over the henna on my palms.
From the hot iron bars of jail
You tormented my children
You who were love's captive
How did the world come to know!!][29]

These lines encapsulate the domestic themes of marriage, love, desire and captivity in a spirit of restrained protest voiced in the line, 'you tormented my children'. It is through her children's eyes that Naheed seems to recognize the cost of her love for Kamran. Her confessional persona shines through as she lets the reader into the disappointments of lived experience when the subject of her love cast a shadow over her life. She recounts for her readers an image of Kamran behind 'hot iron bars', a vivid memory of his imprisonment in 1971 during the regime of General Yahya Khan. The poem doesn't tell the story about why Kamran was in jail. The imprisonment, she confesses to Shahla Haeri, came about because Kamran and his father had insulted the army colonel who had come to collect rent from them for the house they lived in and because Jalil Niazi, the Punjab administrator, had demanded to be with her and she had refused.[30] Perhaps this was a deliberate omission to avoid any repercussions from the army. Instead the poem is a mixture of conflicted emotions, voicing her dissatisfaction with Kamran as someone whose fickle love put barriers between them rather than bringing them closer. The personal is paramount in the act of retrieving memory and the poem can be read as 'truth-telling' masked in the anguish of an unrequited love. By writing about how she was struggling on several fronts to sustain a marriage, a career, a job and a family, while Kamran made no changes to his carefree lifestyle, she lends agency to women in the Urdu milieu to break the silence about domestic power dynamics and to acknowledge the central role they play both emotionally and economically.[31] Yet at the same time this poem is rich with ambivalence as it taps into the mystical tradition of love by deploying metaphorical language and in its use of form. She inverts the gender binary of social structures by using the familiar trope of the lover and the beloved to project the insanity of her love for Kamran as the lover, while his persona is imbued with the characteristics of the cruel beloved who took pleasure in her distress. Masculinity and femininity as imagined in the poem don't map onto the known genders of Naheed and Kamran. The mood is borrowed from the love lyric. The last line, 'How did the world come to know?', again draws the listener to a material reality. By narrating her experience of familial dysfunctionality Naheed lays bare her soul for the listener. This is a sharif woman confessing to a love marriage, prevaricating between speech and silence using idiomatic language. The choice of who to love is not independent of how to love and she underlines how the behaviour of those who take part in this bond can rely on a predetermined emotional landscape mapped out in the contours of language.

Naheed's poems echo a statement of survival for women and speak out against their oppression, relaying vivid descriptions of violence against women, the disfigurement of their bodies from beatings, attempted strangulations and stove burnings. A particularly gruesome poem such as 'Face the Pan', with its simile of frying eggs and women's lips cooked in oil, and 'Clearance Sale', relating the existence of women to cattle in a marriage market, are emblematic of her hard-hitting politics of representation.[32]

Poetry as Performance: The Mother

In her autobiography, *Buri aurat ki katha*, Naheed writes:

> Shairi ne mujhe bohat dukh diye. Shairi chorh deti to shaid naik parvin biwi man li jati. Khidmat guzar man ka aizaz milta, behn bhaiyon se aur qurbat hoti, dunya ko kam samajh pati, sach kam bol sakti, kam dushman bana pati and tanha rahne men kam khushi mehsus karti.

Magar shairi ne mujhe bohat sukh diye. Pura mulk and puri dunya mujhe apna maika lagta hai. Itne dost aur itne chahne vale diye ke mohabbat ki garmi mujhe unthak kam karne par mayal rakhti hai. Shairi ne itni dosarahat di ke rafaqat ke sare rishton ki chadar mere sar par tani hai.

[Poetry has made me very unhappy. If I had abandoned poetry then I might have been accepted as a pure and dutiful wife. I would have been held in esteem as a devoted mother, been closer to my sisters and brothers, understood less of the world, mostly spoken with dishonesty, succeeded in making fewer enemies and felt that living alone curtailed my happiness.

But poetry has made me content. The entire country and the entire world seem like my maternal home. I have been given so many friends and well wishers and the warmth from their love inspires me to keep working non-stop.][33]

Her autobiography challenges the expectations of society and interestingly sets up poetry as performativity, challenging stereotypical perceptions of a bad woman with its deliberate lack of self-censorship. Naheed's use of '*katha*' in her book title nods to nineteenth-century autobiographical writings by Bengali women known as *smrtikatha* (stories from memory). A feature of these memoirs that seems to have influenced Naheed is the way they were structured around the social history of the times. In fact, these stories have provided key source material to scholars mapping out the social history of nineteenth-century Bengal. Naheed is canny in her choice of generic label: historically, anyone could narrate a *smrtikatha*, and the 'artlessness' of its form was considered 'appropriate for an authentic "feminine" literary voice'.[34] By investing her persona into the storytelling theme she makes herself vulnerable to other women and colleagues who have similar experiences, lending authenticity to her narrative. This is not just another romantic deception by the poet; it is testimonial 'truth-telling' from a secular perspective.[35]

In Naheed's own words her story has been layered with different voices. The voices belong to 'seven' women who range from the ordinary to extraordinary: they are Mah Laqa, Layla, Zarin Taj, Mira Bai, Sana, Yashodhra and Hawwa, encapsulating worldly mythical and mystic women from courtesans to queens both Indic and Islamic with histories of prostitution, romance, royalty and so on, including the mother of all,

Eve.[36] The chapter titles of her autobiography pay homage to these icons and she retells her story in the guise of their personae.[37] The irony for her as the writer is her inability to overcome their tragedy with her pen; instead the power of her pen is beyond her control and turns into the proverbial dagger stabbing the very writer (herself) who has undertaken the role of representation. Mapping her circle of influences from poets to mothers, she links women from multilingual geographical locations. 'Sometimes you have named yourself Anna [*sic*] Sexton and announced your correct date of birth at twenty-nine years of age. Sometimes you became Forough Farrokhzad, sometimes Sara Shagufta and sometimes my mother!'.[38] Sexton and Shagufta, both poets who committed suicide, are translated into the figure of her mother to challenge the tradition–modernity paradigm. Amongst these women she also mentions a minority figure, Jacob – an 8-year-old Christian boy kept behind bars in Sargodha for his misdemeanour of scribbling on the walls of a mosque.[39] Through a reference to Jacob's case Naheed highlights the trauma of blasphemy that marks minorities in Pakistan. In doing so, she intertextually connects the marginalities and traumas of both women and minorities and how the law has been deployed to serve sacred ideologies in Pakistan, disempowering those who are peripheral to the national family.[40] Naheed's story is riddled with rejection from her family and her peers, but she reaches out to her readers and listeners through fictional mothers as alternative role models who have sustained her during her years of loneliness. She finds solace in rewriting national politics, reflecting her identifications with the motherland through poems such as 'Apahaj ma mitti ki goldan jubilee' (The Golden Jubilee of a Crippled Motherland) and 'Apni jaisi aurat vazir-e azam se mukalima' (Dialogue with a Woman Prime Minister like Myself), adopting the role of the mother-narrator to retell the stories of Partition and post-Partition violence.[41]

These themes of birth mother and surrogate mother are defined in terms of the Pakistani nation in 'Apahaj ma mitti ki goldan jubilee'. In this poem, on the occasion of the golden jubilee of the nation, nationalist concerns reign supreme. This golden jubilee actually took place in 1997 and Naheed's poem, written in advance, predicts a hollow ring to the celebrations:

میری سنو!
میں تم سے مخاطب ہوں
میں پاکستان ہوں!
تمہاری ماں مٹی
میں نے ان لوگوں کی اُمیدوں کی
کوکھ سے جنم لیا تھا
جواب ہم تم میں نہیں ہیں۔
وہ سچے لوگ
جنہوں نے ایک علیحدہ مملکت کا خواب دیکھا تھا
ایک ایسی مملکت کا خواب
کہ جس میں وہ اور ان کی آئندہ آنے والی نسلیں
آزادی اور فخر سے خود کو انسان کہہ سکیں
وہ سچے لوگ
جنہوں نے اس خواب کی تعبیر کے لیے
اپنی زندگیوں کا سودا کیا تھا۔
میں ان ہی سچے لوگوں کے
خوابوں کی تعبیر ہوں۔
میں چوبیس سال کی ہوئی
تو جھوٹ کے گماشتوں نے مجھے اپاہج کر دیا۔
میں ۴۳ سال کی ہو کے بھی
خوفزدہ اور غیر محفوظ ہوں
اُمیدیں مجھ سے چھپتی پھر رہی ہیں
میں کوئی بھولا ہوا سبق نہیں ہوں
میں کوئی ٹوٹی ہوئی شاخ نہیں ہوں

مگر یہ کیسا دھواں ہے
جو میری آزادی کی آنکھوں کو دھند لانے چلے جا رہا ہے
یہ کون سے شعلے ہیں
جو میرے اسلاف کی فتح مندیوں کو جھلسائے دے رہے ہیں
یہ کیسا خوف ہے
جو میری رگوں میں جوش مارتے خون کو شرمساری کی
برف میں دھنسنے دے رہا ہے
میں نے تو ہوا کے پروں پر بھی
"لے کے رہیں گے پاکستان" لکھا تھا
میرے زمانے میں تو تتلیوں نے بھی
میرے پرچم کا رنگ پہنا تھا
میں نے اپنی دہلیز پر آزادی کا دیا
اس لیے رکھا تھا
کہ غلام قومیں اس کی روشنی میں
آزاد ہونا سیکھیں گی
وہ کون تھا
جو میرے گونجتے نعرے لے کر
زہر ناک سرگوشیاں چھوڑ گیا ہے ۔
میرے بچو !
میرے سچے لوگوں کے بچو
تم اپنی وراثت کو بھول کر

کب تک اپنے ضمیر کو جھٹلاتے
اور جھوٹے وعدوں کو پہنتے رہو گے
میرے بچو!
مجھے تمہارے لفظ نہیں چاہئیں
پھٹی ہوئی تصویر یا پھٹے ہوئے نقشے کی
تاریخ رقم کرنا، تمہارا مقدر نہیں ہے۔
میری بنتی سنو!
مجھے میرے سفید بالوں کا وقار واپس لوٹا دو
مجھے میری کوکھ میں پلنے والا امن واپس لوٹا دو
اٹھو میرے بچو! میں تم سے مخاطب ہوں
ماں! بھلا اور کس سے بات کر سکتی ہے!

Meri suno!
Main tum se mukhatib hun
Main Pakistan hun!
Tumhari ma mitti
Main ne un logon ki umidon ki
Kukh se janam liya tha
Jo ab hum tum main nahin hain.
Voh sache log
Jinhon ne ek alehda mumlikat ka khvab dekha tha
Ek aisi mumlikat ka khvab
Ke jis men voh or un ki ainda ane vali naslen
Azadi aur fakhar se khud ko insan keh saken
Voh sache log
Jinhon ne is khvab ki tabir ke liye
Apni zindagion ka sauda kiya tha.
Main un hi sache logon ke
Khvabon ki tabir hun.
Main chobis sal ki hui
To jhut ke gumashton ne mujhe apahaj kar diya.
Main 43 sal ki ho ke bhi

Khaufzada aur ghair mahfuz hun
Umeeden mujh se chupti phir rahi hain
Main koi bhula hua sabaq nahin hun
Main koi tuti hui shakh nahin hun
Magar ye kaisa dhuan hai
Jo meri azadi ki ankhon ko dhundlae chale jar aha hai
Ye kon se shole hain
Jo mere aslaf ki fatah mandion ko jhulsai de rahe hain
Ye kaisa khauf hai
Jo meri ragon men josh marte khun ko sharmsari ki
Barf men dhanse de raha hai
Main ne to hawa ke paron par bhi
'le ke rahen ge Pakistan' likha tha
Mere zamane men to titlion ne bhi
Mere parcham ka rang pehna tha
Main ne apni dahliz par azadi ka diya
Is liye rakha tha
Ke Ghulam qaumen is ki roshni men
Azad hona sikhen gi
Vo kaun tha
Jo mere gunjte nare le kar
Zahrnak sargoshian chor gaya hai.
Mere bacho!
Mere sache logon ke bacho
Tum apni virasat ko bhul kar
Kab tak apne zamir ko jhutlate
Aur jhute vadon ko pehante raho ge
Mere bacho!
Mujhe tumhare lafz nahin chahiyen
Phati hui tasvir ya phate hue naqshe ki
Tarikh raqam karna, tumhara muqaddar nahin hai.
Meri binti suno!
Mujhe mere safaid balon ka vaqar vapas lota do
Mujhe meri kukh men palne vala aman vapas lota do
Uttho mere bacho! Main tum se mukhatib hun
Ma! Bhala aur kis se bat kar sakti hai!

[Hear me!
I am addressing you
I am Pakistan!

Your mother earth
From the womb of those
Who are not amongst us now was I born.

Those honest people
Who saw the dream of a separate nation
A dream of such a nation
In which they and their future generations
Would with pride and freedom count themselves as part of a human race
Those honest people
Who for the realisation of that dream
Bartered their lives.
I am the realisation of that dream
Belonging to those honest people.

As I turned twenty four
Whirlpools of dishonesty crippled me.

Now forty-three years old
I am still frightened and unsafe

Hopes keep eluding me
I am not a forgotten lesson
I am not a broken branch
But what kind of smoke is this
That keeps misting over my sight of freedom
What sparks are these
That are scorching the triumph of my ancestors
What kind of fear is this?
That is freezing over the running blood of my veins to an icy shame
On the wings of wind, I too
Wrote, 'we will have Pakistan'
The butterflies in those days too
Wore the colours of my flag
I had placed the oil burner of freedom
On my doorstep so that
From its light the enslaved nations
Would learn to be free

Who was it?
That took my reverberating slogans
Leaving behind poisonous machinations.

My children!
The children of my honest people
For how long will you cheat your conscience?
And wear false promises

My children!
I don't need your words
It is not in your stars to rewrite the history
Of a moth eaten map or a torn picture.

Listen to my request!
Return the stature of my white hair to me
Return the peace of my womb to me
Rise my children! I am addressing you
Who else can a mother speak to!][42]

The poem begins with the mother lamenting the decline of the dream of those 'honest' people now dead, who infused optimism and ambition into the birth of their new homeland, and ends with the mother's sense of a cheated reality in present-day corruption. In paying tribute to those people who lost their lives in the realization of their new home, the poem idealizes the past and echoes the romantic lyricism of Faiz. Her negative assessment of the present is reflected through a remembering of key moments from Pakistan's troubled political history, the years 1971 – a moment of permanent separation from East Pakistan, and the creation of Bangladesh – and 1990, marking the just-past, turbulent decade of the 1980s on the occasion of the golden jubilee. Naheed's motherland urges a return to the past to restore order in the present. Crucially, this is not a gendered rendition of motherhood; in fact, it reiterates a statist idea of mother as nurturer and protector.

The mother is a central figure in almost all of Naheed's collections. In this particular collection she appears in the guise of the nation, asking for accountability from her children. This mother, we are told, was born from the womb of those 'who are not amongst us now' – a possible reference to the early rulers of Pakistan, Jinnah and Liaquat Ali Khan. It may seem that the poet is eliding ordinary life histories and the female narrative of that time by only referring to key political personalities, except for her mention of the womb, conceptualizing the reproductive female body and Fatima Jinnah known as madr-e millat (mother of the nation), Jinnah's sister and staunch supporter who stood for election in 1965. Appropriating the garb of mother earth rooted in the soil, Naheed presents an organic picture of the natural saviour and guardian of the nation. It is interesting to note whether Naheed's nationalistic mother is a feminist awakening, or a duplication of earlier reformist representations of the nation as mother.[43]

If we contrast this with another poem that deals with the theme of the nation and women, entitled 'Apni jaisi aurat vazir-e azam se mukalima' (Dialogue with a Woman Prime Minister like Myself), we again see a poetic persona that cannot be read in isolation from the nation; in this case it seems to be referring the reader to Benazir Bhutto's first term in office as prime minister and the return of democracy after a long spell of martial law under General Zia. Written in the style of a lyric, the poem locates its message in the bruised and battered body of the poet/caretaker who looks after the garden, a metaphor for the country. The poet narrates a tale of woe written as an informal confidence to the prime minister, conferring upon her the title of mother, a theme from her previous poem, 'Apahaj ma mitti ki goldan jubilee'.

میں باغ کی راکھی ہوئی میّا
مجھے باغ پہ حق بھی دو میّا

مرے بازو نیلو نیل ہیں سب
مری آنکھوں میں سوئیاں ہیں چھپی
مرے ہونٹوں پہ ہیں زخم سجے
مرے پاؤں میں چھالے ہیں بہت

میں کیسے بھولوں اے میّا
وہ کوڑے جو میری کمر پہ ہیں
وہ قید جو میرے وجود پہ
سانپ سپولے بن بیٹھی
وہ سارے فیصلے یاد مجھے
جو نام پہ مذہب کے آئے
جو میری گواہی پہ چھائے
جو نام شریعت کا پائے
جو حق و صداقت کہلائے
جو زخم لگے، الزام آئے

تمہیں یاد دلاؤں اے میّا
وہ ہاتھ سلامت ہیں اب تک
جن ہاتھوں نے سنگسار کیا
مرے ننھّے پھول سے بچّوں کو

جن ہاتھوں نے چادر چھینی
مری بہنوں کو زد و کوب کیا
جو چاٹ گئے دیواریں بھی
جو نیچ گئے ذرّہ ذرّہ
جنہیں لاج نہ آئی مٹی کی
تمہیں یاد تو ہوگا اے میّا
کیا جیل بنے تھے گھر اپنے
کیا اُجلے تن دُھند لاتے تھے
ہم اپنے دیس میں بے گھر تھے
ہم بے قیمت کہلاتے تھے۔

تمہیں یاد تو ہوگا اے میّا
جو حشر اُٹھے جو گھر اُجڑے
جو مقتل میں جاں ہار گئے
خوں ان کا کم عظمت تو نہ تھا
جاں ان کی بے ہمّت تو نہ تھی
ان سب کی گواہی لے کے میں
ان سب کی دُہائی لے کے میں

یہ نم کو جناؤں اے میّا
مت بھُولنا تم پہ قرض ہے یہ
مت بھُولنا تم پہ قرض ہے یہ
میں باغ کی راکھی ہوئی میّا
مجھے باغ پہ حق بھی دو میّا!

Main bagh ki rakhi hui mayya
Mujhe bagh pe haq do mayya

Mere bazu nilo nil hain sab
Meri ankhon men suyian hain chubhi
Mere honton pai hain zakhm saje
Mere paon men chale hain bohat

Main kaise bhulon ai mayya
Voh kore jo meri kamar pai hain
Voh qaid jo mere vajud pe
Samp sampole ban bethi
Voh sare faisle yad mujhe
Jo nam pai mazhab ke aye
Jo meri gawahi pai chaye
Jo nam shariat ka paye
Jo haq o sadaqat kehlaye
Jo zakhm lage, Ilzam aye

Tumhen yad dilaon ai mayya
Voh hath jo salamat hain ab tak
Jin hathon ne sangsar kiya
Mere nanhe phul se bachon ko
Jinhon ne chadar chini
Meri behnon ko zad-o kob kia
Jo chat gaye divaren bhi
Jo bech gaye zarra zarra
Jinhen laj na ayi mitti ki
Tumhen yad to ho ga ai mayya
Jo hashr uthe jo ghar ujre
Jo maqtal men jan har gaye
Khun un ka kam azmat to na tha
Jan un ki behimmat to na thi
In sab ki gawahi le ke main
In sab ki duhai le ke main

Ye tum ko jitaon ai mayya
Mat bhulna tum pe qarz hai ye
Mat bhulna tum pe farz hai ye
Main bagh ki rakhi hui mayya
Mujhe bagh pe haq bhi do mayya!

[I am a caretaker of this garden, mother
Let me have rights over the garden too, mother!

My arms all are blue with bruises
Needles they have pricked my eyes
My lips they are dressed in wounds
My feet are many blistered

How can I forget, ay mother!
Those lashes imprinted upon my back
That imprisonment which is mine
Sticking like a snake to its newborn

All those decisions I remember
Which came out on the behest of religion
Which cast a shadow upon my witness
Which found name under Shariat
Which were called truth and honesty
Those wounds incurred, allegations made

O mother shall I remind you
That those hands are still alive
Those hands which performed the stoning
On my tiny flowerlike children
Those hands which snatched the *chadur*
Aimed at and beat up my sisters
They were obsessed
They sold each and every particle
They who could not respect the earth

You must remember, ay mother
How our homes turned into jails
How sparkling bodies faded
We were homeless in our homeland
We had been labelled worthless

You must remember, ay mother
The raging hell, the ruined homes
They who lost their lives in execution
Their blood was not less honourable
Their life was not without courage

> With witnesses which I have heard from all
> With the reports which I have taken from all
>
> Shall I admonish you, ay mother
> Do not forget that this is a loan to you
> Do not forget that this is your obligation
> I am a caretaker of this garden, mother
> Let me have rights over the garden too, mother.][44]

The poem is written in the style of a dialogue between a poet and a prime minister. It advocates the rights of women and minorities that have been undermined by the previous regime under Sharia law. According to the poem, those rights need to be restored by the new mother, as a return of the trust that has been invested in her election by the women of the nation. Ironically, Benazir Bhutto answered the call for social justice in a public speech on her wedding day in 1987:

> Today, on an occasion so personal and solemn for me, I want to reaffirm my public pledge to the people of Pakistan, and restate my most solemn vow to devote my life towards the welfare of each citizen and the freedom of this great nation of ours from dictatorship, I'd written in a statement released the morning of the wedding. 'I will not hesitate to make any sacrifice, be it large or small, as in the past. I will work shoulder to shoulder with my brothers and sisters – the people of Pakistan – to create an egalitarian society that is free from tyranny, from corruption and from violent tensions. This was my goal yesterday, this is the dream I share with you, and this will remain our unwavering commitment forever'.[45]

However, Hamza Alavi, in his review of the status of Pakistani women evaluating women's persecution during General Zia's time, reiterated the lack of intervention by Benazir's government regarding women's rights in Pakistan:

> Sadly, the eleven years of the so-called policy of 'Islamisation' under General Zia, have produced in Pakistan a culture of intolerance. This culture, above all, has persecuted women and subjected them to all kinds of humiliation and ill treatment, not to speak of inhuman punishment under the Hudood Ordinances. […]

It was hoped that the democratic government of Benazir Bhutto would reverse this and, in particular, repeal the Hudood Ordinances (including Zina Ordinance). But it has shown no inclination to change the laws.[46]

Naheed's verse also offers an introspective lens on women's rights in Pakistan.[47] Adopting the persona of a national poet, she takes on the role of spokesperson for Pakistani women, bearing witness and reminding the mother of her duty to the nation. However, what she doesn't take into account in this narrative are the difficulties of reputation that also confronted Benazir Bhutto and her followers. The feudal connections and tribal interrelations within the party membership and representation meant that securitization and policing could be used toward reiterating an honour and shame based *biradari* system of social justice with women being held to ransom over their character.[48]

The mother in 'Apni jaisi aurat vazir-e azam' is also double-cast as the prime minister. It can be read as an answering back to the motherland of 'Apahaj ma mitti', enlisting the helplessness of the people as a reason for their ineffectual response to their distressed mother's call for rescue. The poem gravitates between the voice of the poet-narrator and the mother/prime minister and at times both voices blend into one. It reiterates the violence inscribed on women's bodies to establish power. But the important difference between the two poems lies in the characterization of the mother.

The figure of the mother is useful to look at in one of Naheed's earlier poems, 'Mom Mahal' (Wax Palace) from her collection *Siyah hashiye men gulabi rung* (Pink Hue in a Black Margin). In this poem, we see the narration of a dream sequence in which mother and daughter are connected by the shared space of their home but separated by dreams.

موم محل

میرے بیاہ سے پہلے میری ماں
خواب میں ڈر جایا کرتی تھی
اس کی خوفناک چیخوں سے میری آنکھ کھل جاتی تھی
میں اسے جگاتی ماجرا پوچھتی
اور وہ خالی آنکھوں سے گھورتی رہتی
اسے خواب یاد نہیں رہتے تھے

ایک رات خواب میں ڈر کر
اس نے چیخ نہیں ماری
خوف زدہ ہو کر مجھے اپنے ساتھ چمٹا لیا
میں نے ماجرا پوچھا
تو اس آنکھیں کھول کر شکرانہ ادا کرتے ہوئے کہا
میں نے خواب میں دیکھا تھا
تم ڈوب رہی ہو اور میں نے تمھیں بچانے کے لیے
دریا میں چھلانگ لگائی ہے
اور اس رات بجلی کے گرنے سے
ہماری بھینس اور میرا منگیتر جل گئے تھے

ایک رات ماں سو رہی تھی اور میں جاگ رہی تھی

ماں بار بار مٹھی بند کرتی اور کھولتی

اور یوں لگتا کہ جیسے کچھ پکڑنے کی کوشش میں تھک کر

مگر پھر ہمت باندھنے کو مٹھی بند کرتی

میں نے ماں کو جگایا

مگر ماں نے مجھے خواب بتانے سے انکار کر دیا

اس دن سے میری نیند اڑ گئی

میں دوسرے صحن میں آ گئی

اب میں اور میری ماں دونوں خواب میں چیخیں مارتے ہیں

اور جب کوئی پوچھے

تو کہہ دیتے ہیں

ہمیں خواب یاد نہیں رہتے

Mere byah se pehle meri ma
Khvab men dar jaya karti thi
Us ki khaufnak chikhon se meri ankh khul jati thi
Main usay jagati, majra puchti
Aur voh khali ankhon ghurti rahti
Usay khvab yad nahin rahte the.
Ek rat khvab men dar kar
Us ne chikh nahi mari
Khaufzada ho kar mujhe apne sath chimta liya tha
Main ne majra pucha
To us ne ankhen khol kar shukrana ada karte hue kaha,
'Main ne khvab dekha tha
Tum dub rahi ho aur main ne tumhe bachane ko darya men chalang lagali hai'
Aur us rat bijli girne se
Hamari bhains aur mera mangetar jal gaye the.
Ek rat man so rahi thi or main jag rahi thi,
Ma bar bar muthi band karti aur kholti
Aur yun lagta ke jaise kuch pakarne ki koshish men thak kar
Magar phir himmat bandhne ko muthi band karti hai.

Main ne ma ko jagaya
Magar ma ne mujhe khvab batane se inkar kar diya.
Us din se meri nind ur gai,
Main dusre sahn men a gai,
Ab main or meri ma donon khvab men chikhen marte hain
Aur jab koi puche
To keh dete hain
Hamen khvab yad nahin rehte.

[Before my marriage my Ma
Would get frightened in her dreams
Her terrified screams would awaken me
I would wake her, ask what had happened
And with vacant eyes she kept staring.
She could not remember those dreams.
One night frightened in her dream
She did not scream,
Fearfully she had held me tight
I asked, what is it?
Offering a prayer she opened her eyes as she said
'I had seen in my dream,
That you were drowning and I jumped into the river to save you'
And that night from lightning
Our buffalo and my fiancé were electrocuted.
One night Ma was sleeping and I was awake,
Ma kept clenching and unclenching her fist over and over,
And it seemed as if she had wearied from holding on to something,
Yet again mustering up courage she clenched her fist once more
I awakened Ma
But Ma declined to tell me her dream.
Since that day I have lost my sleep
I have come into the other courtyard,
Now both Ma and I scream in our dreams.
And when someone inquires,
We say
We cannot remember our dreams.][49]

'Mom Mahal' begins enigmatically with the mother's nightmares and ends with hallucinations plaguing both mother and daughter. We are introduced to the mother from the start as someone who habitually suffers from nightmares. The narrating voice is that of the woman about to get married, who is constantly kept awake by her mother's screams. Ironically, by the end of the poem the daughter is also afflicted with dream-led delusions, and like her mother adopts silence over speech. The turning point in 'Mom Mahal' is triggered by the death of the fiancé, implying that marriage should not be the only future envisaged for a woman as it spells disaster in a low-income family. Naheed's juxtaposition of the buffalo with the fiancé brings home women's enslavement by the ritual of marriage and dowry. Natural disaster saves the daughter once but then the wax palace melts as the mother and daughter descend into separate personal psychoses, unable to communicate with each other. The mother refuses to share her dreams with her daughter, presumably because she can't save her, and the daughter, burdened by this knowledge, retreats into an inner world. They preserve a mask of sanity for the outside world by maintaining an amnesiac silence about their dreams because to cross that threshold would mean relinquishing a defensive state of depersonalization for a more permanent mental trauma.

One of the questions confronting the reader is the articulation of silences in the poem. The mother's silence goes through many stages. Initially she is silent because she cannot remember her dreams, in the middle she breaks that silence to retell her dream, in which she saves her daughter from drowning, and by the end she once again returns to silence. This silence could be read in a number of ways: first, Ma preserves a deliberate silence with her blank expression and amnesiac memory to exclude her daughter from her mental processes. The daughter keeps asking for inclusion and when her mother finally lets her in, it is only in a controlled manner. She shares the content of her nightmare because the nightmare ends positively. Finally, the mother retreats into the safety net of her unspoken nightmares again and a world beyond language. According to Simone de Beauvoir, one of Naheed's muses, the ambivalence and irony of a mother–daughter relationships is one in which:

> the daughter is for the mother at once her double and another person, the mother is at once overweeningly affectionate and hostile towards her daughter; she saddles her child with her own destiny: a way of proudly laying claim to her own femininity and also a way of revenging herself for it.[50]

Naheed's poem can partially be read in the context of de Beauvoir's analysis as the exploration of a love/hate mother–daughter relationship, in which the mother prepares her daughter for a fate similar to her own and keeps her anxieties hidden in a silent web of dreams. The sacred pact of marriage and family that the mother is committed to is something that is never dialogized other than the mention of the fiancé who dies. Naheed's gendered representation of an emotionally charged mother–daughter relationship subverts the national trope of women as devotional, dutiful and obedient. These women are dissenting silently through their dreams. Relegated to the private realm of the home, she depicts how their social exclusion has far-reaching consequences for their mental well-being. By making these women the addressees of her poem, Naheed is deliberately lifting the burden of modesty as the only story that is relevant to their lives. Through her articulation of dreams she signifies deeper anxieties than just a national critique; she is engaging with contexts of community beyond the nation and stories that remain untold.

The title, 'Mom Mahal', symbolizes the poignancy of the narrative with its imagery of a palace made from wax. Wax, a soft malleable substance secreted by bees to make honeycombs, is a secondary source dependent on the bee for its creation. The wax palace is a metaphor for the hive dependent on the queen bee and here the poem takes an interesting turn. The role of the mother, like the queen bee, is primarily one of reproduction to ensure a new generation, but she is not able to control the behaviour of those who inhabit or visit the beehive. Naheed's title can be read as a metaphor for women as vessels of fertility who nurture their progeny for the same destiny. At some point, the beehive begins to melt as communication channels break down between mother and daughter. We are never told exactly why the mother and daughter are in a hysterical state by the end of the poem but, given the rural landscape, the loss of the fiancé and the cow signifies an economic, social and natural breakdown. From a theoretical perspective it could be argued that their hysteria marks a 'sexual origin of neurosis' and is deliberately evoked by Naheed through a Freudian dream sequence.[51] Both mother and daughter, hounded by their individual nightmares, choose to reject the rules of the beehive and descend into mental chaos. Economically, this can be read as a disavowal of a new patriotism that reads women through their fertility and the logic of capital.[52] There is also an Islamic reading of the beehive if we consider the Qur'anic reference to the bee in *Sura al-Nahl*.

The mother–daughter poems in Naheed's collections bring together the public and the private, ranging from her autobiographical voice to her poetic voice. The mother takes on multiple personae and the poet maps both the expectations and the psychoses of the mother. She seems torn between a nature–nurture national mother and the ravaged at-home mother. Another key aspect of 'Mom Mahal' that is characteristic of Naheed's work is the motif of dreams. In her poems, dreams play a considerable role as they present altered states for women. Mahwash Shoaib has explored the significance of dreams in Naheed's seventh poetry volume, *Khayali shakhs se muqabala* (Confronting an Imaginary Person), published in 1992. Shoaib extends Carlo Coppola's observations of how dreams seem to serve the purpose of sexual fantasy, encoding women's unsaid desires, by analysing the dreams as an expression of the failure of everyday language to absorb women's erotic thoughts and needs.[53] Their continual presence in the poems marks an unwritten language of desire that shapes an inner world for women bearing little resemblance to the outer world they inhabit.[54]

A poem in one of her collections, *Main pehle janam men raat thi* (I Was Night in My First Life), entitled 'Taluq ki be-simti' (The Aimlessness of Contact), underlines how the poet-narrator survives through dreams and the emotional geography of her home. The poem opens with the image of the poet narrator struggling to read a letter by fading lamplight and conveys how her touch disintegrates metaphors of light and love. In the second stanza she writes:

تعلق کی بے سمتی

میں بجھا ہوا چراغ ہاتھ میں لیے
تمہارا خط پڑھنے کی کوشش کرتی ہوں
ماچس جلاتی ہوں
چراغ کے بجائے، انگلی جل جاتی ہے۔
ٹہنی سے پھول توڑتی ہوں
پھول پتیاں پتیاں بکھر جاتا ہے۔

آنکھ بند کرتی ہوں
خواب دیکھنے کو
مجھے اپنا آپ، خالی سوٹ کیس میں رکھا نظر آتا ہے۔
سوٹ کیس کی نچلی سطح پہ
بہت سے پنجوں کے نشان ہیں
کہیں بھی پورا پیر نہیں، پورا قدم نہیں۔
میں ایک نشان پر انگلی لگاتی ہوں۔
میری کھال ادھڑ جاتی ہے۔
اوپر دیکھتی ہوں
بادل سرخ نظر آتے ہیں۔

اوپر سرخ بادل
سامنے بکھرتے ہرسرخ گلاب
پیچھے سے آتی خون کی لہر
اور بندوق کی آواز
میں اداس ہو کر بھی گھر پہنچ جاتی ہوں
دروازہ خود کھلنا ہو تو انتظار کی خواہش
فنا ہو جاتی ہے۔

Ankh band karti hun.
Khvab dekhne ko
Mujhe apna app, khali suitcase men rakha nazar ata hai.
Suitcase ki nichli sata pe

Bohat se panjon ke nishan hain.
Kahin bhi pura per nahin, pura qadam nahin.
Main ek nishan par ungli lagati hun.
Meri khal udhar jati hai.
Upar dekhti hun.
Badal surkh nazar ate hain.

Upar surkh badal
Samne, bikharte, surkh gulab
Piche se ati khun ki lehar
Aur banduq ki awaz
Main udas ho kar bhi, ghar puhanch jati hun.
Darvaza khud kholna ho to intizar ki khvahish
Fana ho jati hai.

[I close my eyes
So I can dream
I can see my self locked up in an empty suitcase
In the lower part of the suitcase
There are many toeprints
There is no imprint of a footstep.
I put my finger on one spot
My skin rips open.
I look up.
The clouds are looking red.

Above red clouds
Below a host of red roses
From behind a wave of blood
And the sound of a gun
Despite my sadness, I reach home
When you have to open the door yourself then the desire to wait
Is no more.]⁵⁵

Home for Kishwar Naheed is like a suitcase in which she channels the experience of exile marked by bloodshed and self-sacrifice. The red symbolism in the poem is also a nod to the fate of Communist thought in Pakistan. Home is unhomely, and when she dreams the self begins to annihilate but she cannot break away from her material self. The feminist prose writer Khalida Husain evaluates Naheed's poetry as a manifesto of survival because it conveys a message of love. This love is not the traditional love between two people but a spiritual love for wo/mankind. Husain applauds Naheed's collection *Malamaton ke darmiyan* for its messages of 'survival', 'healing power' and 'communication'.⁵⁶ This assessment rings true of later collections as well, although we find the poetic self, as in the poem above, becoming more prominent with each new collection.

The Limits of Language

'Khud kalami' (Soliloquy), a free verse poem from the collection *Malamaton ke darmiyan*, is reflective of what Naheed does best: talking to herself.

مجھے سزا دو
کہ میں نے اپنے لہو سے تعبیرِ خواب لکھی
جنوں بریدہ کتاب لکھی

مجھے سزا دو
کہ میں نے تقدیسِ خوابِ فردا میں جاں گزاری
بہ لطفِ شب زادگاں گزاری

مجھے سزا دو
کہ میں نے قاتل کو وصفِ تیغ و علم سکھایا
سروں کو اور جُ قلم سکھایا

مجھے سزا دو
کہ میں عدو کی صلیب کی محتسب رہی ہوں
ہوا کی زد پہ جلے چراغوں کی روشنی ہوں

مجھے سزا دو
کہ میں نے دوشیزگی کو سودائے شب گماں سے رہائی دی تھی
گھروں کے بجھتے دیوں کو شانِ خدائی دی تھی

مجھے سزا دو
کہ میں جیوں تو تمہاری دستار گر نہ جائے
مجھے سزا دو
کہ میرے بیٹوں کے ہاتھ اٹھے تو تم نہ ہو گے
کہ ایک بھی تیغ حرف قوسِ میاں سے نکلے تو تم نہ ہو گے

مجھے سزا دو
کہ میں تو ہر سانس میں نئی زندگی کی خو گر
حیات و بعدِ حیات بھی زندہ تر رہوں گی

مجھے سزا دو
کہ پھر تمہاری سزا کی میعاد ختم ہو گی

Mujhe saza do
Ke main ne apne lahu se tabir-e khvab likhi
Junun barida kitab likhi
Mujhe saza do
Ke main ne taqdis-e khvab-e farda men jan guzari
ba lutf-e shab zadgan guzari
mujhe saza do
Ke main ne qatil ko wasf-e tegh-o alam sikhaya
Saron ko auj-e qalam sikhaya
Mujhe saza do
Ke main udu ki salaib ki muhtasib rahi hun
Hawa ki zad pe jale chiraghon ki roshni hun
Mujhe saza do
Ke main ne doshizgi ko sauda-e shab guman se rihai di thi
Gharon ke bujhte diyon ko shan-e khudai di thi
Mujhe saza do
Ke main jiyun to tumhari dastar gir na jaye
Mujhe saza do
Ke mere beton ke hath uthe to tum na ho ge
Ke aik bhi tegh-e harf qaus-e mian se nikle to tum na ho ge
Mujhe saza do
Ke main to har sans men nai zindagi ki khugar
Hayat-o bad-e hayat bhi zinda tar rahun gi
Mujhe saza do
Ke phir tumhari saza ki miad khatm ho gi

[Punish me
For I have scrawled the meaning of a dream
in my own blood
I have written a book riddled with insanity
Punish me
for I have spent my life chasing tomorrow's sacred dream

Punish me
For I have taught the murderer how to master the sword and the flag
I have taught heads how to sever themselves
Punish me
For I have been an officer lying in wait to be crucified by the enemy
I am the illumination from the burning lamps blowing with the wind

Punish Me
For I have freed virginity from going on sale during lost evenings

I made those extinguished women believe in God again
Punish Me
Because if I live your turban might fall
Punish Me
Because if my sons rise up then you will be no more
Because if even one pointed word comes out from my scabbard then you will be no more

Punish Me
For with every breath I am desirous of a new life
I will be livelier than life when I live and after I die
Punish Me
Because then the time for your punishment will end]⁵⁷

In a poem projected as a soliloquy, the poet makes known to the reader and listener the secret thoughts paramount in her mind. Naheed effectively uses the personal pronouns in her poem to develop an intimate relationship between the subject of her poem, the poet-narrator and her own subjectivity as the poet. Using the refrain 'Punish me', she offers an ironic intervention from a female subject mocking the forces of oppression. The female voice is unlocked in two verb endings in the poem that reflect the subject in line 11 and line 23. The first stanza establishes the mood as one of insanity and anger and the first half of the poem creates a persona that is complicit in bloodshed. The second half of the poem echoes heroic deeds that go against the grain of victimizing women as sacrificial lambs being led to the slaughter. It is interesting to note that her critique is aimed at community practices of honour. In the penultimate stanza, she takes on the persona of the mother with the line, 'Because if my sons rise up then you will be no more'. The last stanza is defiant and confrontational, rejoicing in death, projecting a timeless moral victory over oppression.

The imagery of the poem enacts a battlefield, recalling the symbolic imagery used in the marsiya, an elegiac form written to commemorate the martyrdom of the Prophet's grandson Imam Husain at Karbala. The sword and the standard are real and typical marsiya motifs known to the audience as part of the historic story of Karbala.⁵⁸ They recall for the reader or listener the tragedy of the historical moment, and revive the hope for recognition and survival of the Prophet's bloodline. Naheed's poem borrows some of these motifs to construct her modern interpretation of martyrdom. The female voice, through its reference to her sons, can be read as an emblematic reference to the sacred image of Fatima, the Prophet's daughter, wife of Ali and mother of Husain, a key representative of women's agency in Islam. She presents a feminine ideal that has been mythologized by both secularists and Islamists.⁵⁹ The valorization of Fatima is a key inspiration of the Shi'i marsiya where she is mythologized as a sacred role model for women.[60] Naheed's poetic persona articulates how the optimism and self-belief of Fatima can equivocate between life and death. She concludes the poem by observing the intangibility of hope that cannot be touched and censured. Yet it is the same expectation that makes dreams tangible.

In 'Kare Kos' (A Distance of Two Miles) she pares down linguistic registers to a single letter of the alphabet, highlighting the social construction of language. Beginning on a general note, she speculates on the formation of words from letters of the alphabet, and ends on a personal note by writing herself into the text:

حرف،

گویائی کی زنجیر میں جب قید ہوا

اِسم بنا

عہد بنا

نظم بنا

قصۂ کام و ذہن کا غمِ مطلوب بنا

خوب و ناخوب بنا

حرفِ ناگفتہ

مگر ذہن کا آزار بنا

دل کی دیوار بنا

راہِ دشوار بنا۔

قصۂ شوق کی وارفتہ کہانی نہ بنا

حیلۂ وصل کی غمِ دیدہ نشانی نہ بنا۔

دار ہے منزلِ گویائی

سبھی جانتے ہیں

حرفِ ناگفتہ کے یہ زخم مگر میرے ہیں

جن کو تنہائی مری،

مجھ سے سوا، جانتی ہے

Harf,
Goyai ki zanjir men jab qaid hua
Ism bana
Ehad bana
Nazm bana
Qissa-e kam-o dahn ka gham-e matlub bana
Khub-o na-khub bana
Harf-e nagufta
Magar zahn ka azar bana
Dil ki divar bana
Rah-e dushwar bana.
Qissa-e shauq varafta kahani na bana
Hila-e vasl ki gham dida nishani na bana.
Dar hai manzil-e goyai
Sabhi jante hain
Harf-e nagufta ke ye zakhm magar mere hain
Jin ko tanhai meri,
Mujh se siwa, janti hai.

[A letter of the alphabet
When it was captured in the shackles of speech
It became a noun
It became a covenant
It became a poem
It became the sorrowful quest of labour and the narration of desire
It became effective and ineffective
It became an unsaid letter of the alphabet
It became but an affliction of the mind
It formed a wall around the heart
It formed an arduous path
It did not become the lost tale of a passionate story
It did not become a tragic sign of fraudulent union
The destination of speech is the gallows
Everyone knows
The wounds from an unspoken word are mine alone
Whom my loneliness
Apart from myself, knows.][61]

The poet's references to a symbolic letter that became a 'covenant', 'poem' and 'speech' evoke memories of the poetic style of Faiz who inspired poets to reflect a 'blood-stained world' in their poetry. For Faiz, poets were 'the warriors / the riders of dawn', the Progressive activists who inspired the revolutionary act of anticolonialism and later the conscience of the postcolonial post-Partition nation speaking against a state discourse of censorship.[62] Naheed too writes against official gagging by echoing the lines, 'The destination of speech is the gallows'. She narrates how 'free speech' can be stifled through fear of capital punishment. Grammar, it seems, is irrelevant when it comes to the state and its treatment of multilingual perspectives There is only one singular story that is pushed onto people and it has the authority of sacred ideology to stop people from questioning the context of their surroundings, encouraging them to accept God's will as an all-encompassing force. The poem's final reference is to loneliness as the existential condition that is both inflicted and self-imposed; however, she does not share the context of her story, unlike Fahmida Riaz who chose to speak out. This lack of access to speech comes full circle in her poem 'Censorship', which conveys the hegemony of martial law and the obliteration of civil liberties in Pakistan in the 1980s.

سنسر شپ

جن زمانوں میں کیمرہ ظلم کو ہمیشہ کے لیے
مجسم نہیں کر سکتا تھا
تمہیں ان زمانوں تک ہی
ظلم کو بہادری کا نام دینے کی تاریخ لکھنی چاہیے تھی
آج سلو لائیڈ پہ منتقل منظروں کو دیکھ کر اندازہ ہوتا ہے
کہ پہاڑی ڈھلوانوں پہ جڑوں سے ٹوٹے درختوں کی آواز اور
منظر نامہ کیسا ہوتا ہے
چاہے تم خوش ہو یا افسردہ
سانس تو لیتے ہو
آنکھیں کھولنے یا بند کرنے سے
ذہن پہ نقش منظر نہیں بدلتا
دریا میں کھڑے درخت کا تنا
لکڑی کا ہی رہتا ہے
مگر مجھ نہیں بنتا ہے

ہم کب سے کہانیوں کی چھت پہ چڑھے
یہ سوچ رہے ہیں
کہ یہ شہر ہمارا ہے
بنیاد کی دیواروں کی زمین بیٹھ گئی ہے
مگر اب تک ہم کہانیوں کی چھت پہ چڑھے
پھیکی دو پہروں کی اجڑی گلیوں کی ٹوٹی اینٹوں کی
چوڑی دراڑوں کو زندگی سمجھ رہے ہیں

Jin zamanon men camra zulm ko hamesha ke liye
Mujasm nahin kar sakta tha
Tumhe un zamnon tak hi
Zulm ko bahadri ka nam dene ki tarikh likhni chahiye thi.
Aj celluloid pe muntaqil manzaron ko dekh kar andaza hota hai
Ke pahari dhalvanon pe jaron se tutte darakhton ki avaz aur
Manzar nama kaisa hota hai.
Chahe tum khush ho ya afsurda
Sans to lete ho.
Ankhen kholne ya band karne se

Zehn pe naqsh, manzar nahin badalta hai,
Darya main khare darakht ka tana
Lakri ka hi rehta hai
Magarmach nahin banta hai.
Hum kab se kahanion ki chaton pe charhe
Ye soch rahe hain
Ke ye shahr hamara hai
Bunyad ki diwaron ki zamin beth gayi hai
Magar ab tak hum kahanion ki chaton pe charhe
Phiki dopahron ki ujri galyon ki tuti inton ki
Chauri dararon ko zindagi samajh rahe hain

[In those days when the camera could not frame injustice for all times
You should have kept to those times only
When the history of inequity could be presented as courage
Today through moving images images on celluloid we can imagine

The sound and the vision
Of trees crumbling from their disintegrating roots on mountainous slopes
Whether you are happy or unhappy
You still breathe
By blinking eyes open or shut
The impression or view in our heads does not change
The uprooted branch of a tree in the river
Remains woody growth
It does not transform into a crocodile
Since when are we stood on the rooftops of stories
Thinking this
That the city is ours
The ground beneath the foundation walls has collapsed
But we are still perched on the rooftops of stories
Thinking that life is
Colourless afternoons in ruined alleys with broken bricks with wide chasms][63]

Naheed sketches the strangulation of creativity and freedom of expression in the grip of an authoritarian state. Using the symbol of a camera, she utilizes the modernist technique of photographic fragmentation in the visualization of time.[64] This imagining brings in the differentiation of time: time as a memory of the past recalled through photographs, and the present time. The stoppage of information by dictators is belied by the camera that takes pictures and human memory that can't be erased. The latter half of the poem switches mood to the inspirational theme of storytelling and storytellers who continue to dream despite the ground being removed from under their feet. The city space is reimagined through the minds of its creative artists who can still think of life in ruined alleys. Stories, it seems, have the power to subvert censorship and instil belonging. For Naheed, stories are a means of survival in her adopted country and she emphatically reclaims the city for its storytellers who have seen and heard everything. The foundation walls of Naheed's city have collapsed, signifying the hollow structure that supported those dreams from the 1960s to the 1980s. Naheed questions the continued presence of nostalgia amongst a new generation which keeps them rooted to an imaginary past.

Driving this outlook is her poem 'Kishwar Naheed!' from her collection *Galyan, dhup, darvaze*. In this poem, she establishes her persona as the subject of her poetry, marking herself as the keeper of secrets, a female representative who is not popular or liked but who has kept afloat in times that mythologize.

عمر کے ازتیں برس
تمہارے بالوں اور گالوں میں
اترتی خزاؤں
اور دہلتے جذبوں کی آندھیوں میں
کچے ٹوٹتے پھلوں کی طرح
سارے رشتے
زندگی کے چندن روپوں کی طرح
گدرا گئے ہیں۔

کشور ناہید!
تم منہ بند پیپی کی طرح
زندگی کے سمندر میں
ہواؤں سے باتیں کرتے
پہاڑوں کی بنیاد ہلاتے
اور لہروں کو اپنے بالوں کی طرح کاٹ کر
ساحل پہ
گذشتہ کی روایتی
اور آج کی مضطرب
عورت بن کر سوچ رہی ہو۔

کشور ناہید!
یہاں نہ کوئی بولتا ہے
نہ کوئی بولتی آنکھوں کے
لفظوں کو سمجھنا چاہتا ہے۔

ہاتھ سے پھسلتی مچھلی
میں بدل دیتی ہے۔

کشور ناہید!
تمہیں خاموش دیکھنے کی چاہت
قبروں سے بھی امڈی آ رہی ہے
مگر تم بولو!
کہ یہاں سننا منع ہے
مجھے جن جذبوں نے خوف زدہ کیا تھا
اب میں ان کے اظہار سے
دوسروں کو خوف سے لرزتا دیکھ رہی ہوں۔

Umr ke artis bars
Tumhare balon aur galon men
Utarti khizaon
Aur dhalte jazbon ki andhion men
Kache tutte phalon ki tarah
Sare rishte
Zindagi ke chandan rupon ki tarah
Gadra gae hain.

Kishwar Naheed!
Tum munh band sipi ki tarah
Zindagi ke samundar men
Hawaon se baten karte
Paharon ki bunyad hilate
Aur lehron ko apne balon ki tarah kat kar
Sahil pe
Guzashta ki rivayati
Aur aj ki muztarib
Aurat ban kar soch rahi ho.

Kishwar Naheed
Yahan na koi bolta hai
Na koi bolti ankhon ke
Lafzon ko samajhna chahta hai.
Hath se phisalti machli
Khauf ko nafrat men badl deti hai.

Kishwar Naheed!
Tumhe khamosh dekhne ki chahat
Qabron se bhi umdi a rahi hai
Magar tum bolo!
Ke yahan sunna mana hai
Mujhe jin jazbon ne khauf zada kiya tha
Ab main un ke izhar se
Dusron ko khauf se larazta dekh rahi hun.

[Thirty eight years of life
Visible in the deepening shadows
Of your hair and cheeks
And in the mellowing storms of passion
Like fallen immature fruit

All associations
Like the changing sandalwood tree of life
Have dimmed.

Kishwar Naheed
You are like a pearl oyster
In the ocean of life
Speaking to the wind
Moving mountains from their foundations
Cutting through waves, like you did your hair
You are stood thinking
On the shoreline
Like a traditional woman of the past
And like today's revolutionary woman

Kishwar Naheed
Nobody speaks here
Nor do they wish to understand
What is intimated through glances
When a trapped fish slips through the hands
It transforms fear into hate

Kishwar Naheed!
The desire to see you quiet
Emanates from the graves
But speak out!
Because listening here is forbidden
The passion for which I was made to be fearful
Now by expressing it
I see others tremble in trepidation.][65]

She distances her voice from the poem by using the second-person singular pronoun to write herself into the text in the 38th year of her life. The year is important as it refers to 1978 when General Zia had taken over power and Bhutto was under trial before he was incarcerated in 1979. She constructs her self in response to her reflection, tactically moving between two images. The use of her name as a refrain is more in keeping with the repetitive style of lamentation in a *musaddas*-style lengthy poem, but it also evokes the ghazal as does her imagery of the pearl oyster, the ocean, her hair and her cheeks. Overall, the form is that of a modern nazm layered with the hybridities of traditional influence. The poem reflects the mask she wears as a civil servant and the fear that surrounds her. By cleverly using her name as the centrepiece, she deflects attention from her criticism of a state in crisis, functioning through the medium of fear and intimidation. It is a place where everyone is under surveillance and the power of speech has been shut down.[66] This poem develops the unnamed storyteller of 'Censorship'; here the protagonist is Kishwar Naheed, who is the one being silenced. She personifies herself as the woman of the past and the future who, through storytelling, holds the key to unlock the trauma imposed by enforced silence. In the last stanza, the voice slips from the third person to the first person as she brings in the personal pronoun to project herself as an active speaking subject rather than a passive subject who is acted upon.

Grassroots Activism

Kishwar Naheed refers to 'Hum gunahgar auraten' (We Sinful Women) as her alternative national anthem for Pakistan. It is a poem that has been put to music by the Norwich-based British Pakistani musician and artist Samia Malik in 1990.[67] In the United States, it has been choreographed by Janaki Patrik of the contemporary Indian dance collective The Kathak Ensemble and Friends as a contemporary interpretation of modern 'messy reality' deploying Indo-Pakistani influences.[68] In Pakistan, the poem has become part of the activist-led International Women's Day celebrations, translated into dance by Indu Mitha and performed by Amna Mawaz Khan. Mawaz is a classical dancer specializing in Bharatnatyam and secretary of the Rawalpindi Islamabad youth wing of the left-wing Awami workers' party.[69] These global and local contexts connect Pakistani and South Asian diaspora audiences, bringing them together over the shared project of social justice for women. The poem itself underwrites Naheed's commitment to resistance and the project of women's empowerment as an urgent response to the legal and religio-cultural backlash against women's rights in 1980s Pakistan. With its mocking refrain of 'we sinful women', the poem challenged the military state's adoption of Sharia laws that policed sexuality to protect the spiritual purity of the nation's women. The imagery of these women coming out to raise the banner of truth is a tribute to the women's movement in Pakistan and indicative of Naheed's grassroots activism and membership of the Women's Action Forum (WAF). The poem encapsulates her secular agenda of forcefully rewriting sinful women, who are deemed as such by religious discourse but are in actuality speaking, thinking and self-aware women. 'Hum gunahgar auraten' is her most iconic poem:

ہم گنہگار عورتیں

یہ ہم گنہگار عورتیں ہیں
جو اہلِ جبہ کی تمکنت سے نہ رعب کھائیں
نہ جان بیچیں
نہ سر جھکائیں
نہ ہاتھ جوڑیں۔

یہ ہم گنہگار عورتیں ہیں
کہ جن کے جسموں کی فصل بیچیں جو لوگ
وہ سرفراز ٹھہریں
نیابتِ امتیاز ٹھہریں
وہ داورِ اہلِ ساز ٹھہریں۔

یہ ہم گنہگار عورتیں ہیں
کہ سچ کا پرچم اٹھا کے نکلیں
تو جھوٹ سے شاہراہیں اٹی ملی ہیں،
ہر ایک دہلیز پہ سزاؤں کی داستانیں رکھی ملی ہیں،
جو بول سکتی تھیں، وہ زبانیں کٹی ملی ہیں،

یہ ہم گنہگار عورتیں ہیں
کہ اب تعاقب میں رات بھی آئے
تو یہ آنکھیں نہیں بجھیں گی۔
کہ اب جو دیوار گر چکی ہے
اسے اٹھانے کی ضد نہ کرنا!

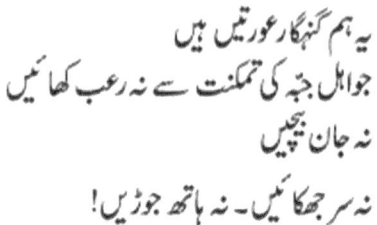

Ye hum gunahgar auraten hain
Jo ahl-e jubba ki tamkinat se na rob khayen
Na jan bechen
Na sar jhukayen
na hath joren.

Ye hum gunahgar auraten hain
Ke jin ke jismon ki fasl bechen jo log
Voh sarfaraz theren
Nayabat-e Imtiaz theren
Voh davar-e ahl saz tehren.

Ye hum gunahgar auraten hain
Ke such ka parcham utha ke niklen
To jhut se shahrah-en ati mile hain,
Har ek dehliz pe sazaon ki dastanen rakhi mile hain,
Jo bol sakti thin, voh zabanen kati mile hain.

Ye hum gunahgar auraten hain
Ke ab taqub men rat bhi aye
To ye ankhen nahin bujhen gi.
Ke ab jo divar gir chuki hai
Use uthane ki zid na karna!
Ye hum gunahgar auraten hain
Jo ahl-e jubba ki tamkinat se na rob khaen
Na jan bechen
Na sar jhukayen, na hath joren!

[It is we sinful women
who are not awed by the grandeur of those who wear gowns
who don't sell our lives
who don't bow our heads
who don't fold our hands together

It is we sinful women
while those who sell the harvests of our bodies
become exalted
become distinguished
become the just princes of the material world.

It is we sinful women
who come out raising the banner of truth
up against the barricades of lies on the highways
who find stories of persecution piled on each threshold
who find the tongues which could speak have been severed.

It is we sinful women.
Now, even if the night gives chase
those eyes shall not be put out.
For the wall which has been razed
don't insist now on raising it again.
It is we sinful women
who are not awed by the grandeur of those who wear gowns
who don't sell our bodies
who don't bow our heads
who don't fold our hands together.][70]

Historically, members of the women's movement experienced totalitarian law enforcement from the state when they held peaceful protest marches against the implementation of Hudood Ordinances.[71] Through her poem Naheed was directly responding to the impact of Sharia law on the lives of women, who were being treated as voiceless and whose vulnerability was taken advantage of in a discourse designed to restore a hypermasculine state. The protest against the state's support of Sharia law and its restrictive impact on women's rights was led by the WAF. Kishwar Naheed speaks of her instrumental role in commissioning a poem from the poet Habib Jalib for the 1983 march against the Zina Ordinance. Jalib, a Progressive who spoke out against Ayub and Zia, was a lyrical supporter, reflecting the spirit of activist response through his verse. His poem 'Dastoor' critically responded to Ayub's 1962 constitution as did his poem 'Zulmat ko Zia' to the Zia regime. Jalib was committed to *baghawat* (rebellion) and he was attached to a people-led politics with the National Awami Party (NAP).[72] For his politics he was tried for treason and jailed. That didn't stop him from marching and speaking for women to support the WAF. His style borrowed from the ghazal and built on the emotive power of the Urdu language, performing thunderously to avidly listening audiences. I quote below a small section of Jalib's poem that is known as the WAF anthem:

> Ab dahr men be-yar-o madadgar nahin hum
> Pehle ki tarah be-kas-o lachar nahin hum
>
> [We are not friendless and helpless in the desert
> We are not powerless and vulnerable like before][73]

Naheed narrates how Jalib, who was committed to the cause for justice and empathetic toward women who were subjected to targeted injustice, joined the historic WAF march on the Mall Road in Lahore. When this small group of protestors was kettled and brutalized by the police with batons, Jalib experienced the physical violence along with women, some of whom had to be taken to hospital and others to Kot Lakhpat jail. From that day Jalib's poem became synonymous with Women's Day in Pakistan. Naheed writes of her huge admiration for Jalib and for Faiz, and her differences from them as a woman poet. Recalling her relationship with Faiz in her book of essays *Shanasaiyan, Rusvaiyan*, she tells us that Faiz (sahib) used to ask her, 'Tum aurat ban kar kyun shairi karti ho' and she would reply, 'Faiz sahib, I am a woman. But not that woman who is the beloved of your poetry.'[74] Never afraid to speak her mind, Naheed has always responded directly to her critics.

A poem that perhaps explains Faiz's response to her work is 'Ghas to mujh jaisi hai' (The Grass Is Like Me), which is representative of Naheed's mixture of tradition and modernity. Speaking from memory, Naheed recalls that this poem raised some eyebrows amongst her male colleagues, who were shocked by its blatantly sexual undertones. On the other hand, it was a poem they enjoyed reading not for its elevation of women, but for its suggestive sexualized imagery.[75] This contradictory reaction has frustrated her with its sidelining of her theme of women's emancipation, but confirmed her scepticism regarding her male contemporaries as biased critics.

گھاس تو مجھ جیسی ہے

گھاس بھی مجھ جیسی ہے
پاؤں تلے بچھ کر ہی زندگی کی مراد پاتی ہے
مگر یہ بھیگ کر کس بات کی گواہی بنتی ہے
شرمساری کی آنچ کی
کہ جذبے کی حدت کی

گھاس بھی تو مجھ جیسی ہے
ذرا سر اٹھانے کے قابل ہو
تو کاٹنے والی مشین
اسے مخمل بنانے کا سودا لیے
ہموار کرتی رہتی ہے

عورت کو بھی ہموار کرنے کے لیے
تم کیسے کیسے جتن کرتے ہو
نہ زمیں کی نمو کی خواہش مرتی ہے
نہ عورت کی
میری مانو تو وہی پگڈنڈی بنانے کا خیال درست تھا
جو حوصلوں کی آنچ نہ سہہ سکیں
وہ پیوند زمیں ہو کر
یونہی زور آوروں کے لیے راستہ بنا دیتے ہیں
مگر وہ پر کاہ ہیں
گھاس نہیں
گھاس تو مجھ جیسی ہے

Ghas bhi mujh jaisi hai
Paon tale bich kar hi zindagi ki murad pati hai
Magar ye bhig kar kis bat ki gawahi banti hai
Sharmsari ki anch ki
Ke jazbe ki jiddat ki

Ghas bhi mujh jaisi hai
Zara sar uthane ke qabil ho
To katne vali machine
Use makhmal banane ka sauda liye
Hamwar karti rehti hai.

Aurat ko bhi hamvar karne ke liye
Tum kaise kaise jatan karte ho.
Na zameen ki namu ki khwahish marti hai
Na aurat ki

Meri mano, to vohi pagdandi banane ka khayal durust tha
Jo hoslon ki shikaston ki anch na seh saken
Voh pewand-e zamin ho kar
Yunhi zor avaron ke liye rasta bana dete hain.
Magar voh par-e kah hain
Ghas nahin
Ghas to mujh jaisi hai!

[Grass too is like me
Cushioning feet, she fulfils her meaning in life
But upon being drenched, what does she bear witness to?
The heat of shame or the limit of passion

Grass too is like me
When she can barely lift her head up
The grass-cutting machine
In the business of transforming her to velvet
Keeps trimming her down.
In order to cut woman down too
You make every kind of effort
But neither the earth's desire to grow dies
Nor the woman's
Listen to me, that idea of making a pathway was right
They who cannot stand the blaze from ambition's
    defeat
Graft themselves onto the soil
And in doing so build a path for the powerful
But they are only straw
Not grass
Grass too is like me.][76]

In this poem, Naheed conveys the object status of women as sexual beings and likens them to grass, which can sometimes serve only aesthetic purposes but in this poem is symbolic of life itself, as it supports the earth and by extension its climate, clean water and air quality. Naheed doesn't fully develop the symbolic reference to grass and the natural environment. She compares grass that is grown to please aesthetically to sharif women who can be nurtured in a similar way. Both are shown to be downtrodden and Naheed draws on the analogy that grass continues to grow unless it is cut back. Starting from an image of grass that is seemingly pliant, she ends by referring to its quality of resilience. In line 4, 'The heat of shame or the limit of passion' encapsulates the stereotypical two-fold characterization of women in patriarchal societies as either modest (virgins) or passionate (whores).[77] With these links, she reiterates the classification of women as soft, pliant, shameful and willing in the traditional setting of Urdu poetry.[78] The grass-cutting machine symbolizing power is shown to be a masculine associative tool of aggression, feeding ambition. But a machine, the poem tells us, can only manage the grass; it can neither feed it nor make it grow. She compares the resilience of women to grass, highlighting their ability to grow despite being used as pawns by those in power to further their ambitions. Toward the end of the poem, Naheed reverses the gendered order of pliancy as feminine by suggesting that those who are ambitious are the ones who are victims and likens them to weak fly-away men – 'par-e kah' (men of straw). The poet-narrator personifies the grass as herself throughout the poem and there is a slippage in the last stanza from every woman to a singular persona. At the same time, her symbol of wet grass has been read metaphorically by male colleagues as an expression of women's state after sexual intercourse. Naheed finds this reading frustrating and limiting as she feels it undermines the powerful message that is contained in her poem. At times, Naheed's self-conscious persona can overpower her own verse and take away from it the subtleties of nuance and allusion that have been the trademarks of Urdu poetry. The process of innovation can lead to a compromise over aesthetics, and critical judgements within Urdu circles have reflected this, as seen with the Progressives. Kishwar's continuation of the Progressive journey shows that little has changed when it comes to the primacy of form, which always holds an upper hand over revolutionary thought.

A more recent poem, 'Taliban se qibla ru guftugu' (A Conversation with the Taliban), characterizes Kishwar's attachment to the revisionist national project of girls' education in the wake of the Taliban blowback and the repercussions of Pakistan's involvement in the Global War on Terror after 9/11. As is typical of her style and in keeping with the persona of a poet laureate, she zooms in on a moment of national crisis and delivers her unique perspective. In this particular poem, she expresses her opposition to the targeting of young girls by the Taliban after the historic *lal masjid* (red mosque) clash in Islamabad in 2008 by using the same sarcastic tone she deployed in 'Hum gunahgar auraten'. More broadly, it can be read as an ode to the plight of Malala Yousafzai and many others like her, whose bodies and right to education became the target of the Taliban's project of a radical Islam using soft targets to spread a message of fear and tyranny. Naheed's voice speaking about the context of local Muslim women offers an important counterpoint and wake-up call from within the nation to reflect and change the fate of young girls who are being used as weapons in a larger warfare. This poem is not about the West saving Pakistan; it is about Pakistan saving itself through critical reflection.

طالبان سے قبلہ رو گفتگو

وہ جو بچیوں سے بھی ڈر گئے
وہ جو علم سے بھی گریز پا
کریں ذکرِ ربِ کریم کا
وہ جو حکم دیتا ہے علم کا
کریں اس کے حکم سے ماورا
یہ منادیاں

نہ کتاب ہو کسی ہاتھ میں
نہ ہی انگلیوں میں قلم رہے
کوئی نام لکھنے کی جا نہ ہو
نہ ہو رسمِ اسمِ زناں کوئی

وہ جو بچیوں سے بھی ڈر گئے
کریں شہر شہر منادیاں
کہ ہر ایک قدِ حیا نما کو
نقاب دو
کہ ہر ایک دل کے سوال کو
یہ جواب دو
نہیں چاہیے
کہ یہ لڑکیاں
اڑیں طائروں کی طرح بلند
نہیں چاہیے
کہ یہ لڑکیاں
کہیں مدرسوں، کہیں دفتروں کا بھی رخ کریں

کوئی شعلہ رَو، کوئی با صفا
ہے کوئی تو صحنِ حرم ہی
اس کا مقام ہے۔
یہی حکم ہے
یہ کلام ہے

وہ جو بچیوں سے بھی ڈر گئے
وہ یہیں کہیں ہیں قریب میں
انہیں دیکھ لو، انہیں جان لو
نہیں ان سے کچھ بھی بعید
شہرِ زوال میں
رکھو حوصلہ، رکھو یہ یقین

کہ جو بچویں سے بھی ڈر گئے
وہ ہیں کتنے چھوٹے وجود میں۔
کرو شہر شہر منادیاں
رکھو حوصلہ، رکھو یہ یقیں
کہ جو بچیوں سے بھی ڈر گئے
وہ ہیں کتنے چھوٹے وجود ہیں۔

Voh jo bachion se bhi dar gae
Voh jo ilm se bhi gurez pa
Karen zikr rab-c karim ka
Voh jo hukm deta hai ilm ka
Karen us ke hukm se mavra
Ye manadian

Na kitab ho kisi hath men
Na hi unglion men qalam rahe
Koi nam likhne ki ja na ho
Na ho rasm-e ism-e zanan koi

Voh jo bachion se bhi dar gae
Karen shahr shahr manadian
Ke har ek qad-e haya numa ko
Niqab do

Ke har ek dil ke saval ko
Ye javab do
Nahin chahiye
Ke ye larkiyan
Uren tairon ki tarah buland
Nahin chahiye
Ke ye larkian
Kahin madrason, kahin daftaron ka bhi rukh karen
Koi shola ru, koi basafa
Hai koi to sahn-e haram hi
Is ka maqam hai.
Yehi hukm hai
Ye kalam hai

Voh jo bachion se bhi dar gae
Voh yahin kahin hai qarib men
Inhen dekh lo, inhen jan lo
Nahin in se kuch bhi baid
Shahr-e zawal men
Rakho hosla, rakho ye yaqin
Ke jo bachion se bhi dar gae
Voh hain kitne chote wajud men.
Karo shahr shahr manadian
Rakho hosla, rakho ye yaqin
Ke jo bachion se bhi dar gae
Voh hi kitne chote wajud hain.

[They who became scared of little girls
They who are fugitives to knowledge
They speak of God Almighty

Who gave the command to seek knowledge
Yet they make proclamations beyond what is divine obligation

No hand should grasp a book
No fingers should grip a pen
There should be no occasion to write a name
Nor a ceremony for a female naming

They who became scared of little girls
They go from city to city making proclamations,
To cover up
Those shameful sexual female bodies

And quell every question from those hearts
With this answer
We do not want
These girls
To soar above like winged birds
We do not want
That these girls
Should go to seminaries even, leave alone offices
Some are fiery sparks and some toe the line
At least there are some
Whose destination is the sacred courtyard in Mecca
This is the obligation
This is the word

They who became scared of little girls
They are close, not far from here
See them, recognise them
There is not much expectation from them
In the fallen city
Keep your faith and uphold your belief
That they who became scared of little girls
Are very small in stature.
Make proclamations in every city
Keep your faith and uphold your belief
That they who became scared of little girls
Are very small in stature.]⁷⁹

When it comes to women's rights and gender justice, Naheed is committed to modernity and highlights the Taliban as symbols of backwardness who misinterpret Islam, encouraging the people to hold on to their faith as resistance. The city is reflected as a confined space that has been taken over by the Taliban to establish the supremacy of their sacred narrative with a nod to Mecca and Saudi Arabia. In this poem, she takes care to maintain an anonymous tone, avoiding naming names except in the title that is pitched as a conversation facing God rather than a confrontation. The strong words for the Taliban are expressed in the last stanza, calling into question their integrity. By doing so she taps into the language of an honour-based culture, using her words as 'soft weapons'.[80] Naheed understands the power of storytelling in a society that lives in fear of speaking out. As a Progressive poet she upholds her commitment to secular ideals and a critique of an ideological society that relies on the rule of majoritarianism to establish its power. She continues to write poems that respond to the politics of a country in which women and girls are undermined. Her poem 'Zainab ka noha' (Zainab's Elegy) remembers the rape and murder of 6-year-old Zainab Amin Ansari in Kasur in 2018.[81] She narrates the poem in the voice of Zainab conversing with her father. The conversation takes the shape of a monologue in which Zainab both recounts what happens and instructs her father on what to do after her death. It is a poem that elevates Zainab while speaking of her rape in the language of an honour crime: 'Baba Zainab to kul alam ke liye / baseerat vala nam hai / mera kalank is nam ko kyun lage' (Baba Zainab is for the whole world / a respectable name / why would my stain attach to this name).[82] It is an odd ending as it seems to be a plea for an honourable death by Zainab, yet in a country where honour-based violence is a concern amongst feminist and women's groups this wording takes Zainab back into a sharif discourse.

Her poem 'Mujhe bhai ne sangsar kiya' (My Brother Stoned Me) is an earlier protest poem about the violence against women that takes place in the name of honour. This poem is prescient as it anticipates the murder of a rising social media star of Pakistan, Qandeel Baloch. In 2016, at the age of 26, Baloch was killed by her brother Waseem for defaming the family honour through her 'illicit' and 'provocative videos' on social media and her shaming of a religious cleric, Mufti Abdul Qavi.[83] The circumstances around her murder illustrate how families are coerced and killers allowed to walk free because the 'honour crime' can be paid for through *qisas* and *diyat* blood money laws. The law was amended in 2016 following a public appeal made to the prime minister at the time, Nawaz Sharif, by the documentary film-maker Sharmeen Obaid Chinoy, on the occasion of a public screening of her film *A Girl in the River: The Price of Forgiveness*. But it wasn't until after Baloch's death that the law changed to ensure a life sentence for the murderer, closing the loophole that allowed them to walk free by seeking forgiveness from another family member and legal pardon.

Naheed's poem imagines the love between siblings literally ripped apart when a girl is prepared for murder by her brother because of a disagreement over her marriage partner. Much has been written on honour crimes and my purpose in referring to the poem below is to illustrate the Progressive arc in Naheed's writing that preserves and nurtures the tone set by Rashid Jahan's prose writing.

مجھے بھائی نے سنگسار کیا

وہ صبح سنہری صبح نہ تھی
وہ دن تو ادھورا دن بھی نہ تھا
مرے دل میں کوئی خوف نہ تھا
میں عشق دلاری، چمپئی رنگ پہن کے
اپنے آنگن میں پھول پروتی، مہندی لگائے
سوچ رہی تھی
میرا راج دلارا بھائی، مجھ سے خفا
بھلا کیسے صبح سے شام کرے گا
یاد ہے مجھ کو
کیسے اپنی گود میں لے کے
باغوں باغوں گھومتا تھا
کیسے مجھے ہنساتا تھا
روتی تھی تو، پیار کٹورا بھر کے
مجھ پہ دلار لٹاتا تھا
مجھے دکھ کی کوکھ میں
بھائی مرا، کب دیکھ سکے گا

میرا ابلتا خون یہ مجھ سے پوچھ رہا ہے
کیسے مانوں! میرے اپنے راج دلارے
بھائی سارے

میرے جسم کو ریشہ ریشہ کرنے
چاروں طرف سے، سنگ دخشت کی بارش کرنے
میرے سامنے آن کھڑے ہیں

تو نے تو اب رب میرے
مجھ سے کہا تھا
جینا، مرنا سب کچھ تیرے حکم سے
تیری رضا سے ممکن ہوگا
کیسے مانوں!
تو نے اپنے حکم کو، میرے اپنوں کے ہاتھوں میں
سونپ دیا تھا
میرا جرم تو صرف یہی تھا
میں نے اپنے دل کی بات کو اپنی گہری چاہت میں ڈوب کے
اپنے ہاتھ میں اس کا ہاتھ لیا تھا
اے رب تیرے سامنے، تجھ کو مان کے
میں نے اپنا جیون ساتھی ڈھونڈ لیا تھا

کتنی خوش ان بانہوں میں تھی
کتنی خوش اپنے دلبر کی سانسوں میں تھی
میرے پاس تو بوند بوند ٹپکتی رحمت
تیری یہی تھی
اے میرے رب!
میرے ہاتھ میں دھانکی بانکیں

تجھے منظور نہیں تھیں
مجھے ہنستے دیکھ کے، میرے راج دلارے اپنے بھائی نے
میرے شہر کے ناہنجار جوانوں کے ہاتھوں میں
خود ہی پتھر لا کے دیئے تھے
سب ہاتھوں میں پتھر تھے، سب کے چہرے پتھر تھے

میرے حال پہ رویا کون
بس وہ شجر کہ جس کے ساتھ مجھے
اور مرے دلبر کو
میرے راج دلارے توانا بھائی نے
خون کے آخری قطرے تک بے ہوش کیا، بے جان کیا
اور خوش ٹھہرے

عزت کے رکھوالے خوش ہیں
اے رب میرے!
کیا تو بھی خوش ہے!

Voh subh sunehri subh na thi
Voh din to adhura din bhi na tha
Mere dil main koi khauf na tha
Main ishq dulari, champai rang pehn ke
Apne angan men phul paroti, mehndi lagaye
Soch rahi thi
Mera raj dulara bhai, mujh se khafa
Bhala kaise subh se sham kare ga
Yad hai mujh ko
Kaise apni god men le ke
Baghon baghon ghumta tha
Kaise mujhe hansata tha
Roti thi to, pyar katora bhar ke

Mujh pe dular lutata tha
Mujhe dukh ki kukh men
Bhai mera, kab dekh sake ga

Mera ubalta khun ye mujh se puch raha hai
Kaise manun! Mere apne raj dulare
Bhai sare
Mere jism ko resha resha karne
Charon taraf se, sang-o khasht ki barish karne
Mere samne aan khare hain

Tu ne to ai rab mere
Mujh se kaha tha
Jina, marna sab kuch tere hukm se
Teri raza se mumkin ho ga
Kaise manun!
Tu ne apne hukm ko, mere apnon ke hathon men
Somp diya tha

Mera jurm to sirf yehi tha
Main ne apne dil ki bat ko
Apni gahri chahat men dub ke
Apne hath men us ka hath liya tha
Ai rab tere samne, tujh ko man ke
Main ne apna jivan sathi dhund liya tha

Kitni khush in bahon main thi
Kitni khush apne dilbar ki sanson men thi
Mere pas to bund bund tapakti rehmat
Teri yehi thi
Ai mere rab!
Mere hath men dhanki banken
Tujhe manzur nahin thin
Mujhe hanste dekh ke, mere raj dulare apne bhai ne
Mere shahr ke nahnjar jawanon ke hathon men
Khud hi pathar la ke diye the
Sab hathon men pathar the, sab ke chehre pathar the

Mere hal pe roya kaun
Bas voh shajr ke jis ke sath mujhe
Aur mere dilbar ko

Mere raj dulare tawana bhai ne
Khun ke akhri qatre tak behosh kiya, bejan kiya
Aur khush tehre

Izzat ke rakhwale khush hain
Ai rab mere!
Kya tu bhi khush hai!

[That morning was not golden
That day had not ended
My heart was free of fear
I was wearing purple, ready to be loved
With henna on, I was threading flowers in my home
I was thinking
My darling brother is angry with me
How will he get through the day
I remember
When he used to take me in his lap
And roam around parks
He used to make me laugh
When I used to cry, his love would cushion me
How will my brother cope
With seeing me in pain

My boiling blood is asking me
How can I believe it! My own darling brothers
Have torn me from limb to limb
They are surrounding me
Ready to pelt me with stones and bricks

My lord you said this to me
Life and death is in your hands
It is determined by you
How can I listen!
You gave your command to my flesh and blood
My only crime was
That I spoke my heart
And lost in the passion of my love
I took his hand in my hand
With you as my witness my lord
I found my life partner

I was so happy in those arms
How happy I was in my darling's every breath
I was showered with blessings

O my lord!
Those yellow green bangles on my arms
Did not agree with you

My darling brother who saw me laughing
Handed me over to the city yobs
Giving them stones for weapons
All of them had stones, their faces were stone

Did anyone cry for me
Only the tree to which I
and my beloved were bound
My darling strong brother
Squeezed every last drop of blood out of me
Made me lifeless
Then they were happy

Those keepers of my honour are happy
O my lord!
Are you satisfied too!]⁸⁴

This concluding poem illustrates Naheed's grassroots activism and showcases the poet's development of a personal archive of national memory and traumas that affect women. Her first loyalty in her poetry is to her activism and to creating political consciousness about women's rights as citizens.

The Traveller

Naheed's travelogue entitled *A jao Afriqa* (Come, Africa) interrogates the old ways of 'seeing and being' in a geographical setting outside the borders of her own home.⁸⁵ She adopts the role of storyteller to tell the tale of the 1985 International Women's Conference held in Nairobi. The contents of her travelogue list the workshops held at the conference, including debates on female circumcision, the veil and Arab women, and her 'Lesbian nama' (story) – topics with the potential to provoke controversy in an Islamic republic. Naheed's report is liberally interspersed with her own commentary, reiterating her gaze as a Third World feminist in an international arena.

In their introduction to *Travellers' Tales: Narratives of Home and Displacement*, the editors write of the 'travelling narrative' as one which explores 'space and difference'; transporting us to foreign lands, it has to interact with 'new concepts, new ways of seeing and being'.[86] *A jao Afriqa* falls into the category of a travelling narrative where Naheed comes into contact with difference. Her encounter with the space and 'contact zone' of a non-European country gives voice to a new transcultural expression.[87] Her ways of looking and identification may remind some Urdu readers of Faiz, who interacted with new ideas of space and change from his restricted space inside a Pakistani prison. Naheed's title echoes his poem 'A jao Afriqa', and on the last page she quotes directly from it: 'Come for I have freed my arms from fear', confirming the inspiration behind her chosen title.[88]

Faiz wrote an imaginary travel narrative as a poem entitled 'Aa jao Afriqa' in the late 1950s. Living inside prison walls, he was dreaming of Africa – a free Africa:

Aa jao, main ne sun li tere dhol ki tarang
Aa jao, mast ho gayi mere lahu ki tal
'Aa jao Afriqa'
Aa jao main ne dhul se matha utha liya
Aa jao main ne chhil di ankhon se gham ki chhal
Aa jao, main ne dard se bazu chhura liya
Aa jao, main ne noch diya bekasi ka jal
'Aa jao Afriqa'
Panje men, hathkari ban gayi hai gurz
Gardan ka tauq tor ke dhali hai main ne dhal
'Aa jao Afriqa'
Jalte hain har kachhar men bhalon ke mirg nain
Dushman lahu se rat ki kalak hui hai lal
'Aa jao Afriqa'
Dharti dharak rahi hai mere sath Afriqa
Darya thirk raha hai to ban de raha hai tal
Main afriqa hun, dhar liya main ne tera rup
Main to hun, meri chal hai teri babar ki chal
'Aa jao Afriqa'
Aao babar ki chal
'Aa jao Afriqa'

[Come, I have heard the ecstasy of your drum –
Come, the beating of my blood has become mad –
'Come, Africa!'

Come, I have lifted my forehead from the dust –
Come, I have scraped from my eyes the skin of grief –
Come, I have released my arm from pain –
Come, I have clawed through the snare of helplessness –
'Come, Africa!'
In my grasp a link of the manacle has become a mace,
I have broken the iron-collar on my neck and moulded it into a shield –
'Come, Africa!'
On every riverside burn the deer-eyes of spears,
With enemy blood the blackness of night has turned red,
'Come, Africa!'
The earth is throbbing along with me, Africa,
The river dances and the forest beats time;
I am Africa, I have taken your figure,
I am you, my walk is your lion walk:
'Come, Africa!'
Come with lion walk –
'Come, Africa!']{.sup}[89]

Faiz uses the first-person pronoun and the present tense to form the text of his poem and the mood is imbued with the philosophy of negritude and the celebration of decolonization in Africa. The poem is narrated in the manner of a tribal dance, its climactic stages performed to the rhythmical frenzy of drumbeats echoing the sounds of nature, the forest and the river speaking out against slavery and oppression. This emotional narration highlights the mood of immediacy and urgency of African nations breaking free from colonial domination. An empathetic belief in self-determination and the struggle against imperialism is conveyed, emphatically recognizing that a revolutionary mobilization of the people is the only way forward in the struggle toward the establishment of democracy. Africa is on his mind but he can only dream from within Pakistani prison walls, whereas Naheed 37 years later is in Africa.[90]

Naheed published her travelogue *A jao Afriqa* in 1987 with no other overt references to Faiz. In contrast to Faiz's poem, her travelogue is situated inside Africa and includes a summary of the International Women's Conference in Nairobi. It includes snapshots of speakers at the conference, an account of sightseeing trips in and around Nairobi and her personal diary of events. Her own agenda in this travelogue is to reflect on the conference as a space/place where she encounters her 'other' selves and the subsequent effect it has on her feminist poetics. She writes in her preface:

> Many people ask me the length of time I intend to portray myself as a woman. I reply that I am a woman and will remain one. If you manage to write the kind of book which you would want to read, then to quote Van Gogh if you find the model as well it is a happy coincidence. In Nairobi I found fourteen thousand models.⁹¹

Viewing her position through the eye of an expressionist painter, locating herself in modernity, Naheed prepares her canvas for bold brushstrokes. The stars of the show are prominent women's rights activists ranging from the American Betty Friedan to the Egyptian Nawal el Saadawi. One of her main aims is the recounting of international feminist activities to women in Pakistan, and through her presentation she offers alternative female role models to her readership. As a report, *A jao Afriqa* anticipates its audience amongst the women's organizations in Pakistan but as an anecdotal travelogue that contains her personal diary entries it offers us an unusual insight into the persona of the poet.

Naheed begins her narration with a chapter entitled 'Sheherazade ki pehli rat ki pehli kahani' (Sheherazade's First Story of the First Night). Her sequence of stories continue into the second night with 'Dusri kahani' (Second Story), then the theme is broken with other titles and is brought back at the end with 'Sheherazade ki akhri rat ki akhri kahani' (Sheherazade's Last Story of her Last Night). Naheed's choice of Sheherazade, the female narrator of *Alf Laila wa laila* (Arabian Nights), as her leading lady who opens and closes the narrative displays her attachment to the Arabic storytelling tradition encapsulated through a female voice.⁹² It recreates the myth of an imprisoned female narrator with a death sentence hanging over her head, who in order to survive the following day has to regale her male audience with a new story each night. In Sheherazade, the 'saving stereotype' of the 'oriental' woman is replicated, showing desirable qualities of 'duty, consideration, love [and] care' suited to the needs of a patriarchal environment.⁹³ Moving away from the stereotype, she focuses on Sheherazade's power as the storyteller controlling the narration. The re-appropriation of female myths is, for South Asian feminist writers, a crucial means of challenging patriarchal perceptions of women in written discourses.⁹⁴

Naheed introduces her first *kahani* (story) with the sentence, 'Virginia Woolf asked "[…] who shall measure the heat and violence of the poet's heart when caught in woman's body?"' and begins her account with diary-style entries.⁹⁵ Her reference first to Sheherazade, and to Virginia Woolf immediately after, is an interesting and telling example of the way in which her writing is poised between two worlds, periphery and metropolis, poetry and prose. It indicates the shifting perspective and influences on Muslim women's lives in South Asia.

Her first diary entry is dated 8 July 1985, Moi Avenue, on her way to the Nairobi University:

> The traffic police inspector, dressed in a black skirt, white top and white hat, on seeing women waiting to cross immediately stops the flow of cars. All steps are in the direction of the Nairobi University, the churidar pajama, sari, shorts, trousers, skirt, gown, shalwar...
>
> 'America has sent two plane loads of lesbians'
> 'It's heard that two hundred TERRORIST women have come'
> 'An emergency should be called. The conference should not be allowed to run smoothly.'[96]

She visualizes the university as a utopian space where there are no boundaries of culture, class or clothing. The conference and its location represent the kind of space she has been searching for in her writings as a feminist. However, casting a shadow over the women's conference is the sensational reporting of the Nairobi press and the conference's association with American funding. A gathering of women is imagined as a national disaster, posing threats to national security, and a means of importing lesbians from America. She narrates the tale of the conference as three stories, wrapping them in references from American feminists such as Betty Friedan and Anne Sexton while also speaking of the difficulties faced by local women in Nairobi when they speak out. Kenyan women who participated in the conference were photographed to ensure their punishment because they spoke in favour of women and against the Kenyan government. Here, her reference to Sheherazade can be seen as a comparative act of symbolic empathy, reaching out to the organizers of the conference who are shackled to the demands of the Kenyan government. The parallels between Kenya and Pakistan are many at this point. Naheed's mimicry of Sheherazade's narration is also personal, as it draws parallels with her own life, reminding us of the time when she was banished from her workplace as a government official, and also when her work as a poet and writer was snipped by the state censor's scissors.

According to Naheed, the conference provided the *mashriqi* (Eastern) women with the opportunity to state an agenda for Third World feminism, which would not tolerate oriental stereotypes of women. In the hybrid atmosphere of the conference, Naheed is confronted with the pedagogical tendencies of Euro-American feminism and the flaws in its performative applicability for Third World women. She redresses the situation by identifying the collective bond which African and Asian women share as second-class citizens of the world. For her, the conference is also a place for commemorating injustices carried out by First World nations against Third World nations, and the shared experiences of repressive postcolonial states as a means to create new alliances, bringing women together across continents and the Indian Ocean. The journey to Africa therefore transforms her feminist vision.

Conclusion

Naheed has contributed a large body of work to the field of women's Urdu poetry. She has been an icon, a civil servant, an editor and someone who still holds the power of influence. Her role as an activist is well known and she has been at the heart of women's protest marches since the 1980s. Recently, she fell on the outer edges of the movement as she came into conflict with a younger generation over the question of language and permissibility in Urdu when it comes to women's voices. In 2019, at the Sindh *aurat tanzeem* (women's collective) celebration marking the success of the *aurat* march, she gave her views on the controversy on social media over the 'offensive' language used on placards. She remarked that the stark language and images represented on the *aurat* march posters – of women cooking while men kept the bed warm, *azadi* (freedom), *awargi* (licentiousness) and others – were too strong and out of sync with our '*tehzib*' (culture), likening the fervour of the marchers to jihadists.[97] Her response created a furore on social media and in the news media. She was criticized for being out of touch by a younger generation of feminists, including the academic activist Nida Kirmani, because of her conservative stance on women's right to protest.[98] The question is, which culture does Kishwar Naheed affiliate with and who is she speaking for? The new middle class, the 'old' ashraf middle class or hybrid groupings in between? The conundrum is that when an iconic feminist such as Kishwar Naheed, who has carved a niche for herself in feminist circles in Pakistan, comes up short as a role model for aspiring young feminists, does it suggest that there is an unbridgeable generational divide between middle-class feminists? As someone who has fallen both outside and inside the cultural expectations of Urdu-speaking publics, she presents an interesting case.

In her defence, Naheed's argument that Pakistani society was not ready for a bold reclaiming of Urdu terms such as '*awara*' (licentious) or images of women with their legs wide apart (understood out of context) is marked by her own traumatic experience of inhabiting the world of Urdu poetry, which has been a tightrope act for sharif women as they traverse a literary territory that associates writing and performative poetry with a Lakhnavi courtesan class. Hence the term '*awara*' has cultural resonances that Naheed is deeply uncomfortable with. This cultural prejudice is embedded in a literary history that includes the rejection of Miraji by the Progressives, who thought him to be an *awara* persona and therefore not fit for their type of modernity.[99] On the surface, the difference of opinion between Naheed and a younger group of feminists represents the iron fist of Urdu literary culture and its linguistic conservatism when it comes to women's prestige. At a deeper level, this intergenerational altercation can be read as a signifier of class differences in a fast-changing Pakistani society. To understand the shifting aspirations of middle-class women, it is useful to refer to Ammara Maqsood's analysis of the new middle class in Lahore that emerged in the 1980s. These women, she argues, are second-generation migrants from rural and surrounding areas in Punjab and those who live in the walled city. She sees them as integral to the shifting perception of modernity between what she calls an 'old' ashraf middle class and the new middle class.[100] This has changed the dynamic of expectations and behaviours.

The question remains, who is Kishwar Naheed speaking to with her self-professed feminist status and call for change in the present? She has alliances with Progressive groups and has been a role model for the women's movement. But a strong criticism of the movement has been that it is representative of a particular elite class of women. Kishwar Naheed's career as a civil servant, a poet and a broadcaster has catered to these tastes and, while her activism is built around empowering and increasing mobility for women from working classes, the Urdu she writes and communicates in is not reflective of their worlds. The bigger problem that emerges from this is whether Urdu's tightly managed borders as a literary and national language allow for a hybridization that is more inclusive. While it has been possible for Urdu feminist voices such as Naheed's to command a presence in the twentieth-century canon, it is clear that an increasingly mediatized twenty-first century demands more inclusivity and a different type of politics from women poets.

Notes

1 Kishwar Naheed, 'Censorship', in *Siyah hashye men gulabi rang* (Lahore: Sang-e meel, 1986), 92.
2 Naheed, personal communication, 19 April 2000.
3 On the categorization of *Mah-e nau* as an anti-radical journal, see Hafeez Malik, 'The Marxist Literary Movement in India and Pakistan', *Journal of Asian Studies* 26, no. 4 (1967): 649–64, https://www.jstor.org/stable/2051241.
4 Asghar Nadeem Sayyid and Afzaal Ahmad, eds, *Nae zamane ki birhan* [A Beloved for a New Age] (Lahore: Sang-e meel, 1990).
5 Asif Furrukhi, '"*Banu-e guft ashna* (A Woman Devoted to Discourse)": An Interview with Kishwar Naheed', in *Nae zamane ki birahan*, ed. Asghar Nadeem Sayyid and Afzaal Ahmad (Lahore: Sang-e meel, 1990), 254.

6   Intizar Husain, 'Nae zamane ki birhan', 'Kishwar Naheed – Nazm se nasr tak', in Sayyid and Ahmad, *Nae zamane ki birahan*, 19–22, 23–25.
7   Ibid., 22.
8   I had the opportunity to ask Intizar Husain this question directly at the Karachi Literature Festival in 2014.
9   Naheed, quoted in Shahla Haeri, 'Marriage: Making a Culture of Her Own', in *No Shame for the Sun: Lives of Professional Pakistani Women* (Syracuse, NY: Syracuse University Press, 2002), 229–304 (265).
10 Kishwar Naheed, *Lab-e goya* (Lahore: Sang-e meel, 1991), 86.
11 Kishwar Naheed, *Aurat mard ka rishta – mazamin* [selected writings from Simone de Beauvoir's and Jean-Paul Sartre's published letters and articles], (Lahore: Sang-e meel, 1994), foreword.
12 Interview in Haeri, *No Shame for the Sun*, 287. I am grateful to Ayesha Siddiqa for pointing me in the direction of this book.
13 Simone de Beauvoir, *The Second Sex*, trans. H. M. Parshley (London: Picador, 1988). Also see Kate Kirkpatrick, *Becoming Beauvoir: A Life* (London: Bloomsbury, 2019). Kirkpatrick offers new insights from previously unavailable diaries and letters before and after she met Sartre. She talks about the status of de Beauvoir as a feminist icon and delves into the reasons why she might have edited herself. This is interesting to contrast with Naheed as she too edits.
14 Kishwar Naheed, *Buri aurat ki katha* (Lahore: Sang-e meel, [ca.1993]), 95.
15 Emma Tarlo's ethnographic study *Clothing Matters: Dress and Identity in Colonial India* (London: Hurst, 1996) is a must-read as an exploration of dress, identity and power politics.
16 Jamila Hashmi was a well-known and successful Urdu short story writer and novelist. She is the author of *Atish-e raftta* (Lahore: Dastan go, 1961); *Chehra bachehra rubaru* (Lahore: Writer's Book Club, n.d.); *Talash-e baharan* (Chandigarh: Rajdhani, n.d.); *Dasht-e sus* (Lahore: Frozsons, 1988). Also see Ayesha Siddiqa's newspaper article, 'The Reluctant Feminists', *Friday Times*, 8 November 2013.
17 Haeri, *No Shame for the Sun*, 285.
18 On the power of dressing and identity politics in India, see Tarlo, *Clothing Matters*.
19 See Haeri, *No Shame for the Sun*, 286.
20 On performativity, see Judith Butler, *Gender Trouble: Feminism and the Subversion of Identity* (New York: Routledge, 1990). Also see Naheed's *Buri aurat ki katha* on her relationship with the burqa, her interview with Shahla Haeri in *No Shame for the Sun* and her travelogue *A jao Afriqa* (Come, Africa).
21 See Naheed's interview in Haeri, *No Shame for the Sun*, 300.
22 Naheed, *Lab-e goya*, 74.
23 Kishwar Naheed, 'Likhne valiyon ki tanhai', in *Apni nigah: auraton ki likhi takhliqat aur tanqidi jaize*, ed. Javeria Khalid and Samina Rehman (Lahore: ASR, 1995), 72–75.
24 Haeri, *No Shame for the Sun*, 300.
25 Mustansar Husain Tarar, *Lahore Awargi* (Lahore: Sang-e meel, 2018), 280.
26 Haeri, *No Shame for the Sun*, 241.
27 Harris Khalique, 'An Interview with Feminist Poet Kishwar Naheed', *Herald*, 8 March 2017, https://herald.dawn.com/news/1153170.
28 Nira Yuval-Davis has interrogated how national literature excludes women and why in gender relations 'manhood' and 'womanhood' are necessary to our understanding

29 Kishwar Naheed, *Be nam musafat* [The Anonymous Journey] (Lahore: Sang-e meel, 1991), 107–8.
30 See Haeri, *No Shame for the Sun*, 268–70.
31 I have critiqued both the genre of life writing and the 'truth-telling' in Kishwar's autobiography in my article 'Autobiography and Muslim Women's Lives', *Journal of Women's History* 25, no. 2 (2013): 171–84, https://muse.jhu.edu/article/510537/pdf.
32 Kishwar Naheed, *Fitna samani-e dil* [Chaos Ridden Heart] (Lahore: Sang-e meel, 1985), 511–12, 517–18, 555–56.
33 Naheed, *Buri aurat ki katha*, 98–99.
34 This analysis is borrowed from my article, 'Autobiography and Muslim Women's Lives', p. 177. See also, Partha Chatterjee, *The Nation and Its Fragments: Colonial and Postcolonial Histories* (Princeton, NJ: Princeton University Press, 1993), 138–40. Also see my article, 'Truth, Fiction and Autobiography in the Modern Urdu Narrative Tradition', *Comparative Critical Studies* 4, no. 3 (2007): 379–402. For an in-depth reading of Naheed's autobiography and her travelogue, see my PhD thesis 'The Intertextuality of Women in Urdu Literature (SOAS, University of London, 2001), 202–12.
35 Don Cupitt makes an interesting intervention on storytelling from a religious and philosophic point of view in a Western context in his book *What Is a Story?* (London: SCM Press, 1991). His argument offers a useful comparative context on the idea of truth in relation to storytelling and how it has shifted over time.
36 Susie Tharu and K. Lalita, eds, *Women Writing in India: 600 BC to the Present*, vol. 1 (London: Pandora Press, 1991), 90–94, 120–22.
37 Naheed, *Buri aurat ki katha*, 100–141.
38 Ibid., 13.
39 Ibid., 12.
40 Naheed also speaks of the subjectivities of women poets themselves and the problems they face in being taken seriously as intellectuals. I have referred to this in my article '"Badan darida" (The Body Torn): Gender and Sexuality in Pakistani Women's Poetry', *Pakistan Journal of Women's Studies (Alam-e Niswan)* 13, no. 1 (2006): 45–66; republished in *The Body and the Book: Writings on Poetry and Sexuality*, ed. Glennis Byron and Andrew J. Sneddon (Amsterdam: Rodopi, 2008), 235–52.
41 See Yaqin, 'The Intertextuality of Women in Urdu Literature'. The two poems are discussed in Chapter 5, 'Kishwar Naheed: A Feminist for the Third World', 192–99.
42 Kishwar Naheed, *Khayali shakhs se muqabala* (Lahore: Sang-e meel, 1992), 84–87.
43 Chatterjee, *The Nation and Its Fragments*, 91. For an interesting historical discussion about Katherine Mayo's *Mother India* and the Indian feminist response that connects the social and political, see Mrinalini Sinha, *Specters of Mother India: The Global Restructuring of an Empire* (Durham, NC: Duke University Press, 2006).
44 Naheed, *Khayali shakhs se muqabala*, 99–102.
45 Benazir Bhutto, *Daughter of the East: An Autobiography* (London: Mandarin, 1994), 365.
46 Hamza Alavi, 'Pakistani Women in a Changing Society', in *Economy and Culture in Pakistan: Migrants and Cities in a Muslim Society*, ed. Hastings Donnan and Pnina Werbner (New York: Palgrave Macmillan, 1991), 124–42 (141).

47 See Ayesha Khan, *The Women's Movement in Pakistan: Activism, Islam and Democracy* (London: I.B. Tauris, 2018).
48 See Shahla Haeri's chapter on 'Violence: Woman's Body, Nation's Honour', in *No Shame for the Sun*, 107–68, detailing the story of 24-year-old student activist with the Pakistan People's Party, Rahila Tiwana's experience of police brutality in 1991.
49 Naheed, *Siyah hashiye men gulabi rang*, 104–5.
50 De Beauvoir, *The Second Sex*, 309.
51 Elaine Showalter, *The Female Malady: Women, Madness and English Culture, 1830–1980* (London: Virago, 1987), 18.
52 See Jasodhra Bagchi, 'Representing Nationalism: Ideology of Motherhood in Colonial Bengal', *Economic and Political Weekly* 25, nos. 42/43 (20–27 October 1990): WS65–WS71, http://www.jstor.com/stable/4396894. Also see Tanika Sarkar, 'Nationalist Iconography: Image of Women in 19th Century Bengali Literature', *Economic and Political Weekly* 22, no. 47 (27 November 1981): 2011–15, http://www.jstor.com/stable/4377759.
53 Carlo Coppola, 'Echoes and Exuberances: Baidar Bakht's Recent Translations of Urdu Poetry', *Annual of Urdu Studies* 8 (1993): 142–57. On Kishwar Naheed, see 152–56.
54 For Shoaib this is an expression of Naheed's protest against the national imaginary. Mahwash Shoaib, '"A Dictionary to Define my Dreams": The Politics of Remembrance and Forgetting in Kishwar Naheed's Poetry', *Women's Studies Quarterly* 39, nos. 3 & 4 (2011): 153–70. On dreams, see 163–65.
55 Naheed, *Main pehle janam men rat thi* (Lahore: Sang-e meel, 1988), 33.
56 Khalida Husain, 'Malamaton ke darmiyan – kyun!', in Sayyid and Ahmad, *Nae zamane ki birahan*, 109–15 (115).
57 Kishwar Naheed, 'Khud kalami' (Soliloquy), *Malamaton ke darmiyan*, in *Fitna samani-e dil*, 741–42.
58 See C. M. Naim, 'The Art of the Urdu Marsiya', in *Islamic Society and Culture: Essays in Honour of Professor Aziz Ahmad*, ed. Milton Israel and N. K. Wagle (New Delhi: Manohar, 1983), 101–16.
59 See Firoozeh Kashani-Sabet's 'Who Is Fatima?: Gender, Culture and Representation in Islam', *Journal of Middle East Women's Studies* 1, no. 2 (2005): 1–24, https://www.jstor.org/stable/40326855.
60 S. A. Husain, *Khavatin-e karbala: kalam-e Anis ke aine men* (The Women of Karbala in the Mirror of Anis's Poetry) (Karachi: Shahnil Traders, 1974); M. H. M. A. Jirajpuri, *Khavatin* (Women) (Delhi: Sangam Kitab Ghar, 1951), 22–35.
61 Naheed, *Be nam musafat*, 59–60.
62 Faiz in *The Unicorn and the Dancing Girl: Poems of Faiz Ahmad Faiz*, trans. Daud Kamal, ed. Khalid Hasan (London: Independent, 1988), 74.
63 Naheed, *Siyah hashiye men gulabi rang*, 91–92.
64 Brian McHale, *Postmodernist Fiction* (London: Routledge, 1987).
65 Kishwar Naheed, *Galyan, dhup, darvaze*, anthologized in *Fitna samani-e dil*, 487–89.
66 Two other poems linked to the theme of silence and censorship in the postcolonial nation and critiquing the patriarchal authoritarianism of the Pakistani state are 'Dafa 144' (Section 144 – the title refers to a section of the law banning public gatherings) and 'Speech Number 27'; Naheed, *Galyan, dhup, darvaze*, in *Fitna samani-e dil*, 531–32, 533–36.
67 This relationship emerged from a meeting at the Asian women writers' collective with the translator of Naheed's work, Rukhsana Ahmad, who encouraged her to undertake the task.

68 See Ela Dutt, 'Kathak Exponent Janaki Patrik, Kiran Ahluwalia to Showcase "We Sinful Women" in New York', *News India Times*, 7 February 2017, https://www.newsindiatimes.com/we-sinful-women/.
69 See Feriyal Amal Aslam, 'Choreographing [in] Pakistan: Indu Mitha, Dancing Occluded Histories in the "Land of the Pure"' (PhD thesis, University of California, 2012). Aima Khosa, '"Aurat Jagi": The Left Way', *Friday Times*, 13 March 2015, https://www.thefridaytimes.com/aurat-jagi-the-left-way/.
70 Translation by Rukhsana Ahmad in her *We Sinful Women: Contemporary Urdu Feminist Poetry Including the Original Urdu* (New Delhi: Rupa, 1994), 31–33.
71 Bhutto, *Daughter of the East*, 312.
72 See Jungu Mohsin, 'Habib Jalib: An Archetypical Lahori', in *City of Sin and Splendour: Writings on Lahore*, ed. Bapsi Sidhwa (New Delhi: Penguin, 2006), 279–83.
73 Personal communication with Ayesha Khan. Also see Khan, *The Women's Movement in Pakistan*, 87–95.
74 Kishwar Naheed, *Shanasaiyan Rusvaiyan* (Lahore: Sang-e meel, 2008), 23.
75 Baqar Mehdi, 'Nisai botiqa', in Sayyid and Ahmad, *Nae zamane ki birahan*, 55–102 (68–81); Naheed, personal communication, 2 March 1998.
76 Kishwar Naheed, *Galyan, dhup, darvaze*, in *Fitna samani-e dil*, 495–96. The feminine gender for grass has been retained from the original Urdu.
77 Neelam Hussain, 'Woman as Objects and Women as Subjects within Fundamentalist Discourse', in *Locating the Self: Perspectives on Women and Multiple Identities*, ed. Nighat Said Khan, Rubina Saigol and Afiya Sheherbano Zia (Lahore: ASR, 1994), 108–34.
78 M. Kaleem Raza Khan, 'Anti-feminism in Urdu: A Study in Linguistics and Gender', *Pakistan Journal of Women's Studies* 1, no. 2 (1994): 64–72 (72). Also see my chapter on '"*Badan darida*" (The Body Torn): Gender and Sexuality in Pakistani Women's Poetry' in *The Body and the Book: Writings on Poetry and Sexuality*, ed. Glennis Byron and Andrew J. Sneddon (Amsterdam: Rodopi, 2008), 235–52.
79 Naheed, *Main pehle janam men rat thi*, 88–90.
80 I borrow this phrase from Gillian Whitlock's book *Soft Weapons: Autobiography in Transit* (Chicago: University of Chicago Press), 2007.
81 'Justice for Zainab: Timeline of the Kasur Rape, Murder Case That Gripped the Nation', *Dawn*, 17 October 2018. The news about Zainab's murder was covered globally by the BBC, NPR, Al-Jazeera.
82 Kishwar Naheed e-mailed this poem to me directly on 15 January 2018.
83 See Sanam Maher, *The Sensational Life and Death of Qandeel Baloch* (New Delhi: Aleph, 2018).
84 Kishwar Naheed, *Vehshat aur barud men lipti hui shairi* (Lahore: Sang-e meel, 2009), 42–45.
85 Susan Bassnett, *Comparative Literature: A Critical Introduction* (Oxford: Blackwell, 1993), 92–114. Also see the interpretation of the border as a space of structural hegemony in Gloria Anzaldua's *Borderlands / La Frontera: The New Mestiza* (San Francisco: Spinsters/ Aunt Lute, 1987). Like Anzaldua, Naheed presents an alternative cultural critique through her hybrid use of form.
86 George Robertson, Melinda Mash, Lisa Tickner, Jon Bird, Barry Curtis and Tim Putnam, eds, *Traveller's Tales: Narratives of Home and Displacement* (London: Routledge, 1994), 2.
87 Mary Louise Pratt' 'Arts of the Contact Zone', *Profession* (1991): 33–40, http://www.jstor.org/stable/25595469.
88 Kishwar Naheed, *A jao Afriqa* (Lahore: Sang-e meel, 1995), 214.

89 Faiz Ahmad Faiz, 'A jao Afriqa', trans. V. G. Kiernan in his *Poems by Faiz* (London: Vanguard Books, 1971), 208–11.
90 On negritude see Aimè Cèsaire, *Notebook of a Return to My Native Land*, 2nd ed. (Columbus: Ohio State University Press, 2000). Faiz had participated in Afro-Asian conferences and served as editor of its linked publication *Lotus* magazine in Beirut. The Asian-African Bandung Conference brought together a legacy of decolonisation alongwith international writers' conferences. On Faiz's links to *Lotus*, see Sumayya Kassamali, ' "You Had No Address": Faiz Ahmad Faiz in Beirut', *Caravan: A Journal of Politics and Literature*. https://caravanmagazine.in/reviews-essays/you-had-no-address-faiz-beirut, accessed 20 September 2021.
91 Naheed, *A Jao Afriqa*, 3.
92 Eva Sallis, *Sheherazade through the Looking Glass: The Metamorphosis of The Thousand and One Nights* (London: Curzon, 1999), 85–107.
93 Rana Kabbani, *Europe's Myths of Orient* (London: Pandora Press, 1988), 50–51.
94 Githa Hariharan, *The Thousand Faces of Night* (London: Women's Press, 1996) and *When Dreams Travel* (London: Picador, 1999); Suniti Namjoshi, *The Blue Donkey Fables* (London: Women's Press, 1988) and *Feminist Fables* (London: Virago, 1994); Gayatri Chavrakorty Spivak, trans., *Imaginary Maps: Three Stories by Mahasweta Devi* (London: Routledge, 1995).
95 Naheed, *A Jao Afriqa*, 6.
96 Ibid., 7.
97 See her speech posted, by Taimur_Laal, 'Kishwar Naheed on the Aurat March' 12 March 2019. https://www.youtube.com/watch?v=tY80utu_UiY
98 See Nida Kirmani's posts on Twitter/Xhttps://x.com/NidaKirmani/status/1105564612886446086
99 See Geeta Patel, *Lyrical Movements, Historical Hauntings: On Gender, Colonialism and Desire in Miraji's Urdu Poetry* (Stanford, CA: Stanford University Press, 2001; reprint, New Delhi: Manohar, 2005).
100 Ammara Maqsood, *The New Pakistani Middle Class* (Cambridge, MA: Harvard University Press), 2017.

CONCLUSION

Aaj mere andar koi isteara sirf thakan se mar gaya hai
Lafz hairan khare hain
Aur qafiya hath chura kar chala gaya hai
Banjar ho gayi hai zamin
Aur vazn – munh ke bal gir para hai
Kahan kho gaya mera aahang?
Aadhe raste men……

Kya tu bhi –
Meri shairi, tu bhi?
Munh phair le gi? Ankhen churaye gi?

[Today only exhaustion has been the cause of death of a metaphor inside of me
Words are staring in surprise
And the rhyming qafiya has freed itself from my hand
The domain has become barren
And metre – has fallen flat on its face ……

Will you too –
My poetry, you too?
Will you turn your face away? not meet my eyes?][1]

In this book, I have argued that women poets have been overlooked in literary histories of Progressive writing. I have attempted to redress that balance by presenting an overview across the twentieth century of how a unique chapter of Progressive women's poetry was unfolding alongside the more radical group of prose writers in the first half of the twentieth century. In tracing their narratives, I note a unique secular and sacred aesthetic in the work of Progressive women poets in Pakistan. I suggest that the world of Urdu literary culture does not always follow geographical boundaries; it is transnational and global but has been subject to ideological interventions and culture wars in

Pakistan and India. Reflecting on anticolonial nationalist mobilization in the pre-independence period, I consider the post-Partition phase and Pakistani women's poetry as an alternative sphere, where the representation of self and subjectivity signalled the entry of a new Pakistani woman whose writing reflected the traumas of the new nation. This new woman was a patchwork of influences who came to the fore with a resistance-led feminist aesthetic in the 1980s. Progressive women's poetry was a notionally secular response to the religious nation, embodying alternative middle-class values that embraced intimacy, sexuality and opposition to the state's affiliation with the conservative Jamaat-e Islami party. In my argument I have demonstrated that there is a strong connection between Progressive poetry and the women's movement committed to social justice. I also underline a concern with patriarchal hierarchies within left alliances: to what extent are women welcomed within those spaces as equals? This was something that bothered Fahmida Riaz very much. Therefore what emerges from feminist activism and poetic intervention is a recognition that entrenched patriarchies contribute to women's sense of displacement from an inner circle of the radical Left as well as the political manipulations of the Right. At the same time there is a strong critique of the state and religious groups demanding a new kind of citizenship free from the burden of honour and shame in the cultural landscape.

As part of my argument, in Chapter 2 I recount the historic heritage of the Deoband and Aligarh schools of reform and their influential foundational Urdu texts on educating the zenana. Reformist texts are crucial to understanding the class aspirations of an ashraf community and offer major insights on how gender was constructed in the late nineteenth century. It is this sensibility that reigns supreme in printed texts, which benefited from increased circulation during the colonial period. Critical studies have often focused on an anthropological understanding of women's lives through these texts. I extend that lens to examine the relationship between form and text. I argue that canonical texts such as *Mirat-ul Arus* and *Umrao Jan Ada* must be read alongside hybridities of language, sexuality and gender and the lyric form. They also have to be understood in relation to the genre of women's travel writing and diaries. This type of reflective and embedded reading can give us a more rounded understanding of how sexualities and the family were being negotiated in the period of colonial influence and Enlightenment thought. Women's published poetry that had previously remained confined to zenana circles from writers such as Ze khe shin and Haya Lakhnavi became a sanctuary for women who had to leave their homes during Partition. Departing the safety of 'home and harem', middle-class women found they could gain access to educational establishments in the public arena in the new nation.[2]

Chapter 3 focuses on the politics of the Progressive Writers' movement in Urdu, emphasizing the effect on writers of an antifascist Left agenda that mobilized anticolonial sentiment, as well as class consciousness and gender equality. The Progressive Writers' experience of censorship and religious offence confirmed an orientalizing East–West divide, reiterating secular as Western and sacred as an Eastern preserve. The story of the movement is focused around patterns of sexualities and offence. I offer close readings of controversial short stories from Saadat Hasan Manto and Ismat Chughtai to illustrate how the open stance toward sexualities in their writing continued to disrupt the status quo after the banning of the foundational Progressive text *Angare*. I juxtapose their experiences of censorship with the strikingly different canvas presented by the metaphorical transformation of language in Faiz Ahmed Faiz's poetic oeuvre. Faiz's lyric voice successfully conveyed the politics of social justice to the public, who responded to the spiritual connection with God and the nation in his poetry as an articulation of home. His incarceration as a Left-wing political activist and his prison years in the 1950s recall a turning point in Pakistani politics and a new relationship with the West during the Cold War. Interestingly, while Faiz was a liberator of justice and advocate of women's rights, he was also influenced by expectations of sharafat from this group. The gendered tradition–modernity relationship created a powerful and transformative new spirit.

The journey from home to nation was fraught with trauma and women's writing echoed an experiential reality in which they were both homemakers and freedom fighters. Ada Jafri was able to step outside the zenana and express a new transnational self, adapting classical metaphors to communicate a new persona that was in turmoil. Zehra Nigah caused a sensation amongst mushaira audiences with her performances and mastery over the lyric form. Her genteel poetic voice brought a new articulation of women's silences, giving expression to poems about spirit possession and her own experience of suppressed speech. In contrast to the safe haven of middle-class life captured by their poetry were the dangers and prohibitions that drove Sara Shagufta to her suicide and made Parvin Shakir a target of gossip and an icon of romance. Urdu poetry was no longer the preserve of the elite and began to reflect the experiences of a rapidly changing sociopolitical environment.

In Chapters 4 and 5, on Fahmida Riaz and Kishwar Naheed, respectively, I argue that the political legacy of Progressive women's poetry reaches its zenith in their writing, which articulated a fierce feminist aesthetic of the personal as political, generating debate, disagreement and censorship. Their life and writings reflect the tensions and closure of the Left in Pakistan, the strong affiliation of the women's movement to left alliances and a resistance to the military state. Fahmida Riaz combines the truth-telling of journalism with the power of protest poetry. Her experience of exile adds to an explosive poet persona never at ease with herself. She is the modern-day Sufi rebel inflecting a gendered aesthetic in her writing. Kishwar Naheed, on the other hand, established herself through the conventional route of the civil service, but wrote against conformity and maintained an activist persona through her lifelong affiliation to the women's movement. She uses intergeneric poetic and prose forms to convey difference, offering alternative storytelling modes to her readers and listeners. Both women graft transnational feminist influences and experiences onto their writing.

Overall, I suggest that women poets negotiate an alternative vision of the sacred–secular divide by rewriting female subjectivities and sexualities, and subverting stereotypes. In doing so, they offer a new *jadidiyat* (modernity) of sunshine, blood and tears, transforming the metaphorical henna on their hands into a call for change. These activist middle-class women reframe the struggle for gender justice through their transnational connections, ushering in a new aesthetic and politics through adaptations of form, voice and persona. It is also important to note comparative instances of activist identification by women writing in other Pakistani languages such as Punjabi, Sindhi and Pashto. Nosheen Ali has done excellent work on this, and her website *Umang Poetry* offers an alternative and important oral and visual archive recording the lived tradition of poetry across regions. Attiya Dawood and Amar Sindhu present two powerful voices from Sindh speaking to feminism and women's activism in local and transnational contexts.[3] The Christian verse-maker Nasreen Anjum Bhatti is an influential bilingual poet who has left her imprint on Punjabi and Urdu poetry as well as Sindhi. She is multilingual and multi-ethnic, connecting across Balochi, Sindhi and Punjabi ethnicities through birth, migration and marriage. Her work offers an insight into the organic emotions of a mother tongue Punjabi and its devotional routes connecting with the Sufi voices of Waris Shah and Bulleh Shah. In Khyber Pakhtunkhwa, the woman writer Dr Roshan Kalim Sarhindi from Malakand has been identified as an emerging resistance writer in Pashto whose voice incorporates the everyday lives of Pakhtun women.[4]

Alongside the older experienced generation of resistance women poets is the rising popularity of new dystopian voices emerging in protest marches and on the streets of Lyari in Karachi where Urdu expression is following new directions. Women in the *aurat* march are demanding a change to how gender is constructed in Urdu. With slogans such as '*Khud khana garam kar lo*' (Heat up your own food) and '*dick pics apne pas rakho*' (Keep your dick pics) they are removing Urdu from its comfort zone as a genteel language populating the imaginative worlds of Urdu novels, women's digests, television drama and film.⁵ The metaphorical language of poetry is thus experiencing a major shift and the women's movement that previously found motivation in Kishwar Naheed's anthem 'We Sinful Women' in the 1980s is now looking for a new expression that calls out class privilege. Beyond the march and on the peripheries of Urdu's well-heeled literati is the voice of Eva B, a female rapper from Karachi who brings both her Baloch background and her identity as a hijab-wearing woman to the fore in her rap song 'Gully Girls'.⁶ Her voice brings to the Urdu literary sphere something that has been missing: a gritty street texture independent of ashrafization that captures the darkness of city life in a ghetto of gangland culture, drugs and poverty. Her rap is inspired by the Bollywood film *Gully Boy*, set in Mumbai, signalling the living oral tradition of Urdu verse form in film songs from across the border. Eva B's home is Lyari in Karachi, host to both Pakistan's African diaspora known as Sheedi and the Baloch community. These migrant ethnicities and new utterances are important to Urdu's lived futures, echoing the politics of young women negotiating multiple identities and articulating differences of class, language and gender.

Notes

1 Fahmida Riaz, 'Pehla bab', in *Kya tum pura chand na dekho ge*, anthologized in *Main mitti ki murat hun* (Lahore: Sang-e meel, 1988), 313.
2 See Inderpal Grewal, *Home and Harem: Nation, Gender, Empire, and the Cultures of Travel* (Durham, NC: Duke University Press, 1996).
3 See Attiya Dawood's poetry translated by Fahmida Riaz, 'Pyar ki sarhaden', 'mohabbaton ke fasle', 'Sharafat ka pul sarat', in *Apni Nigah: auraton ki likhi takhliqat aur tanqidi jaize*, ed. Javeria Khalid and Samina Rahman (Lahore: Asr, 1995), 138–43; her autobiography is available in translation, *Images in my Mirror*, trans. Amina Azfar (Karachi: Oxford University Press, 2014); *The Poems of Attiya Dawood*, trans. Asif Aslam Furrukhi (Karachi: Maktaba-e Danyal, 1995). Amar Sindhu's columns are available to read in *Dawn* newspaper and various interviews and literature festival appearances are available to view on YouTube and social media.
4 Sher Alam Shinwari, 'New Pashto Poetry Book Termed a Strong Voice for Women Rights', *Dawn*, 2 March 2019, https://www.dawn.com/news/1467076/new-pashto-poetry-book-termed-a-strong-voice-for-women-rights. See also, Nasreen Anjum Bhatti, *Nil karaiyan nilkan*. Lahore: Suchet Kitab Ghar, 1979.
5 See my article '*Mera jism, meri marzi*: Claiming Ownership of Her Body', *Equator Line* 31, nos. 8.2–3 (April–September 2020): 17–30. See also, Sadia Khatri, 'Should feminists claim Aurat March's "Vulgar" Posters: Yes Absolutely', *Dawn* (Prism), Accessed 30 May 2020 (https://www.dawn.com/news/1469815.)
6 I'm grateful to my postgraduate taught Masters student Cem Guler for introducing me to Eva B's work. He interviewed her for his inspirational review essay on my module 'Imagining Pakistan: culture, politics, gender' with the title, 'Nationalism, Gender and Hip Hop in Pakistan: Thoughts on Eva B'. Submitted on Turnitin, 6 April 2020, SOAS, University of London.

BIBLIOGRAPHY

Aftab, Tahera. 'Negotiating with Patriarchy: South Asian Muslim Women and the Appeal to Sir Syed Ahmed Khan'. *Women's History Review* 14, no. 1 (2005): 75–98.
Ahmad, Aziz. 'Urdu adab ki jadid tehrik'. In *Taraqqi Pasand Adab*, 43–59. Delhi: Chaman Book Depot, 1945.
———. 'Sayyid Ahmad Khan, Jamal Al Din Afghani and Muslim India'. *Studia Islamica* 13 (1960): 55–78.
Ahmad, Nazir. 'Introduction'. In *The Bride's Mirror: A Tale of Life in Delhi a Hundred Years Ago*, translated by G. E. Ward, 8–10. London: Henry Frowde, 1903; Delhi: Permanent Black, 2001.
Ahmad, Rukhsana, ed. and trans. *We Sinful Women: Contemporary Urdu Feminist Poetry Including the Original Urdu*. New Delhi: Rupa, 1994.
Ahmad, Sadaf. *Transforming Faith: The Story of Al-Huda and Islamic Revivalism among Urban Pakistani Women*. Syracuse, NY: Syracuse University Press, 2009.
Ahmad, Shazia. 'A New Dispensation in Islam: The Ahmadiyya and the Law in Colonial India, 1872–1939'. PhD thesis, SOAS, University of London, 2015.
Ahmed, Asad. 'Advocating a Secular Pakistan: The Munir Report of 1954'. In *Islam in South Asia in Practice*, edited by Barbara Daly Metcalf, 424–37. Princeton, NJ: Princeton University Press, 2009.
Ahmed, Safdar. 'Literary Romanticism and Islamic Modernity: The Case of Urdu Poetry'. *South Asia: Journal of South Asian Studies* 35, no. 2 (2012): 434–55.
Ahmed, Shahab. *What Is Islam? The Importance of Being Islamic*. Princeton, NJ: Princeton University Press, 2016.
Akhtar, Asim. 'Interview with Zehra Nigah'. *Baithak*, 1 November 2005. http://baithak.blogspot.co.uk/2005/11/zehra-nigah-aasim-akhtar.html.
Akhtar, Mohammad Khalid. 'Fahmida Riaz'. *Funun* 2, nos. 4–5 (1966): 294–95.
Alavi, Hamza. 'The State in Post-Colonial Societies: Pakistan and Bangladesh'. *New Left Review* 1, no. 74 (July/August 1972): 59–81.
———. 'Pakistani Women in a Changing Society'. In *Economy and Culture in Pakistan: Migrants and Cities in a Muslim Society*, edited by Hastings Donnan and Pnina Werbner, 124–42. New York: Palgrave Macmillan, 1991.
Ali, Ahmed, and N. M. Rashed. 'The Progressive Writers Movement in Its Historical Perspective'. *Journal of South Asian Literature* 13, nos. 1/4 (1977–78): 91–97.
Ali, Kamran Asdar. 'The Other Side of the "Tracks": Sara Shagufta and the Politics of Gender and Class'. In *Gender, Politics and Performance in South Asia*, ed. Sheema Kermani, Asif Farrukhi and Kamran Asdar Ali, 431–62. Karachi: Oxford University Press, 2015.
Ali, Nosheen. 'From Hallaj to Heer: Poetic Knowledge and the Muslim Tradition'. *Journal of Narrative Politics* 3, no. 1 (2016): 2–26.

Ali, Tariq, Hilal Bhatt, Angana P. Chatterjee, Habbah Khatun, Pankaj Mishra and Arundhati Roy. *Kashmir: The Case for Freedom*. London: Verso, 2011.
Amjad, Rashid. 'Pakistan ki Urdu shairat'. In *Ibarat: Pakistan men Urdu adab ke pachas sal*, edited by Nawazish Ali, 99–112. Rawalpindi: Rabita, n.d.
Anantharam, Anita. *Bodies That Remember: Women's Indigenous Knowledge and Cosmopolitanism in South Asian Poetry*. Syracuse, NY: Syracuse University Press, 2012.
Anidjar, Gil. 'Secularism'. *Critical Enquiry* 33, no. 1 (2006): 52–57.
Ansari, Usamah. 'Producing the Conjugal Patriarchal Family in Maulana Thanavi's Heavenly Ornaments: Biopolitics, "Shariatic Modernity" and Managing Women'. *Comparative Islamic Studies* 5, no. 1 (2009): 93–110.
Anzaldua, Gloria. *Borderlands / La Frontera: The New Mestiza*. San Francisco: Spinsters/Aunt Lute, 1987.
Asad, Talal. *Formations of the Secular: Christianity, Islam, Modernity*. Stanford, CA: Stanford University Press, 2003.
Askari, Muhammad Hasan. *Jadidiyat ya maghribi gumrahiyon ki tarikh ka khaka*. Lahore: Iffat Hasan, 1979.
———. 'Musalman adib aur musalman qaum'. In *Majmu'a Muhammad Hassan Askari*, 1111–19. Lahore: Sang-e meel, 2008.
Aslam, Feriyal Amal. 'Choreographing [in] Pakistan: Indu Mitha, Dancing Occluded Histories in the "Land of the Pure"'. PhD thesis, University of California, 2012.
Awn, Peter J. *Satan's Tragedy and Redemption: Iblis in Sufi Psychology*. Leiden: E. J. Brill, 1983.
Badran, Margot. *Feminism beyond East and West: New Gender Talk and Practice in Global Islam*. New Delhi: Global Media, 2007.
———. *Feminism in Islam: Secular and Religious Convergences*. Oxford: Oneworld, 2009.
Bagchi, Jasodhra. 'Representing Nationalism: Ideology of Motherhood in Colonial Bengal'. *Economic and Political Weekly* 25, nos. 42–43 (20–27 October 1990): WS65–WS71. http://www.jstor.com/stable/4396894.
Baksh, S., ed. *Pakistani adbiyat men khavatin ka kirdar*. Islamabad: Allama Iqbal Open University, 1996.
Barker, M. A. R., S. A Salam and M. A. Siddiqi, eds. *A Reader of Classical Urdu Poetry*. 3 vols. Ithaca, NY: Spoken Language Services, 1977.
Bassnett, Susan. *Comparative Literature: A Critical Introduction*. Oxford: Blackwell, 1993.
Bayly, Chris. *Rulers, Townsmen and Bazaars: North Indian Society in the Age of British Expansion 1770–1870*. Cambridge: Cambridge University Press, 1983.
Bettelheim, Bruno. *The Uses of Enchantment: The Meaning and Importance of Fairy Tales*. Harmondsworth: Penguin, 1978.
Bhatnagar, R. S. *Mysticism in Urdu Poetry*. New Delhi: Department of Islamic Studies, Jamia Hamdard, 1995.
Bhutto, Benazir. *Daughter of the East: An Autobiography*. London: Mandarin, 1994.
Blachère, R., and A. Bausani. 'Ghazal'. In *Encyclopaedia of Islam*, edited by P. Bearman, Th. Bianquis, C. E. Bosworth, E. van Donzel and W. P. Heinrichs. 2nd ed., online. Leiden: Brill, 2012. Accessed 18 February 2021. http://dx.doi.org/10.1163/1573-3912_islam_COM_0232.
Brennan, Timothy. *Wars of Position: The Cultural Politics of Left and Right*. New York: Columbia University Press, 2006.
Britannica, Editors of Encyclopaedia. 'Hetaira'. *Encyclopaedia Britannica*. Accessed 29 November 2013. https://www.britannica.com/topic/hetaira.

Burton, Antoinette. *Dwelling in the Archive: Writing House, Home and History in Late Colonial India.* New York: Oxford University Press, 2003.
Butler, Judith. *Gender Trouble: Feminism and the Subversion of Identity.* New York: Routledge, 1990.
Chatterjee, Partha. *Nationalist Thought and the Colonial World: A Derivative Discourse.* Minneapolis: University of Minnesota Press, 1993.
———. *The Nation and its Fragments: Colonial and Postcolonial Histories.* Princeton, NJ: Princeton University Press, 1993.
———. 'The Nationalist Resolution of the Women's Question'. In *Recasting Women: Essays in Colonial History*, edited by Kumkum Sangari and Sudesh Vaid, 233–53. New Delhi: Kali for Women, 1999.
Chhachhi, Amrita. 'Identity Politics, Secularism and Women: A South Asian Perspective'. In *Forging Identities: Gender, Communities and the State*, edited by Zoya Hasan, 74–95. New Delhi: Kali for Women, 1994.
———. 'Forced Identities: The State, Communalism, Fundamentalism and Women in India'. In *Writing the Women's Movement*, edited by Mala Khullar, 218–42. New Delhi: Zubaan, 2005.
Chughtai, Ismat. *Choten.* Delhi: M. Azad Mirza Malik Book Depot., 1953
———. *Chui mui.* Bombay: Kutab Publishers. 1952.
———. *Kulliyat Ismat Chughtai* (Navil), ed. Asif Nawaz. Lahore: Maktaba-e sher-o adab, n.d.
Chughtai, Ismat. '*Mahfil* Interviews Ismat Chughtai'. *Mahfil* 8, no. 2/3 (1972): 169–88.
———. *The Quilt and Other Stories*, translated and edited by Tahira Naqvi and S. S. Hameed. New Delhi: Kali for Women, 1990.
———. *A Life in Words: Memoirs*, translated from the original Urdu *Kaghazi Hai Pairahan* by M. Asaduddin. India: Penguin Books, 2012.
Cixous, Hélène. 'The Laugh of the Medusa'. *Jalibi* (1991): 182–87.
Coppola, Carlo. 'Urdu Poetry, 1935–1970: The Progressive Episode'. PhD thesis, University of Chicago, 1975.
———. 'The Angare Group: The Enfants Terribles of Urdu Literature'. *Annual of Urdu Studies* 1 (1981): 57–69.
———. 'Premchand's Address to the First Meeting of the All-India Progressive Writers Association: Some Speculations'. *Journal of South Asian Literature* 21, no. 2 (1986): 21–39.
———, ed. *Marxist Influences and South Asian Literature.* New Delhi: Oxford University Press, 1988.
———. 'Echoes and Exuberances: Baidar Bakht's Recent Translations of Urdu Poetry'. *Annual of Urdu Studies* 8 (1993): 142–57.
Coppola, Carlo, and S. Zubair. 'Rashid Jahan: Urdu Literature's First "Angry Young Woman"'. *Journal of South Asian Literature* 22, no. 1 (1987): 166–83.
Cupitt, Don. *What Is a Story?* London: SCM Press, 1991.
Dang, Kokila. 'Prostitutes, Patrons and the State: Nineteenth Century Awadh'. *Social Scientist* 21, no. 9/11 (September–October 1993): 173–96.
Datta, Amaresh, ed. *Encyclopaedia of Indian Literature, Volume 2: Devraj to Jyoti.* New Delhi: Sahitya Akademi, 1988.
Dawood, Attiya. *The Poems of Attiya Dawood*, translated by Asif Aslam Furrukhi. Karachi: Maktaba-e Danyal, 1995.
———. 'Sara meri dost'. In *Apni nigah: auraton ki likhi taakhliqat aur tanqidi jaize*, edited by Javeria Khalid and Samina Rahman, 76–89. Lahore: ASR, 1995.
———. 'Sharafat ka pul sarat'. In *Apni nigah: auraton ki likhi taakhliqat aur tanqidi jaize*, edited by Javeria Khalid and Samina Rahman, 141. Lahore: ASR, 1995.

———. *Images in My Mirror*, translated by Amina Azfar. Karachi: Oxford University Press, 2014.

de Beauvoir, Simone. *The Second Sex*, translated by H. M. Parshley. London: Picador, 1988.

Deol, Jeevan. 'Sex, Social Critique and the Female Figure in Premodern Punjabi'. *Modern Asian Studies* 36, no. 1 (2002): 141–71.

Devi, Mahasweta. 'Douloti the Bountiful', translated by Gayatri Chakravorty Spivak. In *Imaginary Maps: Three Stories by Mahasweta Devi*, translated by Gayatri Chakravorty Spivak, 19–94. New York: Routledge, 1995.

Douglas, Mary. *Purity and Danger: An Analysis of Concepts of Pollution and Taboo*. London: Routledge and Kegan Paul, 1966.

Dutt, Ela. 'Kathak Exponent Janaki Patrik, Kiran Ahluwalia to Showcase "We Sinful Women" in New York'. *News India Times*, 7 February 2017. https://www.newsindiatimes.com/we-sinful-women/.

Eliot, T. S. *The Waste Land and Other Poems*. London: Faber and Faber, 1971.

Emig, Rainer. *Modernism in Poetry: Motivations, Structures and Limits*. London: Longman, 1995.

Faiz, Faiz Ahmed. *Poems by Faiz*, translated with an introduction and notes by V. G. Kiernan. Lahore: Vanguard Books, 1971.

———. *The Unicorn and the Dancing Girl: Poems of Faiz Ahmad Faiz*, translated by Daud Kamal, edited by Khalid Hasan. London: Independent, 1988.

———. 'Dibacha' to *Shama ka pehla tara*. In Zehra Nigah, *Majmua-e Kalaam*. Lahore: Sang-e meel, 2012.

Fanon, Frantz. *The Wretched of the Earth*, translated by Constance Farrington. London: Penguin, 1967.

Faruqi, Mehr Afshan. *Urdu Literary Culture: Vernacular Modernity in the Writing of Muhammad Hasan Askari*. New York: Palgrave Macmillan, 2012.

Faruqi, Shamsur Rahman. 'Images in a Darkened Mirror: Issues and Ideas in Modern Urdu Literature'. *Annual of Urdu Studies* 6 (1987): 43–54.

———. *Early Urdu Literary Culture and History*. New Delhi: Oxford University Press, 2001.

Fatehpuri, Farman, and Umrao Tariq, eds. *Ada Jafri: fan-o shakhsiat*. Karachi: Halqa-e niazo nigar, 1998.

'Fehmeeda Riaz's Son Drowns'. *The News*, 27 October 2007. https://www.thenews.com.pk/archive/print/76606-fehmeeda-riaz%E2%80%99s-son-drowns.

Flemming, Leslie A. *Another Lonely Voice: The Urdu Short Stories of Saadat Hasan Manto*. Berkeley: University of California, Center for South and Southeast Asia Studies, 1979.

Forbes, Geraldine. *Women in Modern India*. Cambridge: Cambridge University Press, 1996.

Ford, Heidi A. 'Hierarchical Inversions, Divine Subversions: The Miracles of Rabia al-Adawiya'. *Journal of Feminist Studies in Religion* 15, no. 2 (1999): 5–24.

Freud, Sigmund. *Totem and Taboo*, translated by James Strachey. London: Routledge and Kegan Paul, 1950.

Furrukhi, Asif. ' "*Banu-e guft ashna* (A Woman Devoted to Discourse)": An Interview with Kishwar Naheed'. In *Nae zamane ki birahan*, edited by Asghar Nadeem Sayyid and Afzaal Ahmad, 254. Lahore: Sang-e meel, 1990.

———. 'Nazm-i Nigah'. *Dawn*, 12 January 2014.

Gandhi, Leela. Review of Susie Tharu and K. Lalita, eds, *Women Writing in India*. *Manushi* 81 (March/April 1994): 31–33.

Gardezi, F. 'Islam, Feminism and the Women's Movement in Pakistan: 1981–91'. In *Against All Odds: Essays on Women, Religion and Development from India and Pakistan*, edited by K. Bhasin, Ritu Menon and Nighat Said Khan, 51–58. New Delhi: Kali for Women, 1994.

Gauhar, Ghulam Samdani. *Hayat-e Mah laqa*. Hyderabad: Nizam al-Matabi, 1904.

Ghosh, Anindita. 'An Uncertain "Coming of the Book": Early Print Cultures in Colonial India'. *Book History* 6 (2003): 23–55.

Gilmartin, David. 'Democracy, Nationalism and the Public: A Speculation on Colonial Muslim Politics'. *South Asia* 14, no. 1 (1991): 123–40.

Glassé, Cyril. *The Concise Encyclopaedia of Islam*. London: Stacey International, 1989.

Gopal, Priyamvada. *Literary Radicalism in India: Gender, Nation and the Transition to Independence*. London: Routledge, 2005.

Grewal, Inderpal. *Home and Harem: Nation, Gender, Empire, and the Cultures of Travel*. Durham, NC: Duke University Press, 1996.

Guler, Cem. 'Nationalism, Gender and Hip Hop in Pakistan: Thoughts on Eva B'. Unpublished essay, SOAS, University of London, 6 April 2020.

Haeri, Shahla. *No Shame for the Sun: Lives of Professional Pakistani Women*. Syracuse, NY: Syracuse University Press, 2002.

Hafeez, Sabiha. 'Social Discrimination of Women in Folk Literature and Culture'. In *Women: Myth and Realities*, edited by Kishwar Naheed, 286–98. Lahore: Sang-e meel, ca.1993.

Hali, Altaf Husain. *Muqaddama-e sher-o shairi*. Lahore: Sartaj Book Depot, [1893] 1950.

———. *Voices of Silence: English Translation of Hali's Majalis-un-nissa and Chup ki dad*, translated by Gail Minault. Delhi: Chanakya, 1986.

Hameed, Yasmeen. 'Beyond the Glamorous Façade'. *News International*, 7 January 1996: 9.

Hariharan, Githa. *The Thousand Faces of Night*. London: Women's Press, 1996.

———. *When Dreams Travel*. London: Picador, 1999.

Haroon, A. 'The Women's Movement in Pakistan'. In *Unveiling the Issues: Pakistani Women's Perspectives on Social, Political and Ideological Issues*, edited by Nighat Said Khan and Afiya Sheherbano Zia, 178–86. Lahore: ASR, 1995.

Hasan, Fatema. *Ze Khe Shin: hayat-o shairi ka tahqiqi aur tanqidi jaiza*. Karachi: Anjuman Taraqqi-e Urdu Pakistan, 2007.

, ed. *Zahida Khatun Sherwania: intikhab kalam*. Karachi: Oxford University Press, 2015.

Hasan, Mushirul. 'Aligarh's "Notre Eminent Contemporain": Assessing Syed Ahmad Khan's Reformist Agenda'. *Economic and Political Weekly* 33, no. 19 (9–15 May 1998): 1077–81.

Hasan, S. 'Urdu shairi men jadid Pakistani aurat ki haisiyat ka'. In *Apni nigah: auraton ki takhliqat aur tanqidi jaize*, edited by Javeria Khalid and Samina Rahman, 9–26. Lahore: ASR, 1995.

Hashmi, Ali Madeeh. *Love and Revolution: Faiz Ahmed Faiz: The Authorized Biography*. New Delhi: Rupa , 2016.

Hay, Stephen, ed. *Sources of Indian Tradition, Volume Two: Modern India and Pakistan*. 2nd ed. New Delhi: Penguin, 1992.

Hisam, Zeenat. 'Fahmida Riaz: Life and Work of a Poet'. *Pakistan Journal of Women's Studies* 2, no. 1 (1995): 43–52.

Hodgson, Marshall G. S. *The Venture of Islam: Conscience and History in a World Civilization*, 3 vols. Chicago: University of Chicago Press, 1974.

Hooke, S. M. *Middle Eastern Mythology*. London: Penguin, 1963.

Hossain, Rokeya Sakhawat. *Sultana's Dream and Padmarag: Two Feminist Utopias*, translated by Barnita Bagchi. New Delhi: Penguin, 2005.

Husain, Intizar. 'Nae zamane ki birhan', 'Kishwar Naheed – Nazm se nasr tak'. In *Nae zamane ki birahan*, edited by Asghar Nadeem Sayyid and Afzaal Ahmad, 19–22, 23–25. Lahore: Sang-e meel, 1990.

Husain, Khalida. 'Malamaton ke darmiyan – kyun!'. In *Nae zamane ki birahan*, edited by Asghar Nadeem Sayyid and Afzaal Ahmad, 109–15. Lahore: Sang-e meel, 1990.

———. 'Nisai khud shinasi aur Fahmida Riaz'. In *Feminism or Hum: Adab ki gavahi*, edited by Fatema Hasan, 183–94. Karachi: Vada Kitab Ghar, 2005.

Husain, S. A. *Khavatin-e karbala: kalam-e Anis ke aine men*. Karachi: Shahnil Traders, 1974.

Hussain, Fahmida. *Image of 'Woman' in the Poetry of Shah Abdul Latif*, translated by Amjad Siraj Memon. Karachi: University of Karachi, 2001.

Hussain, Iqbalunnissa. *Changing India: A Muslim Woman Speaks*. Karachi: Oxford University Press, 2015.

———. *Purdah and Polygamy*, edited by Jessica Berman. Karachi: Oxford University Press, 2019.

Hussain, Neelam. 'Woman as Objects and Women as Subjects within Fundamentalist Discourse'. In *Locating the Self: Perspectives on Women and Multiple Identities*, edited by Nighat Said Khan, Rubina Saigol and Afiya Sheherbano Zia, 108–34. Lahore: ASR, 1994.

Hussein, Aamer. 'Aamer Hussein Reviews Ismat Chughtai's Short Stories'. *Asymptote* (n.d.). Accessed 1 December 2020. https://www.asymptotejournal.com/criticism/ismat-chughtais-short-stories/#.WJhP4mHenQg.facebook.

———. 'Forcing Silence to Speak: Muhammadi Begum, *Mir'atu'l-'Arus*, and the Urdu Novel'. *Annual of Urdu Studies* 11 (1996): 71–86.

Iqbal, Muhammad. *Javid-nama*, translated by A. J. Arberry. London: Allen and Unwin, 1966.

———. *Shikwa and Jawab-e Shikwa (Complaint and Answer): Iqbal's Dialogue with Allah*, translated by Khushwant Singh. Delhi: Oxford University Press, 1981.

———. *Kulliyat-e Iqbal*. Lahore: Iqbal Academy and National Book Foundation, 1990.

Jaffery, Yunus. *History of Persian Literature*. Delhi: Triveni, 1981.

Jafri, Ada. *Ghazalan tum to vaqif ho*. 2nd ed. Lahore: Ghalib, 1982.

———. *Jo rahi so bekhabri rahi*. Karachi: Maktaba-e Daniyaal, 1995.

———. *Main saz dhundhti rahi*. Lahore: Maqbool Academy. 1988.

———. *Saz-e sukhan bahana hai*. Lahore: Maqbool Academy, 1988.

———. *Shahr-e dard*. Lahore: Maqbool Academy, 1988.

Jahan, Rashid. 'Dilli ki sair' and 'Parde ke piche'. In *Angare*, ed. Khalid Alvi. Delhi: Educational Publishing House, 2013.

Jahangir, Asma, and Hina Jilani. *The Hudood Ordinances: A Divine Sanction?* Lahore: Rhotas Books, 1990.

Jalal, Ayesha. *Self and Sovereignty: Individual and Community in South Asian Islam Since 1850*. Lahore: Sang-e meel, 2001.

———. *Partisans of Allah: Jihad in South Asia*. Cambridge, MA: Harvard University Press, 2008.

———. *The Pity of Partition: Manto's Life, Times and Work across the India–Pakistan Divide*. Princeton, NJ: Princeton University Press, 2013.

———. *The Struggle for Pakistan: A Muslim Homeland and Global Politics*. Cambridge, MA: Harvard University Press, 2014.

Jalil, Rakshanda. *Liking Progress, Loving Change: A Literary History of the Progressive Writers' Movement in Urdu*. New Delhi: Oxford University Press, 2014.

———. *A Rebel and Her Cause: The Life and Work of Rashid Jahan*. Karachi: Oxford University Press, 2015.

Jamal, Amina. 'Transnational Feminism as Critical Practice: A Reading of Feminist Discourses in Pakistan'. *Meridians: Feminism, Race, Transnationalism* 5, no. 2 (2005): 57–82.

———. *Jamaat-e Islami Women in Pakistan: Vanguard of a New Modernity?* Syracuse, NY: Syracuse University Press, 2013.

Jamal, Farida. 'Fatema Sughra Haya: She Dwelt among the Untrodden'. *Lucknow Observer*, 5 June 2015.

Jameson, Fredric. 'Third World Literature in the Age of Multinational Capitalism'. *Social Text* 15 (1986): 65–88.

Javed, Rafaqat. *Parvin Shakir jaisa main ne dekha*. Islamabad: Parvin Shakir Trust, 2014.

Jeffery, Patricia. *Frogs in a Well: Indian Women in Purdah*. London: Zed, 1979.

Jaffrey, Yunus. *History of Persian Literature*. Delhi: Triveni Publications, 1981.

Jinnah, Muhammed Ali. *Speeches and Writings of Mr Jinnah*, edited by Jamil-ud-din Ahmad, 2 vols. Lahore: M. Ashraf, 1942.

Jirajpuri, M. H. M. A. *Khavatin*. Delhi: Sangam Kitab Ghar, 1951.

Joshi, Priya. *In Another Country: Colonialism, Culture and the English Novel in India*. New York: Columbia University Press, 2002.

'JSAL Interviews Dr Hamida Saiduzzafar: A Conversation with Rashid Jahan's Sister-in-Law, Aligarh, 1973'. *Journal of South Asian Literature* 22, no. 1 (Winter/Spring 1987): 158–65.

'Justice for Zainab: Timeline of the Kasur Rape, Murder Case that Gripped the Nation'. *Dawn*, 17 October 2018.

Kabbani, Rana. *Europe's Myths of Orient*. London: Pandora Press, 1988.

Kandiyoti, Deniz. *Women, Islam and the State*. Basingstoke: Macmillan, 1991.

Karachi Literary Festival. 'Adab kay sitaray: Zehra Nigah, Kishwar Naheed, Masood Ashar, Mustansar Hussain Tarar', 10 February 2017. https://www.youtube.com/watch?v=YiaC6fQtXX4.

Kashani-Sabet, Firoozeh. 'Who Is Fatima?: Gender, Culture and Representation in Islam'. *Journal of Middle East Women's Studies* 1, no. 2 (2005): 1–24. https://www.jstor.org/stable/40326855.

Kazmi, Sara. 'Don't Make My Corpse Apologise: Lessons in Dissidence from Fahmida Riaz'. *Dawn*, 4 December 2018.

Kermani, Sheema. 'Tehrik-e-Niswan's Tilismati Tees Aur Aik Saal'. In *Gender, Politics, and Performance in South Asia*, edited by Sheema Kermani, Asif Furrukhi and Kamran Asdar Ali, 3–34. Karachi: Oxford University Press, 2015.

Khalique, Harris. 'An Interview with Feminist Poet Kishwar Naheed'. *Herald*, 8 March 2017. https://herald.dawn.com/news/1153170.

Khan, Ayesha. *The Women's Movement in Pakistan: Activism, Islam and Democracy*. London: I.B. Tauris, 2018.

Khan, Insha Allah. *Darya-i Latafat*. Aurangabad: Anjuman-e taraqqi-e Urdu, 1935.

Khan, M. Kaleem Raza. 'Anti-feminism in Urdu: A Study in Linguistics and Gender'. *Pakistan Journal of Women's Studies* 1, no. 2 (1994): 64–72.

Khan, Shahnaz. *Zina, Transnational Feminism, and the Moral Regulation of Pakistani Women*. Chicago: University of Chicago Press, 2006.

———. 'What Is in a Name? Khwaja Sira, Hijras and Eunuchs in Pakistan'. *Indian Journal of Gender Studies* 23, no. 2 (2016): 218–42. DOI: 10.1177/0971521516635327.

Khatun, Habba. *The Way of the Swan: Poems of Kashmir*, translated by Nilla Cram Crook. Bombay: Asia Publishing House, 1958.

Khoja-Moolji, Shenila. *Forging the Ideal Educated Girl: The Production of Desirable Subjects in Muslim South Asia*. Oakland: University of California Press, 2018.

Khosa, Aima. '"Aurat Jagi": The Left Way'. *Friday Times*, 13 March 2015. https://www.the fridaytimes.com/aurat-jagi-the-left-way/.

Kirkpatrick, Kate. *Becoming Beauvoir: A Life*. London: Bloomsbury, 2019.

Kugle, Scott. 'Mah Laqa Bai and Gender: The Language, Poetry and Performance of a Courtesan in Hyderabad'. *Comparative Studies of South Asia, Africa, and the Middle East* 30, no. 3 (2010): 365–85. http://muse.jhu.edu/journals/cst/summary/v030/30.3.kugle.html.

———. *When Sun Meets Moon: Gender, Eros and Ecstasy in Urdu Poetry*. Chapel Hill: University of North Carolina Press, 2016.

Kulkarni, Damini. 'An Urdu Poet, Her Activist Niece, and Two Faces of Rebellion at Lucknow's Farangi Mahal'. *Scroll.in*, 18 September 2017. https://scroll.in/reel/850967/an-urdu-poet-her-activist-niece-and-two-faces-of-rebellion-at-lucknows-farangi-mahal.

Lal, Ruby. *Coming of Age in Nineteenth-Century India: The Girl-Child and the Art of Playfulness*. Cambridge: Cambridge University Press, 2013.

Lambert-Hurley, Siobhan. 'Fostering Sisterhood: Muslim Women and the All-India Ladies' Association'. *Journal of Women's History* 16, no. 2 (2004): 40–65.

———. *Muslim Women, Reform and Princely Patronage: Nawab Sultan Jahan Begam of Bhopal*. New York: Routledge, 2007.

———, ed. *A Princess's Pilgrimage: Nawab Sikander Begum's 'A Pilgrimage to Mecca'*. Bloomington: Indiana University Press, 2008.

———. 'Forging Global Networks in the Imperial Era: Atiya Fyzee in Imperial London'. In *India in Britain: South Asian Networks and Connections, 1858–1950*, edited by Susheila Nasta, 64–79. Basingstoke: Palgrave Macmillan, 2013.

Lawrence, Bruce B. 'Islamicate Civilization: The View from Asia'. In *Teaching Islam*, edited by Brannon M. Wheeler, 61–76. New York: Oxford University Press, 2003.

Lelyveld, David. *Aligarh's First Generation: Muslim Solidarity in British India*. Princeton, NJ: Princeton University Press, 1996.

———. '*Ashraf*'. In *Keywords in South Asian Studies*, edited by Rachel Dwyer, SOAS South Asia Institute (online resource, n.d.). Accessed 12 December 2020. https://www.soas.ac.uk/south-asiainstitute/keywords/file24799.pdf.

Lewis, Reina. *Rethinking Orientalism: Women, Travel and the Ottoman Harem*. London: I.B. Tauris, 2004.

Lokuge, Chandani. 'Dialoguing with Empire: The Literary and Political Rhetoric of Sarojini Naidu'. In *India in Britain: South Asian Networks and Connections, 1858–1950*, edited by Susheila Nasta, 115–33. Houndmills: Palgrave Macmillan, 2013.

Loomba, Ania, and Ritty A. Lukose, eds. *South Asian Feminisms*. Durham, NC: Duke University Press, 2012.

Macaulay, Thomas Babington. *Speeches by Lord Macaulay with his Minute on Indian Education*, selected with an introduction and notes by G. M. Young. Oxford: Oxford University Press, [1835] 1979.

McClintock, Anne. 'Family Feuds: Gender, Nationalism and the Family'. *Feminist Review* 44 (Summer 1993): 61–80.

———. *Imperial Leather: Race, Gender and Sexuality in the Colonial Conquest*. New York: Routledge, 1995.

———. '"No Longer in a Future Heaven": Gender, Race and Nationalism'. In *Dangerous Liaisons: Gender, Nation and Postcolonial Perspectives*, edited by Anne McClintock, Aamir Mufti and Ella Shohat, 89–112. Minneapolis, MN: University of Minneapolis Press, 2004.

McHale, Brian. *Postmodernist Fiction*. London: Routledge, 1987.
Madni, A. H. *Jadid Urdu shairi*. Karachi: Anjuman-e taraqqi-e Urdu, 1990.
Maher, Sanam. *The Sensational Life and Death of Qandeel Baloch*. New Delhi: Aleph, 2018.
Mahmud, Shabana. '*Angare* and the Founding of the Progressive Writers' Association'. *Modern Asian Studies* 30, no. 2 (1996): 447–67.
Majeed, Javed. 'Nature, Hyperbole, and the Colonial State: Some Muslim Appropriations of European Modernity in Late Nineteenth-Century Urdu Literature'. In *Islam and Modernity: Muslim Intellectuals Respond*, edited by John Cooper, Ronald L. Nettler and Mohamed Mahmoud, 10–37. London: I.B. Tauris, 1998.
Malaqa Bai Chanda. *Divan*, edited by Shafqat Rizvi. Lahore: Majlis-e taraqqi-e Urdu, [1798] 1990.
Malik, Hafeez. 'The Marxist Literary Movement in India and Pakistan'. *Journal of Asian Studies* 26, no. 4 (1967): 649–64. https://www.jstor.org/stable/2051241.
Mani, Lata. *Contentious Traditions: The Debate on Sati in Colonial India*. Berkeley: University of California Press, 1998.
Manto, Saadat Hasan. *Mantonama*. Lahore: Sang-e meel, 1999.
———. *The Armchair Revolutionary and Other Sketches*, translated by Khalid Hasan, edited by Ali Mir and Saadia Toor. New Delhi: Leftword Books, 2016.
———. *My Name is Radha: The Essential Manto*, translated by Muhammad Umar Memon. Gurgaon, Haryana: Penguin Books India, 2016.
Maqsood, Ammara. *The New Pakistani Middle Class*. Cambridge, MA: Harvard University Press, 2017.
Matthews, D. J., and Christopher Shackle, eds. *An Anthology of Classical Urdu Love Lyrics*. London: Oxford University Press, 1972.
Maududi, Abul A'la. *Purdah and the Status of Women in Islam*. Lahore: Islamic Publications, 1972.
Mehdi, Baqar. 'Nisai botiqa'. In *Nae zamane ki birahan*, edited by Asghar Nadeem Sayyid and Afzaal Ahmad, 55–102. Lahore: Sang-e meel, 1990.
Menocal, Maria Rosa. *The Ornament of the World: How Muslims, Jews, and Christians Created a Culture of Tolerance in Medieval Spain*. New York: Black Bay Books, Little Brown, 2002.
Menon, Nivedita. 'Outing Heteronormativity: Nation, Citizen, Feminist Disruptions'. In *Sexualities: Issues in Contemporary Indian Feminism*, edited by Nivedita Menon, 3–51. New Delhi: Kali for Women, 2007.
Mernissi, Fatima. *Hidden From History: Forgotten Queens of Islam*. Lahore: ASR, 1994.
Metcalf, Barbara Daly. *Perfecting Women: Maulana Ashraf Ali Thanawi's Bihishti Zewar: A Partial Translation with Commentary*. Berkeley: University of California Press, 1990.
Milani, Farzaneh. 'Formation, Confrontation and Emancipation in the Poetry of Forugh Farrokhzad'. In *A Rebirth: Poems by Foroogh Farrokhzaad*, translated and edited by David Martin, 123–33. Costa Mesa: Mazda, 1985.
Minault, Gail. 'Begamati Zuban: Women's Language and Culture in Nineteenth Century Delhi'. *India International Centre Quarterly* 11, no. 2 (1984): 155–70.
———. 'Making Invisible Women Visible: Studying the History of Muslim Women in South Asia'. *Journal of South Asian Studies* 9, no. 1 (1986): 1–14.
———. 'Sayyid Mumtaz Ali and "Huquq un-Niswan": An Advocate of Women's Rights in Islam in the Late Nineteenth Century'. *Modern Asian Studies* 24, no. 1 (1990): 147–72.
———. *Secluded Scholars: Women's Education and Muslim Social Reform in Colonial India*. New Delhi: Oxford University Press, 1998.
———. '"Tahzibi Bahin": Four Early Indian Muslim Women Writers'. Keynote address for the workshop 'Women's Autobiographies in Islamic Societies: Context and

Construction', Delhi 2010. http://www.columbia.edu/itc/mealac/pritchett/00urd uhindilinks/srffest/txt_minault_zaykaysheen.pdf.

Mir, Farina. *The Social Space of Language.* Berkeley: University of California Press, 2010.

Mir, Safdar M. *Modern Urdu Prose: Essays in Literary History.* Lahore: Azad, 1998.

Mirza, Begum Khurshid. *A Woman of Substance: The Memoirs of Begum Khurshid Mirza*, edited by Lubna Kazim. Delhi: Zubaan, 2005.

Mohanty, Chandra. 'Under Western Eyes: Feminist Scholarship and Colonial Discourses'. *Feminist Review* 30, no. 1 (1988): 61–88.

———. *Feminism without Borders: Decolonizing Theory, Practicing Solidarity.* Durham, NC: Duke University Press, 2003.

———. 'Under Western Eyes: Revisited'. *Signs* 28, no. 2 (Winter 2003): 499–535.

Mohsin, Jungu. 'Habib Jalib: An Archetypical Lahori'. In *City of Sin and Splendour: Writings on Lahore*, edited by Bapsi Sidhwa, 279–83. New Delhi: Penguin, 2006.

Mufti, Aamir R. 'Auerbach in Istanbul: Edward Said, Secular Criticism, and the Question of Minority Culture'. *Critical Inquiry* 25, no. 1 (1998): 95–125.

———. 'Towards a Lyric History of India'. *boundary 2* 31, no. 2 (2004): 245–74.

———. *Enlightenment in the Colony: The Jewish Question and the Crisis of Postcolonial Culture.* Princeton, NJ: Princeton University Press, 2007.

Muhammadi Begum. 'A Long Way from Hyderabad: Scholarly Dreams and a Modern Dilemma for a Young Muslim Woman', translated by Zehra Ahmad and Zainab Masud, edited by Kulsoom Husein. Unpublished manuscript.

Mukherjee, Meenakshi. *Realism and Reality: The Novel and Society in India.* Delhi: Oxford University Press, 1985.

Munir, M., and M. R. Kayani. *Report of the Court of Inquiry Constituted Under Punjab Act 11 of 1954 to Enquire into the Punjab Disturbances of 1953.* Lahore: Government Printing, Punjab, 1954.

Naheed, Kishwar. *Aurat ek nafsiyati mutala*, translation of Simone de Beauvoir's *The Second Sex.* Lahore: Vanguard, 1982.

———. *Fitna samani-e dil.* Lahore: Sang-e meel, 1985.

———. *Siyah hashye men gulabi rang.* Lahore: Sang-e meel, 1986.

———. *Main pehle janam men rat thi.* Lahore: Sang-e meel, 1988.

———. *Leila Khalid*, translation of her *My People Shall Live.* Lahore: Sang-e Meel, 1990.

———. *Be nam musafat.* Lahore: Sang-e meel, 1991.

———. *Lab-e goya.* Lahore: Sang-e meel, 1991.

———. *Khayali shakhs se muqabala.* Lahore: Sang-e meel, 1992.

———. *Buri aurat ki katha.* Lahore: Sang-e meel, ca. 1993.

———. *Women: Myth and Realities.* Lahore: Sang-e meel, 1993.

———. *Aurat mard ka rishta – mazamin.* Lahore: Sang-e meel, 1994.

———. *A jao Afriqa.* Lahore: Sang-e meel, 1995.

———. 'Likhne valiyon ki tanhai'. In *Apni nigah: auraton ki likhi takhliqat aur tanqidi jaize*, edited by Javeria Khalid and Samina Rehman, 72–75. Lahore: ASR, 1995.

———. *Zaitun*, translation of Bapsi Sidhwa's *Bride.* Lahore: Sang-e meel. 1996.

———. *Dukan mata-e hunar.* Lahore: Sang-e meel, 1999.

———. *Sokhta Saamani-e dil.* Lahore: Sang-e meel, 2002.

———. *Buri aurat ke khatut: nazaeda beti ke nam.* Lahore: Sang-e meel, 2003.

———. *Shanasaiyan Rusvaiyan.* Lahore: Sang-e meel, 2008.

———. *Vehshat aur barud men lipti hui shairi.* Lahore: Sang-e meel, 2009.

———. *Zakhm bardashta: Pakistan kahani.* Lahore: Sang-e meel, 2010.

———. *Gumshuda yadon ki wapsi*. Lahore: Sang-e meel, 2012.
———. *Abad Kharaba*. Lahore: Sang-e meel, 2016.
———. *Hazar dastan*. Lahore: Sang-e meel, 2019.
Naim, C. M. '*Ghazal* and *taghazzul*: The Lyric, Personal and Social'. In *The Literatures of India: An Introduction*, edited by Edward C. Dimock, Edwin Gerow, C. M. Naim, A. K. Ramanujan, Gordon Roadarmel and J. A. B. van Buitenen, 181–97. Chicago: University of Chicago Press, 1974.
———. 'The Art of the Urdu Marsiya'. In *Islamic Society and Culture: Essays in Honour of Professor Aziz*, edited by Milton Israel and N. K. Wagle, 101–16. New Delhi: Manohar, 1983.
———. 'Prize-Winning *Adab*: A Study of Five Books Written in Response to the Allahabad Government Gazette Notification'. In *Moral Conduct and Authority: The Place of Adab in South Asian Islam*, edited by Barbara Daly Metcalf, 290–314. Berkeley: University of California Press, 1984.
———. 'How Bibi Ashraf Learned to Read and Write'. *Annual of Urdu Studies* 6 (1987): 99–115.
———. 'Poet–Audience Interaction at Urdu Musha'iras'. In *Urdu and Muslim South Asia: Studies in Honour of Ralph Russell*, edited by Christopher Shackle, 167–73. London: SOAS, 1989.
———. 'Parveen Shakir: A Note and Twelve Poems'. *Annual of Urdu Studies* 7 (1990): 181–91.
———. 'Transvestic Words?: The *Rekhti* in Urdu'. *Annual of Urdu Studies* 16, no. 5 (2001): 3–26.
Najmabadi, Afsaneh. 'The Erotic Vatan [Homeland] as Beloved and Mother: To Love, To Possess, and To Protect'. *Comparative Studies in Society and History* 39, no. 3 (1997): 442–67.
Namjoshi, Suniti. *The Blue Donkey Fables*. London: Women's Press, 1988.
———. *Feminist Fables*. London: Virago, 1994.
Nandy, Ashis. *The Intimate Enemy: Loss and Recovery of Self under Colonialism*. Delhi: Oxford University Press, 1988.
Naqvi, Tahira. 'Introduction'. In Ismat Chughtai, *The Quilt and Other Stories*, translated and edited by Tahira Naqvi and S. S. Hameed, vii–ix. New Delhi: Kali for Women, 1990.
Narang, Gopi Chand. 'Tradition and Innovation in Urdu Poetry'. In *Poetry and Renaissance: Kumaran Asan Birth Centenary Volume*, edited by M. Govindan, 415–34. Madras: Sameeksha, 1974.
———. *Adbi tanqid aur aslubiyat*. Lahore: Sang-e meel, 1991.
Nigah, Zehra. *Sham ka pehla tara*. Lahore: Asatir, 1998.
———. *Varq*. Lahore: Asatir, 1998.
———. . *Majmua Kalam: Sham ka pehla tara, Varq, Firaq*. Lahore: Sang-e meel, 2012.
———. *Gul Chandni*. Lahore: Sang-e meel, 2018.
Noman, Omar. *The Political Economy of Pakistan 1947–85*. London: KPI, 1988.
Oesterheld, Christina. 'Nazir Ahmad and the Early Urdu Novel: Some Observations'. *Annual of Urdu Studies* 16 (2001): 27–42.
O'Hanlon, Rosalind. 'Issues of Masculinity in North Indian History: The Bangash Nawabs of Farrukhabad'. *Indian Journal of Gender Studies* 4, no. 1 (1997): 1–10.
———. 'Manliness and Imperial Service in Mughal North India'. *Journal of the Economic and Social History of the Orient* 42, no. 1 (1999): 47–93.
Oldenburg, Veena Talwar. *The Making of Colonial Lucknow 1856–1877*. Princeton, NJ: Princeton University Press, 1984.
Pakistan Academy of Letters. 'Special Issue on Women's Writing'. *Pakistani Literature* 3, no. 2 (1994): 231–34.

Pakistan Writers Guild, ed. *Muraqqa musanafin*. Sukkur: Pakistan Writers Guild, ca. 1966].
Pamment, Claire. '*Police of Pig and Sheep*: Representations of the White Sahib and the Construction of Theatre Censorship in Colonial India'. *South Asian Popular Culture* 7, no. 3 (2009): 233–45.
———. 'A Split Discourse: Body Politics in Pakistan's Popular Punjabi Theatre'. In *Gender, Politics and Performance in South Asia*, edited by Sheema Kermani, Asif Furrukhi and Kamran Asdar Ali, 203–34. Karachi: Oxford University Press, 2015.
Patel, Geeta. *Lyrical Movements, Historical Hauntings: On Gender, Colonialism and Desire in Miraji's Urdu Poetry*. Stanford, CA: Stanford University Press, 2001; reprint, New Delhi: Manohar, 2005.
Pemberton, Kelly. *Women Mystics and Sufi Shrines in India*. Columbia: University of South Carolina Press, 2013.
Petievich, Carla. *Assembly of Rivals: Delhi, Lucknow and the Urdu Ghazal*. Lahore: Vanguard Books, 1992.
———. *When Men Speak as Women: Vocal Masquerade in Indo-Muslim Poetry*. New Delhi: Oxford University Press, 2007.
Pillai, Sharon. '"Tell … the Truth but Tell It Slant": Form and Fiction in Rusva's *Umrao Jan Ada*'. *Journal of Commonwealth Literature* 50, no. 2 (June 2015): 110–26.
Pollock, Griselda, and Victoria Turvey Sauron, eds. *The Sacred and the Feminine: Imagination and Sexual Difference*. New York: I.B. Tauris, 2007.
Poulos, S. M. 'Feminine Sense and Sensibility: A Comparative Study of Six Modern Women Short Fiction Writers in Hindi and Urdu: Rashid Jahan, Ismat Chughtai, Qurratulain Hyder, Mannu Bhandari, Usha Priyamvada, Vijay Chauhan'. PhD thesis, University of Chicago, 1975.
Pratt, Mary Louise. 'Arts of the Contact Zone'. *Profession* (1991): 33–40.
Pritam, Amrita. *Ek thi Sara: Sara Shagufta ka zindagi nama*. Lahore: Fiction House, 1994.
———. *Life and Poetry of Sara Shagufta*, translated by Gurdev Chauhan. New Delhi: B. R. Publishing, 1994.
Pritchett, Frances W. 'Afterword: The First Urdu Bestseller'. In Maulvi Nazir Ahmad, *The Bride's Mirror: A Tale of Life in Delhi a Hundred Years Ago*, translated by G. E. Ward, 204–21. London: Henry Frowde, 1903; Delhi: Permanent Black, 2001. http://www.columbia.edu/itc/mealac/pritchett/00fwp/published/txt_mirat_intro.html.
———. 'Umrao Jan Ada: A Study Site' (n.d.). Accessed 6 March 2018. http://www.columbia.edu/itc/mealac/pritchett/00urdu/umraojan/.
Pue, A. Sean. 'Rethinking Modernism and Progressivism in Urdu Poetry: Faiz Ahmad Faiz and N. M. Rashed'. *Pakistaniaat: A Journal of Pakistan Studies* 5, no. 1 (2013). https://pakistaniaat.org/index.php/pak/article/view/184.
Qadir, S. A. *The New School of Urdu Literature: A Critical Study of Hali, Azad, Nazir Ahmad, Rattan Nath Sarshar and Abdul Halim Sharar*. Lahore: Shaikh Mubarak Ali, 1932.
Qureshi, Regula B. 'Female Agency and Patrilineal Constraints: Situating Courtesans in Twentieth-Century India'. In *The Courtesan's Arts: Cross-Cultural Perspectives*, edited by Martha Feldman and Bonnie Gordon, 312–31. Oxford: Oxford University Press, 2006.
Rahman, Munibur. 'The Mushairah'. *Annual of Urdu Studies* 3 (1983): 74–83.
Rahman, Tariq. 'Boy-Love in the Urdu Ghazal'. *Annual of Urdu Studies* 7 (1990): 1–20.
Rajan, Rajeswari Sunder. *Real and Imagined Women: Gender, Culture and Postcolonialism*. London: Routledge, 1993.
Reddy, Sheshalatha. 'The Cosmopolitan Nationalism of Sarojini Naidu, Nightingale of India'. *Victorian Literature and Culture* 38, no. 2 (2010): 571–89.

Reddy, William. *The Making of Romantic Love: Longing and Sexuality in Europe*. Chicago: University of Chicago Press, 2012.
Riaz, Fahmida. *Pakistan: Literature and Society*. New Delhi: Patriot, 1986.
———. Letter to the Prime Minister of Pakistan, reproduced from *Mainstream*, 11 July 1987, 30. *Annual of Urdu Studies* 6 (1987): 131–32.
———. *Main mitti ki murat hun*. Lahore: Sang-e meel, 1988.
———. *Godavri*. Islamabad: Dost, 1995.
———. *Karachi: A Novel*. Lahore: Takhliqat, 1998.
———. 'Naya Bharat' (The New Bharat), *Aaj* 31 (April–June 2000): 141–43.
———. 'Us ne kaha tha'. *Dunyazad* 3 (2001): 146–71.
———. *Aurat ki nisai radd-e shakl*. Karachi: Vada Kitab Ghar, 2006.
———. *Ye khana-e ab-o gil*. Karachi: Scheherzade, 2006.
———. 'Ek Bhuli hu'i kahani'. *Dunyazad* 29 (2010): 248–61.
———. *Sab Lal-o Guhar: Kulliyat 1967–2000*. Lahore: Sang-e meel, 2011.
———. 'Akhit Jadoo', translated by Amna Zafar. *Critical Muslim* 5: *Love and Death* (2013): 183–96.
———. *Tum Kabir*. Karachi: Oxford University Press, 2017.
———. *Qila-e Faramoshi*. Karachi: Oxford University Press, 2017.
Roberts, Michèle. 'The Fallen Woman: Prostitution in Literature'. *The Guardian*, 14 April 2017.
Robertson, George, Melinda Mash, Lisa Tickner, Jon Bird, Barry Curtis and Tim Putnam, eds. *Traveller's Tales: Narratives of Home and Displacement*. London: Routledge, 1994.
Robinson, Francis. *Separatism among Indian Muslims: The Politics of the United Provinces Muslims, 1860–1923*. Cambridge: Cambridge University Press, 1974.
———. 'Religious Change and the Self in Muslim South Asia since 1800'. *Journal of South Asian Studies* 20, no. 1 (1997): 1–15.
Rumi, Raza. *Being Pakistani: Society, Culture and the Arts*. n.p.: HarperCollins India, 2018.
Russell, Ralph. 'The Pursuit of the Urdu Ghazal'. *Journal of Asian Studies* 29L (1969): 107–24.
Rusva, Mirza Muhammad Hadi. *Umrao Jan Ada*, edited by Zahir Fatehpuri. Lahore: Majlis-e taraqqi-e adab, [1899] 1988.
———. *Umrao Jan Ada*, translated by David Matthews. Calcutta: Rupa, 1996.
Sadiq, Mohammad. *Twentieth Century Urdu Literature*. Karachi: Royal Book, 1983.
———. *A History of Urdu Literature*. Lahore: Sang-e meel, 1995.
Safadi, Alison. 'The "Fallen" Woman in Two Colonial Novels: *Umrao Jan Ada* and *Bazaar-e Husn/Sevasadan*'. *Annual of Urdu Studies* 24 (2009): 16–53.
Said, Edward. *Orientalism: Western Conceptions of the Orient*. London: Routledge and Kegan Paul, 1978.
Saigol, Rubina. *Feminism and the Women's Movement in Pakistan: Actors, Debates and Struggles*. Islamabad: Friedrich-Eburt-Stiftung, 2016.
———. 'The Past, Present and Future of Feminist Activism in Pakistan'. *Herald*, 15 July 2019. https://herald.dawn.com/news/1398878.
Sallis, Eva. *Sheherazade through the Looking Glass: The Metamorphosis of The Thousand and One Nights*. London: Curzon, 1999.
Sangari, Kumkum. 'Mirabai and the Spiritual Economy of Bhakti'. *Economic and Political Weekly* 25, no. 27 (1990): 1464–75.
Sangari, Kumkum, and Sudesh Vaid, eds. *Recasting Women: Essays in Colonial History*. New Delhi: Kali for Women, 1999.

Sarkar, Tanika. 'Nationalist Iconography: Image of Women in 19th Century Bengali Literature'. *Economic and Political Weekly* 22, no. 47 (27 November 1981): 2011–15.
Sayyid, Asghar Nadeem, and Afzaal Ahmad, eds. *Nae zamane ki birahan*. Lahore: Sang-e meel, 1990.
Schimmel, Anemarie. *Islam in the Indian Subcontinent*. Leiden: E. J. Brill, 1980.
———. *My Soul Is a Woman: The Feminine in Islam*. New York: Continuum, 2003.
Schofield, Katherine. 'Reviving the Golden Age Again: "Classicisation", Hindustani Music, and the Mughals'. *Ethnomusicology* 54, no. 3 (2010): 484–517.
Shackle, Christopher. 'Ghazal'. In *South Asian Keywords*, edited by Rachel Dwyer, SOAS South Asia Institute [online resource, n.d.]. Accessed 23 December 2020. https://www.soas.ac.uk/south-asia-institute/keywords/file24804.pdf.
Shackle, Christopher, and Rupert Snell. *Hindi and Urdu since 1800: A Common Reader*. London: SOAS, University of London, 1990.
Shackle, Christopher, and Stefan Sperl, eds. *Qasida Poetry in Islamic Asia and Africa*. Leiden: E. J. Brill, 1996.
Shackle, Christopher, and Javed Majeed, eds. *Hali's Musaddas: The Ebb and Flow of Islam*. New Delhi: Oxford University Press, 1997.
Shahnawaz, Jahan Ara. *Father and Daughter: A Political Autobiography*. Lahore: Nigarisht, 1971.
Shaikh, Farzana. *Community and Consensus in Islam: Muslim Representation in Colonial India 1860–1967*. Cambridge: Cambridge University Press, 1989.
Shakir, Parvin. 'Women Poets of Pakistan' (reproduced from *The News International*, 9 October 1994). *Pakistan Journal of Women's Studies* 2, no. 1 (1995): 22–30.
———. *Sukhan ki shahzadi: Parvin Shakir*, edited by Rifat Haider. Islamabad: Dost, 1997.
———. *Mah-e tammam: kulliyat*. Islamabad: Murad, n.d.
Shamsie, Kamila. *Offence: The Muslim Case*. Calcutta: Seagull Books, 2009.
Shibli, M. *Maqalat-e Shibli*, vol. 4. Lahore: Majlis-e traqqi-e adab, 1956.
Shinwari, Sher Alam. 'New Pashto Poetry Book Termed a Strong Voice for Women Rights'. *Dawn*, 2 March 2019. https://www.dawn.com/news/1467076/new-pashto-poetry-book-termed-a-strong-voice-for-women-rights.
Shoaib, Mahwash. '"A Dictionary to Define My Dreams": The Politics of Remembrance and Forgetting in Kishwar Naheed's Poetry'. *Women's Studies Quarterly* 39, nos. 3/4 (2011): 153–70.
Showalter, Elaine. *The Female Malady: Women, Madness and English Culture, 1830–1980*. London: Virago, 1987.
Siddiqa, Ayesha. 'The Reluctant Feminists'. *Friday Times*, 8 November 2013.
Sikander Begum, Nawab of Bhopal. *A Pilgrimage to Mecca*, translated by Mrs Willoughby Osborne. London: W. H. Allen, 1870.
Sinha, Mrinalini. *Specters of Mother India: The Global Restructuring of an Empire*. Durham, NC: Duke University Press, 2006.
Spivak, Gayatri Chakravorty. 'Can the Subaltern Speak?'. In *Colonial Discourse and Postcolonial Theory*, edited by Patrick Williams and Laura Chrisman, 66–111. Hemel Hempstead: Harvester Wheatsheaf, 1994.
———, trans. *Imaginary Maps: Three Stories by Mahasweta Devi*. London: Routledge, 1995.
Starke, Ulrike. *An Empire of Books: The Naval Kishore Press and the Diffusion of the Printed Word in Colonial India*. Delhi: Permanent Black, 2007.
Stoler, Ann Laura. *Race and the Education of Desire: Foucault's History of Sexuality and the Colonial Order of Things*. Durham, NC: Duke University Press, 1995.
Tarar, Mustansar Husain. *Lahore Awargi*. Lahore: Sang-e meel, 2018.
Tarlo, Emma. *Clothing Matters: Dress and Identity in Colonial India*. London: Hurst, 1996.

Tharu, Susie. 'Tracing Savitri's Pedigree: Victorian Racism and the Image of Women in Indo-Anglian Literature'. In *Recasting Women: Essays in Colonial History*, edited by Kumkum Sangari and Sudesh Vaid, 254–68. New Delhi: Kali for Women, 1999.

Tharu, Susie, and K. Lalita, eds. *Women Writing in India: 600 BC to the Present*. 2 vols. London: Pandora Press, 1991–93.

Toor, Saadia. 'The State, Fundamentalism and Civil Society'. In *Engendering the Nation-State*, edited by Neelam Hussain, Samiya K. Mumtaz and Rubina Saigol, vol. 1, 131–34. Lahore: Simorgh, 1997.

———. *The State of Islam: Culture and Cold War Politics in Pakistan*. London: Pluto, 2011.

Vanita, Ruth. 'The Lady of Love – The Life and Work of Habba Khatun'. *Manushi* 38 (1987): 25–28.

———. *Gender, Sex and the City: Urdu Rekhti Poetry 1780–1870*. New Delhi: Orient Blackswan, 2012.

Waheed, Sarah. 'Anatomy of an Obscenity Trial'. *Himal SouthAsian*, 1 July 2013. https://www.himalmag.com/anatomy-obscenity-trial/.

Watt, Ian. *The Rise of the Novel*. 2nd ed. Berkeley: University of California Press, 2001.

White, Hayden. *Tropics of Discourse: Essays in Cultural Criticism*. Baltimore, MD: Johns Hopkins University Press, 1978.

Whitlock, Gillian. *Soft Weapons: Autobiography in Transit*. Chicago: University of Chicago Press, 2007.

Yakta, Ahad Ali Khan. *Dasturu 'l-Fasahat*, edited by Imtiaz 'Ali Khan 'Arshi. Rampur: Rampur State Library, 1943.

Yaqin, Amina. 'The Intertextuality of Women in Urdu Literature'. PhD thesis, SOAS, University of London, 2001.

———. '"*Badan darida*" (The Body Torn): Gender and Sexuality in Pakistani Women's Poetry'. *Pakistan Journal of Women's Studies (Alam-e Niswan)* 13, no. 1 (2006): 45–66. Republished in *The Body and The Book: Writings on Poetry and Sexuality*, edited by Glennis Byron and Andrew J. Sneddon, 235–52. Amsterdam: Rodopi, 2008.

———. 'Family and Gender in Rushdie's Writing'. In *The Cambridge Companion to Salman Rushdie*, edited by Abdulrazak Gurnah, 61–74. Cambridge: Cambridge University Press, 2007.

———. 'Islamic Barbie: The Politics of Gender and Performativity'. *Fashion Theory* 11, nos. 2-3 (2007): 173–288.

———. 'Truth, Fiction and Autobiography in the Modern Urdu Narrative Tradition'. In 'Novelization in the Islamic World'. Special issue, *Comparative Critical Studies* 4, no. 3 (2007): 379–402.

———. 'Variants of Cultural Nationalism in Pakistan: A Reading of Faiz Ahmad Faiz, Jamil Jalibi and Fahmida Riaz'. In *Shared Idioms, Sacred Symbols and the Articulation of Identities in South Asia*, edited by Kelly Pemberton and Michael Nijhawan, 115–42. London: Routledge, 2009.

———. 'Faiz Ahmad Faiz: The Worlding of a Lyric Poet'. *Pakistaniaat* 5, no. 1 (2013): i–ix. http://pakistaniaat.org/index.php/pak/issue/view/12.

———. 'Autobiography and Muslim Women's Lives'. *Journal of Women's History* 25, no. 2 (2013): 171–84. https://muse.jhu.edu/article/510537/pdf.

———. '*La Convivencia, La Mezquita* and Al-Andalus: An Iqbalian Vision'. *Journal of Postcolonial Writing* 52, no. 2 (2016): 136–52.

———. 'Islamic Feminism in a Time of Islamophobia: The Muslim Heroines of Leila Aboulela's *Minaret* and Elif Shafak's *Forty Rules of Love*'. In *Contesting

Islamophobia: Anti-Muslim Prejudice in Media, Culture, Politics, edited by Peter Morey, Amina Yaqin and Alaya Forte, 123–46. London: Bloomsbury/I.B. Tauris, 2019.

———. '*Mera jism, meri marzi*: Claiming Ownership of her Body'. *The Equator Line* 31, nos. 8.2–3 (April–September 2020): 17–30.

Yuval-Davis, Nira. *Gender and Nation*. London: Sage, 1997.

Zaidi, A. J. *A History of Urdu Literature*. Delhi: Sahitya Akademi, 1993.

Ze khe shin. *Aina-e Haram*. Lahore: Dar-ul ishat, 1921. https://www.rekhta.org/ebooks/aaina-e-haram-ebooks-1.

Zeb, Sanam. 'From My Bookshelf: "*Akhir-i-Shab* Haunts Me because I Was Associated with the Left"'. *Dawn*, 22 March 2017. https://www.dawn.com/news/1321991.

Zia, Afiya. *Faith and Feminism: Religious Agency or Secular Autonomy*. Brighton: Sussex Academic Press, 2018.

INDEX

Adb-e Latif 77, 78, 181
Ahmad, Aziz 70, 75
Ahmad, Nazir 52–53, 58
    Mirat-ul Arus 27, 40, 52, 57, 254
Ahmad, Sadaf 25
Ali, Kamran Asdar 109
Ali, Nosheen 1, 256
Aligarh movement 16, 20, 39, 47–48, 254; *see also* Deoband movement; reformists
Allahabadi, Akbar 9–11
Angare 68, 70–73, 77, 255
Ansari, Usamah 53
anti-Ahmadi riots 22, 35n87
anticolonial resistance
    1857 Rebellion 5
    Progressive Writers' movement 2, 68, 70, 72, 216
    women 2, 26
ashraf class
    literary representation 39, 40, 51, 76, 129
    literature 1, 11, 48
    modernity 246–47
    morality 43
    Urdu 14
    women poets 12, 27, 67–69, 92, 111, 189, 246
    women's behaviour 58, 83, 92, 123, 131, 186, 229, 235
    women's dress 10
    women's education 47
    see also sharafat
Ashraf, Bibi 58, 63n46
Askari, Muhammad Hasan 78, 81–82
Atiya Fyzee, Begum 58
Ayub Khan 21–22, 81, 180, 225

Badran, Margot 24–25
bhakti poetry 1, 7
Bhatti, Nasreen Anjum 3, 256
Bhutto, Benazir 120, 121, 198, 202–203
Bhutto, Zulfiqar Ali 22, 120, 221

Chatterjee, Partha 6, 114n32
Chughtai, Ismat
    Kaghazi hai pairahan 75, 76, 78
    'Lihaf' 74–75, 76
    radical literature 2, 74, 76, 255
    reaction to work 69, 70–71, 74–75, 77, 152
    'Terhi lakir' 76
colonialism
    censorship 68, 70, 71
    control of sexuality 3, 45, 72, 77, 254
    legislation under 45, 68, 77
    modernizing agenda 6, 12, 39, 46, 47, 58, 68
communalism: *see* nationalism; religious
Communism
    Communist Party of India 73, 78
    Communist Party of Pakistan 81, 116n66, 120, 125
    influence on Progressive Writers' movement 3, 68, 70, 80
    opposition to 13, 81
courtesans: *see* tawaifs

Dawood, Attiya 123, 256
de Beauvoir, Simone 182–83, 207
Delhi 19, 39, 61n18, 120
Deoband movement 20, 39, 40–41, 46–48, 52, 101, 254; *see also* Aligarh movement; reformists
devotional poetry 4, 11, 16, 44; *see also bhakti* poetry

education of women 6, 8–10, 12, 46–50
Eva B 257

Faiz, Faiz Ahmed
  'A jao Afriqa' 242–43
  Fahmida Riaz and 123, 127, 146, 152, 168
  imprisonment 13, 80
  Kishwar Naheed and 179, 181, 197, 215–16, 226, 242–43
  modernization of lyric poetry 18, 67, 69, 79, 80–82
  'Mujh se pehli si mohabbat meri mahbub na mang' 18, 79–80
  Progressive politics 72, 78, 80–82, 215–16, 252n90
  representation of beloved 80, 127
  women's movement and women poets 14–15, 67, 82, 255
  Zehra Nigah and 90, 91, 92
Farrokhzad, Forough 123, 146, 191
feminism
  Euro-American 12, 131, 182, 245
  global 14–15, 25, 243–44, 256
  Islamic 11, 24, 123
  Pakistani 24–26, 131, 246
  Third World 241, 245
  see also education of women; gender; women's movement; women's rights
Furrukhi, Asif 83, 91, 181

gender
  biological determination 146
  construction 23, 53, 122, 183, 213, 252
  grammatical 16–17, 34n68, 153
  literary representation 3–4, 13, 26, 39
  male writers ventroliquizing women 26, 40, 43
  masculinity 10, 26, 76
  poetic voice 4, 40, 41–43, 135
  symbolic role of women 5, 6, 13, 24
  traditional roles 46, 76
  see also education of women; feminism; women's movement; women's rights
ghazal poetry
  Ada Jafri 82, 90–91
  conventions 34n68, 45, 88, 91, 221
  Fahmida Riaz 123, 153
  figure of the beloved 18, 69, 127, 152

form 15–16
Parvin Shakir 106
reform 17, 40
Zehra Nigah 68
see also mushairas
Gopal, Priyamvada 72, 76, 114n28, 114n32

Habba Khatun 4, 5
Hali, Altaf Husain 11, 16–17, 26
  Chup ki dad 46
  Muqaddama sher-o shairi 16, 61n18
Halqa-e arbab-e zauq 13, 78
Hasan, Fatema 105
Haya Lakhnavi 2, 11, 12, 83, 254
Hinduism: *see* Indic culture
Hir Ranjha 4, 5, 29n15, 30
Hossain, Rokeya Sakhawat 11
Hudood Ordinances 14, 23, 162, 168, 202–203, 225
Husain, Intizar 181–82
Hussain, Iqbalunnisa 11
Hussein, Aamer 75
Hyder, Nazar Sajjad 58

Indic culture
  erotic love 3, 5
  music 4, 67
  Sufi poetry 4
  Urdu language 39, 41, 42
  Urdu poetry 1, 7, 44
Insha Allah Khan 42–43
Iqbal, Muhammad 12, 19, 21, 58, 80, 136
Islamicate culture
  cosmopolitanism 19, 39, 41–42, 57
  term 28n5
  Urdu poetry 1, 5, 45
Islamic feminism 11, 24, 123
Islamic state: *see* Pakistan as Islamic state
Islamic thought 18–20, 48

Jafri, Ada
  'Barhte hue sae' 84
  'Honton pe kabhi un ke mera nam hi aae' 82
  Jo rahi so bekhabri rahi 83
  life 82–83, 111
  'Milad-e Bahar' 84

'Phul sehraon men khilte hon ge' 87–91
Progressivism 3, 91, 25
reputation 69, 82, 111
'Us ko nazdik aane na do' 84
Jahan, Rashid 2, 72, 73–74, 78, 82, 236
Jalal, Ayesha 1–2, 19
Jalib, Habib 13–15, 92, 225–26
Jamaat-e Islami 21, 25, 182, 254
Jamal, Amina 25
Jinnah, Mohammad Ali 21, 197

Kamran, Yusuf 180, 185–86, 188–89
Karachi 91, 109, 122, 172–75, 256–57
Khan, Sayyid Ahmad 16, 20, 32n41, 46, 47
Khoja-Moolji, Shenila 48
Kugle, Scott 3, 42, 64n62

Lahore 91, 180, 186, 226, 247
Lalla Ded 4
Liaquat Ali Khan 80, 197
Lucknow
  courtesan culture 148, 246
  literary representation 54–55, 57
  Muslim religious groups 72
  Progressive Writers' movement 68, 71
  Urdu poetry 11, 39, 41–43, 61n18
lyric poetry: *see* Faiz, Faiz Ahmed: modernization of lyric poetry; ghazal poetry

Mah Laqa Bai Chanda 3, 5, 41–42, 55, 190
Mahmood, Saba 25
Manto, Saadat Hasan
  'Bu' 76–77
  censorship and ostracization 69, 71, 109, 152, 255
  Ismat Chughtai and 74, 75, 76, 78
  relationship with PWA 68, 77
Metcalf, Barbara Daly 19, 52
Minault, Gail 11, 47–48
Mira Bai 4, 7, 76, 190
Miraji 77, 82, 83, 113n25, 247
mothers
  literary representation 191–208
  symbolic of nation 24, 37n111, 84, 191–97
  see also nationalism: symbolic importance of women

Mufti, Aamir 20, 34n75, 76
Muhammadi Begum (diarist) 58–59
Muhammadi Begum (novelist) 58
mushairas 16–18, 55, 56, 91–92, 180, 184; *see also* ghazal poetry
Musharraf, Pervez 21, 23

Naheed, Kishwar
  A jao Afriqa 241–42, 243–46
  activist poetry 222–41
  'Apahaj ma mitti ki goldan jubilee' 191–97, 203
  'Apni jaisi aurat vazir-e azam se mukalima' 191, 198–203
  attendance at Zehra Nigah's mushairas 92
  Buri aurat ki katha 183–84, 191
  'Censorship' 179, 216–18, 222
  dreams 208–11
  female voices and influences 190–91, 213, 245–45
  feminism 14–15, 182–89, 243–47, 256
  'Ghas to mujh jaisi hai' 226–30
  'Hum gunahgar auraten' 222–25, 257
  'Kare Kos' 214–16
  'Khud kalami' 211–14
  'Kishwar Naheed!' 218–22
  life 180–81
  Malamaton ke darmiyan 181, 211
  'Mom Mahal' 203–8
  mothers 191–209
  'Mujhe bhai ne sangsar kiya' 235–41
  Progressivism 3, 14
  'Taliban se qibla ru guftugu' 230–35
  'Taluq ki be-simti' 209–11
  'Yousaf Kamran' 186–89
  'Zainab ka noha' 235
Naidu, Sarojini 7
Naim, C. M. 42–43, 45, 52, 107
nationalism
  nation as beloved 18, 78, 80
  Progressive Writers' movement 72, 81
  religious 5, 18–19, 77
  symbolic importance of women 6, 13, 24, 76
  women's participation in public life 2, 12, 24, 76
nazms 83, 91, 106, 123, 186, 221

Neruda, Pablo 121, 146
Nigah, Zehra
  'Ek larki' 97
  'Gul chandni' 98–100, 110
  'Jurm vada' 93
  'Meri saheli' 97
  performances 68, 90–91, 255
  Progressivism 3
  reputation 69, 91, 111
  'Samjhota' 92–93
  'Zehra ne bohat din se kuch bhi nahin likha hai' 101–106, 111
Noor Jehan 67, 79

Pakistan as Islamic state 14, 21–24, 35n87, 78, 168, 222
Pamment, Claire 68
partition in literature 20, 84, 191
Patel, Geeta 72–73
Persia
  language 34n68, 39, 42, 146
  poetry 4, 15–16, 18, 34n68, 44, 79
  Zoroastrianism 121
poetic forms: *see* ghazal poetry; nazms; rekhta poetry; rekhti poetry
post-secularism 25
Pritam, Amrita 109–110, 120
Pritchett, Frances 55, 64n63
private sphere: *see* public and private spheres
Progressive Writers' movement
  activism 78, 80, 225, 254
  Ada Jafri 83, 89–91
  advocacy for women 13, 70, 93, 98
  advocacy for working class 73
  anticolonialism 2, 72, 216
  cultural prejudices 247
  Fahmida Riaz 125, 169
  Kishwar Naheed 230, 23
  lack of gender equality 12
  legacy 3, 13–15
  nationalism 72
  Progressive Writers' Association 13, 14, 22, 68, 70, 77, 81
  relationship with state 129
  representation of sexualities 68–69, 70–71, 72, 77, 80, 12, 127
  secularism 70, 71–72, 235, 253
  split 13–14, 77–78, 81
  women's activist poetry 14, 67, 111
  Zehra Nigah 98
public and private spheres 12, 17–18, 20, 52, 58, 78, 208
purdah: *see* seclusion; zenana

Qasimi, Ahmad Nadeem 78, 120

Rajan, Rajeswari Sunder 23, 116n70
Rashed, N. M. 82, 83
reformists 5–6, 39–40, 48; *see also* Aligarh movement; Deoband movement
rekhta poetry 40, 42, 61n21, 61n27
rekhti poetry 40–46, 61n21, 64n64, 75
Riaz, Fahmida
  '23 March 1973' 153
  activist poetry 122–23, 256
  'Aqlima' 137–39
  awards 123
  Badan darida 122, 130–53
  'Bakira' 134
  'Chadar aur divari' 162–68
  Communism 120, 125
  'Ek aurat ki hansi' 150–52
  exile from Pakistan 120–21, 124
  feminism 15, 121
  Godavri 121
  'Jhijhak' 129–30
  Kya tum pura chand na dekho ge? 172–74
  'Lao, hath apna lao zara' 143–46
  life 119–22
  literary influences 121, 123
  'Lori' 153–62
  'Main to mitti ki murat hun' 153
  Marxism 122
  'Naya Bharat' 169–72
  Pathar ki zaban 132
  Progressivism 3, 14, 111, 125
  Qila-e Faramoshi 111
  Raj singhasan 125–27
  'Sahil ki eek sham' 153
  'Sura-i yasin' 139–43
  'Tasvir' 132–33
  Tum Kabir… 121
  'Voh ek zan-e napak hai' 146–50
  Ye Khana-e Aab-o gil 121
  'Zabanon ka bosa' 122, 127–29

Rumi, Jalaluddin 15, 19, 121, 123
Rusva, Mirza Hadi
  Umrao Jan Ada 41, 54–58, 67, 254

sacred: *see* secular and sacred
Said, Edward 20, 116n80
Sarhindi, Roshan Kalim 256
Schimmel, Anemarie 4
seclusion
  literary representation 11
  protection of women 17
  under Zia 15, 23
  women challenging 12, 46, 58
  see also zenana
secular and sacred
  combined in literature 2, 4, 15, 27, 101, 122, 153, 172, 181, 213, 253
  ideological separation 21–22, 40, 48, 255, 256
secularism
  Fahmida Riaz 121, 153, 172
  Kishwar Naheed 179, 190, 235
  modernity 20
  Progressive Writers' movement 70, 72, 235, 253
  secular criticism 20
  state 21–22, 168
  Urdu writing 67, 179
  Westernization 12, 19, 20, 71, 255
  women's movement 24–26, 222
sexualities
  changing literary representation 13, 80
  colonial control 3, 45, 72, 77, 254
  controlled literary representation 17, 69, 70–72, 74, 78, 127
  open literary representation 42–43, 57, 68–69, 129, 255
  state control 23–24, 222
  Sufi poetry 4
  women's literary representation 125, 127–29, 146, 152, 226
Shagufta, Sara
  life 15, 69, 109–10, 255
  literary representations of 108–9, 191
  poetry 3, 110–11
Shakir, Parvin
  Khushbu 106–7
  reputation 69, 106–9, 111, 255

'Tanqid aur takhliq' 107–8
'Tomato Ketchup' 108–9
'Wasteland' 107
sharafat 28n1, 39, 72, 109, 127, 180, 185, 255; *see also* ashraf class: women's behaviour
Sharar, Abdul Halim 42
Sharia
  Islamic philosophy 18
  legislation in Pakistan 14, 22–23, 225
  women's behaviour and rights 52, 53, 168, 202, 222, 225
sharif. *See* ashraf class
Sharif, Nawaz 23, 235
Sherwania, Zahida Khatun: *see* Ze Khe Shin
Sindhu, Amar 3, 256
Sohini Mahiwal 4, 5
Sorabji, Cornelia 7, 31n38
Spivak, Gayatri Chakravorty 6
Sufi poetry 1, 4–5, 15, 82, 150, 256
Sufism 4, 16, 19, 34n75, 37n111, 48, 72, 122, 256

tawaifs
  literary representation 55, 57
  performative poetry's association with 13, 16, 68, 91, 246
  poetry by 3
  symbolic of regressive past 5
  women's roles 3–4, 76
Thanawi, Ashraf Ali 52, 101
  Bihishti Zewar 40, 52–53, 57
Toor, Saadia 13–14, 81

Urdu
  Dakani 39, 41–42
  gendered voice 41–43
  linguistic development 39, 45–46
  linguistic variations 41–42

veiling 9–10, 23, 91, 162

Waliullah, Shah 19, 48
West, the
  Islam's influence on 18
  modernity 5, 19, 21
  secularism 12, 19–21, 71, 168, 255
  threat to morality 6, 8–11, 12, 73

women's movement
  in India 2, 13
  in Pakistan 3, 13–15, 23–25, 183, 222, 256
  protests 225
  see also education of women; feminism; gender; women's rights
women's rights
  groups 6–7, 225
  legislation 6–7, 22–23
  men's attitudes to 11, 47, 255
  restriction of 23, 202–203, 222, 225
  see also education of women; feminism; gender; women's movement

Yahya Khan 180, 188

Zaheer, Sajjad 71, 72, 77, 78, 116n66
Ze Khe Shin 8, 11, 12, 32n41, 254
  Musaddas Aina-e Haram 8
Zebunnisa Begum 3, 49
zenana
  literary representation 49, 51, 75
  modernization 20
  reform through education 39–40, 46–47, 69, 254
  target of colonial reform 6, 12
  threatened by modernity 52, 53, 73
  women leaving 67, 90, 255
  writing from 2, 7–8, 11, 69, 254
  see also seclusion
Zia, Afiya 25
Zia-ul Haq 15, 22–23, 120, 162, 180, 202, 221, 225

www.ingramcontent.com/pod-product-compliance
Lightning Source LLC
Chambersburg PA
CBHW021137230426
43667CB00005B/150